Asian Maritime Power in the 21st Century

The **Institute of Southeast Asian Studies (ISEAS)** was established as an autonomous organization in 1968. It is a regional centre dedicated to the study of socio-political, security and economic trends and developments in Southeast Asia and its wider geostrategic and economic environment. The Institute's research programmes are the Regional Economic Studies (RES, including ASEAN and APEC), Regional Strategic and Political Studies (RSPS), and Regional Social and Cultural Studies (RSCS).

ISEAS Publishing, an established academic press, has issued more than 2,000 books and journals. It is the largest scholarly publisher of research about Southeast Asia from within the region. ISEAS Publishing works with many other academic and trade publishers and distributors to disseminate important research and analyses from and about Southeast Asia to the rest of the world.

Asian Maritime Power in the 21st Century

Strategic Transactions
China, India and Southeast Asia

VIJAY SAKHUJA

INSTITUTE OF SOUTHEAST ASIAN STUDIES
Singapore

First published in Singapore in 2011 by ISEAS Publishing
Institute of Southeast Asian Studies
30 Heng Mui Keng Terrace
Pasir Panjang
Singapore 119614

E-mail: publish@iseas.edu.sg
Website: bookshop.iseas.edu.sg

All rights reserved. No part of this publication may be reproduced, stored in a retrieval system, or transmitted in any form or by any means, electronic, mechanical, photocopying, recording or otherwise, without the prior permission of the Institute of Southeast Asian Studies.

© 2011 Institute of Southeast Asian Studies, Singapore

The responsibility for facts and opinions in this publication rests exclusively with the author and his interpretations do not necessarily reflect the views or the policy of the publisher or its supporters.

ISEAS Library Cataloguing-in-Publication Data

Sakhuja, Vijay.
 Asian maritime power in the 21st century: strategic transactions : China, India and Southeast Asia.
 1. Sea-power—Asia—21st century.
 2. Asia—Strategic aspects.
 3. Southeast Asia—Strategic aspects.
 I. Title.
V55 A8S15   2011

ISBN 978-981-4311-09-0 (soft cover)
ISBN 978-981-4311-10-6 (E-book PDF)

Typeset by International Typesetters Pte Ltd
Printed in Singapore by Utopia Press Pte Ltd

CONTENTS

Acknowledgements	vii
Introduction	ix
1. Maritime Power: A Tour D'Horizon	1
2. Maritime Geography, Law of the Sea and Geostrategy	35
3. Military Maritime Power: China and India	65
4. Economics and Maritime Power	124
5. Political Components of Maritime Power	175
6. Techno-Military Dimension of Asian Maritime Power	215
7. Strategic Transactions: China, India and Southeast Asia	251
8. Conclusion	308
Selected Bibliography	313
Index	335
About the Author	363

ACKNOWLEDGEMENTS

It has indeed been a long voyage sailing through the Indian and the Pacific Ocean transiting through the Straits of Malacca and attempting to determine the maritime power of India and China in the 21st century and its impact on Southeast Asian security. In endeavouring to venture into these relatively dangerous waters through which I had sailed several times during my naval service, I drew enormous strength from a number of individuals who constantly supported me to complete this study. It is impossible to list them all here due to constraints of space. In particular, I must acknowledge my thanks to the following:

Ambassador K. Kesavapany, Director, Institute of Southeast Asian Studies (ISEAS), Singapore, for giving me the opportunity to undertake research and also publish the volume. The two-year fellowship was indeed very inspiring and a rewarding experience.

Dr W. Lawrence S. Prabhakar, Associate Professor, Department of Political Science, Madras Christian College, Chennai, India for sharing his perspectives on matters maritime and also diligently going through the manuscript.

Mr Daljit Singh, Visiting Senior Research Fellow, ISEAS, who was a constant source of encouragement and who very painstakingly went through the manuscript.

My wife Sangeeta and daughters Neha and Nayan for being supportive while I finished my research in Singapore.

I must also acknowledge that a large number of senior naval officers in India gave me their valuable time to discuss matters maritime.

Last but not least, I record my gratitude to my uncle Shri Satyapal Sakhuja, who very early during my formative years brought home the importance of the seas and navies. Without his inspiration and guidance throughout my childhood and naval career, this study could never have achieved fruition and maturity.

Vijay Sakhuja
2010

INTRODUCTION

The rise of Asian power and its transformed strategic profile in the 21st century is predicated on the robust economic performance of several countries in the region. Globalization and rapid economic development of these Asian countries has induced a new sense of confidence which is reflected in their strategic profile and standing in the West-led global order. In Asia, China and India are states with a long civilizational history of pre-eminence, and are now embarking on the process of economic-industrial transformation reflected in the trajectories of their phenomenal and sustained economic growth, socio-economic development, and strategic transformation. Their ability to adapt to the needs of a modern society has resulted in a powerful and resilient capacity to absorb the western institutional processes and indices of national power. These processes and indices have been gradually assimilated in their unique socio-cultural-political-strategic matrices.

The maritime history of the world shows that states have relied on maritime power for a full realization of their power potential. The Minoans, Phoenicians, Egyptians, Greeks, Romans, Arabs, Indians and Chinese have all exhibited a strong proclivity to maritime power that had expeditionary roles factored in them even as they launched their mercantile trade criss-crossing the Mediterranean Sea, the Indian Ocean and Asian waters through Southeast Asia as far as China. The quest for new lands and the necessity to trade with the affluent East encouraged the colonial powers such as the Portuguese, Dutch, British and French to invest significantly in maritime power. These colonial powers came to adorn the Asian littorals with forts and factories to support the domestic demands and in the process built strong maritime foundations.

The rise of Asian maritime power in the 21st century is now featuring the dynamic and determined rise of China and India. Their maritime rejuvenation is premised on high economic growth, burgeoning maritime trade, a promising maritime science and technology base, evolving military-industrial-technological transformation driven by the ongoing information revolution and a desire to build a robust maritime military capability. Further, the development of their industrial complex has led to several indigenously developed technologies aimed at self reliance to avoid overdependence on external sources of military hardware. Significantly, the Asian maritime power emerges amidst the overarching supremacy of the West, an emergence ironically brought about by globalization and liberal economic paradigm of global interdependence that has been introduced to the world by the United States-led West. China and India are poised to be the anchors of globalization in the Asia Pacific and could chart the course of globalization for the region.

Maritime power in its scope could be classified in the broad typology of "benign" and "coercive". The constituents of maritime power have been time immemorial, however navies over the years have defined their roles and missions in accordance with the politico-military milieu that conditioned the purposes of maritime power. Maritime power could also be envisaged as the vanguard of globalization. As states become more and more interdependent for their growth and prosperity, the salience and criticality of maritime infrastructure is clearly visible among those that seek to build their economic power. Maritime power is thus the "externalized" essence of national security strategy and its indivisibility is quite important and cannot be ignored.

There is a complex relationship between the state and the sea that is based on the degree of seaborne trade, the merchant marine, shipbuilding capability, and the ability to exploit living and non-living resources. Maritime transformation as evident in technological developments and in the 1982 United Nations Convention of the Law of the Sea (UNCLOS) nautical regime has also been an important consideration in a state's maritime power. Under the UNCLOS states can claim Exclusive Economic Zones (EEZ) and continental shelf and develop technological capability to exploit offshore resources.

Trade and naval power constitute the twin pillars of the globalized state's reliance on the sea for its economic growth. The reliance of the state on its navy essentially arises from its dependence on the sea and the ability of the naval force to secure sea lanes for maritime trade and its ability to secure its littoral, extended littoral-continental shelf and the EEZ. In essence, the role of the navies is to secure the national maritime interest.

In that context, this study aims to determine the growth of Asian maritime power in the 21st century centred on China and India. Given that Southeast Asia is the convergent maritime hub of the dynamics of China and India that is reminiscent of the ancient times, the study examines the nature of maritime transactions among China, India and Southeast Asia. The increasing sensitivities about safety of sea lanes, forward presence of navies, and naval nuclear developments in China and India are issues of significant concern to Southeast Asian countries.

There are at least five important reasons for this study. First, Asia maritime history confirms that China, India and Southeast Asia made a seminal contribution and played a significant part in Asian prosperity in the pre-colonial history of the region. In fact, Asian seas had facilitated movement of people, cultures, and trade otherwise constrained by difficult and challenging overland geography. Traders from China, India, Southeast Asia, Rome, Greece and Persia sailed through Asian waters and engaged in a flourishing maritime enterprise resulting in interdependence. Importantly, a sophisticated maritime trading system emerged in Asia that contributed not only to the growth of Asia but was linked with other trading systems in the Indian Ocean and the Mediterranean.

The rise of Asian maritime power in the 21st century emerges against the backdrop of this ancient legacy that goes back to the far-sighted maritime vision of the Song and Ming Dynasties of China, the Chola Kings in India and the Srivijaya Empire in Southeast Asia. Asia's maritime power declined as the key countries engaged in several internecine feuds and wars which was indeed the reason for the colonial domination in the 18th, 19th and 20th centuries.

Second, in the 21st century, China, India and several Southeast Asian countries have experienced substantial growth in their maritime power. The 1990s and the first decade of the 21st century is indeed an important period for the rediscovery of maritime power in the Asian context. Impressive economic growth rates, increased trade, high energy demands, recognition of the importance of security of sea lanes, and the safety of marine resources in the EEZ have led to the modernization of their navies. Other catalysts have been the need for modernization to overcome years of military obsolescence, and the imperatives to secure littorals against asymmetric challenges.

Third, the study is important from the perspective of the strategic cultures of China, India and Southeast Asia. These draw their political theory and statecraft from the respective ancient schools of thought epitomized in the eras of their antiquity and golden ages that had firm maritime foundations, i.e. *Shih* (Sun Tzu), *Mandala* (Kautilya) and *Mandala-Negara*, a Hindu-Buddhist cosmological thought.

Fourth, the growth of maritime power of China, India and Southeast Asia is also impelled to develop security strategies to preclude the littoral dominance by the extra-regional powers that have well-developed access and basing strategies in Asia. Of particular consequence for China, India and Southeast Asia are Japan, a leading maritime power in Asia, and the United

States, the pre-eminent maritime-naval power engaged in the region through alliances, partnerships, security arrangements and economic engagements.

Fifth, during the past six decades, conflict has been the characteristic in China–India and China–Southeast Asia relations. In 1951, China annexed Tibet leading to mounting nervousness in New Delhi about the permanent stationing of the Chinese military on its northern borders. The capture of Aksai Chin in 1962 (claimed by India as part of Jammu and Kashmir), the border dispute involving 90,000 square kilometres in Arunachal Pradesh, and the extensive military infrastructure built in Tibet also impacted on Indian security and added to uneasiness in New Delhi. The situation worsened in 1963 when Pakistan ceded more than 5,000 square kilometres of territory in Pakistan-Occupied Kashmir (POK) to China that culminated in the construction of the Karakoram Friendship Highway. Indian threat perceptions are well grounded in China's nuclear capability, and New Delhi's efforts at redressing the nuclear asymmetry have led Beijing to help Pakistan acquire nuclear weapons, and build significant conventional capability, including military infrastructure developments, thus complicating India's security calculations. Similarly, China is actively engaged in a competition for influence in South Asia among the small states, Bangladesh, Myanmar, Nepal, Pakistan, and Sri Lanka. In response, India is building relations with the United States which China views as the only global competitor and Japan, the other Asian power, a balancing strategy by India. Given Indian and Chinese economic growth, neither side is willing to accommodate the other and be the junior partner.

Competing territorial claims in the South China Sea emerge as a serious source of interstate tension in China–Southeast Asia relations. The six claimants (China, Taiwan, Vietnam, Malaysia, the Philippines, and Brunei) except Brunei have sought to consolidate their claims by occupying islets, stationing forces on them and building sophisticated military infrastructure. Overlapping territorial claims led to serious friction between China and the Philippines and China and Vietnam during the 1970s and 1990s, while bilateral and multilateral efforts to ease tensions have so far met with mixed success. Although these political disputes remain intractable, the logic of economic engagement generates interdependence among China and Southeast Asian countries.

Also of significance is China's rationale to secure and monitor its critical oil jugular through the Straits of Malacca. China's real strategic intent would be to nurture a long-term relationship with Southeast Asian countries, particularly the Straits of Malacca littorals, to counter extra-regional military powers that seek naval presence in the area through access and basing arrangements. So far China has projected its benign intent in the region but as it leverages its political, economic and military power, it will be in a position to pursue its geostrategic and geoeconomic interests more assertively. An adept diplomacy by China disguised to influence Southeast Asian countries to view China's rise as benign and non-threatening appears to have paid off. China has engaged in multilateralism, security dialogues and economic engagements but in the end, its ever-increasing political, economic and military power has the potential to upset regional security.

In the past, several scholars and experts have written on the diverse facets of maritime power of China and India[1] and offered some interesting insights into the Asian understanding of maritime power. The present study seeks to examine Asian maritime power in the 21st century and argues that China and India are engaged in building their power potential based on maritime power as a key component. Also, China and India draw their political theory and statecraft from the respective schools of thought rooted in their antiquity. It is hoped that this study will contribute to a greater understanding of the maritime ambitions of China and India, and how this instrument of power is employed in the overall building of their power potential and the resultant impact on Southeast Asia.

The study is based on an analysis of qualitative and empirical data accrued from varied sources. An attempt has been made to discuss maritime infrastructure, naval equipment and capabilities, the impact of information technologies on maritime power, and the maritime environment in India and China. Several primary sources like official government publications, white papers and interviews with practitioners and naval planners have supported the study. Likewise, visits to maritime infrastructure (ports, shipyards and dockyards) in India have provided a rich source of data. It was not possible to visit China during the study. However, an earlier visit to Chinese and Taiwanese naval bases, shipyards, ports, and recent interaction with Chinese maritime specialists during Track II and informal meetings provided valuable data for the study. Inputs for this study include the author's meetings with the Chinese, Taiwanese, Southeast Asian and Indian practitioners and experts including naval commanders-in-chief. These meetings provided important perspectives in terms of strategic thinking in China, India and Southeast Asia and the China threat as perceived by the Asians.

It is true that a realistic assessment of maritime power is an extraordinarily complex empirical problem given that the input elements of maritime power are both objective and subjective, i.e. it is possible to quantify and size up the military strength, economic potential and technological capability, but an assessment of intangible factors such as national will, motivations and intentions is indeed a complex mathematical problem. In this study, an attempt has been made to determine the maritime power of China and India as systematically as possible. The study has relied on Ray S. Cline's formula for calculating the power of nations.[2] Based on this, the study created a mathematical equation to determine the maritime power of a nation. This model is suitable because it encompasses the changes in the nautical regime brought about by UNCLOS III and the impact of information technology on the maritime power of a state.

The study has been divided into seven chapters. These chapters in turn look at maritime power comparatively, i.e. they discuses various constituents of maritime power in both the Chinese and Indian context. The chapters seek to identify developments in maritime power and bring to the fore the commitment of the respective governments to build maritime power. An attempt is also made to understand the contemporary Asian maritime thought through the prism of ancient political theory and statecraft, given that there is a symbiotic relationship between the state and the navies.

Chapter 1 examines the concept of maritime power (sea power) as it has evolved over the years in Britain, the United States, Soviet Union/Russia, Japan, China and India. It analyses the writings of several maritime strategists, academics and practitioners, and argues that the constituents of maritime power have undergone a change with UNCLOS III and the ongoing revolution brought about by information technology. It develops an input/output model and a mathematical equation for computing the maritime power of a state. It also highlights how states have used their maritime power to safeguard their national interests.

Chapter 2 establishes a link between geography and maritime power. It argues that the two are closely linked to each other and are vital determinants in a country's march towards becoming a maritime power. The chapter examines in detail the maritime geography of China and India.

Chapter 3 analyses Chinese and Indian naval strategy, force structure and capabilities to achieve strategic objectives set by the leadership. It argues that both countries are building their naval muscle to preclude littoral dominance by external powers as well as to project power in their respective areas of maritime interest that overlap in the Indian Ocean and the South China Sea.

Chapter 4 examines the economic components of maritime power. It examines shipbuilding, shipping, port infrastructure and the fishing industry of China and India. It shows that both countries have intensified their efforts to build maritime infrastructure to harness the wealth available from the sea.

Chapter 5 examines the political component of maritime power. It argues that there is continuity from the past with regard to the use of navies for coercion and gunboat diplomacy. Importantly, the navies and the coastguards are the only instrument of the state that can be legally deployed in peace or war anywhere on the seas for political purposes. Both China and India have used their navies for diplomacy in the Asia-Pacific region.

Chapter 6 examines the impact of information-based technologies on the growth of maritime power in China and India. Both countries have kept abreast of developments in information warfare and are slowly adapting to changes brought about by the Revolution in Military Affairs (RMA). The chapter also highlights critical deficiencies in the RMA capabilities of China and India.

Finally, Chapter 7 traces the ancient maritime exchanges between China and India and the impacts of these interactions on Southeast Asia. The chapter argues that in their strategic conduct, China, India and Southeast Asia draw liberally from their ancient practice of international relations and that there are a number of positive as well as negative political, economic and military consequences of the rejuvenated maritime power of China and India on Southeast Asia.

Notes

1. David G. Muller, Jr., *China as a Maritime Power* (Colorado: Westview Press, 1983); Gang Deng, *Maritime Sector, Institutions, and Sea Power of Premodern China* (Westport: Greenwood, 1999); Bernard D. Cole, *The Great Wall at Sea: China's Navy Enters the Twenty-first Century* (Annapolis: Naval Institute Press, 2001); Srikanth Kondapalli, *China's Naval Power* (New Delhi: Knowledge World, 2001); John Wilson Lewis and Xue Litai, *China's Strategic Seapower: The Politics of Force Modernization in the Nuclear Age* (Stanford: Stanford University Press, 1994); G.V.C. Naidu, *Indian Navy and South East Asia* (New Delhi: Knowledge World, 2000); K. Raja Menon, *Maritime Strategy and Continental Wars* (London: Frank Cass, 2000); Geoffrey Till, *Seapower: A Guide for the Twenty-First Century* (London: Frank Cass, 2004); Toshi Yoshihara and James R. Holmes, *Asia Looks Seaward: Power and Maritime Strategy* (Westport, Connecticut: Praeger Security International, 2008).
2. Ray S. Cline, *World Power Trends and U.S. Foreign Policy for the 1980's* (Colorado: Westview Press, 1980), p. 27. Cline put forth a formula to determine the power of nations for planning American defence and foreign policy.

1

MARITIME POWER: A TOUR D'HORIZON

Since ancient times, states have depended on sea-based commerce for growth and affluence. Seafarers travelled distant lands in search of raw material, critical resources, luxury goods and markets for their products and these activities resulted in several trading systems that emerged in the Mediterranean of Greece and Rome; Egypt, Persia in Southwest Asia; India, Southeast Asia and China in the Asian littoral. The maritime trading systems featured intense competitive rivalries as contending states outdid one another, and at times states contested to limit and control trade as a means of containing the rising power with the consequences of trade-related wars. The struggle for the maritime commercial power induced several maritime developments that featured the build-up of navies to protect trade as well as to fight piracy.[1]

Sea-based commerce necessitated the development of naval and civilian maritime shipping. It resulted in the technological innovation of vessels for commerce and warfare. Naval supremacy assured the tranquillity of the seas and the securing of uncharted waters as well as guaranteed access to ports, thus sustaining the economy. At another level, human resources deployed at sea were dichotomous for naval and civilian maritime roles. States enacted land battles at sea and also embarked armies on board ships as marines to fight naval battles to achieve maritime dominance and supremacy. Naval power was the critical offshore leveraging power that shaped and influenced the strategic and tactical outcomes of battles on land.

Ancient maritime history informs us that the Mediterranean Sea located at the junction of Africa, Asia, and Europe was the first centre of maritime power. The Minoans based in Crete were perhaps the first civilization (3000 BC to 1500 BC) that developed extensive maritime trading relations[2] as well as significant naval power without being significantly threatened by external forces. The Minoan maritime empire and enterprise was the epitome of ancient maritime trade and maritime supremacy. The nemesis of the Minoan civilization was however due to a catastrophic natural disaster owing to a volcanic eruption around 1500 BC.[3]

The Phoenicians succeeded Minoans and emerged as a dominant maritime power. Their seafaring skills encouraged them to expand their trade well beyond the Mediterranean to the west coast of Africa and their shipbuilding capability enabled them to build warships to project power and emerge as a formidable navy.[4] The Phoenicians sustained their maritime trading hegemony in the Mediterranean until the Greeks neutralized them.

The Egyptians were yet another maritime power with extensive maritime trade links with Ethiopia and Sudan in the Mediterranean and with the Arabs in Persia. The Egyptians were proficient seafarers and possessed excellent shipbuilding techniques.[5] Seaborne commerce was critical to the Pharaohs and they developed a navy to safeguard trade. Land-based archers trained as naval warriors manned the Egyptian ships and these vessels enjoyed a distinctive advantage being propelled with both oars and sails. The origins of a naval infantry were quite evident as the Egyptians began building dedicated naval infantry forces for their naval vessels that were the vanguard of their maritime trade.

Ancient Greece, built around city-states, though not unified, was a great ancient maritime power centred on huge fleets. Interestingly, there is a belief that Homer's *Iliad* is a poetic portrayal of Greek sea power and the siege of Troy was aimed at securing the Hellespont (Dardanelles) that would result in control of Black Sea trade.[6] No wonder then that the Greek kings acknowledged the importance of a strong merchant marine and a powerful navy. Under Alexander the Great, Greek influence was visible in Persia and as far as India through conquests[7] and under his patronage, Admiral Nearchos, established new trading links in the Persian Gulf and India. The expansion of the Roman trading links was catalytic to new trading links with Southeast Asia and as far as China. The origins of the trans-oceanic Mediterranean-Persian-Asian sea-based commerce were thus evident.

The Romans too developed a significant maritime power due to their location astride the River Tiber through a trading system and built a navy; however the disastrous loss in the First Punic War[8] encouraged Rome to build a strong navy, which, in later years, patrolled not just the Mediterranean, but was instrumental in Roman victory over Sicily, Spain and North

Africa. It also engaged in fighting piracy. The Roman maritime power was perhaps a good precursor to the European maritime quest for trade and later colonization.

In the archipelagic Southeast Asia, the late 7th century saw the emergence of the Srivijaya Kingdom as the most powerful maritime empire supported by burgeoning trade, a powerful navy and an ambitious political leadership.[9] In the 10th century, the Cholas in Southern India emerged as the pre-eminent power.[10] Seafaring was at its peak in China during the 11th century and by the 13th century, the Chinese had captured the bulk of the Indian Ocean trade and Zheng He, the famous eunuch mariner led seven expeditions (1405 to 1433).[11] These expeditions showcased China's maritime power but that was short-lived and could not be sustained. By the late 16th century, the Asian powers had declined resulting in a vacuum filled in by the Europeans. The ancient Asian maritime developments are discussed in greater detail in Chapter 7.

The arrival of the Portuguese in the Indian Ocean heralded the presence of an extra-regional naval power that ventured into the Indian Ocean in support of the state policy that looked upon the seas as their possession.[12] Notwithstanding the initial resistance, the Portuguese established themselves as the only naval power in the Indian Ocean that had a significant presence across the entire swath of the Indian Ocean as far as Macao in China. Their naval capability helped them annex Sacotra, gain suzerainty over Hormuz, and hold Malacca, the three strategic maritime gateways of the Indian Ocean, thus ensuring a total monopoly over Indian Ocean trade and enabling them to sustain their supremacy over the next 150 years.[13]

Like the Portuguese, the Dutch were interested in commerce and had launched expeditionary forces in the Asian littorals.[14] The French and the British launched into the Indian Ocean as traders and their rivalry resulted in numerous naval bases in the Indian Ocean. Several setbacks for the French, particularly the near annihilation of their navy at Trafalgar in 1805,[15] and the opening of the Suez Canal in 1869,[16] resulted in Britain enjoying undisputed sway in the Indian Ocean. By the dawn of the 20th century, the Indian Ocean had turned into a "British lake" with the British enjoying undisputed command over the transoceanic trade supported by a tough control over the colonies that served as the source of raw materials as well as forward bases for projection of power into Asia as far as China.

The colonial dominance of Asia spanned the 18th, 19th and 20th centuries. It signified the era of European dominance with an overt emphasis on maritime-based trade and military preponderance. The European maritime-based economic order ushered in economic growth and prosperity from the end of the Napoleonic wars until the outbreak of World War I and II. The consequences of economic growth and maritime power had several states in Europe particularly Britain, Germany, France, Italy and also the United States enter the high stakes of maritime-based economic growth and expansion of maritime power that was evident in their naval power. The two World Wars were thus the violent culmination of competitive economic growth and naval expansion. In the 21st century, maritime power continues to be the defining paradigm with the emergence of the economic order of globalization. The current economic growth trends among several Asian countries have provided an impetus and enormous lateral capacity for industrialization and military-strategic expansion manifest in their naval order of battle.

From the above it is evident that the tendency of maritime powers in history has always been the augmentation of economic power through high rates of economic growth that has come with extensive trade. Significantly, maritime power emerges as the primary facilitator of the mercantile-based trading system of global capitalism and the military corollary emerges with the build-up of the navy of the state. Also, maritime powers have an aggregation of economic-industrial power that is sustained by a strong penchant for science and technology.

CONCEPT OF MARITIME POWER

The term maritime power implies various meanings and interpretations. Strategists, practitioners and analysts of maritime power have re-examined its constituents, importance and utility. Some prefer to use "sea power" while others have a preference for "maritime power".[17] In its narrower scope, sea power is understood as "navy" for distant interventions and is synonymous with warships, submarines, aircraft carriers and navies.[18] At the other end of the spectrum, it is broadly understood as the ability of a state to use the sea to its optimum. It has also been argued that a great sea power may not be a maritime power although one follows from the other.[19] In that context, sea power is defined as a state that has formidable naval capabilities (ships, submarines, shipping in support of the military for specific missions) and maritime power is defined as the state that makes widespread access to the seas to sea resources for economic purposes that in turn provide the state with a significant position in its power relations. Thus there is no necessity for a maritime power to develop a navy and in theory a great sea power need not necessarily be a maritime power. However, historical evidence tells us that maritime powers do develop their navies to safeguard their interests and project power.

Notwithstanding that, "sea power" or "maritime power" has a long and a well-documented history and its importance and exercise has come to be realized by one and all including kings, statesmen, politicians, policy-makers and practitioners. Maritime power is a dynamic concept and has experienced constant change with newer dimensions evolving based on changes in international legal regimes, technology and naval warfare. The nautical regime created by the UNCLOS III has led to the establishment of sovereignty on the seas resulting in a transformed maritime intercourse among states with significant ramifications for interstate relations. Similarly, technological developments over the years have led to major transformations in maritime affairs and naval war fighting has undergone major changes.

Globalization too drives the triangular process of trade, technology and interdependence. Globalization and maritime economy has emerged as a significant issue in the growing debate on globalization and national security. Propelled by rapid changes in technology and communications, globalization is essentially an effort at integration of trade, services, markets and thus the economies. There are varied perceptions of globalization on how it opens the economies of the nation-states to global integration and its implications for national security of states that are considered the monolithic entities of state sovereignty. Globalization apparently seeks to provide equal access to the global economic pie, though not necessarily on an equal distribution basis. This has an important implication for maritime power of states even as states vie for trade and the access to resources critical for their economies. The rapid pace of economic growth gulps enormous resources that are finite and have to be accessed and transported on the transoceanic routes. The advances made in information and communication technologies too have accelerated the process of globalization. At another level, proliferation of information-technological innovations has had a far-reaching impact on the concept of future wars.

Globalization has thus left a profound impact on both landlocked and littoral states. Most countries have experienced buoyant economic and trade prosperity with access to global markets. The global system is predominantly dependant on international trade that has 90 per cent of trade moving by sea establishing a symbiotic relationship between globalization and maritime power.[20] There is also a transformation in the global logistic system with accents on seamless maritime supply chains focused on door-to-door delivery systems comprising mega ships and hub ports. This mega phenomenon is sparking a new coalescence of power, which is globalizing the supply chain system along the lines of volume, strength, and reach. The impacts of globalization have been felt in the development of maritime infrastructure with a revolution in port operations, shipping movement and transformed transactions that are now based on information technology. The transformation is evident in the foreign and domestic investment-driven innovation that has enabled several countries such as China and India into predominance of maritime activity. Globalization has been viably facilitated by information-age technology systems that make it increasingly difficult for countries or firms to pursue independent, much less autarkic, maritime policies in this globalized industry.

As discussed earlier, maritime power in its civilian and military importance has been the primary constituent for any rising power in any historical epoch. The aggregation of maritime power provides for the state's economic power in the global domain. In essence, maritime power in its comprehensive scope is built around the political, economic, military and technological dimensions while the constants of geography remain fundamental to the development of maritime power. To accrue an ambient understanding of the same, this chapter will deal with maritime power in its conceptual foundations. Maritime power needs to be contextualized and assessed in terms of its interrelationship between elements of maritime power, naval missions and force structure of navies along with a quantitative assessment. The chapter also attempts to highlight how states have exercised maritime power to achieve national objectives.

The chapter begins by undertaking a survey of the evolution and understanding of the concept of maritime power that evolved in Britain, the United States, Soviet Union, Japan, China and India. It postulates the constituents of maritime power and places them in the context of the leading maritime thinkers. It is quite essential that maritime power should be located in its derivative context that can be assessed from the quantitative dimensions and the mathematical matrices that denote national power and maritime power. The chapter culminates by demonstrating how states have deployed/employed maritime power to safeguard maritime interests.

It is purposeful to explore very briefly the schools of maritime thinking that have been characteristic of the dominant maritime powers in different historical epochs. At this juncture it is useful to point out that it would not be an exaggeration to state that the dominant discourse on contemporary maritime thought and practice has been from the oceanic powers of the Anglo-American tradition. This is so because maritime strategy and naval power has been the dominant niche of the Western world of scholarship and analysis among the strategic community. Besides, these powers were able to propound theories of maritime power and practised them. It will also be an interesting insight to perceive how the continental powers such as Russia have evolved notions of maritime power that were in contrast to the Anglo-American tradition. Also of significance is the understanding and practice of maritime power by the civilizational states of China and India who were the epitome of maritime prowess during the ancient period.

BRITISH MARITIME THOUGHT

In 1588, the defeat of the Spanish Armada in the English Channel by Sir Francis Drake resulted in British maritime pre-eminence.[21] With the exit of the Spanish naval dominance and the British ascendancy to a pre-eminent naval power, the Royal Navy emerged as the unchallenged naval power of the colonial and European world that crucially facilitated the rise of British mercantile-colonial-imperialism. Also, the dominance of the American continent and the command of the American, African and Asian littorals catapulted Britain to the position of a global power for nearly 300 years.

Britain's hegemony during the colonial period has been singularly attributed to their naval supremacy and the role the Royal Navy played in Britain's strategic power. The Royal Navy exercised colonial domination and sea-control by the tenacious control of the Indian Ocean and in that context, Panikkar notes that "It was the Century in which, it could legitimately be said that Britannia ruled the waves. The mere presence of the British Gunboat anywhere in the seven seas had decisive effects both for maintenance of peace and enforcement of policy."[22] He also points out that "Colonies away from the Motherland, unless dependent on their own strength, are only hostages to naval powers" and "nations who do not enjoy mastery of the seas are no more than hostages in the hands of the enemy", clearly highlighting the fact that the British Royal Navy was the vanguard of global mercantilism of that period.

Contemporary British maritime thought owes a great deal to Sir Julian Corbett. From his historical research, Corbett derived the principles governing the conduct of maritime warfare.[23] He offered "no general theory of sea power; instead, Corbett focused his thoughts on the nature of maritime strategy and the purpose of naval warfare."[24] By strategy he meant the principles governing a war in which the sea is a substantial factor, while naval strategy determined the movement of the fleet after maritime strategy had determined what part the fleet should play in relation to land forces. Command of the sea is the central issue in Corbett's thinking about naval warfare. It is identified with the ability to use sea communications for military and civil purposes and to deny such use to the enemy. Corbett makes an important distinction between land and sea warfare. In land warfare, the objective is seizure and holding of enemy territory; in a naval war the objective is to gain and secure the use of the seas.

In 1890 Corbett wrote that the real importance of maritime power is its influence on military operations. Admiral Jackie Fisher, British First Sea Lord (1904–10) summed up Corbett's views by stating "The army is a projectile to be fired by the navy."[25] Corbett was convinced that sea raiding or attack against seaborne trade was an indecisive and wasteful form of warfare. He appeared to be more interested in commerce protection than commerce destruction. Corbett's insistence that naval strategy was but part of a larger maritime whole also influenced British maritime practice.

In 1995, the Royal Navy released a publication entitled *The Fundamentals of British Maritime Doctrine, BR 1806*.[26] Earlier, the U.K. Army had published British Military Doctrine and the Air Force produced *AP 3000*. *BR 1806*, the number assigned to the old Naval War Manual, was retained in order to reflect the fact that doctrine is a long-standing concept for the Royal Navy.[27] *BR 1806* is specifically concerned with the application of maritime power at sea and maritime power projection from sea. It notes that maritime power is inherently joint in nature and emanates from forces drawn from all three services, both sea- and land-based, supported by national and commercial resources, exercising influence over the sea, land and air environment. The document does not define maritime power but discusses the nature of maritime power. Maritime power is "military, political and economic power exerted through an ability to use the sea". It points out that power at sea has been traditionally used for "general economic well being" or "survival of sea dependent states". The publication does not specify the constituents of maritime power and leaves it open to the extent that it also encompasses commercial maritime interests, size of resource zone, shipbuilding capacity and others, which are often seen by both classical maritime strategists and modern practitioners as elements of maritime power.

AMERICAN MARITIME THINKING

The discourse on American maritime thought emerged as a sequel to the dominant imperial maritime traditions of British naval and maritime dominance that held sway for almost three centuries. In the United States, Rear Admiral Alfred Thayer Mahan, United States Navy, through his most famous work, *The Influence of Sea Power Upon History 1660–1783*,[28] introduced the concept of sea power. He sought to explain sea power in its broadest context and discovered that British dominance of the sea was a major factor that allowed it to challenge its opponents. Mahan explained Britain's success by developing a simple deduction: greatness and strength are the products of wealth derived from trade: to protect this wealth, Britain possessed a powerful navy.[29] Mahan described sea power as the ability of a country to use the oceans for national advantage and argued that nations seek sea power as "a great highway" that provides a means of cheap transport. His thesis was that no nation could aspire to be a great power unless it effectively used the sea for both commercial and military purposes. For Mahan, the use of oceans and seas for one's own purpose and to preclude its use by the enemy was critical, and this could be achieved through the application of naval power. Thus the primary task of the navy was to gain ascendancy and challenge the opponent navy and drive shipping off the oceans thus facilitating unimpeded and unchallenged utilization of the seas.

Interestingly, Mahan remarked that sea power was "at once an abstraction and a concrete fact" and did not clearly distinguish it from the ideas of "command of the sea" and "sea control" as if these terms were synonymous.[30] However, he was convinced that sea power was based on the trilogy of the navy, commerce and colonies. The fighting instrument, i.e. the navy, enabled a state to acquire colonies and territories. This encouraged trade and commerce resulting in wealth and prosperity. He concluded that being a great power meant being a sea power and that sea power meant commercial and naval strength.

As for America (his own country), Mahan was convinced that it did not possess any of the characteristics of a sea power. The essence of American thinking was centred on the old tradition of coastal defence and commerce raiding and the navy was intended for and employed for limited roles. Mahan dismissed commerce raiding as the weakest form of naval warfare.[31] To substantiate his argument, he cited the French experience. British ships had successfully challenged the French commerce raiding forces, and this experience had highlighted the importance of sea power.

The Mahanian philosophy about the nature of sea power rested on six factors, which he called "elements of sea power". These included: (a) geographical position, (b) physical conformation, (c) extent of territory, (d) population (size and character of the people, their maritime orientation and an ability to absorb technology), (e) character of people, and (f) character of the government.[32]

Expounding on his views, Mahan stressed that geographical conditions determined the sea power of a state. Britain's geographical location served strategic advantage both in terms of access to seas, as well as to control the "great thoroughfare of the world's sea borne trade route". Similarly, for the

United States, the Panama Canal and the Caribbean Sea offered comparable conditions to the Channel to England and Suez to the Mediterranean states.[33] Further, a country with a long coastline but no ports could never aspire to be a sea power. It would be at a great disadvantage because it would be unable to engage in seaborne trade, have no shipping or navy of its own. Thus ports and harbours are a source of strength and wealth, and more so if located on navigable rivers. This would naturally facilitate and encourage both domestic and foreign trade. However, these could become a source of weakness if not properly defended. Citing the example of France, Mahan argued that it had few military ports in the channel but excellent harbours in the Mediterranean.[34] These were favourably located for both internal and external trade. The "extent of territory" of a nation also determined sea power of a state. It is not the area in square miles that a country possesses that is important but rather the length of its coastline and the disposition of its harbours that are to be considered in evaluating sea power.[35]

Similarly, the number of people that earned their livelihood from the sea and were available for employment on board ships was another significant factor for the growth of sea power.[36] National character, though abstract, constitutes an important element of sea power and Mahan observed that the character of the government and the institutions were an important factor in determining sea power of a state.[37] He noted that it is the government that can provide directions for growth of maritime enterprise. Britain reached the greatest height of sea power because the government aimed at becoming a great maritime power.

SOVIET/RUSSIAN MARITIME APPROACH

Russian maritime traditions reflect the continental state's dilemma with regard to sea power. Unlike Britain, the United States and Japan who enjoyed unhindered access to the warm water ports and access to the sea for resources and markets for their economic survival, geography and climate constrained Russia's access to the seas resulting in a maritime dilemma, but it exploited the sea for political and military purposes.[38] Russia has been in continuous quest for warm water ports for trade and naval power projection and it was the grand strategic objective of Peter the Great to build Russia into a great naval power that resulted in victory during the Northern Wars (1700–21) and provided the much needed access to the Baltic Sea resulting in direct relationships with the European countries.[39] During later years, Russian naval power was challenged by the emergent Japanese maritime power resulting in the climactic defeat of Russia's naval fleets in July 1904 under Admiral

Rojdestvensky in the fateful Battle of Tsushima where the Russian Fleet was obliterated with massive casualities. During World War I, the Russian Navy did not participate in major engagements at sea, but some squadrons of the Baltic and Black Sea fleets had several confrontations. However during World War II, the Soviet Navy played a major role and engaged the navies of Germany and Japan with great success.

The Cold War was quite a fertile period of renaissance in Soviet maritime thinking under Admiral Sergei Gorshkov, Commander-in-Chief of the Soviet Navy. Sergei Gorshkov's understanding of sea power was quite similar to Mahan but was partly flavoured with communist ideology, especially relating to access to resources and territories/colonies.[40] Expounding his views on sea power, Admiral Gorshkov wrote a series of articles entitled "Navies in War and Peace" that appeared in the Soviet journal *Morsky Sbornik* (the naval review) in 1972–73. These articles examined the historical importance of sea power and their relevance to Russian sea power. An expanded work comprising these articles along with some more writings on modern uses of the navies appeared in the English translation of a book *Sea Power of the State*, published in 1976. The volume received accolades in Russia and Marshal Bagramayan in *Izvestia* noted, "For the first time in Soviet literature the author formulates the concept of sea power as a scientific category"[41] and other commentators praised the work as a major contribution to military science for developing an accurate understanding of sea power. Indeed, the volume reflects Admiral Gorshkov's grasp of maritime affairs and a critical evaluation of the elements, requirements and advantages of a modern sea power.

Admiral Gorshkov argued that the fundamental difference in the understanding of sea power by the Soviet Union and the imperialist powers stem from the latter's "class essence". It (sea power) also determined the goals, tasks and means of applying various components, notably the navy, which in the imperialist states were assigned the role for world dominance.[42] For the Soviet Union, the main goal was to build communism, and sea power was one of the important factors in strengthening its economy and consolidating links with countries friendly to it.[43]

Like Mahan, Gorshkov believed that geography, economics and the character of the leadership determined sea power.[44] He defined sea power as "the ability of a state to study (explore) the oceans and harness its wealth; the merchant and fishing fleet and their ability to meet the needs of the state and a navy matching the interests of the state".[45] The importance of a strong navy was a predominant theme in Gorshkov's writings and the force was considered as the guarantor of security. Also the sea was an important source of food, hydrocarbons, energy and minerals.

Gorshkov was convinced that shipping and shipbuilding formed an important component of sea power and served a nation both during war and peace. Besides being an important means of economy, the mercantile marine of a state was an important support element for the navy during war. He observed that the merchant fleets of capitalist countries were being developed keeping in mind the requirements during war as a means to transport men and material.[46] Perhaps the most unique facet of Gorshkov's understanding of imperialist sea power was his appreciation of big businesses involved in the economies of overseas countries. These businesses used raw materials of the host country and produced goods for exports which had resulted in enhanced seaborne trade, and the expansion of economic monopolies. Gorshkov considered these institutions as accomplices in exploiting the peoples of these countries.[47] This in turn made them dependent on the imperialists for economic, political and military assistance.

JAPAN'S MARITIME DEVELOPMENTS

In the 13th century, Japan had established commercial contacts with India and Samurai warriors had fought against the forces of Korea and Mongolia and Kublai Khan had retreated after a shocking defeat in 1281 due to a typhoon, the "divine wind".[48] In later years, Imperial Japan watched Asian colonization with concern (Japan had a significant Portuguese presence) and it was the considered policy of the Tokugawa Shogunate to insulate Japan from the outside world. In 1635, the Shogunate had barred Japanese citizens from making contact with foreigners, and travel both into and outside Japan was forbidden.[49] Interestingly, in 1638, Japan banned construction of large merchant vessels and only coastal trade was permitted that resulted in a near total isolation of Japan to the global maritime developments, scientific innovations and markets. Limited access was permitted to Chinese businessmen and the Dutch were permitted one ship visit per year that traded in silk.

For nearly 250 years Japan survived in isolation until the arrival of the Americans in July 1853. Commodore Matthew C. Perry acting under the orders of the U.S. President Franklin Pierce sailed into Japan with four warships and was successful in opening Japan to the outside world with the signing of the Treaty of Amity and Commerce.[50] The Meiji Restoration in 1868 was a turning point in Japanese history and the ruling elite began to rapidly develop military industry keeping in mind that if Japan was to preserve its independence, it must invest in defence. By 1890, Japan was commercially strong enough to correct unequal treaties it had been subjected to by the United States, Britain and other western countries.

The political and military coercion by the United States encouraged the Shogunate to invest in military building and permitted construction of ocean-going vessels. It was a coincidence arising from the repairs of a Russian wooden frigate that the Japanese were able to obtain the drawings to build more vessels and the Russians also provided guns and assisted gunsmiths.[51] In the run-up to the development of the Japanese military industry, it was the Japanese Navy that benefited the most and the impact was visible during the Sino-Japanese war of 1905 and the Russo-Japanese war of 1905, where the Soviet fleet was totally decimated.

At a time when Alfred Thayer Mahan was developing his ideas for the magnum opus *The Influence of Sea Power Upon History, 1660–1783*, in Japan Sato Tetsutaro had developed a sophisticated maritime thought for Japan that was based on Japan's own historical experiences.[52] Sato Tetsutaro had vehemently argued with the Shogunate on the importance of the navy to Japan and sought increased funding. Sato travelled to Britain and the United States visiting naval facilities and on return concluded that Japan's defence lay in building deterrence and preventing the enemy form threatening the nation's coast. In a controversial volume on Imperial defence, Sato concluded that the navy, and not the army, stood as Japan's first line of defence. At about the same period, another Imperial Japanese Navy Officer Akiyama Saneyuki, came to be acknowledged as "a brilliant naval strategist and tactician and a pivotal figure who exerted a dramatic and comprehensive impact on Japanese naval thinking". Interestingly, modern Japanese naval thought begins with Akiyama Saneyuki.[53] Akiyama was the chief architect of the Japanese victory in the battle of Tsushima in May 1905, and had developed a conceptual defensive framework that laid the foundation for Imperial Japanese Navy's defensive maritime posture until 1940. Notwithstanding that, Mahanian thought impacted vigorously on Imperial Japanese naval thinking.[54]

The robust strengths of the Imperial Japanese Navy and its diligent naval build-up enabled it to compete with the tonnage and firepower of the United States and Britain. This resulted in the 1921 Naval Conference in London that sought to confine the strength of the Imperial Japanese Navy.[55] The argument for containing the Japanese was based on the premise that a strong Imperial Japanese Navy was a sign of problems for the Far East particularly Britain. This was a major setback to the Japanese maritime industry as the treaty sought a ten-year moratorium on capital shipbuilding that dropped by nearly 80 per cent from 1921 to 1932. After denouncing the Washington and London treaties and refusing to sign the Second London Naval Treaty, Japan launched a massive warship shipbuilding programme of heavy battle ships, carriers, destroyers, submarines and auxiliary vessels.[56] By 1937, Japanese shipyards were competing with Britain and producing one-fifth of the global shipping production.

The long history of the Imperial Japanese Navy had developed a rich tradition of strategic maritime thought that was indigenous to Japan. The Imperial Japanese Navy was the crucial enabler for the imperial-hegemonic dominance of the Asia with their grandiose strategy that had a naval dominance of the region. Japan entered World War II along with Germany and Italy with strong assents on expansionism, thinking that there would be no resistance from Asian powers. In December 1941, the Imperial Japanese Navy deployed its aircraft carriers in the Pacific Ocean and attacked Pearl Harbor. Later during the War, it took the combined military and naval might of the United States, Britain and the allied naval powers deployed in the Pacific and Indian Ocean to counteract the Japanese might through a series of naval battles leading to the surrender in 1945.

CHINESE MARITIME UNDERSTANDING

China's maritime history has several epochs of maritime glory and is best understood through the maritime developments that took place during ancient times. The Song Dynasty and Ming Dynasty endeavoured to build China into a major maritime power that resulted in several successful maritime expeditions to Southeast Asia and the Indian Ocean. China certainly was the strongest sea power in Asia in that period. The Ming Emperor Ren-Song noted "To make China rich and strong, we (China) must control the seas. But while wealth comes from the sea, danger does also."[57]

China's regime and dynasty changes had serious impacts on its maritime culture. Its preoccupation in the north and the weakening of the mercantile economy also served to weaken its maritime legacy in the subsequent period. In the 19th and 20th centuries, it was the external sea power that came to haunt China and subjugated it. China was frequently attacked from the sea. For instance, between the period of the Opium Wars (1839–42 and 1856–60), till the founding of the People's Republic in 1949, China was invaded from the littorals more than 470 times and as many as 14,697 naval visits were undertaken by the Colonial powers.[58] Sun Yat-sen understood the neglect of naval power by Chinese feudal rulers resulting in China losing its territory and sovereignty to Western powers and noted that "since the great changes in world forces, national might often depends on the navy, not the army, with the naval victor often having the superiority of national might".[59] But after his death, the quest for Chinese maritime innovation and thinking declined.

After the communists came to power in China in 1949, the leadership once again began to salvage the maritime significance of the state. The maritime infrastructure was developed with the Soviet Union's assistance and several merchant ships and naval combatants, including nuclear submarines were built. There was a maritime ambition that was limited in outlook primarily due to the continental mindset of the Chinese leaders influenced by the Soviet military doctrine. Deng Xiaoping's four modernizations programme had a very important impact on coastal zone development programmes and contributed to the national economy. At the same time Chinese academics began studying the significance of maritime power. The focus of these studies was the transformation of China into a strong maritime power. Significant investment was made into studies relating to marine environment, resource exploitation and the sinews of maritime power were built on the foundations of a strong navy that would safeguard China's maritime interests. Contemporary maritime developments in China are discussed in succeeding chapters.

Significantly, Admiral Liu Huaqing is a contemporary exponent of Chinese maritime thought and ambitions. Trained at the Soviet Voroshilov Naval Institute, Liu was the Commander-in-Chief of the PLA Navy from 1982–86.[60] Later, he was appointed as the Vice Chairman, Central Military Commission and is often referred to as the Chinese "Mahan" or "Gorshkov".[61] As a practitioner and a strategist, Liu was convinced of the relevance of maritime power for China.[62] Liu strongly advocated the robust development of China's maritime power and its operational capabilities and had consistently argued that sea power was crucial and China must develop a navy capable of defending her maritime interests. It was his strong belief that there was intense competition among nations to carve out resource-rich areas and the navy had an all-important task of guarding China's maritime interests.[63] Thus, formal and formidable foundations were laid for furthering maritime power.

INDIAN MARITIME DEVELOPMENTS

India has a distinguished ancient maritime history that was nurtured on strong commerce, trade, movement of peoples, spread of culture and the rooting of Indian influences in the Mediterranean, Persia, Southeast Asia and China. The Mauryas, Satavahnas, Chalukyas, Cholas, and Chera kingdoms had a flourishing maritime enterprise and some of them had developed powerful navies that engaged in warfare. These global links were significant for the growth of Indian influences and trade that flourished on high growth rates and expanding trade and India and the Indian Ocean emerged as the centres of maritime activity and maritime enterprise.[64] Historical maritime and naval developments in India are discussed in greater details in Chapter 7.

Significantly, abundance of raw materials and goods, prosperity, and wealth were the magnet for the European initiative to trade with India that later turned into colonial subjugation. In the colonial times, the British had developed a minimal maritime infrastructure in India that was to cater to transport raw materials and goods to England and also for sustaining the expeditionary British forces in Asia. Engaging the vast Indian human resources, the British exploited both civilian and military labour to support their overseas colonial operations in Southwest Asia, Southeast Asia and Africa. The Royal Indian Marine (RIM) was established in 1892 with an initial force of seven ships and about 2,000 men.[65] The RIM was the principal force that was deployed in campaigns in the Mediterranean, Persian Gulf and Burma. The RIM also saw action in terms of convoy duties in the Atlantic and the Pacific Oceans. In subsequent years, the British did not expand the RIM, since it was tailored to a minimal auxiliary force to the Royal Navy.

The British strategy for India rested on commercial interests aimed at maintaining trade links with the homeland.[66] It inhibited Indian initiatives to develop parallel capacities in mercantile trading and also served to shun Indian participation in maritime matters that resulted in a total lack of indigenous maritime thought in India. The British of course had to leave a few elderly platforms that for reasons of sea-worthiness were not worth a journey to Britain.[67]

For India, the geo-spatial location in the Southern Asian-Indian Ocean regions confers its "maritimeness".[68] It was thus *fait accompli* that the Indian Ocean derived from its Indian epistemological root. Although this fact is deeply rooted in Indian maritime strategic thinking, no theories on the application of maritime power have been developed. Much of the understanding of matters maritime is still based on British and American thought and practice.[69] This is notwithstanding the fact that during the 1970s and 1980s there was a major influx of Soviet/Russian military hardware, but these were adapted to Western maritime thought.[70]

Indian writings on "sea power" or "maritime power" draw inspiration from Mahan and British articulations. Sea power is described as "the ability of a state to use the sea. This depends in large measure on its possession of a naval force, merchant marine, fishing and oceanographic fleet, port facilities, shipbuilding industry and the system of marine finance and insurance."[71] This falls short of including important constituents such as the EEZ, seabed area, and technological capability to exploit these resources and the all-important factor of geography. Sea power is also described as "that part of the maritime strategy with which a nation attempts to achieve predetermined economic and political goals", and maritime strategy is defined as "the total response of a nation to the ocean around it".[72] Similarly, it is also argued that there is a mistaken belief that "sea power" is a synonym for a strong navy.[73] At yet another level, it is noted that "Sea power is an important commodity. A country like India without sea power is a weak state."[74]

The more contemporary writings and articulations describe maritime power as military, political and economic power exerted through an ability to use the seas. A distinction is however made by explaining military maritime power as the ability of a state to influence events through amphibious and ship-launched attack operations.[75] Naval forces are considered an element of maritime power to further national interests, be they economic, diplomatic or strategic. Indian naval practitioners note that naval power is that element of military power associated with forces, ships, submarines, and aircraft, naval marines that operate primarily on, over, under or from the sea.[76]

It has also been argued that sea power is not merely warships and Prime Minister Jawaharlal Nehru was quoted to have observed that mercantile marine represents power of a different type; not power of armed might but the power of a country's growing wealth and prosperity.[77] Jawaharlal Nehru was truly visionary to look beyond the naval roles and operations of India's maritime power to envision that economic growth and trade had an inextricable link with maritime power. Nehru's ambient vision of the economic premises of maritime power also had a strong naval vision that was quite evident in the early procurements that India made to justify that its subcontinental territorial domain had both continental and maritime elements in that context. This perception has thus an ambient definition that goes beyond the naval dimensions of sea power encompassing the economic and marine resources of the state that augments national power. Nehru is reported to have said "To be secure on land, we must be supreme at sea."[78]

THE MARITIME KEYBOARD: SOURCES AND ELEMENTS

The concept of maritime power has an ambient scope for its conceptual definition and they are contextualized to their respective national maritime milieus. A *tour d'horizon* of maritime thought over the past centuries highlights that the concept of maritime power has undergone a major transformation and states have been in constant quest for building both civilian and military maritime prowess to further their national interest. Significantly, maritime power, both as a concept and as a force, has become an important component of national power. As a concept, states have in the past and present, continued to exploit the sea for economic, political and military benefits and as a force maritime power has been employed for safeguarding national interests pivoting on sovereignty protection, safeguarding maritime territory, protection of resources at sea, or safety of sea-based commerce. Maritime power is dynamic in nature and reasonably flexible to assimilate several inputs that facilitate a state to use the sea to further its national interests.

From the classical Mahanian maritime thought (sea power) that rested on navy, colony and commerce, to its contemporary interpretations, several new elements have been added and have contributed immensely to a broader understanding of the concept of maritime power. Several technological revolutions in weaponry and warfare, communications, ship design and propulsion and the ongoing Revolution in Military Affairs based on information technology have transformed the nature of naval warfare. Also, the "territorialization"[79] of the seas resulting in a partial sovereignty over the "great commons" evolving from the interpretation and application of the Law of the Sea have resulted in a new understanding of the use of maritime power.

The ever-changing nature of maritime intercourse emergent from the new security environment plagued with violent non-state actors' calls for greater military engagement with regional and extra-regional maritime forces with assents on cooperative arrangements has brought to the fore emerging cooperative roles that the navies are required to perform, and has transformed the politico-military nature of maritime power. Further, in this era of globalization, states have become more conscious of their ability to use the sea to their advantage in their economic, political and military interaction, resulting in a new appreciation of the power that accrues to them by way of promoting interdependence that is assiduously developed by employment of maritime power. There is near unanimity among the maritime strategic and research community of the varied scope of the constituents of seapower or maritime power and the continual and constant state of advancement.[80]

The corpus of maritime thought enunciated by prominent maritime strategists and practitioners has had a profound impact upon the state's desire to possess a certain degree of maritime power. K.M. Panikkar quotes Khaireddin Pasha, the Turkish admiral in the Mediterranean who was confronting the Christian world in the 15th century, as saying, "He who rules on the seas will shortly rule on the land also."[81] It has also been noted that the "sea is not only a medium to fight on but also something to compete",[82] and fight for.

In the course of the development of maritime power, states and their protagonists have been influenced by the prevalent schools of maritime thought and have attempted to emulate them while developing their own concepts of maritime power. While in the case of some, maritime thought is based on their civilizational and historical experiences, they have also been influenced by the prevalent schools of thought. The imperative is to accrue a comprehensive understanding and assessment of maritime power.

Several scholars have synthesized the seminal writings on the concept of sea power and presented input/output model[83] of sea power. In one such model, the inputs are "sources" and "elements" and the output is sea power. The inputs are based on classical Mahanian "elements of sea power" wherein maritime community, resources, styles of government and geography are considered. The model identifies merchant shipping, overseas possessions or bases and the fighting instrument as the three material elements of sea power.[84]

Although this model is in conformity with the basic Mahanian approach, it does not take into consideration the subjectivity and objectivity of the constituents of the input. For instance, it is difficult to determine the quality of the maritime community, determine the nature of resources, measure geography and calculate the style of government. Resources could be material, monetary, living, non-living or even the population as a resource base. The constituents are not segregated into political, economic, geography and military to facilitate a clear understanding of the role of a particular constituent as well as to keep in mind the objectivity and subjectivity of the constituents.

In another model, the inputs are land area, shoreline length, exclusive economic zone, fisheries resources, geographic locale, offshore oil, and so on. The output is population, gross domestic product (GDP), number of ships, shipbuilding, and fish catch and marine treaties. Both the inputs and output are objective and quantifiable. The review of the above model would reveal some lacunae in the output side. Viewed holistically it would be that the constituents in the output are essentially the inputs. For instance, the number of naval ships of a country, shipbuilding capacity, and capability to catch fish are a measure of a state's reaction to sea dependence and not related to sea dependence itself.

The third model divides the constituents of maritime power into three major domains, i.e. physical, economic and political. These have been further subdivided into objective and subjective. The inputs undergo filtration through a decision process. It is noted that the "three groupings are not distinct, nor are they totally black and white in their division. It may be that a particular constituent will find it located in more than one domain." That is, resources living and non-living, located in the physical domain, would find a logical position in the economic domain too. Similarly, shipbuilding can find itself in the economic and political domains based on the resource benefits made available to the shipbuilding industry by a government and maritime tradition.

There are weaknesses in this model. The resultant output of the model is essentially the coercive component of maritime power, i.e. a navy, the fighting instrument, and its employment in for military purposes and in diplomacy as an instrument of state policy. In fact, the fighting instrument is an input component and an instrument to safeguard maritime interests. Also, the model does not include constituents such as level of technological developments arising from the use of information technology that supports its maritime developments both civilian and military.

It is argued that input components of the above models require a revision and a more comprehensive model would include five domains: geographical, military, political, economic and information technology pivoting on RMA. It is clear that the military domain is an input and is subject to decision processes and should be considered separately from the revolution brought about by information technology that has transformed the nature of maritime interaction and therefore needs to be considered as a separate domain. This model is better equipped to undertake an objective assessment of comprehensive maritime power of a nation. The inputs are tangible, and those that are intangible can be computed by using numerical coefficients to obtain an empirical evaluation of maritime power and this is discussed in the next section.

MARITIME CALCULUS

It is evident from the previous section that maritime power is a mix of the geographical, economic, political and technological strengths and weaknesses of a state. It is also determined by the military component (both nuclear and conventional). While some of the constituents are tangible, some are intangible, and are usually described in terms of national will, maritime tradition and national strategy. A sound maritime strategy requires an objective calculus of several elements that constitute the maritime power of a state.

In attempting to determine an empirical evaluation of maritime power, it will be instructive to understand the concept of power. Power *per se* is a subjective concept and is built and employed by states based on perceptions of their own power and that of the opponent. More often than not, the end game is generally known, and is perceived based on the character and the strategic culture of the antagonists. Only in desperate conditions, do states enter themselves into conflict as the last resort. Thus the antagonists would normally engage in the exercise of determining motivations, intentions and capabilities of each other.

It is true that a realistic assessment of power is an extraordinarily complex empirical problem. The inputs to the power of a state have varied from time to time and can encompass a large number of elements. Ray S. Cline envisaged the calculus that determines the power of nations in the international context as a basis for planning American defence and foreign policy.[85] The formula reads as follows:

$$Pp = (C + E + M)(S + W)$$

Its terms are defined as:

- Pp = Perceived Power
- C = Critical Mass = Population + Territory
- E = Economic Capability
- M = Military Capability
- S = Strategic Purpose
- W = Will to Pursue National Strategy

In order to undertake an empirical analysis of maritime power, this study has adapted Cline's equation. For the purpose of assessment of maritime power it would be useful to group the constituents into at least five domains: geographic, economic, military, technological and political. The terms for these domains can be referred to as:

- Pmp = Perceived maritime power
- G = Geographical factors
- E = Economic capability
- M = Military capability
- T = Technological capability
- P = Strategic purpose of maritime power (S) and a will to pursue maritime Strategy (W).

In sequence with Mahan's footsteps, the first factor for measuring maritime power is geography. This is essentially based on the length of the coastline, island territories, land area ratio, population, size of EEZ, continental shelf for seabed exploitation, number of harbours and size of population and maritime community. Also of significance is the location of a state with respect to choke points, international sea routes, sources of raw materials and markets. These factors are tangible and can be quantified objectively. In the context of geography, the location of allies and friends is significant; in times of crisis, these should be able to reach in time and provide necessary assistance. The first approximation therefore becomes:

$$Pmp = G.$$

Given that the United States, China, India, Indonesia, Canada, Australia, Philippines, Fiji and Brazil have large EEZs, long coastline and seabed exploitation areas, this should mean that these are major maritime powers. But exceptions would have to be made in the case of the Philippines and Fiji who have large EEZs but are not major maritime powers. The above equation would thus be an over simplification of the complex problem and therefore requires additional factors and coefficients to make a more accurate assessment. The above equation becomes more useful if:

$$Pmp = G + E$$

The material and economic wealth of a state are an important source of maritime power. The economic strength of a state is built around the availability of natural resources, production of goods, services, trade and technological capability that provide for the well-being of the society and its people and also build its military power. In that context, the maritime power of a state is dependent on its merchant shipping, fishing fleet, level of development of ports, GDP, critical mineral resources, shipbuilding, ship repairing, maritime trade, energy production, hydrocarbon reserves, size of marine-related industry and sea-based food resources. These elements are also quantifiable and it is possible to rank maritime nations to determine the combined economic strength/weakness of a state.

If the perception of maritime power was based on geographic and economic factors, then the United States, Japan, and Russia would hold the top rank. India and China with good geographic location and impressive economic indicators can be counted as maritime powers but Honduras, Libya, and Panama with large registered mercantile tonnage cannot be considered as maritime powers. At this juncture it is useful to expand the equation to include the military factor. The formula therefore is:

$$Pmp = (G + E + M)$$

Perceptions of military strength are highly subjective. However, a weighting system has to take into account both the nuclear and the conventional component of the fighting instrument. The perceived maritime power of a nation is enhanced if it possesses nuclear weapon-capable naval forces that can act as a deterrent. It is safe to assign a higher maritime power weight to the United States, Russia, the United Kingdom, France and China based on their

SSBN/SSN/ships/aircraft capable of delivering nuclear weapons. Similarly, it is possible to estimate conventional naval power based on manpower figures, number of combatants, and range of weapons. However, the intangibles of military power such as troop skill, morale, quality of military leadership, coherence of military strategies, flexibility, mobility and reach of forces cannot be discounted. By applying a series of conversion factors or coefficients to these factors, estimated maritime power can be computed and navies can be compared hierarchically.

Changes in technology too have had a major impact on matters maritime. The advent of computers, space-based reconnaissance, digital communications and information technology have been instrumental in changing the nature of maritime intercourse. Almost all the elements of maritime power have been influenced by technology. Besides, the networking of knowledge is leading to a new technology in the computational field. Informatics has telescoped the rate of obsolescence. The 1990–91 Gulf War provided a glimpse of high technology in maritime affairs. Therefore, the formula needs to be readjusted to read as:

$$Pmp = (G + E + M + T)$$

The two critical intangible factors in the assessment of maritime power are national maritime strategy and the strength of national will or maritimeness. These are part of the political factors that are involved. National will is the foundation on which national strategy is formulated and carried through to success.[86] The equation therefore now reads as follows:

$$Pmp = (G + E + M + T)(S + W)$$

The "S" factor comprises a clear cut strategic maritime doctrine with plans to exercise maritime power and aggrandizement of influence and strategic maritime culture.[87] The "W" factor is based on national leadership and the relevance of maritime strategy to national interests. This factor needs to be qualified by adding the tradition of earlier success in maritime expeditions. The above calculus thus provides an analysis of perceived maritime power. Many factors included in the equation are subjective and have to be dealt with using numerical coefficients based on the viewpoint of decision-makers.

EMPLOYMENT OF MARITIME POWER

Since ancient times naval power has been an integral dimension of the process of development of maritime power. The navies emerged as the most viable and the primary strategic arm for projecting power across the oceans and safeguarding national interests that ranged from protection of sovereignty, safeguarding territory, safety of commerce at sea, preserving order in the maritime domain and even protection of diasporas.

In the matrices of national power, navies have played crucial roles in foreign policies and diplomatic processes of the state in various roles that are symbolic and substantive. Given the attributes of flexibility, mobility and visibility, naval forces are important tools available to states for conduct of their foreign policies. Significantly, naval platforms emerge in benign and coercive roles and contribute towards the stabilization of a crisis. This is achieved through their ability to cover long distances over the seas that provide seamless and transnational transit, an ability to project power far from the home shores, and the three-dimensional means of power projection, i.e. surface, subsurface and in air-space through a networked operation. Also, the deployments provide subtle and nuanced diplomacy. At another level, nuclear weapons at sea provide for assured deterrence with a viable second-strike capability. The relevance and the leveraging effectiveness of naval power in remote locations as an increasingly effective expeditionary strike and logistical force is amply analysed in the following brief case studies that highlight the roles of navies in contemporary times.

THE FALKLANDS WAR 1982

The Falklands group of islands, located some 8,000 nautical miles from home, is a British Colony in South Atlantic. It comprises the Falkland Islands and South Georgia and in 1883, Britain occupied these islands from Argentina and established a garrison. Argentina's continuing claims to sovereignty encouraged Buenos Aires to seize the islands in April 1982 and the British responded by dispatching a large task force to recapture the islands. A series of sea, air and land battles took place, resulting in the final surrender by Argentina to Britain.

An examination of the Falkland conflict highlights how Britain was able to harness its maritime power and bring it to bear on Argentina. The campaign highlighted how Britain was able to marshal national resources and also its political determination to dispatch a large naval force over a long distance for the restoration of sovereignty of the islands. For Britain, the biggest impediment was geography.[88] As noted earlier, the islands are located 8,000 nautical miles from home in perhaps the most inhospitable maritime environment. It was a long voyage for the British task force to reach the area of operation and the passage had its fair share of both material failure and human fatigue. The British colonies at St. Helena, Ascension and Tristan da Cunha in South Atlantic were invaluable. The Ascension Island, located 3,700 nautical miles from Britain, is also an important base for the Royal Air Force. The force had exercised, recouped and undertook maintenance of its forces before heading for the Falklands. Besides, the Wideawake airfield in the Ascension Island served as an important staging post for British *Vulcans*, *Nimrods* and *Hercules* aircraft. This 10,000-feet runway had earlier been a staging post for the British during World War II.[89] Though such distant territories serve as assets and augment distant operations, they can also be a source of weakness. These need to be militarily equipped to deter an opponent from attacking.

The British task force comprised carriers, destroyers, frigates and Royal Fleet Auxiliaries. The British flagged merchant fleet was augmented to support the task force through its long voyage to the Falklands. These included 3 passenger liners, 15 oil tankers, 4 passenger cargo ships and several general cargo ships, offshore support vessels, tugs and trawlers.[90] Some of these were provided with helicopter landing facilities, replenishment at sea equipment, military communication facilities, satellite navigation and satellite communication equipment. These ships were refitted, repaired and retrofitted to meet the requirements of the taskforce.

The contribution made by the maritime community was well demonstrated. The shipyards and the dockyards played an all-important role. Their ability to convert a large number of vessels for military deployment was indeed noteworthy. That several vessels had to be fitted with helicopter landing decks, fuelling stations and special cargo spaces without much notice was a reflection of the importance of maritime infrastructure and the maritime community worked hard to deliver these vessels on time. A task force comprising two aircraft carriers, two assault ships supporting auxiliary ships and merchant vessels totalling 110 vessels sailed for the Falkland Islands.[91] Some 28,000 personnel were mobilized and these included some 330 officers and 1,170 men of the merchant navy.[92] The Falklands campaign demonstrated that the maritime community is an important component of maritime power.

Turning to an examination of the fighting instruments of maritime power, both the Royal Navy and the *Armada Republic Argentina* were fairly modern, well-trained and balanced forces. Both sides had carriers,[93] destroyers and submarines. The Argentine Navy had been trained in Britain and had even carried out practice missile firings at the British firing range. As a prelude to the Falklands Operation, the Argentine Navy had exercised with the Uruguay Navy and was a well-trained force. Unlike the Argentine Navy, the Royal

Navy had other commitments too. Also, the British fleet had been tailored to NATO requirements and was essentially equipped for anti-submarine warfare role. Despite these constraints and geographical difficulties, the Royal Navy got the better of the *Armada Republic Argentina*. The campaign showcased British maritime power and the determination of the political leadership to use it to protect national interests.

GULF WAR 1990–91

The Gulf War 1990–91 once again showcased the ability of states to exercise maritime power to achieve a decisive victory. After the Iraqi military crossed over into neighbouring Kuwait in August 1990, the United States, along with a thirty-two-nation coalition force, stemmed the misadventure. Iraqi military ambitions were challenged and ultimately subdued.

Accounts of the Gulf War 1990–91 have lauded the relevance of land-based air power.[94] The thirty-eight-day aerial campaign rapidly gained air supremacy and seriously degraded Iraqi command, control and communications, thus facilitating the other objectives of the air campaign and greatly assisting the land offensive. The contribution made by the maritime forces of the coalition is also noteworthy. The flexibility, mobility and lethality of maritime power were suitably exhibited during Desert Shield/Desert Storm. Maritime superiority enabled multinational forces to implement and sustain UN sanctions against Iraq.

The aim of the initial coalition deployment of military forces in response to the Iraqi invasion of Kuwait was to contain the conflict and particularly prevent a further advance into Saudi Arabia and hence keep free the ports and air bases needed for subsequent reinforcements.[95] The build-up began with the deployment of two carriers task groups (*USS Eisenhower* and *Independence*) into the area.[96] These were stationed so as to strike Iraqi targets. This was followed by the deployment of four additional carrier battle groups, a thirty-one-ship amphibious task force under the command ship, *USS Blue Ridge*, and several other combatants and support ships. The first combat aircraft on the scene were the air wings of the *USS Eisenhower* and *USS Independence*. Additional land-based fixed-wing aircraft began arriving shortly afterwards.

Desert Shield/Desert Storm validated the fact that, for sustained distant combat operations, large stocks of equipment and ordnance must be transported by sea. The importance of mercantile marine/special ships is a pre-requirement for a decisive victory. The first Maritime Pre-positioning Ships, with ordnance for the U.S. Marine Corps, arrived seven days after the deployment order. Two Afloat Pre-position Force ships carrying U.S. Air Force equipment followed, and ordnance arrived ten days after the deployment order. Strategic sealift from Diego Garcia and Guam was therefore crucial to operations in the Gulf. Afloat Pre-position Ships, Maritime Pre-positioning Ships, Fast Sea-Lift Ship and Rapid Reserve Force augmented the main force through a rapid build-up of men and material. Similarly, two U.S. hospital ships were on station and ready in the Persian Gulf within about sixteen days of the deployment order. This was perhaps the largest and fastest sea-lift operation with more than 240 ships carrying 18.3 billion pounds of equipment and supplies to sustain Desert Shield/Desert Storm.[97] The naval reservists played an important role. The call-up of reservists in support of the operations was probably the largest since the Vietnam War. Twenty-one thousand naval reserves joined active duty units. They made significant contributions in medical, cargo handling, mine warfare, naval control of shipping and several other duties. Admiral James E. Taylor, USN, Director of Naval Reserves noted that the reservists were motivated and well trained.[98]

On 17 January 1991, Desert Storm unleashed its fury with a barrage of *Tomahawk* Land Attack Missiles (TLAMS). In all, 288 TLAMS were fired from cruisers, destroyers, battleships and submarines with a success rate of over more than 85 per cent.[99] It was a testimony to the uses of advanced technology and constituted a revolution in warfare. *E2C Hawk Eye* operations kept track of Iraqi aircraft and coordinated reconnaissance and combat air patrols. The Unarmed Ariel Vehicles and Remotely Piloted Vehicles were another success story. "Smart" weapons and laser-guided bombs used in the war introduced a new age of weaponry. While these weapons proved to be successful, the C4 I systems proved that future maritime warfare would be technology-intensive. The strategic advantage of high technology was amply demonstrated. Another aspect of the campaign was jointmanship. The success of cooperation and coordination in joint operations confirmed its importance and relevance for the U.S. military and coalition partners. Desert Shield/Desert Storm highlighted the need for synergistically developed combat capabilities. The entire operation was unprecedented in scope, complexity and speed. It underscored the fact that maritime power is an ever-expanding concept. It is no longer restricted to the navy or the maritime components only.

OPERATION IRAQI FREEDOM 2003

After months of warnings to Saddam Hussein's military establishment, United States-led coalition forces launched Operation Iraqi Freedom (OIF) on 20 March 2003. The initial attack comprised air strikes from aircraft carriers, as well as attack by *Tomahawk* cruise missiles from surface ship and submarine in the region, along with air-launched cruise missiles. The primary aim of these concentrated strikes on select targets was to create "shock and awe"[100] and shatter the will of the people to put up resistance. Five aircraft carriers were on station supporting the ground forces from before the war began until things ashore began to shift from battle to peacekeeping.[101] The U.S. Navy fielded some 408 aircraft (232 Fighters, 20 C-2A cargo aircraft, 52 Tankers, 29 ISR, 5 Airlift, and 70 others) that were used for surveillance, intelligence, and carried strikes on targets ashore.[102] On occasions, carrier-based air operations suffered due to sandstorms.[103] Though not usually related to the open sea, during the OIF, sandstorms had prevented carrier air operations on two different occasions clearly showcasing that geography and weather play a significant role in employment of maritime power.

At another level, the OIF witnessed one of the most impressive sea-lifts in the history of warfare. The United States' build-up in support of OIF engaged about 5,000 civilian mariners who crewed more than 100 vessels that delivered men and material for the coalition forces. Ships of the Military Sealift Command (MSC), vessels from the U.S. Ready Reserve Force (RRF) and commercial vessels were activated for the war. These included break-bulk freighters, aviation logistics support ships, auxiliary crane ships, tankers, LASH vessels, and roll-on/roll-off ships. Most of the military hardware and other vital ground equipment was transported via ships. This enhanced U.S. sea-lift capability is the result of an investment of more than US$6 billion by the U.S. Defense Department (DOD) in cargo ships since the 1991 Gulf War. Today, the MSC activates the fleet as needed for various deployments. If necessary, DOD also turns to ships currently operating in commercial markets, beginning with U.S. flagships participating in the Maritime Security Program and those signatory to Voluntary Intermodal Sealift Agreements (VISA). If that does not meet the requirement, the United States draws ships and sea-lift manpower from the deep-draft domestic fleet operating under the 1920 Jones Act. The foreign-flag sea-lift option is not a favoured option. In 1991, the Defense Department relied on a fleet of smaller, commercial cargo ships, but concerns about timely delivery, security and the design of those ships prompted the MSC to buy its own fleet of nineteen ships.[104]

CONCLUSION

In summation, the analysis dwelt on the concept of maritime power in the United States, Britain, Japan and Russia and emerging maritime powers such as China and India. It is evident from the above analysis that the concept of maritime power has a strong element of continuity. Mahan would have little difficulty in understanding and advocating solutions, which would be unlikely to differ fundamentally from those which are current today — whether among major or emerging maritime powers. Perhaps for the previous generation of maritime strategists, UNCLOS III, which has created a new nautical regime (EEZ), and changes in warfare brought about by the RMA would be incomprehensible.

Though Mahan had a broader view of sea power, at that time the dominant view restricted maritime interests primarily to seaborne trade, fishing limited to coastal waters, and a navy to protect maritime interests. Today, a state's maritime power encompasses a much broader definition. It includes a state's dependence on sea, maritime tradition, size of the navy, merchant fleet, shipbuilding capacity, seaborne trade, development level of ports, size of the EEZ, continental shelf, seabed area, marine resources and geographic location with respect to the choke points and waterways, the level of technological development and the capability and the will to exercise maritime power.

Yet another facet of maritime power is the revolution brought about by the RMA, advances in information technology, digitalization, and globalization of the world economy. Finally, maritime power is a dynamic concept and will experience a constant change with newer elements being added based on change both in technology and interstate relations.

Notes

1. E.B. Potter, *Sea Power: A Naval History* (Annapolis: Naval Institute Press, 1982), pp. 1–5.
2. Crete was rich in natural resources, and engaged in intense commercial activities with Egypt, Syria, Cyprus, the Aegean Islands and the Greek mainland.
3. Hans Georg Wunderlich, *The Secret of Crete* (Glasgow: William Collins, Sons and Co., 1976), p. 123. There is also a belief that the destruction of Crete could have been due to an outside invasion by the Mycenaeans in 1650 BC.
4. Robert Shawn Keatts, "Ancient Mariners", *American Society of Oceanographers Journal* 10, no. 4, available at <http://americanoceanographer.com/PDFs/Archive_K4.pdf> (accessed 10 October 2007).
5. Pierre Montel, *Lives of the Pharos* (London: Spring Books, 1974), p. 15.
6. Potter, *Sea Power*, p. 2.
7. Radha Kumud Mookerji, *Indian Shipping: A History of the Sea-borne Trade and Maritime Activity of the Indians from the Earliest Times* (Bombay: Longmans, Green and Co., 1912), pp. 70–71.
8. F.W. Walbank, *The Decline of the Roman Empire in the West* (London: Corbett Press, 1946).
9. K.K. Beri, *History and Cultures of South-east Asia* (New Delhi: Sterling Publishers Pvt. Ltd., 1994), p. 73.

10. B. Arunachalam, *Chola Navigation Package* (Mumbai: Maritime History Society, 2004), p. 42.
11. Chiu Liang-Yeong, *Zheng He: Navigator, Discoverer and Diplomat* (Singapore: Unipress, 2001), pp. 8–16.
12. K.M. Pannikar, *India and the Indian Ocean* (Bombay: George Allen and Unwin (India) Private Ltd., 1971), p. 39.
13. K.M. Pannikar, *Asia and Western Dominance* (London: George Allen and Unwin (India) Private Ltd., 1959), p. 41.
14. C.R. Boxer, *Portuguese Conquest and Commerce in Southern Asia, 1500–1750* (London: Variorum Reprints, 1985), pp. 118–36. Also see Alber Hyma, *A History of the Dutch in the Far East* (Ann Arbor: G. Wahr, 1953).
15. Philip J. Haythornthwaite, William Younghusband, and Martin Windrow, *Nelson's Navy* (UK: Osprey Publishing, 1993), p. 4.
16. Hugh J. Schonfield, *The Suez Canal in World Affairs* (London: Constellation Books, 1952), pp. 37–43.
17. Geoffrey Till, *Seapower: A Guide for the Twenty-First Century* (London: Frank Cass, 2004), pp. 2–4.
18. Sam J. Tangredi, "Globalization and Sea Power: Overview and Context", in *Globalization and Maritime Power*, edited by Sam J. Tangredi (Washington: National Defense University Press, 2002), pp. 1–5.
19. Geoffrey Kemp, "Maritime Access and Maritime Power: The Past, The Persian Gulf and the Future", in *Sea Power and Strategy in the Indian Ocean*, edited by Alvin J. Cottrell and Associates (California: Sage Publications Inc., 1981), p. 26.
20. Tangredi, *Globalization and Maritime Power*, pp. 1–24.
21. Alberto Coll, "England and Spain: 1567–1604", in *Seapower and Strategy*, edited by Colin S. Gray and Roger W. Barnett (Annapolis: Naval Institute Press, 1989), pp. 132–58.
22. Pannikar, *India and the Indian Ocean*, p. 72.
23. Christopher M. Bell, *The Royal Navy, Seapower and Strategy Between the Wars* (London: Macmillan, 2000), pp. xvi–xviii.
24. John Gooch, "Maritime Command: Mahan and Corbett", in *Seapower and Strategy*, p. 37.
25. Ibid., p. 41.
26. *The Fundamentals of British Maritime Doctrine: B R 1806* (London: HMSO, 1995).
27. Andrew Dorman, Mike Lawrence Smith, and Mathew R.H. Uttley, *The Changing Face of Maritime Power* (New York: St. Martin Press, 1999), p. 57.
28. Alfred Thayer Mahan, *The Influence of Sea Power Upon History 1660–1783* (Boston: Little Brown and Company, 1918), p. 29.
29. Geoffrey Till, *Maritime Strategy and the Nuclear Age* (London: Macmillan, 1994), p. 31.

30. Cited in Gooch, "Maritime Command", pp. 31–32.
31. Till, *Maritime Strategy and the Nuclear Age*, p. 33.
32. Mahan, *The Influence of Sea Power Upon History 1660–1783*, p. 29.
33. Allan Westcott, *Mahan on Naval Warfare* (Boston: Prentice Hall, 1991), p. 28.
34. Westcott, *Mahan on Naval Warfare*, p. 35.
35. Mahan, *The Influence of Sea Power Upon History 1660–1783*, pp. 35–42.
36. Ibid., pp. 44–49.
37. Ibid., pp. 58–89.
38. Kemp, "Maritime Access and Maritime Power", p. 37.
39. Robert H. Donaldson and Joseph L. Nogee, *The Foreign Policy of Russia: Changing Systems, Enduring Interests* (Armonk, NY: M.E. Sharpe, 1998), p. 21.
40. Roger W. Barnett, "Soviet Maritime Strategy", in *Seapower and Strategy*, p. 301.
41. Bryan Ranft and Geoffrey Till, *The Sea in Soviet Strategy* (Hong Kong: The Macmillan Press Ltd., 1983), p. 76.
42. S.G. Gorshkov, *The Sea Power of the State* (Oxford: Pergamon Press, 1979), p. 3.
43. Ibid., p. 1.
44. Geoffrey Till, "Luxury Fleet? The Seapower of (Soviet) Russia", in *Naval Power in the Twentieth Century*, edited by N.A.M. Roger (London: Macmillan, 1996), p. 14.
45. Gorshkov, *The Sea Power of the State*, p. 1.
46. Ibid., pp. 29–30.
47. Ibid., p. 2.
48. Robert B. Edgerton, *Warriors of the Rising Sun: A History of the Japanese Military* (New York: Norton, 1997), pp. 21–24.
49. James E. Auer, *The Post War Rearmament of Japanese Maritime Forces, 1945–71* (New York: Praeger Publishers, 1973), pp. 12–13.
50. Malcolm McIntosh, *Japan Re-armed* (London: Frances Pinter, 1986), p. 5.
51. Richard J. Samuels, *"Rich Nation, Strong Army": National Security and the Technological Transformation of Japan* (New York: Cornell University Press, 1994), pp. 81–85.
52. Carlos Rivera, "Sato Tetsutaro: Preparing for the Hypothetical Enemy, 1906–1916", available at The Russo-Japanese War Research Society, <http://www.russojapanesewar.com> (accessed 10 January 2008).
53. Carlos Rivera, "'Smells Like Butter?' The Kaigun's Akiyama Saneyuki", available at The Russo-Japanese War Research Society, <http://www.russojapanesewar.com> (accessed 10 January 2008).
54. James R. Holmes, "Japanese Maritime Thought: If Not Mahan, Who?", in *Asia Looks Seaward: Power and Maritime Strategy*, edited by Toshi Yoshihara

and James R. Holmes (Westport, Connecticut: Praeger Security International, 2008), pp. 148–54.
55. Samuels, *"Rich Nation, Strong Army"*.
56. Arthur J. Marder, *Old Friends, New Enemies: The Royal Navy and the Imperial Japanese Navy: Strategic Illusions, 1934–1941* (Oxford: Clarendon, 1981), p. 15.
57. "Naval Officers on International Chinese Maritime Strategy", *Zhongguo Junshi Kexue* [China Military Science], 20 May 1997, available at website of Foreign Broadcast Information Service at <http://wnc.fedworld.gov> (accessed 31 March 2000).
58. See Srikanth Kondapalli, *China's Naval Power* (New Delhi: Knowledge World, 2001), p. xix.
59. "Naval Officers on International Chinese Maritime Strategy", op. cit.
60. Kondapalli, *China's Naval Power*, pp. 190–96.
61. Branley Haln, "Hai Fang" [Maritime Defence], *U.S. Naval Institute Proceedings* (March 1986): 119.
62. You Ji, "The Evolution of China's Maritime Combat Doctrines and Models: 1949–2001", Working Paper no. 22, The Institute of Defence and Strategic Studies, Singapore, May 2002, pp. 6–7.
63. Jun Zhan, "China Goes to the Blue Waters: The Navy, Seapower Mentality and the South China Sea", *Journal of Strategic Studies* 17, no. 13 (September 1994): 180–223.
64. Rear Admiral Satyindra Singh, *Blueprint to Bluewater: The Indian Navy 1951–65* (New Delhi: Lancer International, 1992), pp. 4–18.
65. In 1829, the Bombay Marine was assigned the new nomenclature, the Bombay Marine Corps but by 1830 this was changed to Indian Navy. This also changed to Indian Marine in 1892, and the navy was rechristened as Royal Indian Marine (RIM) in 1892. The RIM was reconstituted as a combatant force in 1928, and on 2 October 1934, the Royal Indian Navy (RIN) came into being with Naval Headquarters at Bombay.
66. Rahul Roy-Chaudhary, *Sea Power and Indian Security* (London: Brassy's, 1995), p. 16.
67. In 1947, under the Armed Forces Reconstitution Committee (AFRC), the Indian Navy received 4 sloops, 2 frigates, 1 corvette, 12 minesweepers, and 10 minor craft.
68. S.W. Bateman notes that "maritimeness" is based on the state's dependence on the sea and this is an amalgam of factors such as maritime traditions, size of the navy and merchant fleet, dependence on seaborne trade, size of EEZ, value of offshore resources, and the capability of the domestic shipbuilding industry. For more details see his "Sea Change in Asia-Pacific", *Jane's Navy International* (October 1996): 26.
69. The Indian Navy still follows some of the Commonwealth Navies' traditions and practices, and till very recently, the Indian Navy flag had the Royal Navy ensign's "George's Cross".

70. Thomas P.M. Barnett, "India's 12 Steps to a World-Class Navy", *U.S. Naval Institute Proceedings* (July 2001): 41–45.
71. Singh, *Blueprint to Bluewater*, p. 14.
72. R.H. Tahiliani, "Maritime Strategy", *USI Journal* (January–March 1981): 227. Also cited in G.V.C. Naidu, *Indian Navy and South East Asia* (Delhi: Knowledge World, 2000), p. 71.
73. S.N. Kohli, *Sea Power and Indian Ocean: With Special Reference to India* (New Delhi: Tata McGraw-Hill, 1978), pp. 23–26. Admiral S.N. Kohli, former Chief of Naval Staff, Indian Navy, believes that this is a myopic view and cites Mahan: "Sea power embraces all that tends to make a people great upon the sea or by the sea" and examines the Mahanian elements of maritime power against Indian settings.
74. Raju G.C. Thomas, "The Sources of Indian Naval Expansion", in *The Modern Indian Navy and the Indian Ocean,* edited by Robert H. Bruce (Perth: Curtin University of Technology, 1989), p. 90.
75. *Strategic Defence Review: The Maritime Dimension, A Naval Vision* (New Delhi: Naval Headquarters, 1998), p. 25.
76. Vice Admiral R.B. Suri, "Shape and Size of the Indian Navy in the Early Twenty First Century", Project Report submitted to the United Services Institution of India, New Delhi, May 1998.
77. Rear Admiral K. Sridharan, *Sea: Our Saviour* (New Delhi: New Age International, 2000), pp. 157–58.
78. Arthur Herman, "The Eagle and the Elephant", *Wall Street Journal,* 7 March 2006.
79. H.J. Kearsley, *Maritime Power and the Twenty-first Century* (Aldershot: Dartmouth Publishing Company, 1992), p. 17.
80. Till, *Seapower: A Guide for the Twenty-First Century*, pp. 25–112.
81. K.M. Panikkar, *India and the Indian Ocean: An Essay on the Influence of Sea Power on Indian History* (London: George Allen and Unwin Ltd., 1945), cited in K.R. Singh, *Navies of South Asia* (New Delhi: Rupa Co., 2002), p. 14.
82. Kearsley, *Maritime Power and the Twenty-first Century*, p. 3.
83. Ibid., p. 113. Kearsly argues that "model" denotes an orderly set of interrelated concepts and propositions designed to show how foundational maritime elements, naval missions and force structures may interact.
84. Ibid., p. 13.
85. Ray S. Cline, *World Power Trends and U.S. Foreign Policy for the 1980's* (Colorado: Westview Press, 1980), p. 27.
86. Ibid., p. 143.
87. Ibid., p. 145.
88. Kearsley, *Maritime Power and the Twenty-first Century*, p. 131.
89. "Ascension Island: Stepping Stone to Victory", available at <http://www.naval-history.net/F29ascension.htm> (accessed 20 January 2007).

90. Geoffrey Till, *Modern Sea Power* (Washington: Brassey's Defence Publishers, 1987), p. 137.
91. "Falklands 25: Background Briefing", available at <http://www.mod.uk/DefenceInternet/FactSheets/Falklands25BackgroundBriefing.htm> (accessed 20 June 2007).
92. Till, *Modern Sea Power*, p. 137.
93. "Aircraft Carriers and the Falklands War", available at <http://www.btinternet.com/~warship/Feature/falk.htm> (accessed 24 June 2007).
94. Hugh Smith, "Reflections on the Military Significance of the Gulf War", in *The Military Significance of the Gulf War*, edited by Andrew Ross (Canberra: Australian Defence Studies Centre, 1991), p. 5.
95. Andrew Dorman, Mike Lawrence Smith, and Mathew R.H. Uttley, *The Changing Face of Maritime Power* (New York: St. Martin Press, 1999), p. 111.
96. For a detailed account of the war see Department of the Navy, Naval Historical Center, "US Navy in Desert Shield/Desert Storm", available at <http://www.history.navy.mil/wars/dstorm/index.html> (accessed 16 January 2007).
97. "Overview — The Role of the Navy", available at <http://www.history.navy.mil/wars/dstorm/ds1.htm> (accessed 16 January 2007).
98. "The Gathering Storm — The Build-up of U.S. Forces", available at <http://www.history.navy.mil/wars/dstorm/ds2.htm> (accessed 16 January 2007).
99. "Thunder and Lightning — The War with Iraq", available at <http://www.history.navy.mil/wars/dstorm/ds5.htm> (accessed 16 January 2007).
100. "Shock and Awe: The Idea Behind the Buzzwords", *Washington Post*, 30 March 2003.
101. For an account of coalition naval forces in the Persian Gulf prior to commencement of OIF see P.K. Ghosh, "Naval Roles", in *Iraq War 2003: Rise of the New "Unilateralism"*, edited by K. Santhanam (New Delhi: IDSA and Ane Books, 2003), pp. 165–71; also see "Navy May Reduce Gulf Carrier Presence As Iraqi Freedom Winds Down", available at <http://www.news.navy.mil.com> (accessed 18 January 2007).
102. The United States Air Force had the largest number, the U.S. Navy had 408, the Marine Corps 372, the U.S. Army 20 (not counting attack helicopters), the British 113, Australia 22 and Canada 3. For more details see James Dunnigan, "The Air Campaign in Iraq", available at <http://www.strategypage.com/dls/articles2003/20030522.asp> (accessed 18 January 2007).
103. For a detailed account of weather over Iraq, see Ajey Lele, "Military-Meteorological Aspects", in *Iraq War 2003: Rise of the New "Unilateralism"*, edited by K. Santhanam (New Delhi: IDSA and Ane Books, 2003), pp. 142–43.
104. For more details see Michael R. McKay, "AMO Ready for Sealift Service as U.S. Gears for War with Iraq", available at <http://www.amo-union.org/Newspaper/Morgue/10-2002/Sections/Views/Index.htm> (accessed 28 January 2007).

2

MARITIME GEOGRAPHY, LAW OF THE SEA AND GEOSTRATEGY

Geography is a critical determinant of national strategy and plays an important role in its development process. The geographical profile, relative position on the globe and prevalent climatic conditions are the crucial indices and vital strategic factors that bestow upon any state its rightful position in the international system. While the indices of national power may vary over time in terms of capacity, capability and credibility, it is the permanency and constants of geography that confer nations with a sense of security and their relative position in international system. Notably, the crucial and vital indices of the geography provide states with a sense of resilience with determinism of their power and capabilities.

States inherit and develop strategic culture and behaviour derived from their location, topographical settings and environmental conditions that prevail in the geographical realm. The interrelationship among these is a critical determinant of the matrix of strategic culture and behaviours in international relations. States form different perspectives on the constants of geography and transact relationships and businesses based on their understanding of these constants to further national political, social, commercial and strategic ambitions. The ability of a state to correlate its geography into a cogent strategic thinking for an ambient vision would be the perfect example for strategic conduct in this age of globalization. It is not surprising then that Napoleon once observed, "The policy of a state lies in its geography."[1]

Economists, politicians, military and the strategic community highlight geography in their discussions since it provides clarity and helps them to understand and appreciate strategic relationships and requirements. States develop maritime strategy based on several critical inputs that include physical location, access to the seas, nature of coastline, quality of harbours, and position with respect to sources of raw materials, markets and trading routes. At the same time, constants of geography foster the development of naval power of the state. Naval practitioners develop strategy and plan force structure based on national maritime interests that could be regional or global. A variety of variables are at play when formulating force structure and include threat perceptions, the operational environment, hydrographic and hydrological conditions, the extent of sea space, size of littorals to be defended, and the shore and offshore maritime infrastructure to be protected.

Yet at another level, geography is a critical factor that determines effective deployment of forces particularly in the context of the location of friends and adversaries and involves the "spatial dimension" of the sea space that has to be traversed by the naval forces to get to the help of the other or to reach the scene of crisis. It should be pointed out that constants of geography are always at play in naval operations planning and it is the appreciation and exploitation of geography that would determine the outcome of any military action at sea.

Climatic and weather conditions prevalent in the geographical domain endow the state with an advantage or could act as an adversity. For instance landlocked states that experience temperate or harsh climatic conditions are at a great disadvantage compared to maritime powers that may have relatively favourable weather conditions. Russia can be cited as a good example of being a continental power of unparalleled dimensions yet hamstrung by the harsh climatic conditions of the Arctic that dictate limited and partial access to sea. This is a permanent factor in the Russian calculi of national strategy, whereby such powers would be zestful to claim constant access to sea. At the strategic level, climate dictates access to the sea for powers that are in the higher latitudes and closer to the poles and these states are constantly engaged in overcoming the constraints of geography by establishing political and diplomatic relations to seek access to warm water ports. The former Soviet Union had established in the Indian Ocean several military bases and facilities equipped with maritime/naval infrastructure to support forward deployed forces including rapid reaction units. At the tactical level, the navies seek technology that offers optimal exploitation of the geography in conduct of operations. For instance, adverse hydrological conditions in tropical waters can severely hamper anti-submarine operations posing major challenges in terms of detection and prosecution.

Geography can pose major challenges to merchant shipping since these vessels plan the shortest route for saving costs and for timely delivery of "just in time" cargo. There are times when the merchant shipping lanes transit through dangerous waters that are plagued with piracy or areas that are likely to encounter asymmetric actors capable of maritime terrorism. These activities have the potential to adversely impact the global trading system. For instance, Japan is highly dependent on maritime trade for its economic prosperity and any disruption of sea lanes in the Indian Ocean and in Southeast Asian waters could impact on its economy. To overcome and mitigate these threats, it is exploring the possibility of a trans-Arctic route and also attempting to build special vessels that can cut through the Arctic ice. Besides, global shipping is in a constant quest for exploring alternate routes to improve profit margins. Similarly, waters off the Horn of Africa are prone to piracy and there have been several cases of hijacking of ships that necessitated an advisory for ships to sail at least 200 nautical miles from the Somali coast.

There is a vital correlation between geography and demography, particularly in the context of the ratio of the population density and the community that desire to use the sea. The sea serves as a significant provider of food and employment to the people that reside close to seashores. It is an important fact that a majority of the megalopolises are located on the shores that serve as major commercial and trading hubs resulting in large concentration of population. The littoral spaces are home to more than 60 per cent of the global population,[2] and there is a heavy concentration of trading hubs and commercial megalopolises.

Interestingly, the common denominator for both maritime and continental states is their geography. For instance, Mahan's analysis focused on the earth as a "great watery planet speckled with continents" leading him to conclude the primacy of sea power, while for Mackinder, Eurasia was the most prominent feature on the globe, the "world island".[3] For maritime powers, preservation of access and exploitation of seas is a national priority and continental powers are zealous to exploit their continental constraints and limitations and develop sophisticated strategies to gain access to the sea since the oceans and seas provide a seamless conduit for trade, resources and power projection and in that context, navies and the merchant marine are critical for both maritime and continental powers that have the agenda of pre-eminence.

This chapter examines the geographical constants of India and China, and highlights how these have impacted on the growth of their maritime power and the relevance and importance of geography in the formulation of maritime strategy. The chapter is divided into five sections. The first section highlights the relationship between geography and maritime power. It establishes links between maritime geographical features and sea lanes that have direct bearing on the maritime power of a state. The second section analyses 1982 UNCLOS III and establishes a relationship between the nautical regime of EEZ and maritime power. The third and the fourth sections analyse the maritime geography of China and India and the last section highlights the maritime geography of the Asia-Pacific region and argues that maritime geography impacts economic and security dimensions of the region.

THE MATRIX OF GEOGRAPHY AND MARITIME STRATEGY

Geographical features such as islands, straits, rocks, reefs, shoals and nature of coastlines play an important part both in the commercial shipping operations and development of military maritime strategy. To the economists, commercial operators and businesses, the shortest route, low transportation cost and timely delivery of cargo are some of the factors that play a dominant role in developing maritime transport strategy. To a politician it is the state of relations with countries located in the maritime area that is of interest and is a significant driver for growth of maritime power. When the military examines maritime power, the geographical location of friends and adversaries as well as the geography that has to be traversed to get to the assistance of the other is vital. It is quite evident that it is the appreciation of geography and its effects on the state that will determine the maritime strategy.

Given the complexity of naval operations, a multitude of factors are considered when planning strategic and tactical operations on the high seas, in the littorals and underwater.[4] For instance, naval operations on the high seas are conducted with no physical hindrances, there is a seamless sea space for naval engagement and near total absence of chaotic conditions unlike the littorals that are witness to high density of traffic involving neutral vessels, fishing boats, murky waters due to discharge from rivers placing severe constraints on underwater operations, thus offering an advantage to the enemy.[5]

A geostrategic space on the oceans can be defined as a sea space wherein a state's perceived political, economic and military interests converge either individually or collectively. These interests are important enough for the state to use all possible means available to protect its national interests. The geostrategic spaces at sea vary in size, numbers, and location and primarily depend upon the national interests (global or regional). In the case of a state with global interests, there may be more than one geostrategic sea space, e.g. the United States, which is a pre-eminent maritime power, has interests in the Indian and the Pacific Oceans and considers these oceans as critical geostrategic areas. In the same way, the Persian Gulf and Southeast Asian waters are important to both China and India for maritime trade and energy security. On the other hand, for a state with interests in its immediate littorals, the geostrategic space may only be limited to its territorial sea and the EEZ. Such states develop their naval strategy and plan force structure for exercising influence in the geostrategic region encompassing a limited sea space. For instance, Sri Lanka, a small island state, considers its EEZ as its area of geostrategic interests and national interests.

States that need to influence events far beyond their EEZ or have global interests establish more extended geostrategic sea spaces depending upon their perceived interests. Naturally in their case the naval force structure focuses on large platforms that traverse long distances and are able to sustain over extended periods. Such states also establish forward naval bases and facilities in friendly countries to support forward deployment of forces and quick operational turnaround (OTR). For instance, Britain, with its interests in Hong Kong (before 1997), had maintained a permanent naval presence in the area. Similarly, the United States has a permanent and forward naval presence in Manama in the Persian Gulf. China and India have built a regional navy to exercise influence in their respective regions and protect sea lanes. States with small coastline and EEZ have limited and localized interests. For instance, Cambodia has a constabulary navy to safeguard its maritime interest in its EEZ.

Straits and choke points can also be considered as geostrategic spaces at sea. However small in size, they are of significant strategic importance to the state that controls them. For Malaysia, Singapore and Indonesia, the Straits of Malacca is important enough to consider undertaking regular patrolling in the area. Similarly, the Straits of Hormuz is of critical importance to not only Iran and Oman but also to all countries that are dependent on the Gulf oil. The latter countries employ political, diplomatic and sometimes military strategies to protect their interests.

Similarly, sea lanes are geostrategic spaces and have a strong bearing on both commercial and military operations. In the geographical-commercial-operational matrix, a sea lane is the preferred route taken by merchant vessels to transport their cargo and it should be short, economical, and safe for transit. In the geographical-military-operational context, sea lanes are determined by several factors including the location of operational area, proximity to friendly harbours and ports for rest and recuperation including replenishment, and OTR. Both military and commercial sea lanes vary in length and location depending on navigation and geography to be negotiated in terms of landmass, choke points, and other oceanic features and the location of the ports and harbours. Significantly, sea lanes serve as commercial trading routes during times of peace and can be referred to trading lanes that need to be safeguarded against sea piracy and terrorism. During hostilities these routes emerge as strategic spaces that need to be defended against interdiction by the opposing forces or the enemy.

Thus there is a symbiotic relationship between sea lanes and geography in the construction of commercial and military maritime strategy. For instance, the Japanese national interest demands that sea lanes be safeguarded out to 1,000 nautical miles from the Japanese shore and for Tokyo this sea space is a geostrategic region. Also, states that intend to protect the mercantile traffic far beyond their shores establish several geostrategic spaces in different regions through which their respective commercial and military shipping would transit during peace and hostilities. The United States maintains a permanent naval presence in the Persian Gulf through forward deployed forces, military and naval bases and several military alliances/treaties. The safety and security of the sea lane carrying U.S. vital trade and energy supplies has resulted in several bilateral and multilateral maritime arrangements with several navies including naval exercises. Likewise, the United States has strategic relations with Japan and South Korea in East Asia. Northeast Asia, including adjoining sea areas, is of strategic significance to the United States and its alliance partners. The sea lanes in the Indian Ocean place enormous responsibilities on the Indian Ocean littorals particularly India whose peninsula juts out to over 1,000 miles into the ocean, making it the "natural sentinel"[6] of this trade route. For India, this sea lane is of geostrategic importance and its safety and security features prominently in its political articulations, diplomatic initiatives and naval strategy including force structure.

UNITED NATIONS CONVENTION ON THE LAW OF THE SEA (UNCLOS)

In 1949, an international law commission was constituted under the United Nations to study national boundaries at sea and formulate laws of the seas.[7] After a seven-year study (1949–56), eighty-six states met in Geneva for the 1958 Law of the Sea conference to discuss four draft conventions relating to sea boundaries developed by the Commission. The 1958 Law of the Sea Convention deals with: (a) the Territorial Sea and the Contiguous Zone, (b) the High Seas, (c) Fishing and Conservation of Living Resources of the High Seas, and (d) the Continental Shelf. These conventions had drawbacks and were considered inadequate for the demarcation of boundaries. These inadequacies resulted in a second UN conference on the Law of Sea that was convened in 1960 to look into fishing rights and the problems relating to the territorial sea.[8] On 1 November 1967, Arvid Pardo, Malta's Ambassador to the UN, called on the UN to address the following concerns: (a) reserve all non-territorial seabed resources as the common heritage of mankind, (b) establish international control on the use of the seabed, (c) seabed to be proclaimed as the common heritage of mankind, and (d) the UN General Assembly should call for a third LOS conference.[9] The UN General Assembly called for the third Law of the Sea conference and the third Law of the Sea Convention was put to the vote on 30 April 1982. One hundred and thirty states, including India and China, voted yes, four states were against the convention (United States, Israel, Turkey and Venezuela) and seventeen states abstained.

The 1982 UNCLOS III establishes a comprehensive framework for the regulation and management of the ocean space.[10] The convention consists of 320 articles and nine annexes and covers a broad spectrum of issues relating to regulation of navigation, marine protection, scientific research and seabed mining. The salient features of the convention are: (a) drawing of base lines, (b) a twelve-nautical miles territorial sea, (c) unimpeded transit passage through international straits, (d) EEZ extending up to 200 nautical miles, (e) continental shelf regime and rights to manage living and non-living resources of the continental shelf, and (f) concept of archipelagic waters and regulatory power over the ocean for archipelagic states.[11]

The above regimes have facilitated the demarcation of sea spaces into territories under the UNCLOS III that have been designated as Territorial Sea, Archipelagic Waters, Contiguous Zone, Exclusive Economic Zone, Continental Shelf, High Seas, and confers upon states rights in the EEZ for commercial activity.[12] The convention sets out a comprehensive code of legal principles for resolving disputes relating to boundaries, law enforcement, passage rights, exploitation of marine resources, marine environment, military and scientific activities, including safety and security of maritime transport. Under the UNCLOS III, countries claim twelve nautical miles of territorial sea and a 200-nautical miles EEZ that extend out to 350 nautical miles if it is on the continental shelf.[13] The convention is also applicable to archipelagic waters if a country is made up of a number of islands like Indonesia and the Philippines.

Several coastal states have accrued expansive sea space under the UNCLOS III and these have the promise of enormous living and non-living sea wealth. This sea space, designated as Exclusive Economic Zone (EEZ) under the UNCLOS III, provides sovereign rights for commercial activity, be it to catch fish, mine the seabed or exploit any oil and gas in the area. Although the UNCLOS III regime may have brought about "order at sea" in terms of management of the sea spaces and resources, it has generated tensions among states, particularly when states declare national jurisdiction over deputed sea spaces, begin to exercise sovereignty and exploit resources.

Interestingly, geographical features such as rocks, reef, and shoals, have emerged as precious real estate on the seas. Usually considered as unsafe for navigation by a mariner and designated as "dangerous ground" on navigational charts that ships normally steer well clear of to prevent running aground, such features are gaining greater significance as an attractive property at sea for any marine-related commercial enterprise such as resorts, recreational facilities and marine parks. There is also an attempt to declare areas as marine eco-zones. For instance, the Great Barrier Reef off Queensland's east coast, Australia, has been declared as a World Heritage Area that has implications for innocent passage of ships.[14]

What perhaps merits greater attention is the fact that the attraction and commercial value for such features increases considerably when the possibility arises that these may bestow exclusive exploitation rights around the inconspicuous real estate at sea. The situation is further complicated when states respond through nationalist expression, enacting laws, including them in provinces, flag waving, constructing observation posts and meteorological stations, military garrisons, and naval anchorages.[15] In some cases the rhetoric is evident in the domestic political agenda.[16]

Under the convention, rocks that cannot sustain human habitation or economic life of their own cannot claim an EEZ or a continental shelf.[17] This perhaps has led to several countries building artificial structures on these features, dumping building materials for reclamation and even planting corals to claim territory under the UNCLOS III. For instance, Japan plans to invest US$7 million in transplanting 50,000 fast-growing Acropora coral fragments on Okinotorishima, two uninhabited rocks in the Pacific Ocean, 1,700 kilometres southwest of Tokyo.[18] Although Japan has announced that the project would prevent further erosion, China has challenged the Japanese claim and argued that under international law such uninhabited rocky features cannot be termed as islands.

At another level, states are averse to naval surveillance and reconnaissance activity by foreign military ships and aircraft, hydrographic surveys and marine scientific research in their EEZs. These activities are considered intrusive, prejudicial to national security and perceived as challenging sovereignty. Significantly, foreign military and scientific survey research vessels have been deployed by several countries, particularly by major maritime powers such as the United States and Britain who argue that the 1982 UNCLOS III does not prohibit such activities and they are well within their rights to exercise the freedom of the sea, freedom of navigation and overflight as contained in the 1982 UNCLOS III.[19] Some states have even formulated national legislation to keep out foreign military and scientific survey vessels from their EEZs.[20]

CLIMATE CHANGE AND MARITIME GEOGRAPHY

There are several observable impacts of climate change that are consistent with predictions and scenarios such as melting of the polar ice cap, rise of sea water levels, coastal flooding resulting in inundation of cities, and increased frequency of natural disasters causing large movements of people seeking shelter. The governments, international community and environmentalists are engaged in a variety of initiatives to control and slow down the impacts of climate change by developing strategies and building capacities to prevent its adverse impacts on social and environmental facets of human life.

Projected climate change will impact on national economies that are highly dependant on maritime trade. Being critical nodes of global trade, port cities are large industrial and population centres and would be exposed to adverse impacts of coastal flooding. It is estimated that the total value of coastal assets exposed to climate change would increase from US$3,000 billion in 2005 to US$35,000 billion by the 2070s, nearly ten times the current levels and rising to roughly 9 per cent of projected annual GDP in this period.[21] According to the Intergovernmental Panel on Climate Change (IPCC), a large part of the coastal cities will be submerged if sea levels rise.[22] The climate change predictions are indeed worrisome and note that if the global temperature rises by four to five celsius, it would result in a rise in sea level by five metres.[23]

It is feared that large coastal areas will be inundated resulting in shifted coastlines or low-lying island territories submerged resulting in legal tensions over territorial claims between states.[24] For instance, the Maldives is at grave risk of being submerged since it is only 1.5 metres above sea level and some 200 inhabited islands are experiencing severe beach erosion. The 1987 and 1991 stormy high waves flooded a large number of islands, including the capital that is home to 25 per cent of the country's population.[25] Similarly,

Talpatti Island in the estuary of the Haribhanga river on the border between India and Bangladesh emerged from the tidal and cyclonic activity and has been an issue of depute between India and Bangladesh. With the rise in sea level, the formation may simply disappear.

At another level, states have begun to integrate climate change consequences into the national maritime strategy[26] and are engaged in devising a comprehensive strategic and tactical response in humanitarian missions of the navies who have enormous platform and capabilities-orientation to cope with and respond to adverse climate change impacts on national populations. The imperatives therefore lie in the need for a reconfiguration of maritime forces that would perform humanitarian and constabulary roles besides the benign, coercive and compelling roles. Reconfiguration of force structure would imply the need for expeditionary platforms whose focus would be on humanitarian missions. Such missions would be more frequent in occurrence in the future and the offer of assistance as demonstrated during the 2004 Indian Ocean Tsunami would emerge as a new template of multinational maritime operations in the humanitarian spectrum.

EEZ: AN ELEMENT OF MARITIME POWER

Traditionally sea has been an efficient medium of transport, an important source of wealth for humankind and has contributed to its prosperity and well-being in a number of ways including source of food, raw materials, and energy. As the raw material sources on land are fast depleting due to overexploitation, resources from the sea have attracted great interest throughout the world. Further, the pressures of population growth, emergent food shortages due to several reasons including growing population, eating habits, degradation of the environment and climatic change have forced humankind to look to the sea to meet the growing demand. The seas have thus emerged as another reservoir of resources for humankind.

EEZs are thus critical geographical maritime spaces to countries that are keen to protect, safeguard, preserve, and exploit these as a resource base for their power potential. In the context of maritime geography, the EEZ provides the muscle for maritime states as compared to the continental and landlocked states that do not enjoy this unique leverage of ownership, access and connectivity to sea-based resources. Unfortunately, the sea wealth is being exploited with little understanding of the fact that it too has limited resources and thus it is important to exploit these judiciously and in a sustainable manner. Also, seas have become a major dumping ground for the waste created on land thus resulting in depletion as a source of food.

Sea-based resources can be broadly divided into living and non-living. Among the living resources, fish, plankton, salt, seaweeds are the most exploited resources and are a rich source of protein. Some of these have also been used in medical prescriptions. The non-living resources include: hydrocarbon (oil and gas), metals (manganese, copper, gold, coal, tin, found as nodules on the seabed), and commonly seen sand and gravel. Presently, hydrocarbons are by far the highest value marine resources. The commercial value of the global production of oil and gas at sea has been increasing with states engaged in extensive oil exploration in the seas. Most oil exploration activities are being conducted in the EEZs and thus these maritime spaces have emerged as the most valuable assets available to states notwithstanding the fact that there still remain several technological constraints to extract some of the wealth from the seas in a profitable manner.

Similarly, sea has nearly nine times the vegetation cultivated on land.[27] Sea vegetation also referred to as "super foods" such as weeds and plants contain a wide range of nutrients and has found usage in the daily diets of many people, particularly the Japanese who use seaweeds in a variety of ways as a vegetable, in soups and salads. These plants are also a source of potent organic fertilizer and are used in pharmaceuticals and cosmetics. Scientific research has also shown that many plants may contain vegetable oils and vegetable proteins.

The year 1998 marked the bicentenary of Thomas Robert Malthus's essay on population.[28] The global population in 1798 was less than a billion, less than the current figures of China or India. Yet Malthus was concerned about human capability to increase food production to a level needed to meet the demands of the growing population. The current global food situation is quite unfavourable. According to the United Nation Food and Agriculture Organization (FAO), people in several developing countries lack protein in their diet and in 2002 there were nearly 840 million people (14 per cent) who were undernourished.[29] In 2008, the global food situation continued to be unfavourable and some 854 million people, i.e. 12.6 per cent of the global population, most of them living in developing countries, were undernourished.[30] With such an adverse food situation coupled with the rise in the world population, and the future threats arising from phenomena such as climate change, floods, draughts, cyclones and hurricanes, the result could be catastrophic. Perforce, humans are looking towards the sea to supplement their nutritional requirements.

According to FAO, people in developed and developing countries are increasingly dependent on fish as a supplement of proteins. Besides, there is an increasing awareness of the health benefits of eating fish.[31] Fish is the cheapest form of animal protein and in recent times there has been a significant surge in fishing primarily driven by the increasing demand for food. Technology too has kept pace with the growing demands and what used to be a coastal activity, fishing is now conducted in deep seas far into the oceans. In order to obtain preferred species, fishing trawlers are equipped with sophisticated underwater and satellite technology. Some modern fishing vessels are also equipped with processing facilities and serve as mother ships and the merchandise, packed and ready for shipment, is transferred to smaller vessels for onward dispatch. Significantly, oysters, shrimp, mussels, prawns and other variety of fish continue to meet the growing demand of seafood as a vitamin supplement.

It is also a well-established fact that the oceans, which cover two-thirds of the earth's surface, contain vast resources of metals and minerals. In the past, lack of technology had hampered exploitation of these resources, but as the technological advances continue and deep-sea extraction technology becomes affordable, it will be possible to exploit deep-sea resources and would thus offer a promising future both for metals and minerals.

HMS Challenger first discovered seabed resources in 1872[32] and since then with improvements in technology relating to underwater photography, exploration revealed that millions of square miles of ocean bottom are littered with nodules containing important minerals and large quantities of high-grade ores of metals and non-metals. For instance, there are 43 billion tonnes of aluminum (reserves for 20,000 years as compared to known land reserves for 100 years), 358 billion tonnes of manganese (reserves for 400,000 years as compared to known land reserves of only 100 years), 7.9 billion tonnes of copper (reserves for 6,000 years as compared to only 40 years on land), nearly one billion tonnes of zirconium (reserves for 100,000 years as compared to 100 years on land), 14.7 billion tonnes of nickel (reserves for 150,000 years as compared to 100 years on land), two billion tonnes of cobalt (reserves for 200,000 years as compared to land reserves for 40 years only), 0.75 billion tonnes of molybdenum (reserves for 30,000 years as compared to 500 years on land), and the seabed nodules in the Pacific Ocean are estimated to contain 207 billion tonnes of iron, nearly 10 billion tonnes of titanium, 25 billion tonnes of magnesium, 1.3 billion tonnes of lead, 800 million tonnes of vanadium ad several other metals and ores.[33] There are also placer deposits of gold, platinum, zircon and titanium. These are detritus minerals that are washed ashore through rivers.[34] In the coastal areas, scientists have found deposits of bromine, coal, magnesium, sulfur and tin. However, these are yet to be exploited but technology is fast being developed for commercial extraction and use.

It is true that there is a growing demand for resources but there also exists a new source of supplies, i.e. the sea. Rising demand relative to supply is a common socio-economic phenomenon but does not result in tensions among states.[35] As long as access is available and not controlled by one entity, the environment is manageable by adopting controls/rationing strategies. However, states are becoming more conscious of this newfound wealth at sea and do not want the marine wealth in their EEZs exploited by outsiders. Nor are they willing to allow their vital strategic sea spaces, i.e. EEZs to be a dumping ground of foreign waste; they determinedly prevent any hostile activity that threatens national interests. Significantly, this realization and exercise of sovereignty over sea-based resources is a distinct departure from the earlier understanding and practice among states accepting oceans and seas as the common heritage of mankind.

States exercise jurisdiction over their respective EEZs, maintain strict vigilance in the area, subjecting defaulters to penalties, engage in sustainable exploitation, safeguard sea lanes under their jurisdiction, and uphold maritime order. Consequently, the oceans are now subjected to rules of governance both for exploitation, for exercising ownership over resources and for the safety of maritime traffic thus bringing in greater awareness among states to safeguard this newfound wealth. The resources within the EEZ, both living and non-living, are large to sustain humankind and technology is under development for efficient exploitation to meet the ever-growing demand. However, in this era of rising demands, improvements in technology and new oceanic regimes such as the UNCLOS III, freedom to exploit the seas freely has been greatly curtailed.

Mare Liberum (The Free or Open Ocean) and *Mare Clausum* (Closed Sea) has been a subject of aggressive debate during the 16th century. Interestingly *Mare Clausum* was asserted and enforced long before the European debate during the 7th to the 10th centuries when the maritime kingdom of Srivijaya compelled ships to call at its ports.[36] Taken as a whole, the quantity of materials available from the sea is gigantic and all contribute to the maritime power of a state. This power requires constant attention and nurture, bringing additional responsibilities of protection, preservation and judicious exploitation of resources on states.

CHINA, LAW OF THE SEA AND TERRITORIAL DISPUTES

During ancient times, Chinese rulers were quite content with their dominance over land frontiers and had limited focus on sea areas. Much of the Chinese maritime activity was restricted to coastal waters and the vast sea space to the east into the deep ocean had remained unexplored. The realization that interests extend far beyond national borders led the Chinese leadership to appreciate the unexploited maritime frontiers through Southeast Asia, India, and as far as the east coast of Africa establishing social, cultural, trade relations including suzerainty at several places.

In ancient times, the Chinese concept of international law was based on the "theory of the universal state" that required states to submit to the Chinese Emperor and pay tributes.[37] According to historian Joseph Needham, the Chinese developed their own rules and practices which were not necessarily international in nature.[38] However, with the arrival of the Europeans in the 17th century, modern international law was based on sovereignty and equality. The same was introduced and was first invoked in 1864 based on the principles of international law governing maritime territory.[39] During subsequent years, China actively participated in the 1899 and 1907 Hague Peace Conferences and ratified several multilateral conventions dealing with *laws of war* including settlement of disputes through peaceful means.[40] Under Sun Yatsen, China professed "to obtain the rights of a civilized state" and "to place China in a respectable place in international society".[41]

Since independence in 1949, China has been a strong supporter of legal regimes pertaining to the Law of the Sea. For instance, in 1952, China translated the second revised edition of *The International Law of the Sea* exhibiting a desire to follow international practices, and safeguarding its sovereignty, maritime interests including resource exploitation.[42] In accordance with the then international regulations, the Chinese territorial waters were limited to three nautical miles from the coast.

However, on 4 September 1958, at the height of the Jinmen crises, China declared that its territorial waters extended to twelve nautical miles.[43] The Chinese reaction was in response to the U.S. support to Taiwan to defend Quemoy and Matsu, two islands belonging to Mainland China and under the occupation of the nationalist forces. The Chinese Government through the Declaration Concerning China's Territorial Sea unilaterally extended the territorial waters and the situation was further complicated by the fact that instead of establishing baselines from the low-water mark on the mainland coast, an international practice, the Chinese authorities declared territorial waters of twelve nautical miles with a baseline established by connecting the outermost islands along the coast. The U.S. Navy had followed the three-mile territorial water regime with utmost care and never ventured into Chinese territorial waters. It was their belief that the unilateral declaration of territorial waters would automatically keep the U.S. Navy outside twelve nautical miles.

Interestingly, at the time of the outbreak of the Korean War in 1950, China proclaimed three maritime security zones "in the interest of defence security and military needs".[44] These were (a) Maritime Warning Zone, (b) Military Navigation Zone, and (c) Military Operation Zone. The Maritime Warning Zone comprised an area encompassing Yalu River estuary and the eastern end of Shandong Peninsula. The areas comprising these zones were not defined clearly in terms of spatial dimensions and the Japanese fishing vessels would have to enter the area at their own risk. China continued to exhibit assertiveness with regard to its sea areas and it opposed the "right of innocent passage" of vessels in its territorial waters. For instance, in 1958, the Chinese authorities had objected to an Indian Navy vessel when it transited within twelve miles of the Chinese coastline but well outside the then internationally accepted three-mile territorial waters limit.[45]

The Cultural Revolution (1966–69) had its impact on Chinese articulations on the Law of Sea. Maritime legal matters took a back seat and China remained preoccupied with domestic problems. Besides, China did not have many international law experts[46] but by 1970, Chinese statements on matters relating to maritime jurisdiction became more pronounced. By then most countries had extended their respective territorial waters out to twelve nautical miles as against the international stipulation of three nautical miles. Several Latin American countries declared their territorial claims extending to 200 nautical miles and this move was opposed by both the United States and the Soviet Union but not opposed by China. Interestingly, Beijing refrained from declaring a similar territorial zone for itself. The Chinese clarified their position by noting that each county's claim was to be determined "on the basis of equality and reciprocity" and that claim was to be based upon coastal conformation, the width of the continental shelf and coastal resources.[47]

But it was only in 1971, after its recognition and formal admission to the UN as the People's Republic of China, that it made its debut in the UN Seabed Committee 1971–72 and also began participating in the conferences leading to the 1982 Law of the Sea Convention. China made known its views on issues relating to maritime sovereignty, definitions and delimitations of sea areas enshrined in the Law of the Sea Convention, rights of coastal states including regimes for passage of warships through coastal waters, voting procedures and several other substantive issues leading to the 1982 UNCLOS III.

There were important features of the Chinese articulations. China sought to project itself as the champion of Third World countries and took a high moral ground. In a statement on 9 December 1982, Han Xu, Chairman of the Chinese delegation noted that the new Convention had brought several changes from the old law that served the interests of some of the big powers and that the new law would serve to overcome hegemonism, bring about new economic order, facilitate cooperation and exchanges among all the countries.[48]

Although China had participated in the discussions and formulation of the new law, it was still unhappy with some of the provisions of the Convention and made known some of the serious shortcomings particularly with regard to the regime of passage of warships through territorial waters. It was the Chinese principled view that all military vessels and aircraft, when entering its territorial waters must obtain permission from the Chinese Government and there were several supporters for Chinese arguments.[49] The Chinese, however, had agreed to the provision of free passage of international shipping through territorial waters but continued to protest against similar provisions for warships.

During these conferences the issue relating to EEZ became very important. In 1974, China clarified its position by noting that the coastal states were at liberty to reasonably define their territorial seas, exclusive economic or fishery zones of appropriate limits based on specific natural conditions, national economic development and national security.[50] Importantly, the Chinese were constantly aware of their national security interests and economic wealth at sea. They maintained flexibility in their claims but in practice they could be very rigid when their own interests were jeopardized, e.g. in the South China Sea.

China signed the 1982 UNCLOS III in December 1982 at Montego Bay, Jamaica. On 25 February 1992, the Standing Committee of the National People's Congress adopted The Law on the Sea and Contiguous Zone of People's Republic of China, and on 15 May 1996, the Standing Committee of the National People's Congress ratified the United Nations Convention of the Law of the Sea.[51] These provide the legal basis for exercising Chinese sovereignty over territorial seas and jurisdictions over the adjacent zones and safeguarding national maritime rights and interests. In January 1998, the Republic of China on Taiwan promulgated its Law on Territorial Sea and the Contiguous Zone and the Law of the Exclusive Economic Zone (EEZ) and the Continental Shelf and in the same year in June, the People's Republic of China (PRC) promulgated its Law on the EEZ and the Continental Shelf.[52]

Given that Beijing does not support two Chinas and considers Taiwan a renegade province, China does not acknowledge any of the Taiwanese promulgations and announcements relating to law of the sea and sea areas governed under the 1982 UNCLOS III regime. It should also be noted that in 1958 China was represented by the Republic of China during the deliberations and final promulgation of the 1958 Geneva Convention on Territorial Sea and Contiguous Zone. The People's Republic of China has never accepted the legitimacy of the Republic of China on Taiwan and considers the Geneva Convention as an old international law.

Perhaps what is more significant is that China's maritime claims and expressions of jurisdiction in disputed sea areas in the Yellow Sea, East China Sea and the South China Sea have resulted in concerns among its neighbours who are also claimants to disputed islands. Unilateral initiatives by China in the disputed EEZs are catalyst for military build-up by the other claimant states. The likelihood of skirmishes or conflicts remains alive and regional states prefer China to follow international law and demonstrate its intentions to resolve outstanding maritime disputes under the 1982 UNCLOS III.

China's disputes with its maritime neighbours relate to demarcation of maritime boundaries and ownership of islands in the South China Sea and East China Sea. The South China Sea is dotted with islands, reefs, shoals, and rocks, some of which are barely above water during high tide, mostly uninhabited, and even pose dangers to navigation. The area has witnessed a high pitch of regional contention by the littoral states that have competing and contesting claims over boundaries and territories. The Paracel Islands are under Chinese control but also claimed by Taiwan and Vietnam while the Spratly group of islands is claimed by China, Brunei, Malaysia, the Philippines, Taiwan and Vietnam in varying degrees.

The Chinese support their claims to the Paracel Islands through historical records and note that Admiral Zheng He colonized these islands in the 15th century[53] and this claim is substantiated by archeological research.[54] Vietnam rejects this claim and argues that the Paracel were part of its territory since the 18th century and under Emperor Gia Long several research missions were dispatched to the islands till 1836.[55] They further argue that these islands were part of French Indo-China and that Vietnam is the successor state. During the 1950s and the 1960s, the disputes remained dormant and both sides were quite content with *status quo* but thereafter the Chinese were concerned about the American involvement in the dispute.[56]

In 1974, the Chinese Government reacted sharply asserting its claim to the Paracel and dispatched fishermen to set up huts, put up flags on the islands, and even dig up tombs and the Vietnamese reciprocated by occupying Money and Robert Islands. Provoked by the Vietnamese actions, China invaded Pattle, Money and Robert Islands in January 1974. The military action was undertaken by PLA Navy destroyers, gunboats, including fighter jets,[57] and since that operation, the Chinese have occupied the islands. China has built a medium-length runway on Woody Island and operates fighter aircraft that enable China to exercise influence over the South China Sea.

Unlike the Paracel, the Spratly Islands are claimed by six countries who have historical and legal basis for their arguments: China, Taiwan and Vietnam claim all the features, arguing that the islands have been part of their territory and have traditionally been used by their respective fishermen; the Philippines and Malaysia claim a few of the islands while Brunei claims an EEZ. The Vietnamese claim is based on history, the Indo-China French connection, and also on the basis of the statements made by the Vietnamese delegation in 1951 on the eve of the San Francisco Treaty, followed by the 1954 Geneva conference that accepted Spratly and Paracel as part of South Vietnam.[58] The Philippines claim islands in the area on the basis of *terra nullius* (no man's land) and also on the basis of fact that since the sovereignty of the islands had been renounced by the Japanese after the 1951 San Francisco Treaty, a Philippines sailor occupied the islands and later transferred these to the Philippines Government who call them the Kalayaan (Freedom land).[59]

Malaysia claims several features in the southern Spratly because they fall within the continental shelf boundary[60] and has developed an airstrip on the Layang Layang Island (English translation for Layang Layang is Swallows Reef) and part of the island has been converted into a tourist resort and a base for its fishermen.[61] Brunei ratified the UNCLOS III on 16 November 1994 and claims an EEZ as far as the Rifle Bank and has a dispute with Malaysia over the Louisa Reef.[62]

In geostrategic terms, the Spratly Islands sit astride the primary shipping lane passing through the South China Sea. The geographic advantage offers the claimants a strategic observation post to monitor merchant traffic during peacetime and during hostilities the islands can serve as staging posts to interdict enemy shipping. The area is also suitable for small submarine operations since during World War II the Japanese converted the Itu Aba Island into a submarine base for launching offensives in the Philippines.[63]

China, along with Taiwan and Japan, claim the Diaoyutai Islands (T'iaoyutai) but the islands are currently occupied by Japan. The Chinese claim is based on a number of historical records that the islands were under the jurisdiction of the Chinese rulers and during the period 1372–1879, the Chinese emperors dispatched twenty-four investiture missions to the Ryukyu Islands.[64] The Japanese name these islands "Senkaku", a translation of the English name "Pinnacle Islands" and the English name is derived from the Chinese name.

The Taiwanese claim is based on the fact that the Diaoyutai Islands are part of the Taiwanese territory and Taiwan contends that historically the islands became part of Japan and on 14 January 1895 the Japanese incorporated these islands into their territory after Japan had defeated China in the 1894 Sino-Japanese war and Formosa (Taiwan) and its associated islands were ceded to Japan under the Shimoneasky Treaty.[65] The islands came under U.S. control soon after World War II and were returned back to Japan in 1971 along with the Ryukyu group of islands under the Okinawa Treaty. The Japanese position is that the Senkaku group of islands is an integral part of the Ryukyu archipelago and therefore cannot be the object of territorial dispute.

INDIA, LAW OF THE SEA, AND TERRITORIAL DISPUTES

Article I of the Constitution of India defines its territory but there is no mention of territorial waters. However, during the debates in the Constituent Assembly, on the subject matter of what is now Article 297 of the Constitution, references were made for the first time to the concept of India's territorial waters. By virtue of this article "all lands, minerals and other things of value underlying the ocean within the territorial waters or the continental shelf of India shall vest in, and be held for the purpose of the Union".[66]

India's contribution to the process of codification and development of law of the sea has been noteworthy. It actively participated in the Geneva Conferences of 1958 and 1960 and the 1982 Law of the Sea Conference and contributed significantly in the matter of fixing the limit of the territorial sea, retaining the concept of contiguous zone and determining the limits of the continental shelf, issues relating to pollution control, and scientific research on the continental shelf and the EEZ.[67]

India voiced its concern on the inadequacy of the three-mile rule of territorial waters during the Geneva Conference of 1958 and argued for a twelve-mile territorial limit.[68] During the deliberations on the limits of territorial waters, it prevented a U.S.-Canadian proposal, which disregarded the right of the coastal state to call for advance notice from foreign warships of their intention to transit through its waters.[69] The issue of unannounced passage was supported by major maritime powers and was objected to by India during the Geneva Conferences of 1958 and 1960.

At the 1958 Geneva meeting, India facilitated diverse groups to reach a compromise proposal on the limits of the territorial sea limit of three miles.

At that time India was supportive of a six-mile limit and opposed the passage of warships due to security reasons.[70] During the second UN Conference on the Law of the Sea, 1960, the Indian delegation put forward a proposal to extend the territorial waters out to twelve miles against the existing three-mile regime. The Indian arguments were based on the belief that a wider coastal sea meant wider zones of security.[71] It also meant widening the area of peace and reducing the area of high seas that could become a battlefield. With the passage of time and a realization that its warships would also face inconvenience due to time-consuming prior clearances and authorizations for innocent passage, it wanted UNCLOS III to adopt a rule wherein only a notification was necessary. This resulted in confusion, and now state practice varies on the issue of warships.

Through a Presidential Proclamation, on 30 September 1967, India adopted a twelve-mile territorial water limit. This was in response to Pakistan having declared extension of its territorial waters from three to twelve nautical miles.[72] As regards contiguous zones, India adopted a twelve-mile contiguous zone in 1956 on a unilateral basis. The issue was raised and it was argued that, with the new regime of twelve-mile territorial sea and a 200-mile exclusive economic zone, the twelve-mile contiguous zone had become irrelevant. A consensus emerged on a twenty-four-mile contiguous zone limit. India declared four maritime zones and these are identified in the Maritime Zones Act, 1976: (a) the territorial sea, (b) the historic waters, (c) the contiguous zone, and (d) the exclusive economic zone.[73]

Both the 1958 Geneva Convention on the Law of the Sea and UNCLOS III do not contain any provisions on historic waters. These are left to be decided mutually between parties and governed by international law. Both India (under Section 8 of India's Maritime Zones Act, 1976) and Sri Lanka (under Section 9 of Sri Lanka Maritime Zones Law, 1976) have specified the limits of their historic waters in the Palk Strait, Palk Bay and Gulf of Mannar.[74] In 1956 India adopted a twelve-mile contiguous zone for the purposes of customs and sanitary regulations. New Delhi was silent on the issue of security rights of a coastal state but advocated a separate fishery zone of twelve miles beyond a territorial sea of twelve miles. However this was not accepted.[75]

India's rights and jurisdiction in its EEZ are enshrined in Section 7(4) of the Maritime Zones Act, which goes well beyond the 1982 UNCLOS III and declares the designated area as its EEZ. It makes necessary provisions for the safety and security of resources, environment, artificial structure, customs and fiscal matters.[76] India signed the 1982 UNCLOS III in December 1982 and ratified it on 29 June 1995.

MARITIME GEOGRAPHY OF CHINA

Geographically, China is a maritime state and located in the maritime area of the Asia-Pacific region. With 9.6 million square kilometres of landmass, China is endowed with a long coastline of 6,000 nautical miles on the mainland. Its deeply indented coastline is fringed with some 3,500 islands, including Taiwan. There are also a large number of island territories in distant waters and these geographical constants generate an additional coastline of 5,000 nautical miles.

Though blessed with a long coastline, China does not border an ocean except east of Taiwan where the waters of the Pacific Ocean wash its shores. However, small enclosed and semi-enclosed seas border China. These are: the Yellow Sea, East China Sea, and South China Sea. The Yellow Sea is approximately 400,000 square kilometres wide and is relatively shallow with an average depth of about 55 metres and a maximum of 125 metres at the deepest point. The East China Sea is about 700,000 square kilometres and the seabed slopes gently into the Okinawa trough that has depths of nearly 2,300 metres. The East China Sea encompasses Taiwan, the Senkaku group of islands and the Okinawa group. The South China Sea covers an area of 3,400,000 square kilometres and is home to four principal island groups: the Palawan, Spratly Islands, Paracel Islands and the Natuna group.[77]

The Spratly Island group comprises a multitude of reefs, shoals, cays and rocks. Some of them are barely above water during high tide. These pose dangers to navigation, and the maritime traffic transiting the area stay clear of the islands for safety. The Paracels lie to the northwest of the South China Sea and only a few are inhabited. These too, like the Spratly, are reefs and rocks and comprise some 130 barren islets, the largest being Woody Island. The Senkaku Islands comprise a total of seven volcanic rocks, the largest being 4 kilometres long and 1.5 kilometres wide. These are uninhabited and are dangerous to navigation. With the exception of one island, Sekibi Sho, which is 48 nautical miles to the east of the main group, they are a compact group.[78]

There are some important waterways in the Chinese area of maritime interest that have both economic and military significance. These are: Straits of Malacca, Sunda Strait, Lombok Strait, Ombai Wetter Strait, Makassar Strait, Torres Strait, and Taiwan Strait. The Straits of Malacca is the main waterway that connects the Indian Ocean and the Pacific Ocean. The strait is 600 nautical miles long and permits seventy-two feet draught vessels to transit.[79] The Sunda Strait is an alternate to Straits of Malacca and is considered unsafe for navigation by large vessels because it is shallow and dangerous. The route saves only 150 nautical miles as compared to transit from the Lombok Strait but is not popular among mariners. The Lombok Strait is wide and deep which allows safe passage for Very Large Crude Carriers (VLCCs) intending transit to the Philippines, Japan or the west coast of North America. Similarly, the Makassar Strait, between Kalimantan and Sulawesi, is fairly deep and offers safe navigation by VLCCs. There is also a hypothetical choke point between Sabah on Borneo and the southern tip of Vietnam. It is not a choke point *per se* but can be termed as a high seas strategic passageway. It is fairly wide and shipping traffic transits through this keeping well clear of the Spratly group of islands.

INDIA'S MARITIME GEOGRAPHY

Like China, India is a maritime state with a long coastline and island territories off its eastern and western coast. It is surrounded by the world's third largest ocean, the Indian Ocean and occupies a dominant position. The peninsula juts out for almost 1,000 nautical miles thereby providing an extended "sea frontage". India lies between latitude 9 to 37 degrees north and longitude 68 to 76 degrees east and has a coastline of 7,515 kilometres including the Lakshadweep group of islands in the Arabian Sea on the western seaboard and the Andaman and Nicobar group of islands in the Bay of Bengal/Andaman Sea on the eastern seaboard. Most of India's neighbours are maritime states; to the west, it shares a maritime boundary with Pakistan, south with Sri Lanka and to the east with Bangladesh, Myanmar, Thailand and Indonesia. Another feature of India's maritime geography is the shipping lane that transits through Indian waters and serves as the umbilical cord for the Asia Pacific and United States west coast economies.

The Indian Ocean (73,600,000 square kilometres), the third largest body of water and one-seventh of the earth[80] is home to important seas: the Red Sea, Persian Gulf, Arabian Sea, Bay of Bengal and the Andaman Sea. India is located between the Arabian Sea and Bay of Bengal, the two largest water bodies of the Indian Ocean. The Arabian Sea covers an area of 3.86 million square kilometres and its waters wash the shores of East Africa, part of the Persian Gulf, Pakistan, and the Indian subcontinent. Similarly, the Bay of Bengal covers an area of 2.17 million square kilometres and its waters wash the shores of the Indian subcontinent, Bangladesh, Indonesia, Malaysia, Myanmar, Singapore, and Thailand.

The Andaman Sea occupies 0.55 million square kilometres and surrounds the Andaman and Nicobar group of islands. The Andaman and Nicobar Islands comprise 667 islands and islets and stretch along a 900-kilometre axis from north to south. The islands are 250 kilometres from Myanmar (the closest Myanmar territory is only 45 kilometres), 500 kilometres from Thailand and 1,300 kilometres from mainland India. The Lakshadweep and the Minicoy Island groups abound in reefs, islets, shoals and are referred to as danger grounds by mariners. For safety of navigation, maritime shipping steers well clear of the islands.

There are some important waterways in India's maritime areas of interest that have both economic and military importance. These are: the Straits of Hormuz, Straits of Malacca, Ten Degree Channel and two hypothetical choke points between the Lakshadweep Islands and mainland India and Indira Point in the Nicobar Islands and the western edge of Sumatra Island. Some of these are not choke points *per se* but are fairly wide and can be termed high seas strategic passageways where the bulk of merchant traffic funnels in/out. The region's important sea lanes, which serve as the umbilical cord of the economies of several Asia Pacific and European countries, pass through these strategic choke points. They carry critical energy resources from the Persian Gulf as well as providing economical maritime transport routes.

The Straits of Hormuz, nearly twenty nautical miles long, is one of the world's most important strategic choke points. It is fairly deep and vessels of 1,60000 dwt (dead weight tonnage) can pass through this channel. Nearly 88 per cent of the oil exported from the Gulf transits through the choke point accounting for 16 to 17 million barrels of oil per day.[81] On average twenty to thirty tankers enter the Arabian Gulf each day and at peak hours, one tanker leaves the Strait every six minutes. Interestingly, every operational tanker of the world transits through this strait some time or other during the year.[82]

The principal sea lane connecting the Pacific Ocean and the Atlantic Ocean passes through the Indian Ocean. The sea lane runs towards the west to pass through the Suez Canal. One of its arteries runs towards the south to round the Cape of Good Hope. In the east, it passes through the Straits of Malacca before joining the sea lane that transits through the South China Sea with the Paracel and Spratly group of islands on either side. There are other tributaries of the main shipping lane that join the Sunda Strait, Lombok Strait, and the Makassar Strait. The southern straits of the Indonesian archipelago therefore serve as important choke points for the shipping traffic heading towards the Pacific Ocean.

GEOSTRATEGIC IMPORTANCE OF ASIA-PACIFIC REGION TO CHINA AND INDIA

As a geographical entity, the Asia Pacific is an extension of the continental Asian landmass and its large crescent shaped littoral-maritime space has endowed it with immense geoeconomic and geostrategic importance. Significantly, economics and security has been the twin driving factors shaping the contemporary discourse in the region. In its geoeconomic construct, trade and energy flows link the region with the economies of the Indian Ocean and the Persian Gulf states and to its east through the Pacific Ocean to markets in North and South America. In its geostrategic construct, the region is characterized by the presence of two rising powers, i.e. China and India. An arc comprising big and middle-sized powers, i.e. Australia, few Southeast Asian countries (Indonesia, Malaysia, Singapore, Thailand and Vietnam), Japan, Russia, South Korea, and Taiwan play a significant role in the security and economic dynamics of the Asia-Pacific region. Besides these regional powers, the Asia-Pacific region is also of great significance to the United States, the lone superpower, engaged in the region through several bilateral alliances and treaties and trade linkages. The United States can also be called a "resident power"[83] given the nature of alliances and interests it has in the region.

The geostrategic complexities and potential risks in the Asia-Pacific region arise from the prevalence of deep-rooted historical and territorial disputes, tensions in interstate relations, contested sovereignties, and nationalistic interpretations of the UNCLOS III. Some of these are significant flashpoints and the dangers of an armed conflict persist. Given the nature of potential conflict and contestations arising in the maritime domain, Asian powers have been building their naval power in offensive-defence capabilities. The objective being to build robust littoral defences to maximize anti-access measures and area denial means to deprive extra-regional intervention and presence.

At the economic level, the majority of countries in the region have witnessed an economic boom. They have adopted liberal economic policies and opened their markets to integrate with the regional and world economy. The regional rail and road networks are inadequate for accelerating hinterland connectivity, consequently the seas have assumed a importance for regional trade with intensified shipping activity to support economic vitality. The primary interest is to ensure an uninterrupted flow of energy to fuel growing economies as well as unhindered access to sources of raw materials and markets for products.

While there is an enhanced economic dynamism in the region, there is also an increased sensitivity to the safety of sea lanes through the strategic choke points in Southeast Asia and further in to the Straits of Hormuz in the Persian Gulf. In the event of such a situation leading to the closure of the Southeast Asian strategic choke points, maritime traffic would have to sail farther south of Australia, placing increasing demands on vessel capacity, higher costs of transportation and disruption in both energy and material supply chains.

The strategic and economic realities in the region are thus complex, particularly for China and India and these states seek an enhanced role in the region for the safety and security of their long and often vulnerable sea lines of communications. It should be pointed out that a large proportion of raw materials and energy for the economic boom in China and India must be sourced from the Indian Ocean states in the Persian Gulf and Africa. The safety and security of shipping in the Indian Ocean is thus of critical importance to their economies. This is best reflected through the heightened security concerns of sea lines of communications, energy supply chain security, the imperatives of cooperative maritime security demonstrated through bilateral/multilateral naval exercises, a commitment to preserving order at sea and combating piracy and maritime asymmetric threats and countering WMD proliferation in the Asia-Pacific region. These issues are discussed in greater detail in succeeding chapters.

The above analysis endeavoured to highlight the relevance and importance of geography in the formulation of any strategy for building a nation's maritime power. It is evident that maritime power and geography are closely linked to each other and are vital determinants in a country's march towards becoming a maritime power. Also, geographical features like the size and type of coastline seas, location of offshore island territories and the size of EEZs are important components that shape maritime power. Besides, the adjacent seas, location of choke points, length of sea lanes and the geography they have to traverse will shape the strategy a country adopts for building its maritime power. Besides, these physical features also determine the sea lanes that serve as the umbilical cord of the economic vitality of a nation.

Both India and China are endowed with favourable maritime geography: both have a long indented coastline with natural harbours and a large EEZ. India, by virtue of its geography, lies close to the Persian Gulf, the main source of energy, thus lowering the vulnerability of its energy sea lanes. For China, the sea lane from the Persian Gulf to Mainland China must pass through the Indian Ocean, the choke points of Malacca, Sunda, and Lombok, thereby resulting in a high degree of vulnerability. This sea wealth in their

EEZ has also placed added demands on the two countries to invest in marine resource exploitation as well as to build maritime forces to safeguard national maritime interests.

The constants of maritime geography, the imperatives of globalization and the quest for maritime power determine the dynamics of how these rising powers, i.e. China and India contend in the maritime domain of the Asia-Pacific region. Maritime geography will also determine the nature of access and control of the littoral seas and shapes the milieu of the changing naval balance of power in any region. The Asian littoral has strong evidence of rising economic and strategic power. China and India have emerged as the robust rising powers in the Asia-Pacific littoral and the constants of their geography are empowering them to their current status.

Notes

1. James E. Toth, "Military Strategy and Strategic Geography" (Washington: Industrial College of the Armed Forces, 1995), p. 1, cited in Reynold B. Peele, "The Importance of Maritime Chokepoints", *Parameters* (Summer 1997): 61–74.
2. Nearly 60 per cent of the world's population lives within 100 kilometres of the ocean and some 70 per cent live within 320 kilometres. Most cities with populations of more than one million are located in the littorals and of the world cities with a population of 500,000 or more, nearly 40 per cent are located on the shore. For a good discussion on the issue of chaos in the littorals, see "The Landscape: Chaos in the Littorals", *MCDP 3: Expeditionary Operations*, Department of the Navy, Headquarters, United States Marine Corps, Washington, D.C., 16 April 1998, p. 21.
3. Walter A. McDougall, "Why Geography Matters … But Is So Little Learned", *Orbis* 47, no. 2 (Spring 2003): 217–33.
4. Michael S. Lindberg, *Geographical Impact on Coastal Defence Navies: The Entwining of Force Structure, Technology and Operational Environment* (London: Macmillan Press Ltd., 1998), pp. 45–46.
5. Edward Hanlon, Jr., "Taking the Long View: Littoral Warfare Challenges", in *The Role of Naval Forces in 21st Century Operations*, edited by Richard H. Shultz, Jr. and Robert L. Pfaltzgraff, Jr. (Washington: Brassy's, 2000), pp. 156–57.
6. Arun Prakash, "A Vision of India's Maritime Power in the 21st Century", *Air Power Journal* 3, no. 4 (October–December 2006): 2.
7. Clyde Sanger, *Ordering the Ocean* (London: Macmillan, 1988), p. 192.
8. Ibid., p. 17.
9. Sayer A. Swarztrauber, *The Three Mile Limit of Territorial Sea* (Annapolis: United States Naval Institute Press, 1972), p. 55.
10. United Nations, *The Law of the Sea (LOS)* (New York: UN, 1983), p. 192.

11. Ibid., p. ix.
12. LOS. Art. 56, p. 18.
13. LOS. Art. 76, p. 27.
14. Peter Glover, "Marine Casualties in the Great Barrier Reef: 'Peacock', 'Bunga Teratai Satu' and 'Doric Chariot'", *MLAANZ Journal* 18 (2004): 55–72.
15. Mark J. Valencia, "China and the South China Sea Disputes", Adelphi Paper 298 (London: International Institute for Strategic Studies, 1995), p. 8.
16. "Taiwan President to Visit Disputed Spratly Islands: Report", *Intellasia*, 22 January 2008.
17. LOS. Art. 121, p. 39.
18. "Japan to Plant Thousands of Corals to Bolster Claim Over Disputed Pacific Ocean Islets", *Japan Today*, 8 April 2008.
19. For a detailed discussion and legalities of military activities in the EEZ see Hasjim Djalal, Alexander Yankov, and Anthony Bergin, "Military and Intelligence Gathering Activities in the Exclusive Economic Zone: Consensus and Disagreement II", *Marine Policy* 29, issue 2 (March 2005): 175–83. Also see "Guidelines for Navigation and Overflight in the Exclusive Economic Zone EEZ Group 21", Ocean Policy Research Foundation, Japan, 26 September 2005.
20. Sam Bateman, "The Emergent Maritime Future of the Asia Pacific Region", in *The Evolving Maritime Balance of Power in the Asia-Pacific: Maritime Doctrines and Nuclear Weapons at Sea*, edited by Lawrence W. Prabhakar, Joshua Ho, and Sam Bateman (Singapore: World Scientific, 2006), p. 248.
21. R.J. Nicholls, S. Hanson, C. Herweijer, N. Patmore, S. Hallegatte, Jan Corfee-Morlot, Jean Chateau, and R. Muir-Wood, "Ranking of the World's Cities Most Exposed to Coastal Flooding Today and in the Future", OECD Environment Working Paper no. 1 (ENV/WKP(2007)1), available at <http://www.oecd.org/dataoecd/16/10/39721444.pdf> (accessed 15 July 2008).
22. "The Working Group II Contribution to the IPCC Fourth Assessment Report", available at <http://www.ipcc-wg2.org/index.html> (accessed 15 July 2008).
23. "Greenpeace sees Effect of Climate Change in Kochi", *The Hindu*, 26 March 2008.
24. Charles Di Leva and Sachiko Morita, "Maritime Rights of Coastal States and Climate Change: Should States Adapt to Submerged Boundaries?", Law and Development Working Paper no. 5, 2008.
25. "Maldives: State of the Environment 2002", pp. 22 and 31, available at <http://www.environment.gov.mv/Docs2/SoE/MaldivesSoE2002.pdf> (accessed 15 July 2008).
26. "National Security and the Threat of Climate Change", available at <http://SecurityAndClimate.cna.org> (accessed 15 July 2008).
27. R.P. Anand, *Legal Regime of the Seabed and the Developing Countries* (New Delhi: Thomas Press (India) Ltd., 1975), p. 17.

28. Thomas R. Malthus, *An Essay on the Principle of Population* (Illinois: Richard D. Irwin Inc., 1963).
29. Elizabeth Becker, "U.N. Agency Urgently Seeks Food for Afghans and Africans", *New York Times*, 22 October 2002.
30. "World Hunger Facts 2008", available at <http://www.worldhunger.org/index.html> (accessed 24 May 2008).
31. "Nutritional Elements of Fish", Fisheries and Aquaculture Department, Food and Agriculture Organization of the United Nations, available at <http://www.fao.org/fishery/topic/12319/en> (accessed 6 June 2007).
32. Barry Buzan, *Seabed Politics* (New York: Praeger, 1976), p. 3.
33. P. Murugesan, T.T. Ajitkumar, and S. Ajmal Khan, "Marine Resources and their Future", *Journal of India Ocean Studies* 13, no. 1 (April 2005): 132–41.
34. Anthony S. Laughton, "Responsible Ocean Exploration", in *India's Exclusive Economic Zone: Resources, Exploration, Management*, edited by S.Z. Qasim and G.S. Roonwal (New Delhi: Omega Scientific Publishers, 1996), pp. 19–28.
35. Ross D. Eckert, *The Enclosure of Ocean Resources* (Stanford: Hoover Institution Press, 1979), pp. 7–8.
36. So Kee-Long, "Dissolving Hegemony or Changing Trade Pattern? Images of Srivijaya in the Chinese Sources of the Twelfth and Thirteenth Centuries", *Journal of Southeast Asian Studies* 29 (1998): 300.
37. Jeanette Greenfield, *China's Practice in the Law of the Sea* (New York: Oxford University Press, 1992), p. 3.
38. Joseph Needham, *Science and Civilization in China* (Cambridge: University Press, 1954), p. 521, cited in Greenfield, *China's Practice in the Law of the Sea*, p. 4.
39. Greenfield, *China's Practice in the Law of the Sea*, p. 16. The Chinese were able to secure the surrender of a Danish vessel that had been impounded in Bohai Bay, China's territorial waters from the Prussian gunboat *Gazelle*.
40. Jeanette Greenfield, *China and the Law of the Sea, Air, and Environment* (Germantown Maryland: Sijthoff & Noordhoff, 1979), p. 5.
41. Greg Austin, *China's Ocean Frontier: International Law, Military Force and National Development* (New South Wales: Allen & Unwin Australia Pte. Ltd., 1998), p. 18.
42. Greenfield, *China's Practice in the Law of the Sea*, p. 17.
43. Choon-ho Park, "China and Maritime Jurisdiction: Some Boundary Issues", in *The Law of the Sea: Problems from the East Asian Perspective*, edited by Choon-ho Park and Jae Kyu Park (Honolulu: University of Hawaii, 1987), p. 284. Also see David G. Muller, Jr., *China as a Maritime Power* (Colorado: Westview Press, 1983), pp. 82–83 and 145–146. The United States ignored Chinese concerns and warnings but the Chinese continued to challenge the U.S. naval vessels.
44. Ibid., pp. 256–57. Also see Choon-ho Park, *East Asia and the Law of the Sea* (Seoul: Seoul National University Press, 1983), pp. 250–51.

45. Rear Admiral Satyindra Singh, *Blueprint to Bluewater: The Indian Navy 1951–65* (New Delhi: Lancer International, 1992), pp. 486–88.
46. Austin, *China's Ocean Frontier*, p. 21.
47. Ibid.
48. Greenfield, *China's Practice in the Law of the Sea*, p. 203.
49. Ibid., pp. 198–99.
50. Srikant Kondapalli, *China's Naval Power* (Delhi: Knowledge World, 2001), pp. 12–13.
51. Ibid., p. 255.
52. Zou Keyuan, "A Comparative Study of Chinese Basic Maritime Laws: The Mainland and Taiwan", EAI Working Paper no. 17 (Singapore: East Asia Institute, December 1998), p. 1.
53. Muller, *China as a Maritime Power*, p. 80.
54. Chi-kin Lo, *China's Policy Towards Territorial Disputes: The Case of the South China Sea Islands* (New York: Routledge, 1989), p. 30.
55. Bob Catley and Makmur Keliat, *Spratlys: The Dispute in the South China Sea* (Aldershot: Ashgate Publishing Ltd., 1997), p. 34.
56. Lo, *China's Policy Towards Territorial Disputes*, p. 32.
57. Ibid., p. 56.
58. Catley and Keliat, *Spratlys: The Dispute in the South China Sea*, p. 34.
59. Khoo Hao San, "ASEAN and the South China Sea Problems", in *China, India, Japan and the Security of Southeast Asia*, edited by Chandran Jeshurun (Singapore: Institute of Southeast Asian Studies, 1993), p. 194; Sujit Dutta, "Securing the Sea Frontier: China's Pursuit of Sovereignty Claims in the South China Sea", *Strategic Analysis* 29, no. 2 (April–June 2005): 269–94.
60. Victor Prescott, *Limits of National Claims in the South China Sea* (London: ASEAN Press, 1999), pp. 22–23.
61. "Malaysia to Safeguard Sovereignty Over Layang-Layang Atoll", *Bernama*, 12 August 2008.
62. Alan Collins, *Security and Southeast Asia: Domestic, Regional, and Global Issues* (Singapore: Institute of Southeast Asian Studies, 2003), p. 189.
63. Richard D. Fisher, Jr., "Brewing Conflict in the South China Sea", Asian Studies Center Backgrounder 17, The Heritage Foundation, 25 October 1984.
64. Hungdah Chiu, "An Analysis of the Sino-Japanese Dispute over the T'iaoyutai Islets", *Occasional Paper/Reprint Series in Contemporary Asian Studies*, no. 1 (1999): 150.
65. Ibid., p. 16.
66. H.M. Seervai, *Constitutional Law of India* (Bombay: N.M. Tripathi Ltd., 1967), p. 983.
67. Discussions with Rear Admiral O.P. Sharma (retd.), Former Judge Advocate General, Indian Navy, and Indian Delegate at the UNCLOS III deliberations. Also see O.P. Sharma, "India and the United Nations Convention on the Law of the Sea", *Ocean Development and International Law* 26, issue 4 (1995): 391–412.

68. Rama Puri, *India and National Jurisdiction in the Sea* (New Delhi: ABC Publishing House, 1985), pp. 231–33.
69. Ibid.
70. R.C. Sharma and P.C. Sinha, *Indian Ocean Policy* (New Delhi: Khama Publishers, 1994), p. 173.
71. Puri, *India and National Jurisdiction in the Sea*, pp. 49–50.
72. Sharma, "India and the United Nations Convention on the Law of the Sea", p. 392.
73. Ibid., p. 400.
74. Seervai, *Constitutional Law of India*, pp. 66–68.
75. Puri, *India and National Jurisdiction in the Sea*, p. 103.
76. Ibid., pp. 206–7.
77. Park, "China and Maritime Jurisdiction", pp. 246–48.
78. Clive Schofield, "Island Disputes in East Asia Escalate", *Jane's Intelligence Review* (November 1996): 519.
79. John H. Noer, "Chokepoints: Maritime Economic Concerns in South East Asia" (Alexandria, V.A.: Centre for Naval Analyses, March 1996), p. 2.
80. Sharma and Sinha, *Indian Ocean Policy*, p. 25.
81. "Trans-Arabian Oil Pipelines", *Security and Terrorism Research Bulletin*, Gulf Research Center, issue 6 (August 2007): 4.
82. *The Strait of Hormuz: Global Shipping and Trade Implications in the Event of Closure*, Office of Naval Intelligence, 1997, p. 5.
83. U.S. Defense Secretary Robert Gates in his speech at the Shangri-La Dialogue in 2008 described the United States as a "resident power" in the Asia-Pacific region due to its political, economic and security linkages with the region. See P.S. Suryanarayana, "A New Marketplace of Security Ideas", *The Hindu*, 9 June 2008.

3

MILITARY MARITIME POWER: CHINA AND INDIA

There is a strong belief among Asian nations that it was the neglect of ocean frontier security that led to their domination by colonial powers during the 15th to the 19th centuries. For China, its preoccupation with internal wars led to the neglect of the littorals that came to be dominated by the imperialist powers and was the springboard to the domination of the hinterland.[1] Similarly, for India, the littoral dominance by the European powers, first by the Portuguese and then by the British and French resulted in their ascendancy of the Indian heartland.[2] Significantly, for both China and India the colonial-imperial supremacy came from the sea, to the littorals and into the heartland. The foremost strategic objective of China and India therefore is to build autonomous maritime military capability to preclude intrusive dominance of the littorals by any external power.

Soon after independence, China and India were engaged in wars across their land frontiers and military developments were shaped by the strong continental mindset among the ruling elite. It was in this context that the trajectory of the military structures and organization of the two powers was largely built around the army. Naturally the army was the vanguard of the national security structure and entrusted the important role of guarding national frontiers and providing external security. Operationally, the navy and the air force of the two countries were subsumed within the primary role of the army and were adjunct to the land forces. In the Chinese context, its navy was addressed as People's Liberation Army Navy, i.e. PLA Navy and in India it came to be termed as "Cinderella" service.[3] In terms of strategic priorities in decision-making, resource allocation and the formulation of security strategy, the army dominated the national security structure.

However, weakness at sea soon came to haunt the two Asian powers; for China the First and Second Taiwan Strait Crises of 1954–55 and 1958 witnessed U.S. intervention in support of its ally Taiwan.[4] Significantly, both crises witnessed U.S. aircraft carrier task force deployed in the area and precluded any attempt by the PLA to undertake amphibious landing on Quemoy. For India, the dispatch of a naval flotilla by Indonesia to deter India against Pakistan and a threat of opening of another war front in the Andaman and Nicobar Islands during the 1965 India-Pakistan war[5] and the U.S. decision to dispatch Task Force 74 led by *USS Enterprise* in the culminating stages of the 1971 India-Pakistan war[6] were the stark reminders of the dangers of external intervention from the sea, reminiscent of the colonial past. The successive dominance of the littorals by a superior naval power and recurring threats of external intervention from the sea have been the primary causal factors resulting in the rediscovery of the seminal importance of the navies that is today acting as a catalyst for China and India to modernize their naval power.

At another level, the two navies have set strategic visions that envisage building power projection capabilities for regional influence. The current force structure and future acquisitions indicate that the two navies are building platforms capable of long-range sustained operations supported by a host of manned and unmanned surveillance capabilities. Also, the threat of a nuclear intervention impacts on Chinese and Indian strategic thinking and necessitates an appropriate response from the sea.

The navies of the two states also gain salience driven by the imperatives of globalization and economic growth. There is a heavy concentration of economic hubs in the coastal region, which are the engines of economic development. Several maritime infrastructure projects have mushroomed in the coastal areas to support burgeoning trade, which contributes enormously to national economic growth. Thus the naval power of China and India is also derived from the strategic necessity of globalization and economic development that is inevitably predicated on maritime power.

The operational concepts of the PLA Navy and the Indian Navy envision extended strategic depth for projecting power from the littorals into the seas. These pivot on a formidable force structure built around highly manoeuvrable platforms designed to conduct over-the-horizon tactical operations. Besides, the naval doctrines are in the throes of transformation and envisage information-based operations with an ability to transit the sea-space-shore (S3) continuum for tactical surprise and swift introduction of forces. At the operational level, force formulations include a large number of networked, geographically dispersed platforms and off-board systems that complement air power projection achieved through multi-mission assets based at sea and ashore.

Sea-based deterrence finds a prominent place in the maritime strategic formulations of China and India. It pivots on credible deterrence through the dispersal of platforms/payloads that offer survivability and provide an assured retaliatory capability. Ballistic and cruise missiles from submerged platforms afford the advantages of dispersal and contribute to stealth. At another level, sea-based missile defence systems offer China and India the mobility and flexibility and serve as power projection capability built around an offence-defence template. These formulations resonate in the Chinese and Indian strategic thinking and are exhibited in the quest to develop a robust sea-based nuclear deterrent.[7] Naval planners in China and India are also studying the Cold War deployment of strategic submarines in deterrence roles by the United States and Soviet Union. Also, of interest is the post-Cold War deployments of nuclear deterrent; the United States, Russia, France and Britain have moved significant numbers of their nuclear arsenal onto submarines.

Similarly, an aircraft carrier finds a prominent position in the strategic and tactical calculus among Chinese and Indian naval planners. Aircraft carriers are considered power projection platforms that can launch aircraft in support of combat operations both at sea and on land as well as lifting of Special Forces during covert missions. In the tactical role, the aircraft carriers contribute to missions such as sea denial, sea control and long-range offensive operations. Organic air assets equipped with missiles add to the power projection capability of a force, assist in sea control/sea denial functions and contribute effectively to constabulary/benign tasks. Besides, carrier air operations provide speed and agility and can alter the aircraft mix for the entire spectrum of missions, combat crisis-non-combat. Naval planners and tactical commanders in the PLA Navy and the Indian Navy are studying and conceptualizing a wide spectrum of missions and exploit the ability of such platforms to transit the sea-space-shore interface.

The PLA Navy is focused on developing capabilities for its "offshore active defence strategy" to serve as a strategic-tactical force and affirm China's image of a regional maritime power with a robust naval capability. The strategy is also meant to safeguard China's burgeoning coastal economic regions and defend its maritime interests on the high seas. It seeks to defend China's littorals against external intervention and prevent the historical weaknesses that led to its subjugation in the past. The strategy also takes advantage of the navy's strategic and tactical capabilities and integrates these into national defence planning.

The Indian Maritime Doctrine enunciates the strategic missions entrusted to the Indian Navy and the capabilities required for undertaking a wide spectrum of tactical missions involving combat, coercive and benign operations. The doctrine supports the operational tenets of flexibility, battle space dominance and decisive action through sea control, sea denial, *"guerre de course"*, naval blockade, and combat action in surface-subsurface-space-shore continuum.[8] The doctrine further emphasizes the vital need to protect the Exclusive Economic Zone known to contain enormous amounts of marine resources.

With 250,000 naval personnel,[9] more than fifty major surface combatants and an equal number of submarines in its inventory, the PLA Navy is the largest naval power in the Asia-Pacific region. Though not as human resource-intensive, the Indian Navy is a force of nearly 70,000 personnel[10] and about 150 ships and submarines, and is the third largest in Asia after China and Japan. In terms of intent-capability matrix, the PLA Navy and the Indian Navy are developing power projection capability that envisions projecting images of regional maritime power, deployment of sea-based nuclear forces for deterrence across the peace-crisis continuum, anti-access capability and littoral dominance.

This chapter attempts to examine the naval capabilities of China and India that contribute to the maritime power and the ability to use this instrument of maritime power to safeguard respective national maritime interests. It highlights the ongoing naval acquisition programmes to support respective naval strategies. The chapter also undertakes an objective analysis of naval missions, and strengths and weaknesses of the two naval forces. The chapter is divided into two sections: the first section undertakes a critical analysis of the PLA Navy's strategy, its roles and missions and the capabilities of surface, subsurface, land attack capability and naval air force. Similarly, the second section undertakes an assessment of the Indian Navy's strategy, force structure, roles and missions. In that context, the chapter first highlights the complex art of force structuring.

FORCE STRUCTURING

Force structuring is a complex process[11] and involves multifaceted geographical, political, economic, technological and domestic variables that must be considered before arriving at the right combination of a defence force. Neighbourhood tensions and disputes, alliances and treaty obligations, compulsions of modernization, high technology developments, doctrinal changes, evolving missions in support of humanitarian assistance and commitments to international efforts under the United Nations shape the acquisition plans. At another level, foreign policy choices among nations are critical determinants of force structuring. While a force planner seeks the best solution through a comprehensive analysis of important factors, tangible and intangible including perceptions, opinions and viewpoints, there is rarely a single "correct" answer.[12]

With such a wide spectrum of complexity involved in force structuring, military planners are constantly engaged in establishing requirements, defining priorities, taking decisions and finally allocating resources for an optimal and potent military force. Significantly, force planning is a dynamic process and the planner is engaged in a struggle between various components of a force structure, i.e. (a) resources (means), (b) aims (ends), and (c) plans (strategy).[13]

There are several approaches available to a military planner to formulate military hardware acquisition plans to support the military strategy and national interests: The "top down" approach originates from a state's national interest. It focuses on the national grand strategy or national security strategy. The existing force levels, weapon systems and operations doctrines drive the "bottom up" approach. It emphasizes the forces "in being" which determine the national security strategy. The "scenario" approach is driven by the existing situation on the ground. The approach relies on real world information with elements of assumed plans. The "threat" approach is primarily based on the capabilities and limitations of the adversary. It focuses on the potential adversary and takes into consideration both the macro and micro picture of the conflict situation. The "mission" approach is operation-based and looks at capabilities across a wide spectrum of threats and challenges. The force planner examines several general categories of military activities such as strategic deterrence, sea control, littoral operations, and threats emanating from non-state actors such as terrorists and pirates. "Hedging" is a technique that seeks redundancy of specialist weapons/platforms and specialist troops capable of handling a wide range of contingencies. The "technology" approach is primarily driven by the belief that conflicts can be best deterred/stopped by employing superior weapon systems against a potential adversary. The advantage of this approach is that technology reduces casualties, and skilful deployment of capabilities could provide significant military leverage. The budgetary resources made available by a state to its military drive the "fiscal" approach and it also takes into consideration the democratic process.[14]

Each of these approaches has its merits, advantages and disadvantages but a judicious mix can result in a well-balanced force capable of undertaking a variety of missions across a wide spectrum encompassing conflict-peace-OOTW (operations other than war). Force planners are in a constant struggle to balance the "means", "ends" and "strategy" and contend with the issue of obsolescence that is rapid and uncontrolled, particularly in the current age of high technology and information systems. Naval vessels in particular highlight these realities as it can take several years to form plans, meet staff requirements and place orders with shipyards and the subsequent handing over for exploitation. Significantly, the end product may not necessarily be the most sophisticated since the technology may have raced far beyond.

THE CHINESE NAVY

Since its inception on 23 April 1949, the PLA Navy or *renmin jaifangjun haijun*, has witnessed several highs and lows shaped by external and domestic dynamics that had an impact on its strategy, force structure, roles and missions. Drawing inspirations from the ancient Chinese maritime supremacy of the Song and Ming dynasty, successive Chinese leadership has stressed that sea power is critical in China's efforts towards attaining a great maritime power status. That China must build a modern navy to prevent recurrence of imperialist aggression and dominance, safeguard national maritime interests and project its maritime power has been a recurring theme in major politico-maritime policy articulations. In 1953, Chairman Mao stated, "We must build a strong navy for the purpose of fighting against imperialist aggression"; in 1979, Deng Xiaoping called for a powerful navy and in 1999 President Jiang Zemin noted that China must strive to establish a modern navy with a strong comprehensive combat capability.[15] Addressing PLA Navy officers, Chinese President Hu Jintao was quoted as saying "We should endeavour to build a powerful people's navy that can adapt to its historical mission during a new century and a new period ... In the process of protecting the nation's authority and security and maintaining our maritime rights, the Navy's role is very important."[16]

During the last few decades, the PLA Navy has emerged as an important constituent of China's maritime power and is both a strategic and a tactical arm of the Chinese national defence with an extended reach and an expanded operational radius far from the mainland. Contemporary Chinese naval strategic thinking pivots on "limited war under high-tech conditions"[17] and "revolution in military affairs", the latter being the new "mantra". The Revolution in Military Affairs (RMA) in the PLA Navy is discussed in greater detail in Chapter 6. The naval planners are introducing modern warfare concepts by integrating technologies that can help to prosecute new threats in complex battle environments driven by information technologies. In essence, the current strategy aims at building a force capable of safeguarding sovereignty, protection of national maritime interests, serve as a deterrent, and conduct offensive and defensive missions set by the national leadership.

During the last few decades, the PLA Navy was provided with substantial financial resources to build a powerful navy and this aspect is best demonstrated by the fact that several new classes of ships, submarines and aircraft have been inducted in the force and the navy is in the throes of modernization both in terms of force structure and organization. The PLA Navy now sails in distant waters and several indicators point to the qualitative changes in its capabilities towards a powerful and modern navy capable of dominating regional affairs. Notwithstanding these developments, the sophistication and technological superiority of the PLA Navy is much below that of the navies of the United States and Japan and the naval capabilities of the Republic of Korea and Taiwan should offer significant challenges to the might of the PLA Navy.

Strategy

During Chairman Mao's era, the objectives and the capabilities of the PLA Navy were limited to coastal waters.[18] At that time, political thought with a strong continental mindset dominated military and strategic thinking, and the navy was considered to be an extension of the ground forces. In that context, the primacy of the PLA was also evident in the organizational structure and communist army generals commanded the navy.[19] The PLA Navy's roles were limited and it was not required to "wage a decisive battle" in the coastal waters. This was because the combat capability of the force was quite limited and it was ill-equipped for sustained operations in deeper waters due to logistical constraints thus limiting its area of operations. Consequently, the navy neither possessed the image nor the capability to find favour among the political elite and lacked the status and supremacy enjoyed by the army. However, the rude awakening about the importance of sea power dawned on the Chinese leadership when Chiang Kai-Shek's ships successfully evacuated retreating troops from Mainland China.[20] Apparently, the nationalists were able to bring together some 7,000 merchant vessels to transport the troops.[21]

The Cultural Revolution and the national policy under Deng Xiaoping provided an opportunity for the navy to develop its own strategic concepts. This is not to suggest that it was only during Deng's period that the PLA Navy got a boost; indeed, the PLA Navy's modernization had already begun as early as 1975 with the "ocean going navy proposal" endorsed by Mao.[22] By the mid-1980s, Sino-Soviet rapprochement had become probable and the PLA Navy began to transform its strategy. The leadership envisioned projecting China's naval forces further into the high seas[23] and much of the credit for the strategy of "offshore active defence" can be attributed to Admiral Liu Huaqing who advocated interpretations of "offshore operations" and "active defence" at sea, which had significant influence on China's naval modernization.[24] However, there is no conclusive definition provided by the PLA Navy regarding the precise distance implied by "offshore".

Often referred to as the Chinese "Mahan" or "Gorshkov", Liu stressed that the navy should be able to exert effective control of the seas within the first island chain. It was Liu Huaqing understanding that offshore should not be interpreted as coastal; instead, offshore is a concept relative to the high seas.[25] In the geographical context, the first island chain comprises the Aleutians, Kuriles, and Japanese archipelago, Ryukus, Taiwan, the Philippines and Greater Sunda Islands. The second island chain comprises the Bonins, Marianas, Guam and Palau group and relates to waters within the second island chain.

Force Structure

After the communist takeover of the People's Republic of China in 1949, the PLA Navy comprised a few frigates, junks and riverine craft.[26] There were also some amphibious landing vessels of U.S. origin, which had been captured from the retreating Nationalist force and some were imported from the Soviet Union.[27]

In the last six decades or so, the PLA Navy has come a long way and the current naval order-of-battle is built around a credible force for deterrence, power projection, expeditionary operations, and surveillance and reconnaissance in the EEZ. The PLA Navy is capable of undertaking littoral defence, sea control in adjacent sea areas (around mainland and South China Sea), limited naval-air dominance (in the absence of an aircraft carrier force), and includes nuclear submarines for deterrence and second strike and conventional submarines for anti-submarine warfare and naval blockade, anti-ship and land attack cruise missile for tactical superiority, an evolving expeditionary force for safeguarding offshore territories and assets and a variety of smaller vessels for constabulary functions in the EEZ. Much of the new ship construction is based on indigenous ship designs and incorporates both indigenous and imported weapons and sensors.

Deterrence

The concept of deterrence constitutes the core of the PLA Navy's force structure. In numerical terms, the PLA Navy outnumbers the regional navies and with the acquisition of modern ships and aircraft, it has developed significant deterrence capability. Further, nuclear submarines contribute to Chinese ability to deter any adventurism by other major powers. This higher level of deterrence reflects China's resolve to deter both regional and extra-regional powers in an engagement.

In the early years of independence, the spectre and fear of nuclear weapons loomed large in the Chinese thinking. Chairman Mao was convinced of the relevance of nuclear weapons as a currency of power in the conduct of international relations and had argued that if China was not to be bullied, it must develop nuclear capability. Besides, this capability would be significant in boosting courage and deter the others.[28] China launched its nuclear weapons programme in 1955, undertook the first nuclear test in October 1964, and test fired its first missile in 1966. The Soviet Union had provided significant assistance and support to China in its nuclear weapons development programmes but in the late 1950s it suddenly stopped supporting China resulting in a major setback to Chinese nuclear ambitions. However, the leadership was convinced that nuclear weapons were the ultimate guarantor of power and this thought has supported China's nuclear ambitions that continue till date.

Over the years, Chinese nuclear forces have emerged into a powerful and effective force pivoting on land based silo/mobile missile force, air delivery platforms and submarines. Analysts note that China has substantial uranium resources, the plutonium production has been steady and China's fissile material stocks are sufficient to produce 1,000 nuclear warheads.[29] Further, the current inventory is estimated to be between 237 and 246 including 84 sea-based nuclear warheads and in the next five years, the sea-based nuclear warheads are expected to be around 192, including 12 existing warheads on the JL-1A IRBMs.

Nuclear submarines are an important component of China's status as a major maritime power and play a critical role in Chinese defence and naval strategy. Since sea-based missile defence systems offer limited protection against incoming ballistic missiles, in such a scenario, sea-based nuclear weapons deployed on board nuclear submarines provide the much needed second strike capability. The Chinese naval planners consider sea-based nuclear weapons as a currency of power to serve their ambition to emerge as a major maritime power in the 21st century. Admiral Zhang Lianzhong, the former chief of the navy, was quoted as saying, "The development of the nuclear powered submarine is the chief objective of this country."[30] Significantly, the sea-based deterrent offers the PLA Navy an assured retaliatory capability. Over the years, China has developed a strategic force built around land-based platforms, sea-based nuclear submarines and strategic bombers to complete the triad.

The most prestigious among the PLA Navy submarine force is the Xia class SSBN and China built only one such submarine.[31] The Xia class submarine carries a weapon load of twelve Julong I (JL-1) SLBM (submarine-launched ballistic missile), with a single 250 KT warhead but is believed to be noisy and rarely seen at sea. In 2001, China laid the keel for the Type 094 Jin class SSBN at the Huludao Shipyard that was launched in 2004 and recent satellite pictures revealed that two such vessels have been built.[32] Four such units are likely to be built. The submarine is believed to be fitted with twelve three-stage, solid fuel JL-2 (JL-2 SLBM is a modification of the Dong Feng 31 (DF 31) land-based ballistic missile) and capable of hosting single nuclear warheads of one mega tonne or three to eight MIRV of smaller yield. The first vessel commenced sea trails in 2005 and experts are of the opinion that the Jin class SSBN noise control technology is not comparable to that of European or U.S. submarines but this deficency is made up for by the 8,000 kilometre range of the JL-2 SLBM.[33] The only Golf-class ballistic missile submarine, built at Dalian and launched in 1966, serves as the test platform for submarine-launched missiles.[34]

The PLA Navy's SSN fleet comprises four Han class submarines (one submarine was decommissioned in 2003) and three of these are capable of firing YJ-801Q (C 801) surface-to-surface missiles through the torpedo tubes.[35] Two Type 093 Shang class SSNs are under construction and are reported to host Russian technology and would represent a major technological improvement over the Han class SSN. However, according to an evaluation, the Project 093 submarine is similar to the 1980s Russian Victor III SSN.[36] China has also evinced interest in buying Project 971 Akula SSNs and Project 949 Oscar class nuclear-powered cruise missile submarines (SSGN).[37]

Power Projection

The most advanced surface platform in the PLA Navy inventory is the 8,000-tonne Sovermenny class guided missile destroyer.[38] China acquired four such vessels from Russia and commissioned these during 1999–2006. These ships are fitted with the SS-N-22 (Sunburn, 160-kilometre range) missiles and this acquisition has enhanced the PLA Navy's stand-off weapon capability. The SA-N-4 (Gadfly, 25-kilometre range) surface-to-air missiles provide "area defence" against incoming missiles and aircraft, though limited. The integral Ka 27 helicopter has boosted the PLA Navy's anti-submarine capability keeping in mind that in the past there were only a few ships that could carry Z9C ASW helicopters. The Sovermenny class guided missile destroyer equipped with Sunburn missiles was originally conceived for the Soviet/Russian Navy as a response to the U.S. Aegis weapon system. What is perhaps worrisome to the U.S. Navy is that the SS-N-22 has the capability to "destroy American aircraft carriers and other warships equipped with advanced Aegis radar and battle management systems".[39]

Notwithstanding the import substitution from Russia, the indigenous destroyer shipbuilding continues to make significant progress.[40] The most modern indigenous vessel in the PLA Navy inventory is the Luyang I class missile destroyers that entered service in 2004. These vessels are based on Type 052 B hull design, and equipped with both indigenous and imported weapons and sensors that showcase the Chinese ability to integrate different systems on board its warships. The Luyang II class, based on the Type 052 C, are air defence destroyers equipped with forty-eight long-range HHQ 9 surface-to-air missiles with a range of 100 kilometres. The Luhai class is a multipurpose, versatile, sophisticated and modern platform by Chinese standards. These 6,000-tonne Type 051B destroyers are powered by Modern Turbine Union (MTU) diesel, Ukraine gas turbine engines and are fitted with modern weapons. The first of the class was launched in 1997 at the Dalian shipyard and its major armament comprises sixteen CSS-N-8 (Saccade, C-803) surface-to-surface missiles, the HQ-7 Crotale surface-to-air missile system, 324 mm torpedo tubes, and two Z9A helicopters. While modern destroyers make entry into the PLA Navy order-of-battle, various versions of the Luda class still constitute a substantial part of the destroyer force.

In addition to destroyers, the PLA Navy has a variety of frigates. The Jiangkai (Type 054) joined the force in 2005 and incorporates stealth features exhibiting the advancements in Chinese warship design and building capability. These frigates have indigenous missile weapon packages including torpedoes. In addition, French diesel engines are installed to power the vessels, suggesting that western technologies too are finding place in the Chinese naval ships. The two follow-on frigates of Type 054 A host HHQ 16, a thirty-two cell vertical launch system and could possibly be a cold launch system. Among the other frigates, fourteen Jiangwei class Type 053 H2G and 053H3 incorporate modern propulsion systems and weaponry. These frigates are equipped with YJ-1 (C 801) surface-to-surface missiles, the indigenous sextuple HQ 61 (Crotale) surface-to-air missiles and are capable of embarking two Z9A helicopters. The rest of the force of the older twelve Jianghu I//III/IV/V class supports frigate inventory.

The PLA Navy subsurface forces have received priority in recent years and the strategy is to build a variety of subsurface platforms to replace the ageing and old generation vessels to modernize the force as well as to keep pace with the regional submarine acquisition trends.[41] The current submarine building programme aims at different classes of submarines simultaneously; this is a distinct departure from the past practice when one submarine was built and subjected to long operational trails before series production. At another level, the Chinese naval planners see submarines as potent weapon platforms in future naval warfare which is best reflected through a series of surprises made by the PLA Navy against U.S. aircraft carriers.[42] Significantly, the submarine force is listed as first in the order of protocol among the combat branches of the navy.[43]

Among the conventional submarine force inventory, the Romeo class (Soviet designs) and the Ming class, which is a modified version of the Romeo class submarine, make up half of the inventory. Two important developments during the last decade have been the acquisition of the Kilo class submarines from Russia and the development of the Song and Yuan class submarines built indigenously.[44] In 1993, China placed orders for Russian Kilo class attack submarines and the current inventory includes two Project 877 EKM and ten Project 636 submarines.[45] There were plans to acquire the Amur class possibly with SS-N-27 missiles[46] but these plans were shelved. The indigenous submarine programme has seen the production of the Song class and the Yuan class submarines; the Song class is a modern indigenous conventional submarine in the PLA Navy's inventory and is intended to replace the Ming class and the Romeo class submarines. The Song class is fitted with YJ-82 (sub-launched version of the C 801 ship-borne missiles) and six 533 torpedoes with replacements.[47] The Yuan class submarines building programme commenced in 2002[48] and it is believed that it is comparable to the 636 Kilo class in terms of performance and several of its features may have been derived from the Song class and the Kilo class submarines.[49]

The PLA Naval Air Force (PLANAF) is built around a generous mix of vintage (1950s and 1960s) and modern Russian origin and indigenously built aircraft. Since the PLA Navy does not possess an aircraft carrier, it is unable to provide continuous seaborne air cover for its fleet, for which it relies on the shore-based aircraft that include the J-8 I that cover up to 600 nautical miles from the shore.[50] The Russian origin Su 30 aircraft are deployed in the maritime role at Hainan Island in Southeast China and Woody Island in the Paracel group of islands in the South China Sea. These can provide cover over 1,000 nautical miles[51] and with mid-air refuelling these can remain airborne for longer periods; however, crew fatigue can restrict extended deployment. The PLA naval aviation also comprises shore-based Y-8 turboprop aircraft. This aircraft is the licensed copy of the Soviet/Russian An-12 Cub.[52] The first aircraft was delivered in 1984 and the PLA Navy has deployed it for maritime patrol and in anti-submarine warfare. Its electronic suite includes electronic countermeasures systems, optical/infrared cameras, sonobuoys, and sonar receiver. The SH-5 (Shuishang Hongzha-5) is an amphibious aircraft but is fitted with electronic suite and is also used for maritime patrolling and reconnaissance.

China's need for an aircraft carrier has been a subject of intense debate in China and also among foreign military analysts. At the domestic level, issues such as "prestige", "power projection" and "preclude coercion" are some of the drivers that shape the domestic discourse in China on the need for an aircraft. Issues such as the regional security environment, temptation for acquisition by Japan and South Korea, and overall balance of naval power have dominated discussions among foreign analysts and practitioners. Chinese naval experts are of the opinion that the size, shape, propulsion, aircraft and the weapon outfit of the aircraft carrier will be determined by the country's naval strategy which should be in compliance with the overall military and economic strategy reflecting "Chinese characteristics".[53]

The urge to possess an aircraft carrier is best demonstrated through an articulation by Admiral Liu Huaqing who was quoted as saying: "I'll die with an everlasting regret if China does not build an aircraft carrier."[54] Liu Huaqing started the "pilot warship captains" course in Guangzhou Naval Academy for command of surface ships. Rear Admiral Yao, President of the Guangzhou Naval Academy has observed that aircraft carriers are a symbol of the "deterrent power" of a state and have found favour among national security planners.[55] Yao acknowledged the fact that construction of an aircraft carrier is a long dawn process and for some "historical reasons, China has not yet built aircraft carriers". Admiral Shi Yunsheng, the former Commander-in-Chief of the PLA Navy had also emphasized that the PLA

Navy needs an aircraft carrier to provide air cover to the fleet operating in the South China Sea.[56] In more recent times, Lieutenant General Wang Zhiyuan, Vice Chairman of the Science and Technology Commission of the PLA's General Armament Department noted that China was studying the technology to build aircraft carriers to help develop on indigenous platform and "Aircraft carriers are indispensable if we want to protect our interests in oceans."[57] Besides, the American deployment of aircraft carriers in the major crises in the Taiwan Straits in 1958 and 1996 is a significant factor in Chinese thinking.

Chinese naval aviators have practised simulated flight take off and landing using catapults and arrestor wires on the copied flight deck of the HMAS Melbourne (purchased as scrap from Australia) using J8-II fighters.[58] Besides HMAS Melbourne (20,000 tonnes) purchased in 1985, China acquired three decommissioned aircraft carriers, i.e. Minsk (40,500 tonnes) in 1998, Kiev (45,000 tonnes) in 2000, and Varyag (58,500 tonnes). Apparently, these platforms were purchased to examine and understand the technology and develop designs for an indigenous aircraft carrier. Notwithstanding these initiatives, China faces several challenges with regard to the design and building a complex platform such as an aircraft carrier. Chinese shipyards may have the capability to build large vessels but aircraft carriers are sophisticated platforms and their design and engineering complexity goes far beyond building VLCCs. Besides, the integration of systems particularly for flight deck operations is alien to the PLA Navy. There are varying estimates about China's ability to field an indigenous aircraft carrier; these range from end of the Twelfth Five-Year Plan (2011–15) to the end of the Thirteenth Five-Year Plan (2015–20).[59]

Varyag, the second of the Kuznetsov class, purchased in 2001, has undergone three years of extensive and expensive repairs. The vessel is likely to have Pennant No. 83 and be named "Shi Lang" after Admiral Shi Lang, the Chinese Commander-in-Chief of the Manchu fleets that conquered Taiwan in 1681.[60] In 2006, the carrier was docked at the Dalian shipyard and its flight deck had been given a new coat of non-skid deck paint and the vessel's exteriors were shipshape and painted in official PLA Navy colours. However, the island on the carrier deck was devoid of any sensors and it could very well be that the PLA Navy plans to equip the vessel with basic navigation and surveillance systems to be able to put the vessel to sea and may even be planning to use this platform for humanitarian missions and disaster relief operations.[61] Should the PLA Navy decide to deploy Varyag in combat role, then the platform could have an air wing of Su-33 Flanker fighters and for that to fructify a ski jump is a prerequisite and would demand indigenous technology and design. Notwithstanding the technological constraints, by putting Varyag to sea, the PLA Navy will surely gain tremendous experience in operating large platforms and with helicopters deployed on the platform, the learning curve will be much faster.

In October 2006, Beijing signed a US$2.5 billion deal with Moscow to acquire up to fifty Su-33 (naval variant of the Su-27) fighters,[62] currently operated by the Russian Navy on board its carrier Admiral Kuznetsov. The delivery schedule is indeed very ambitious with two aircraft to be delivered in 2007 to the PLA Navy for evaluation and this will be followed by the delivery of twelve more aircraft at a later date.[63] There also exists a possibility for the deal to add another thirty-six Su-33s making the total fifty. The Chinese are also in advanced negotiation with the Russians for the possibility of purchasing the Ka-31 helicopter for use as an AEW platform.

Although the carrier is far from any meaningful naval operations, the ongoing Chinese purchases and investments in Varyag and the associated aircraft and helicopters to make it operationally deployable suggest that the PLA Navy may be thinking of refitting and retrofitting the carrier for operational deployments fully equipped with weapons and sensors at a later stage. Despite its plans to acquire an aircraft carrier, integrating it into Chinese naval tactical doctrine will be a challenge and may take a long time.[64]

Expeditionary Capability

The PLA Navy has noted with interest the acquisition of expeditionary vessels by several navies in the Asia-Pacific region. During the last decade new classes of amphibious and troop transport ships have been inducted in the naval inventory.[65] These platforms have enhanced the PLA Navy's capability to undertake expeditionary-amphibious operations in China's immediate and adjacent waters as well as distant territories in the South China Sea. However, its capability to participate in international/multilateral relief efforts such as the 2004 Indian Ocean Tsunami remain to be seen, bearing in mind the operational constraints. Besides, such deployments are also shaped by the political realities.

The Chinese expeditionary capability is built around the Yukan and Yuting class Landing Ship Tanks (LST) and these vessels complement the Qiongsha class troop carriers. Two ships of the Qiongsha class are fitted out as hospital ships.[66] In 2006, China launched the Type 071 LPD at the Hudong Shipyard in Shanghai and this vessel will boost the PLA Navy's expeditionary potential.[67] With a displacement of nearly 20,000 tonnes, the Type 071 LPD is highly versatile and can perform a variety of mission roles including its classic role as an amphibious assault vessel, platform for humanitarian aid during disasters relief operations and in roles involving casualty and refugee evacuation from conflict zones.

Besides, the PLA Navy has a large inventory of more than 200 amphibious vessels including smaller Landing Craft Utility (LCU), Landing Craft Medium (LCM) and Landing Craft Vehicles and Personnel (LCVP) type that are used to transport troops and materials.[68] There are also LSMs and LSTs that can carry troops and military transport/amphibious tanks. The Jingsha-class Air Cussion Vehicles, based on Russian Zubr design are capable of supporting amphibious operations. In 2001, China signed a US$4 billion deal with Russia to build 100 high-speed amphibious vessels.[69] The PLA Navy is also interested in acquiring wing-in-ground-effect craft that can cruise one metre above the water at speeds of 120 knots or more.[70] Besides, other auxiliary vessels such as tankers, container vessels, a variety of passenger vessels can be mobilized from trade for ferrying stores and troops and numerous boats and trawlers from the fisheries department can support the logistic supply chain during amphibious operations in adjacent waters.

The amphibious and logistic support capability can transport up to one infantry division[71] in the area of operation. There are several other vessels that operate under the paramilitary forces such as the China Maritime Surveillance (CMS), Maritime Safety Agency (MSA), People's Armed Police (PAP), Customs Patrol and Fujian Militia.[72] Both the PLA Navy and the Army have their own landing ship divisions and regiments. For instance the North Sea Fleet has one landing ship Division, East Sea Fleet two Divisions and one Regiment and the South Sea Fleet two Divisions and one Independent Regiment. The South Sea Fleet amphibious capability is for operations in the South China Sea and the East Sea Fleet has Taiwan as its area of responsibility. The Army Landing Formations located in the coastal military regions can also be mobilized for amphibious operations.[73] The 15th Airborne Army, comprising three Divisions is the best trained for amphibious assault operations. There are an additional fifteen Divisions designated as Rapid Reaction Forces (RRF) comprising 200,000 to 300,000 troops that can be mobilized to undertake assault operations in any operation and these are supported by electronic warfare units.[74]

The PLA Navy has conducted amphibious exercises targeted against Taiwan on a regular basis such as the Peace Mission in 2005.[75] According to the U.S. 2006 Annual Report to Congress, China conceptualizes different strategies for invading Taiwan including the Joint Island Landing Campaign that aims to "break through or circumvent shore defences, establish and build a beachhead, and then launch an attack to split, seize and occupy the entire island or important targets on the island".[76]

Littoral and Constabulary Forces

With more then 200 vessels, the PLA Navy has the largest number of small combatants in its inventory in Asia. The bulk of these is the Hainan class (375 tonnes) and the Shanghai class gun/patrol boats (113 tonnes).[77] Two Haijiu class (490 tonnes) are large patrol craft. The PLA Navy has forty Houbei class (220 tonnes) FAC(M) that are fitted with eight C-803 (range of 150 kilometres).[78] These are supported by the Houxin class (478 tonnes) and the Haujian class (520 tonnes) fitted with six YJ-1 SSMs (range of 40 kilometres).

Sea mines features prominently in the Chinese concept of naval warfare and mine warfare is understood and practised as both offensive and defensive. Another dimension of mine warfare is that the PLA Navy sees it as a "poor man's ASW"[79] illustrating the dimension of use of mines as tools of asymmetric warfare. Most of the PLA frontline ships and submarines are capable of laying mines and a variety of civilian vessels and craft can be mobilized for augmenting mine-laying capability. The Chinese sea mine inventory comprises a variety of mines including contact, acoustic, magnetic, pressure, rocket-rising and mobile mines and their numbers are estimated to be between 50,000 and 100,000 mines.[80] Submarines are considered as the most appropriate platform for laying mines due to the stealthy nature of their operations, besides these submerged platforms can be deployed close to the coast and port entrances. Submarine-launched mines are also most suitable for carrying out naval blockades and mine warfare by submarines is a significant part of PLA Navy exercises.

Roles and Missions

The PLA Navy's missions are closely related to the securing of China's maritime interests. Defence of offshore islands is regarded as the most likely form of China's engagement in the near future. In contrast to the Spratly Islands, no serious confrontation in the recent past has occurred in the case of Taiwan or the Senkaku Islands. The PLA Navy's likely engagement in Taiwan is discussed at several places in this study. In the South China Sea, the PLA Navy has clashed with Vietnam and the Philippines over the disputed island territories. There are several disputes of sovereignty and demarcation of boundaries and territory, and those that are not uninhabited have the potential to be captured by other claimants. Recapturing these places formidable demands on the PLA Navy since it would be operating a good distance from home. Such a mission would require proficient training and a high degree of operational readiness. It also calls for efficient ships, timely and effective shore-based air cover against enemy air strikes, effective C4ISR systems and a well organized logistic supply chain. These requirements have been addressed through modernization of on board equipment, acquisition of advanced aircraft, electronic warfare systems and a large number of expeditionary and supply platforms.

Although the PLA Navy has undertaken deployments, and carried out exercises in the South China Sea, its efficacy during conflict remains to be seen, particularly when the claimants are augmenting the existing military infrastructure on the islands. Of particular interest are the four known airstrips of various sizes on the Spratly Islands: Rancudo Airfield (1,300 metres) on the Pagasa, occupied by the Philippines, is the longest and C130 transport aircraft land on a regular basis. Islets occupied by Malaysia (Swallow Reef or Layang Layang), Vietnam (Truong Sa Lon) and Taiwan (Taipingdao) are home to 600-metre airstrips. The islands are unsinkable aircraft carriers and it is possible to stage smaller military aircraft of the VSTOL (vertical short takeoff and landing) variety. The forward deployed ships and submarines serve as a deterrent and can also be put to combat at short notice until reinforcements arrive from the mainland. The airstrips in Spratly and Paracel Islands are very short and VSTOL aircraft will be the platform of choice for deployment, bearing in mind that these can be deployed from several military and civilian platforms such as helicopter carriers, landing ships, and large flat-deck merchant ships and container vessels. VSTOL capability was proven during the 1982 Falkland War in the Atlantic Ocean when Britain successfully forward deployed its Sea Harriers from modified merchant vessels.

Currently none of the claimant states have VSTOL aircraft in their inventory and have to rely on foreign sources. Malaysia may explore the possibility of acquiring the Russian MiG 29 9-17K (K for *Korabelnyi* meaning "ship borne"). It is a carrier-operated aircraft with folding wings, toughened undercarriage and an arrestor hook. This aircraft can be deployed from shore particularly from shorter or damaged airstrips and is being acquired by India for its carrier *Vikramaditya*. In the 1990s, Malaysia acquired sixteen MiG 29 air superiority fighters from Russia, which are operational, and for the Royal Malaysian Air Force operating VSTOL aircraft should not be a big challenge. Vietnam too has a history of operating Soviet/Russian aircraft. Significantly, the bulk of the aircraft inventory of the Vietnam People's Air Force is of

Soviet/Russian origin and thus it has expertise in operating modern Russian aircraft such as the Su-27/Su-30. Hanoi too may be tempted to consider the MiG 29 9-17K. Much of Philippines' military aviation inventory is of U.S. origin with limited numbers of fighter aircraft. Significantly, the current Philippine Air Force efforts are focused on counter-insurgency and are investing in helicopter gunships and troop-lift capability and not much thought has gone into VSTOL aircraft.

For Taiwan there are several challenges for acquisition of military aircraft. Besides what it can develop indigenously, Taiwan has relied on the United States for most of its military needs that remain fraught with Beijing expressing concerns over the sale and accusing the United States of arming the renegade province. Liu Kui-li, the Taiwanese Air Force Chief, has noted that "Because of the strong likelihood that landing strips at airbases will come under intensive missile attack and be destroyed during a war with China, the air force considers fighters with VSTOL capabilities to be most suitable for Taiwan's defense ... The air force is open to any kind of VSTOL fighters, and is not necessarily aiming for the U.S. Joint Strike Fighters (JSF) that is in development."[81] As noted earlier, the Chinese inventory includes a variety of modern military aircraft like the Su-27, Su-30, Su-33 and the JF-10 that can be staged from either Hainan Island or Woody Island that are within short range of the Spratly Islands. With mid-air refuelling, these aircraft have enhanced loiter time and their stand-off weapon capability makes them formidable.

Another important mission for the PLA Navy is to safeguard sea lines of communications that are closely linked to the energy and material (raw and semi-finished goods) supply chains that originate in distant regions as far as Latin America, the Indian Ocean, Africa, Persian Gulf, and Southeast Asia. These are long and often vulnerable to disruption and are critical bearing in mind that China relies heavily on seaborne trade for its economic vitality as well as for its energy needs. In the event of closure of the choke points in Southeast Asia and disruption of merchant traffic in the constricted sea lanes through the South China Sea, China will be adversely affected. The PLA Navy would be tasked to keep the sea lanes open and escort Chinese merchantmen transiting the straits in the Indian Ocean, Persian Gulf and Southeast Asia.

China has long understood the strategic importance of the Straits of Malacca. In contemporary times, Chinese naval planners and practitioners are convinced that the Straits of Malacca continue to dominate the commercial and economic lifelines of China. It is estimated that nearly 60 per cent of Chinese crude is sourced from the Middle East[82] and given growing demand this figure is likely to rise beyond 70 per cent in the near future[83] and the bulk of this would naturally transit through the Straits of Malacca. It is no wonder then that the vulnerabilities in the Straits of Malacca prompted China to articulate the "Malacca Dilemma".[84] Reportedly, in November 2003 President Hu Jintao, without naming the countries, noted that "certain major powers" were actively strategizing to control the Straits and had called for exploring ways to overcome Chinese supply chain vulnerabilities.[85] Interestingly, the Chinese fears of strangulation of their supply chains led to the suggestion that "It is no exaggeration to say that whoever controls the Strait of Malacca will also have a stranglehold on the energy route of China."[86] Further, an observer suggested that whoever controls the Straits of Malacca and the Indian Ocean could threaten China's oil supply route.[87] In response, China plans to build oil storage facilities as a strategic reserve. Four such facilities have been identified at Zhenhai in Luanshan and Zhoushan Island in Zhejiang province, Huangdao in Qingdao in Shandong province, and Dayawan in Guangdong province.[88] A long-term plan envisages an initial reserve of 10 million cubic metres of oil by 2010 followed by 28 million tonnes each in two additional phases. Interestingly, these figures do not include the requirements of the large equipment- and human resource-intensive PLA.

These vulnerabilities have prompted China to position sea lane and choke point security high on its maritime strategy and also as one of the important missions for the PLA Navy. China is also conscious of the vulnerability of its energy supplies sourced from the Persian Gulf and North Africa. These must transit the vulnerable Straits of Hormuz and the Straits of Bab-al-Mandeb. Gwadar is strategically located overlooking the Gulf of Oman and the entrance to the Persian Gulf region. It is 40 nautical miles to the east of Pakistan–Iran border and is 390 nautical miles from the Straits of Hormuz. In March 2002, President Pervez Musharraf of Pakistan and the visiting Chinese Vice-Premier Wu Bangguo laid the foundation stone of the Gwadar Deep Sea Project GDSP[89] and China has provided financial and technical support for the project. In military strategic terms, Gwadar facilitates China to monitor the sea lanes from the Persian Gulf. This issue is discussed in greater detail in Chapter 7.

China has stated that it will use force should Taiwan declare independence.[90] In the event of such a scenario, the PLA Navy could be tasked to enforce sea control in adjacent waters and protect mainland merchant shipping transiting the sea lanes through the Straits of Taiwan. It will also be tasked to execute a naval blockade of all shipping headed by Taiwan and with the current order-of-battle, the PLA Navy is favourably positioned to enforce a naval blockade relying on its surface, subsurface and air superiority. The large fleet of conventional submarines is best suited for this task without intervention by any external power. The underwater conditions, shallow depths in the Taiwan Strait and in sea areas north and south of Taiwan are conducive for mine warfare. However there are some limitations for mine warfare along the deeper waters of the east coast. In case the United States intervene in support of Taiwan or to protect merchant traffic transiting through the area, the blockade may prove less effective.

To obviate that, China may not announce hostilities against Taiwan but the PLA Navy should be able to execute a "notional naval blockade" by positioning its subsurface assets along the international shipping lane and this would be enough reason for the international shipping in the area to move away and avoid calling at Taiwanese ports. There will also be a concomitant economic impact on Taiwan, as insurance agencies would naturally raise their risk assessments of the region and charge higher premiums for ships heading for Taiwan. To make the naval blockade more effective, the PLA Navy may even lay sea mines. Although this initiative will invite international criticism, it can be substantive enough to prevent foreign flag vessels transiting through the Taiwan Strait.

The Chinese shore-based missiles are capable of pinning down Taiwanese military and it is plausible that these missile launches could be a precursor to a naval attack on Taiwan. Currently China has deployed more than a thousand missiles targeted against Taiwan[91] and this figure is increasing at about 100 to 120 missiles annually.[92] The Chinese missile capability was demonstrated during the 1995–96 Taiwan Strait crisis when China fired missiles to intimidate Taiwan. On its part, Taiwan acquired three missile batteries and 200 PAC-2 Plus missiles in 1993 and is currently the first international Patriot customer outside the United States with a perfect record of achievement in live fire exercises. An indigenous version Tien Kung 2 based on the Patriot has been developed and an advanced version Tien Kung 2A is being developed.[93]

In July 2006, during Taiwan's annual military exercise, Han Kuang or "Chinese Glory", the Taiwanese Navy fired the Hsiung Feng III missiles (mach 2.5, range 150 kilometres). The missile, developed by the military-run Chungshan Institute of Science and Technology, is reported to be a match for the Russia origin SS-N-22 Sunburn supersonic anti-ship missile fitted on board the Chinese Sovremenny class destroyers. Both missiles are comparable in precision and capabilities, but the Hsiung Feng III is smaller, thus reducing the chance of its being detected.[94] The PLA Navy also requires air superiority and must prevent Taiwan's naval and airpower from defeating its naval blockade. For that, the PLA Air Force, with its large inventory of a variety of platforms, should be able to suppress Taiwanese air defences and subsequently achieve air superiority in Taiwanese air space resulting in air dominance.

At another level, the Chinese are sure to employ electronic warfare against Taiwanese electronic transmissions. The PLA Navy ships host a variety of electronic warfare systems including ECM and ESM equipment and the shore-based electronic facilities would be able to augment the PLA Navy's electronic warfare capabilities. Also, military satellites could provide electronic intelligence and reconnaissance particularly to monitor naval activity and vessel traffic in the waters around the Taiwan Strait and the South China Sea. This would enhance the PLA Navy's maritime domain awareness and provide early warning of incoming attacks. These issues are discussed in greater detail in Chapter 6.

The use of nuclear weapons against Taiwan is the subject of much debate and discussions ranging from their relevance as weapons of mass destruction to their employability as tactical weapons. Tactical nuclear weapons do find a place in Chinese strategic thinking and China has developed and tested tactical nuclear devices. Some observers believe that the Chinese use of nuclear weapons against Taiwan "rests on rationality, not necessarily on reality"[95] and if used, it would overkill. China surely understands that there are several grave political, diplomatic, military, economic and moral costs involved in the use of nuclear weapons, particularly when they enjoy a marked conventional superiority against Taiwan. Also of interest is the Chinese discussions relating to arming sea mines with tactical nuclear weapons.[96] Although there is no evidence as yet about the development of nuclear sea mines it is important to understand the Chinese thinking in this regard. China can also apply enough political pressure on the countries to stop shipments of critical resources such as oil and gas to Taiwan resulting in supply strangulations. Such a situation is plausible due to the fact that China has been able to wean away several countries that had earlier recognized the Republic of China and established diplomatic and political relations.

Defence of the littorals is the historical naval mission. Today, much of Chinese economic growth is taking place in the coastal regions. Special Economic Zones have been established which have emerged as the nerve centre of the economic boom and a gateway to the world. Nearly 40 per cent of the population, 50 per cent of cities, 70 per cent of GDP, 84 per cent of direct foreign investment and export products is generated within 200 kilometres of the coast.[97] These issues are discussed in greater detail in Chapter 4. In the foreseeable future, the threat to China's coastal safety comes mainly from Taiwan. There have been no clashes between Taiwan and China in the recent past; the likelihood of a conflict may arise should Taiwan decide to declare independence.[98] In such a scenario, Taiwan has the capacity to severely damage China's maritime industrial infrastructure such as dockyards, repair yards, logistics depots and oil storage facilities. As noted earlier, China is building strategic reserves at four sites along its coast and geographically these remain in close proximity to Taiwan and three of these, i.e. Zhenhai, Luanshan, and Dayawan, are precariously within range of the Taiwanese cruise missiles and fighter aircraft.[99]

Military modernization and deployment of missiles by China necessitates an increase in Taiwan's military spending, but domestic politics had blocked a special budget to buy U.S. arms, even though the package had been cut.[100] Taiwan's shopping list included submarines, the Patriot anti-missile system and anti-submarine aircraft. The critics argue that any large budget proposal could further provoke China and heighten cross-Strait tensions. China has the ability to conduct counter strikes and cripple Taiwan by using large numbers of conventional submarines, mine-laying capability, ship-launched missiles and shore-based aircraft. However, if China was to face a major sea power such as the United States in support of Taiwan or Japan, the PLA Navy would not be able to withstand any such attack, and its coastal defence would prove to be thin.

Changes in inventory do not necessarily result in improvements in actual combat capability and in that context it should be pointed out that the PLA Navy has a number of deficiencies which include the inability to undertake distant water sustained operations, limited integral fleet air defence, modern anti-submarine warfare capability, few AIP (Air Independent Propulsion) fitted submarines, and lack of modern electronic warfare equipment. Despite improvements in fleet-air defence and shore-based air cover, PLA Navy units are still vulnerable to incoming missiles. With the fitting of the French Crotale/HQ-7 surface-to-air missiles, limited defence has been provided, and these surface-to-air missiles (10-kilometre range) may prove to be ineffective against the modern misiles such as the Harpoon, Exocet, and the more recent Klub and Brahmos missile attacks which have stand-off capability and can be launched from as far away as 50 to 100 kilometres.[101] Similarly, the naval units are also vulnerable to air-launched missiles. The Su-27, Su-30 and the J8/10 aircraft (shore-based) would improve the air cover for the fleet at sea, but can provide limited air defence and mid-air-refuelling capability is critical. With the current air defence assets, it would be a big challenge to provide air cover over extended periods for the PLA Navy task forces operating in the South China Sea. Besides, the transit time to the scene of action, efficiency of data link between aircraft and the naval ships and command and control pose major challenges for an effective employment of shore-based air cover over extended periods.

Notwithstanding the modernization efforts in the field of missiles, the most conspicuous area where the PLA Navy has been found to be outdated is anti-submarine warfare (ASW). Most of the ASW sensors and weapons fitted on board naval vessels are upgrades of the Soviet models of the 1940s and 1950s.[102] However, the newly acquired Ka 28 from Russia and the indigenously produced Harbin Z9C Haitun helicopters have significantly enhanced the anti-submarine warfare capability of the fleet. In its offensive format, major platforms of the PLA Navy host A 244s torpedoes and multiple-barrel rocket launchers.

Early warning systems such as the radar and Electronic Support Measures (ESM) equipment are still based on Soviet models. For instance, the Jiangwei class frigate is fitted with air surveillance radar based on the Soviet "knife rest" radar of post-World War II vintage. Till the late 1990s, much of the early warning equipment fitted on board the PLA Navy ships was old;[103] however, the new vessels host Chinese/Russian surveillance systems that include the E/F band Top Plate 3D air search systems and the G-band Type 364 Seagull. Similarly, the Chinese ships are now armed with improved naval guns such as the Chinese built 100 millimetre that have replaced the old mounts based on the Soviet naval artillery of the 1950s and 1960s vintage. For instance, the 130-millimetre gun continues to be the primary gun on the Luda class destroyers, 100-millimetre gun on the Jinghu class frigates, and the twin 37-millimetre guns fitted on almost all naval ships. The Chinese on their part have only upgraded these weapons and the associated fire control systems.

Although the PLA Navy's submarine force is quite impressive, there are a number of factors that reduce its effectiveness. First, the majority of the submarines have sonar of Soviet origin of the 1950s vintage (Hercules and Feniks),[104] but the hull-mounted Shark Teeth and Mouse Roar fitted on the Kilo class submarines have improved the underwater detection capability of the PLA Navy to some extent. Further, the operational readiness of the submarines has been a matter of conjecture. China's Romeo class submarines may be spending only a few days at sea each year. For instance, during the 1990s the PLA Navy submarines were engaged in an average of 1.2 patrols annually, but since 2000, the average has improved significantly to 3.4 patrols annually with a maximum of six patrols only during 2000 and 2007.[105] Besides, the older submarine machinery is noisy and vibration-damping technology is still evolving.[106]

Defence Spending

The resolute grip over the political and social order has resulted in a major transformation in the Chinese economy. A continued 9 per cent average growth during the last decade has catapulted China into a position of economic supremacy. The implication of its rapid economic growth has had a profound global impact, alarmed the world and raised fears of the nature and scope of China's "rising power".

China has the world's largest standing military, and its actual defence spending growth rate is on the rise.[107] Since the 1990s, Chinese economy and the defence spending have grown rapidly and if the trends continue, the PLA Navy should be able to keep the modernization drive quite easily without burdening the economy. The Chinese policy-makers should be able to provide substantial fiscal resources in the foreseeable future to meet the diverse needs of the PLA Navy such as new equipment and better training infrastructure.

There has been an internal debate in China on the relationship between defence and economic development.[108] The Chinese believe that excessive defence spending in the early periods of its independence imposed a heavy burden on the economy and hindered its development. In the early 1950s, due to the Korean War, the defence spending was as high as 42 per cent of the total budget. In the early 1970s, the defence spending accounted for 22.99 per cent due to threat by "imperialist and revisionist elements" and suffered a rapid decline (negative growth of 3.99 per cent for seven consecutive years) in the 1980s in their attempts to revive the economy that had been devastated by the "Cultural Revolution".[109] This weakened China's defence modernization considerably. However, since the early 1990s, defence spending has increased in double-digit percentages due to the rapid growth of the national economy.

The year 2008 marked yet another year of sustained rise in the military spending in China. Beijing announced a record 19.4 per cent rise in its military budget to 417.8 billion yuan (US$58.8 billion) from 350 billion yuan in 2007.[110] Although China has been increasing its military spending by double digits nearly every year since the early 1990s, this defence budget increase was the largest rise in five years, For instance, in 2006 the Chinese argued that the defence spending was very low (1.4 per cent of the GDP) and defended the increase on the ground that China had "no intention of vigorously developing armaments", claiming that much of the new spending would be to offset higher fuel costs and increase in salaries and concluded that China was a "peace-loving nation".[111] In 2007, a government official stated that the navy would build its first aircraft carrier by 2010[112] and in 2008, the Chinese Premier Wen Jiabao defended the increase in the defence budget and noted that "We must balance economic development and national defence development to make China prosperous and the armed forces strong as we carry out modernization ... Our aim is to enable the army to fully carry out its historic mission in the new stage in the new century."[113]

The Chinese leadership has dismissed worries among the regional countries of its military modernization and emphasized that it is concentrating on economic development. But the leaders know that there are several benefits that accrue from the growing economy when sustained investments are made to build credible military and naval power and prevent the historical folly of allowing imperial occupation leaving regional countries wondering about its long-term intentions.

THE INDIAN NAVY

The 1947 partition in the Indian subcontinent resulted in the division of the Royal Indian Navy into two different entities, i.e. the Indian Navy and the Pakistan Navy.[114] It was decided to allow British Royal Navy officers to plan the development of respective maritime forces due to a deficiency of higher ranking and experienced officers in the respective navies.[115] In 1948, a ten-year Indian naval expansion plan, prepared under the guidance of British Royal Navy officers was presented to the government. The plan was accepted in principle by the then Governor General of India, Lord Mountbatten and the then Prime Minister of India, Jawaharlal Nehru. However, it did not fructify due to several geopolitical, domestic and financial constraints.[116] Notwithstanding that, the Indian ruling elite were convinced about the significance and importance of sea power and it was generally agreed that a strong navy was critical for India. On 28 March 1958, Jawaharlal Nehru, on board Mysore, the second cruiser acquired by independent India, noted that by virtue of its geography, India is in the "lap of an ocean" and reiterated the importance of the sea to India and that India could not afford to be weak at sea. Reinforcing his argument, Nehru observed that whoever controls the Indian Ocean has influence over India's trade.[117] There is a strong element of continuity from the past and similar sentiments continue to resonate among contemporary political leadership who note:

> The realisation that this gross neglect of maritime security eventually led to the colonisation of the sub-continent and the consequent loss of India's very independence for nearly three centuries should make

a repetition of this strategic error utterly unaffordable. These harsh lessons of history are not lost upon the modern, independent republic that is India.[118]

In recent times, India's political elite, irrespective of their political affiliations, have enunciated a maritime strategic vision and defined the strategic geography in which the Indian Navy will be called upon to operate. Addressing the Annual Combined Commanders Conference,[119] Prime Minister Vajpayee of the National Democratic Alliance (NDA) noted:

> ... As we grow in international stature, our defence strategies should naturally reflect our political, economic and security concerns, extending well beyond the geographical confines of South Asia ... Our security environment ranges from the Persian Gulf to the Straits of Malacca across the Indian Ocean, includes Central Asia and Afghanistan in the North West, China in the North East and South East Asia. Our strategic thinking has also to extend to these horizons.[120]

Under the same government, in 2000, the Indian Defence Minister George Fernandes noted "India's area of interest extends from the north of the Arabian Sea to the South China Sea."[121]

The UPA government under Prime Minister Manmohan Singh has articulated the strategic geography in which India has significant stakes. The Prime Minister stated:

> India's growing international stature gives it strategic relevance in the area ranging from the Persian Gulf to the Straits of Malacca. ... India has exploited the fluidities of the emerging world order to forge new links through a combination of diplomatic repositioning, economic resurgence and military firmness.[122]

Pranab Mukherjee, as Defence Minister, also under the UPA government, reinforced the strategic domain for the Indian Navy and defined a large swath of sea space in the Indian Ocean as the Indian Navy's area of responsibility. He noted:

> Our location on top of the Indian Ocean between the sea routes from the Cape of Good Hope and the Mediterranean and the energy sources of the Gulf to the strategic Malacca Straits gives us a vantage point and responsibility to safeguard the security of our energy supplies and shipping in the Indian Ocean region.[123]

From the above, it is quite evident that there is a perceptible shift in the strategic thinking among the ruling elite from "maritime blindness"[124] and "neglect" and the notion of "Cinderella service" of the Indian Navy to a greater understanding of the capability of the force and its significance in India's economy that is predicated on globalization and maritime trade. The economic reforms in the early 1990s resulted in improved economic growth, and this was a catalyst for the realization that naval capability was critical to protecting sea lanes, safeguard maritime infrastructure, protection of EEZ, and other political, economic and strategic interests on the high sea. The Indian political establishment has understood the efficacy of the navy in the political milieu of international relations and see it as a force with a distinctive profile of being the instrument most suitable for projecting power and influence both in the national and international contexts across the globe. That such a force should project power is a recurring theme in Indian naval articulations too:

> ... if India aspires to don the mantle of even a regional entity, New Delhi must shed diffidence, and find not just the ways and means but the will to project power overseas. This did not mean that India was planning to be the aggressors, or planning to invade someone. It needed enough power to eject intruders from its island territories, to come to the assistance of neighbours, to rescue Indian nationals, and as the Tsunami showed, and to render aid in natural calamities.[125]

Over all, there is an "overt political and military"[126] willingness in India to develop a powerful force that can project power, safeguard littorals against intervention and dominate affairs in the Indian Ocean. It is envisioned that the Indian Navy should be capable of responding to a wide spectrum of tasks and roles ranging from conventional naval operations, the *raison d'etre* of the navies since historical time, to securing the littorals against low-level threats from asymmetric actors such as terrorists and pirates as well as to engage in humanitarian missions and respond to natural disasters like the recent Indian Ocean Tsunami. The above spectrum of threats and responses demand a judicious force mix and importantly a capability of immediate reaction to deter/counter the enemy or act in response to a natural emergency. The Indian Navy also needs capabilities to respond quickly to international crises as well as to contain conflicts in the region to avoid the spillover effects and to prevent escalation. In evidence is a strategic evolution of the Indian Navy in the 21st century that stems from its enhanced capabilities and naval muscle, derived from the continued economic growth, burgeoning military-industrial complex, nuclear military capability and missile technology contributing to its strategic profile.

Contemporary Development in Indian Naval Strategy

The concept of "tous azimuts" resonates in the India naval strategic thinking. It envisions deterrence and in case that fails, the Indian Navy should seize the initiative and engage in battle action and carry the offensive into the adversary's zone.[127] In that context, the navy should be able to exercise control in areas of interest[128] referred to as (a) Zone of Positive Control (ZPC), (b) Zone of Medium Control (ZMC), and (c) Zone of Soft Control (ZSC). The size and extent of these zones is based on the Indian Navy's capability to conduct surveillance, detection, identification and prosecution of the challenger before it can jeopardize national security or damage critical assets at sea or on land. In simple geographic terms, these zones encompass large sea spaces from the coast into the deep seas covering a large swath of the Indian Ocean.[129] This requires the Indian Navy to have the range and endurance for extended deployment well beyond the Andaman and Nicobar and Lakshadweep group of islands and interdict enemy forces approaching the island groups. The islands will thus act as unsinkable carriers and serve as forward bases to host combat aircraft, store missile batteries, electronic pickets as well as to provide logistics support to forces operating far from the mainland.

The Indian Navy's *Strategic Defence Review* published in 1998 observes that navies enjoy complete international legality on the high seas can therefore operate well beyond the territorial limits of a nation in different situations covering a variety of contingencies both during war and peace and that the Indian Navy should have the capability to be regarded "as of consequence in the region".[130] *India's Military Maritime Strategy* envisions the Indian Ocean region as the primary area of interest and operations, which includes the sea space encompassing the Straits of Bab-el-Mandeb, Straits of Hormuz, Straits of Malacca, and Cape of Good Hope.[131] Although the Red Sea, South China Sea, Southern Indian Ocean and East Pacific Region have been classified as the secondary area of interest to the Indian Navy, these would gain primacy should events and incidents in those areas impinge on Indian interests.

Given the primacy of the Indian Ocean (approximately 74 million square kilometres) in the Indian naval thinking, the strategy envisages sustained and long-range airborne surveillance and reconnaissance in the area. The Indian Navy has defined three tiers of sea-air space in the Indian Ocean that would be under surveillance and reconnaissance by a variety of airborne assets controlled both from ships and shore. In the innermost tier, surveillance would be undertaken by UAVs (Searcher and Heron class UAVs) controlled from ships and shore stations. The next tier would be the responsibility of the Medium Range Maritime Reconnaissance (MRMR) aircraft and surveillance and reconnaissance in the outer tier will be undertaken by the Long Range Maritime Reconnaissance (LRMR).[132] The force structure for air surveillance architecture should be such that the air platforms should be able to operate 1,000 miles from the coast and fly for ten to twelve hours.[133] The Indian Navy acknowledges that large sea areas such as the Indian Ocean cannot be kept under constant surveillance through individual efforts and regional naval efforts would need to be mobilized including shore-based international initiatives such as the "Automatic Identification System" (AIS) and the "Long-Range Identification and Tracking" (LRIT) system, and a variety of transnational and regional cooperative and collaborative mechanisms for "Maritime Domain Awareness".[134]

The core of the Indian Navy's strategy is deterrence and if deterrence fails, war fighting and conflict termination on terms favourable to India. During times of peace, the Indian Navy should demonstrate its resolve and readiness to reinforce deterrence.[135] When dealing with a powerful adversary, deterrence can be achieved through leveraging partnerships or alliances/coalitions exhibiting solidarity. However, national policies prohibit the Indian Navy from building or participating in alliances/coalitions outside the ambit of the United Nations. The Indian Navy's deterrence capability thus pivots on (a) combat efficiency, (b) forward presence, (c) reach and sustainability, (d) information capability, and (e) building partnerships.

Towards that end, the Indian Navy has followed a judicious force acquisition programme aimed at safeguarding national interests and supporting naval strategy. The current force structure is built around nearly 140 vessels including 1 aircraft carrier, 8 destroyers, 13 frigates, 25 corvettes, 16 conventional submarines, and a large number of smaller combatants. Besides logistic support vessels and survey/research form the auxiliary force, a host of long/medium range maritime patrol aircraft, fighters jets and helicopters deployed on board ships and ashore provide the requite reconnaissance and surveillance needs of the force.

Force Structure

From a motley collection of few ships in 1947,[136] the Indian Navy has grown in size, capability and sophistication and is the largest in South Asia and the third largest in the Asia-Pacific region after the PLA Navy and the Japanese Maritime Self Defence Force (JMSDF). The Indian naval plans envisage a force of nearly 200 vessels[137] from the current levels of 136.[138] This will include building 75 ships in the Eleventh Defence Plan and during the Eleventh and Twelfth Defence Plans, the navy would emerge as a balanced force with blue water capability centered on two simultaneously-operational carrier strike groups with a suitable mix of escorts comprising destroyers, frigates and corvettes. However, the submarine force is expected to maintain the present level of deployable platforms. The 2005 Maritime Capability Perspective Plan of the Indian Navy envisions a balanced force of 160 ships including 90 frontline combat platforms.[139] Under the plan, a variety of vessels including missile destroyers, frigates, and submarines would be built over the coming decade and a half. As of May 2008, the Indian Navy had placed orders for 34 ships, 6 submarines and 3 aircrafts carriers, out of which 2 would be indigenous carriers.[140] Also, the Indian Navy's focus is on acquiring force multipliers such as maritime reconnaissance aircraft, rotary-wing unmanned aerial vehicles and underwater systems. The 2008 force level of 142 vessels would continue to decrease till 2012 as the number of decommissioned vessels will be larger than new induction due to limited naval shipbuilding plans during the period 1985–95.[141] The Indian Navy's order-of-battle by 2022 could be "a fleet of 160-plus ships, three aircraft carriers and 400 aircraft of different types. Extensive satellite surveillance and networking will be there", and most of these would be indigenously built.[142]

Deterrence

No first use of nuclear weapons is the stated policy of the Government of India. In August 1999, New Delhi made public the Draft Nuclear Doctrine that clearly spells out that India remains committed to global nuclear disarmament and would endeavour to practise arms control measures. Further, the Draft Doctrine states that India is committed to No-First-Use (NFU) against nuclear weapons states and "No-Use" against non-nuclear weapons states. However, in case the non-nuclear weapon states align with nuclear weapons states or seek nuclear protection under treaties and declarations, the NFU may not be applicable.

The Doctrine notes, "India's strategic interests require effective credible nuclear deterrent and adequate retaliatory capability should deterrence fail" and "credibility", "effectiveness" and "survivability" are the cardinal principles under which India's nuclear deterrent will function.[143] The Indian naval leadership argues that the deterrent should be lethal with sufficient yield to inflict unacceptable damage to the intended targets both military and civilian.[144] Further, the lethality factor should account for "inaccuracies of vector and inefficiencies of warhead". Therefore, any nuclear strike on India shall result in a retaliatory strike to inflict unacceptable damage on the attacker. Bearing in mind the doctrine of "no first use", Indian naval planners and strategists view a nuclear submarine as critical and argue that "[nuclear submarine] is much more than just a submarine with a nuclear reactor ... It is the arbiter of power at sea."[145]

In that context, India's naval strategy envisages conventional deterrence to prevail in normal circumstances thus preventing conflict and should that fail, nuclear deterrence is a powerful tool available to the state in achieving security. In order to achieve the desired response, India must possess a credible and survivable nuclear deterrent. Under these circumstances, nuclear submarines are the most suitable platforms to provide states with the desired second strike capability. Nuclear propelled submarines possess unique characteristics of stealth, endurance, flexibility, survivability, responsiveness, and connectivity and provide the most credible and reliable nuclear deterrent in the arsenal.

In 1988, India acquired a nuclear submarine on lease from the Soviet Union and commissioned it as the Chakra.[146] The submarine served as a training ground for the Indian naval personnel and was also a design laboratory for developing and testing indigenous nuclear submarine technology.[147] At the end of the lease period in 1991, Chakra was returned to Russia.

The indigenous nuclear submarine programme, designated as an Advance Technology Vessels (ATV), could begin sea trials in 2009.[148] The ATV submarine is expected to be of 6,000-tonne displacement, and four to five such vessels are to be built. To arm the vessel, India also started to develop the underwater launch-capable missile named Sagarika.[149] In February 2008, a submarine-launched ballistic missile named K-15 was test fired in the Bay of Bengal from a submerged pontoon fifty metres in the sea, thus India joins the United States, Russia, the United Kingdom, France and China which have the capability to launch a variety of missiles from the air, surface and subsurface. According to the DRDO (Defence Research and Development Organization), the K-15 is 8.5 metres long and a two-stage missile capable of carrying a one-tonne nuclear warhead to a range of 700 kilometres. The missile performance during tests was "far higher" compared to the specifications by the Indian Navy and is under production.[150] The ATV submarine is capable of hosting twelve vertical-launched nuclear tipped missiles (SLBMs or SLCMs), however, integrating the K-15 and proving the system will take some more time.[151] The Indian naval chief noted, "The DRDO project will demonstrate the technology of these (nuclear submarines) and we hope someone will develop the nuclear-powered submarine technology for the navy in future."[152] There have been regular reports to indicate that India is planning to lease a Russian SSN to help bolster the development of the ATV.[153] In 2008, the said platform was involved in a major accident during its sea trails in the Sea of Japan and nearly twenty crew members died and another twenty-one had to be hospitalized due to acute freon poisoning.[154] The Indian Navy also has two "dual-tasked" vessels (INS Subhadra and INS Suvarna) that have been modified and fitted with the nuclear-capable Dhanush (variant of Prithvi with a 330-kilometre range) missiles.[155]

Power Projection

Soon after independence, a ten-year naval expansion plan was unveiled and it was decided to build two fleets, one each for the Bay of Bengal and the Arabian Sea, centred on four aircraft carriers and 280 shipborne strike and fighter aircraft.[156] But it was in the 1950s that the Indian Navy first unveiled its blueprint for a three-carrier force. The then naval planners had studied and understood the relevance of aircraft carriers during the Second World War. Besides, the Indian Navy's blue water ambitions were quite clear from its ten-year naval expansion plan.

Indian strategists and naval practitioners have consistently argued that an aircraft carrier is a versatile platform and can support combat operations both at sea and on land as well as support induction of Special Forces during covert missions. In the tactical role, the aircraft carriers contribute to support missions such as sea denial, sea control and facilitate long-range offensive operations.[157] Its organic air assets also contribute effectively to constabulary/benign tasks. Above all, the aircraft carrier serves as a potent deterrent to an invading force.[158]

Aircraft carriers are power projection platforms and can act as a deterrent. They are also powerful political weapons that have the ability to influence events short of war. Indian national security interests include enabling the country to exercise a degree of influence over nations in the immediate neighbourhood as well as to promote harmonious relationships in tune with national interests. To that extent the carrier is an important tool for influencing events in the maritime neighbourhood. Significantly, the aircraft carrier is central to the Indian Navy's concept of operations.[159]

In the Indian context, the aircraft carriers have been cleverly deployed in carrying strikes ashore into East Pakistan during the 1971 Indo-Pak conflict, employed in support of naval diplomacy and several other constabulary and non-combat tasks. However, these deployments have been limited to the northern Indian Ocean in the Persian Gulf and the Bay of Bengal littorals. Given the centrality of aircraft carriers in Indian naval strategic thinking, it is not surprising that these platforms find significance in Indian naval force structure formulations. As an ardent practitioner of carrier operations, the Indian Navy is striving to "fulfil its long-term operational commitment" by deploying two carrier task forces in the Indian Ocean, as enunciated in the naval plans of 1947.[160]

It is also argued that one of the aims of naval forces is to influence events on land. In order to achieve this, naval forces need necessary tools to carry strikes deep inside the enemy territory against strategic targets or in support of land forces. This has blurred the earlier fine line demarcating sea power from land power resulting in the "fusion of land and maritime strategies" which has been further supported by technological developments in tactical and cruise missiles.[161] However, the relevance of an aircraft to carry strikes ashore has come under scrutiny given that long-range missiles and munitions, and increasingly sophisticated UAVs are forming part of the naval inventory resulting in a diminished role for the manned aircraft.

India acquired the INS Vikrant (ex-HMS Hercules), a Majestic class light fleet carrier from the United Kingdom in 1961 and it was tactfully deployed in the Bay of Bengal for combat operations in East Bengal (now Bangladesh) during the 1971 India-Pakistan conflict. The second aircraft carrier, INS Viraat (ex-HMS Hermes), was acquired in 1986 and continues to serve as the only power projection platform of the Indian Navy.

During the 1980s and the 1990s, India was scouting for aircraft carriers in the international market but none was available. The U.S. option was foreclosed due to political considerations and the Soviet carriers were equipped with Yak 36 that was considered inferior to the Sea Harrier already existing in the Indian Navy's inventory. While import substitution is an easy answer to maintain a carrier force, the need for an indigenous platform had been gathering momentum since the 1970s. The naval architects had been experimenting with designs to build an indigenous aircraft carrier but did not receive support. In the late 1980s, the Indian Navy persuaded the government and DCN International of France assistance was obtained, however plans were shelved due to financial constraints. Above all, the need to preserve carrier operation techniques and crew expertise built over three decades dominated the minds of naval planners.

In 1999, the Indian Government sanctioned the Air Defence Ship (ADS) to be built at the Cochin Shipyard. This 37,500-tonne carrier, also known as Project 71 Indigenous Aircraft Carrier (IAC), likely to be named as INS Vikrant, is an ambitious project bearing in mind that Indian shipyards have never attempted to build a warship of such complexity. The vessel is designed to operate MiG-29K and LCA (Navy), the indigenous light combat aircraft built by Hindustan Aeronautics Limited (HAL) from a ramp with arrestor gear.[162] The IAC can host thirty aircraft and helicopters, configured to perform several roles and is likely to join the fleet by 2015.[163]

The Indian Navy's plans to acquire the Russian aircraft carrier, Admiral Gorshkov, renamed INS Vikramaditya, has been the subject of controversy with regard to the cost, size and age of the vessel.[164] The carrier was offered on sale for free to the Indian Navy but its refit cost including upgrade and a ski jump was estimated at US$970 million with an additional cost of nearly US$530 million for the MiG-29K fighter jets, and Kamov surveillance and anti-submarine warfare helicopters. The platform was to be handed over to the Indian Navy in 2008 but ran into delivery time delay and cost overruns. The platform is likely to be delivered to the Indian Navy by 2012 after eighteen months of extensive sea trials jointly by the Russian and Indian naval personnel. Its air compliment comprises twelve MiG-29K fighter jets and six Kamaov helicopters aircraft and these were supplied to the Indian Navy in 2010.

There had been some reports to suggest that after the successful sale of USS Trenton (re-christened as INS Jalashava) to India, the United States offered the sale of USS Kitty Hawk for free provided the Indian Government buy sixty-five F/A 18E/F carrier-based fighters.[165] Apparently, the proposal was to be put forward by the U.S. Defense Secretary Robert Gates, who visited India in February 2008. But both sides denied that there was any such proposal and dismissed the reports as "rumours".

In May 2007, by way of a statement before the parliamentary panel on defence, A.K. Antony, Indian Defence Minister, confirmed in the Rajya Sabha that the Indian Navy would induct a third aircraft carrier by 2017 to make it a three-carrier force by 2017,[166] to include INS Vikramaditya (Admiral Gorshkov), the indigenous Air Defence Ship (ADS) and the third carrier, to be built by Cochin Shipyard Ltd. Significantly, the Indian Navy is seeking a three-carrier force, one carrier each for the two fleets and the third in refit/repair. Bearing in mind that the age of an aircraft carrier is about thirty to forty years, it is envisaged that by the time INS Vikramaditya is due for decommissioning, another carrier would be ready to join the force. To maintain this force level, the naval plans envision a long-term construction arrangement with the Cochin Shipyard Limited.

Other than an aircraft carrier, the most advanced vessels in the Indian Navy inventory are the indigenously built Delhi class guided missile destroyers. Built with the assistance of the Russian Severnoya Design Bureau, these vessels are the largest vessels ever built by Indian shipyards.[167] Designated as Project P15, the three vessels, INS Delhi, Mysore and Mumbai, are large platforms of 6,700 tonnes and form the mainstay of the attacking force and enhance Indian Navy's stand-off capability.[168] These are equipped with quadruple launchers with four tubes each for launching the KH-35E Uran (SS-N-25) anti-ship sea skimmer missiles (range 70 nautical miles, 145-kilogram warhead). The surface-to-air missile package Gadfly is equally impressive and can provide area defence up to 13.5 nautical miles. An important feature of these vessels is the capacity to host two helicopters; Seaking Mk 42 B or the indigenous ALH that can be configured both for an anti-submarine role as well as to launch anti-ship missiles, thereby providing an extended range of attack.

Under Project 15-A, three vessels of Kolkata class Guided Missile Destroyers are under construction at the Mazagon Dockyard Limited[169] and the first vessel is expected to be commissioned in 2010. These 7,000-tonne ships are designed for combat in multi-threat environments, would be fitted with sixteen BrahMos PJ 10 launchers, a DRDO developed twenty-four cell vertical-launch missile system for air defence, multi-function radar system, Humsa-NG (hull-mounted sonar array) sonar and a Nagin active towed array sonar. The ship is designed to operate two multi-role helicopters.

Five Russian-origin Kashin class destroyers were acquired in the 1980s and continue to support the navy's destroyer fleet; one vessel has been modified to be the test platform for the BrahMos series of missiles. These vessels are equipped with SS-N-2d Styx anti-ship missiles with a range of 45 nautical miles. In November 1997, India placed orders with Russia for three Krivak III class 3,620-tonne frigates (Talwar, Trishul and Tabar) built in Russia at an estimated cost of US$1 billion. The Severnoye Design Bureau and Baltisky Zavod shipbuilder of St. Petersburg developed the design and constructed the vessels. Interestingly, some 130 entities and vendors from Russia, India, Britain, Germany, Denmark, Belarus, Ukraine and some other countries were engaged in this project. The frigates are the first Indian Navy vessels that incorporate stealth features and a vertical-launch missile system for the SS-N-27 Klub-N anti-ship cruise missile (ASCM).

The Project 17 (P17) Shivalik class is an enlarged and modified version of the Russian P1135.6 Krivak III class stealth frigates built in collaboration between the Indian Naval Design Bureau (NDB) and Russia's Severnoye Project Design Bureau. Three vessels (Shivalik, Satpura and Sahyadri) of this class are under construction at Mazagon Dockyard Limited, Mumbai, and expected to be commissioned 2008 onwards. To lower the IR (infra-red) signature, Infra-Red Suppression System (IRSS) design tools and training have been supplied by Canada's Davis Engineering. The weapon package and EW suite is still speculative.

With the ageing and subsequent decommissioning of the several British design Nilgiri class (Leander class) frigates, the Indian Navy acquired the Brahmaputra (Project 16-A Godavari class follow-on) ships.[170] A total of three vessels were built and the missile package is similar to the Delhi class destroyers. The important feature of this class of frigates is the indigenous surface-to-air missile suite, namely, Trishul.[171] Trishul is still being tested and will ultimately be fitted on all future missile vessels. In the meantime, the Indian navy fitted the Israeli Barak vertical-launch surface-to-air missile system.[172]

Submarines are an important component of the Indian naval force structure. A thirty-year submarine construction plan stretching to 2025 aims at an inventory of twenty-four submarines and this will boost indigenous production.[173] The current inventory comprises a mix of Russian and German-origin boats and the bulk of these are of the Kilo class and four HDW type 209/1500 boats (two built in India) of German origin. The Indian Navy acquired ten Kilo class (referred to as Sindughosh class in the Indian classification) Project 877EM/8773 SSK submarines from Russia in the late 1980s and 1990s.[174] The last vessel was delivered in 2000. These vessels have undergone modernization and retro-fitment in terms of weapons and sensors. Five of these have been modernized at the Russian shipyards in Severodvinsk and fitted with modern sonar and advanced electronic warfare equipment with a capability to launch SS-N-27 (3M-54 E Klub) cruise missiles with a range of ninety-two nautical miles, associated Lama-ER control system, new sonars (MGK-400EM), electronic warfare systems, new control systems from Avrora such as the Palladij-M machinery control system and the AICS (Automated Information and Control System) integrated weapon control system.[175] Some of these vessels are likely being updated to a Type 636 standard. These vessels are also being fitted with a Panchendriya package that includes an Indian sonar (USHUS) developed by NPOL (Naval Physical Oceanographic Laboratory) of the Indian Navy and a fire control system developed by the WEESE (Weapons Engineering and Electronics System Engineering), another unit of the Indian Navy, both in collaboration with the BEL (Bharat Electronics Limited).

The Shishumar class (Type 209/1500) of German origin were delivered between 1986 and 1994.[176] The first two submarines of the series were built by HDW, Germany, and the remaining two were assembled at the Mazagon Dockyard in Mumbai. There were plans to build two additional Shishumar class submarines but these were shelved in 1987–88. After some prolonged deliberations, India signed a contract in 2005 with France for the licensed production of six Project 75 Scorpene class 1,750 tonne conventional submarines worth US$3.5 billion.[177] The Mazagon Dockyard Limited with technical support from Armaris will build these submarines in India and the first vessel is to be commissioned in 2012 and the balance of five to be delivered by 2017, one per year. The agreement includes the technology transfer for the entire submarine excluding the technology for torpedo tubes. The equipment for the first two units will be sourced from France and the equipment for the balance four vessels will be made in India under various Indo-French collaborations and joint ventures. Reportedly, the agreement has a provision for building an additional nine units but the contract has no provision for fitting of MESMA (Module d'Energie Sousmarin Autonome) AIP (Air Independent Propulsion) module. The Indian navy is hoping to install the system on the last three submarines that would cost an additional US$50 to US$60 million for each MESMA system. Also, installation of sea-skimming SM 39 Exocet anti-shipping missiles is a part of the deal and the submarine design has been modified to include provision for firing two different types of torpedoes. Besides the Scorpene class submarines, the Indian Navy plans to acquire an additional six submarines that have the capability to launch surface-to-surface missiles.[178]

The Indian naval air arm comprises a variety of Russian, British, and French aircraft and helicopters including the indigenously built ALH helicopters (being produced by Hindustan Aeronautics Limited) under licence. The inventory is fairly modern by regional standards and can provide effective air cover to the fleet for the aircraft carrier and for shore strikes. The long-range maritime patrol aircraft are shore-based and provide surveillance to the fleet operating far from the shore. The navy has anti-submarine (ASW), early warning (EW), and missile-capable helicopters that provide both defensive and offensive air capability to support fleet operations. The inventory is spread over sixteen naval air squadrons including fighter jets, both from shore and from the aircraft carrier, maritime patrol aircraft, helicopters, and Unmanned Aeriel Vehicles. The aircraft carrier can host up to eight Sea Harrier fighter jets and at least two-dozen helicopters (configured in anti-submarine and search and rescue roles). The Sea Harrier is V/STOL aircraft of British origin, operated from the aircraft carrier and INS Hansa at Goa on the west coast. Some of these have been upgraded to include ELTA' EL/M-2032 X-band monopulse Doppler radar and RAFAEL's

Derby thirty-six kilometre active radar air-to-air missiles. As noted above, the Indian Navy contracted for sixteen MiG-29 fighters to be deployed from INS Vikramaditya, undergoing refit/modernization in Russia.

The Indian Navy has twenty Dornier-228 short-range maritime patrol aircraft in its inventory. These have been fitted with SAR (Synthetic Aperture Radar) and FLIR (Forward Looking Infrared) systems. The inventory also includes eight to ten Tu-142 acquired from the Soviet Union/Russia and the Indian Navy is looking to replace these with modern aircraft for which the RFP (Request for Proposal) has been issued. Three IL-38 maritime patrol aircraft were upgraded in Russia from SD 1 to SD 6 and equipped with Sea Dragon electronic suite that has enhanced the exploitation potential of the platform. The aircraft is equipped with multiple tracking doppler radar, advanced ASW system including low frequency sonobuoys, MAD (Magnetic Anomaly Detector), IR and night vision capability and a sophisticated ESM (Electronic Support Measure) suite. Its combat capability has been further enhanced with a pair of KH-35 air-to-surface missiles.[179] Sea King 42 of British origin have been in service with the Indian Navy for more than three decades but their operational availability has been suspect due to non-supply of spares. The helicopters are being upgraded in India and are likely to be fitted with indigenous ESM systems including a LRDE-manufactured (Electronics and Radar Development Establishment) radar upgrade. Ka 25 and Ka 28 are shipborne helicopters fitted with indigenous ESM system. The helicopter can fly out to 100–150 kilometres from the mother ship and can monitor targets well beyond that range. The Ka 31 is an AEW (Airborne Early Warning) helicopter and is networked on data link to the Talwar class stealth frigates.

The UAV fleet is built around twelve UAVs (four Herons and eight Searchers II) deployed from both permanent and temporary sites along the east and west coast of India. These platforms have augmented the Indian Navy's surveillance capability. In the future, India plans to acquire rotary UAVs.[180] The current thrust is to enhance the surveillance capability to achieve a greater maritime domain awareness of the Indian Navy by investing in a variety of air platforms. The navy has plans to build a naval aviation force of 250 aircraft up from 170 in 2006.[181] The Indian Navy plans include acquisition of nearly a dozen long-range maritime reconnaissance/anti-submarine warfare aircraft (MR/ASW). For this contract, the contenders include BAE (Nimrod), Boeing (P-8A MMA), IAI/Elta (Dassault Falcon 900 MPA), Lockheed Martin (P-3C Orion), Northrop-Grumman (Global Hawk, presumably), EADS (CN-235MP, AT3 Atlantique, ATR-72MP, modified A319) and Rosoboronexport IL-38 and TU-142, both of which are currently operated by the Indian Navy.[182] There are plans to acquire short-range maritime patrol aircraft such as the Dorneir-228 being built by the state-owned Hindustan Aeronautics limited (HAL).[183] The Indian Navy has also been offered the P3C Orion[184] and Boeing has offered P8I maritime patrol aircraft as direct sale and not under the U.S. foreign military sales (FMS) programme.[185] The deal valued at US$2.2 billion is expected to provide the navy with advanced maritime reconnaissance and surveillance equipment.

Land Attack Capability

It is a well-known fact that sea-based cruise missiles are now capable of delivering the desired quantity and type of ordinance at the designated target on land. The capability to carry strikes ashore has transformed the nature of warfare on land. In the Indian context, the Indian Navy has supported operations on land in the past. For instance, during the 1971 India-Pakistan conflict, the Indian Osa class missile boats attacked several targets including ships and shore-based infrastructure in Karachi and the attack had a major impact on the outcome of the war. The Indian Navy has acquired the Klub (NATO named SS-NX-27) anti-ship missiles to be fitted on submarines, long-range maritime aircraft and new frigates.[186] The latest Kilo class submarine Sindhushastra is equipped with tube-launched Klub anti-ship missiles and the Talwar class frigates carry eight standardized vertical-launch tubes of the Klub-N system. Reportedly, the Indian Navy has test fired the surface-to-surface missile Dhanush (range of 250 kilometres) from the modified offshore patrol vessel INS Subhadra.[187]

In March 2008, India test fired the land attack version of the Brahmos, a supersonic cruise missile that can hit targets both on land and at sea.[188] It is a sea skimmer that can fly at ten metres above the sea surface and has a speed of Mach 2.8, three times faster than the U.S.-made subsonic Tomahawk cruise missile. INS Rajput, the Russian-built guided missile destroyer has served as a test platform for the BrahMos cruise missile tests. Indian missiles are fast emerging as sophisticated weapons and some are comparable to those operated by the West. The fifteen tests of BrahMos so far are pointers towards the development of more modern missiles.

Expeditionary Capability

During the last two decades there has been a substantial increase in the Indian amphibious capability with the induction of INS Jalashwa, (ex-USS

Trenton), the indigenously built Magar class vessels, Polnochny LSM from Poland, and Landing Craft Utility (LCU). INS Jalashwa and the Magar class vessels are capable of hosting helicopters and the latter can land special marine commandoes in enemy areas.

In the absence of substantial organic capability, India has to rely on container, bulk and tankers from trade that transport weaponry such as air defence guns, military vehicles, ammunition, engineering equipment and fuel. The Indian Maritime Doctrine notes that Ships Taken Up From Trade (STUFT) should normally augment operations to transport troops, equipment, materials and logistics. By far the most commonly requisitioned vessels are tankers, passenger and cargo ships and some underway replenishment vessels. In fact the Indian merchant marine is the fourth arm of defence.

Unlike the United States that has global commitments and whose military is constantly forward deployed, the Indian Navy has engaged in wars in its neighbourhood. These wars did not necessitate large-scale transportation of troops, arms and ammunitions and other military stores over sea. During the Kargil conflict, the Indian merchant fleet continued to perform its regular operations of transporting cargo but there were plans to deploy Sea Harrier fighter planes on board a temporarily converted oil tanker since the carrier was under repair. For India, the expeditionary capability gains salience during maritime contingency in the Andaman and Nicobar and the Lakshadweep group of island territories, be it in the form of foreign infiltration or occupation by separatist groups. Bearing in mind the geographic location far from the mainland, the requirement of sealift capability would become obvious. The sealift forces would require support from fleet auxiliaries such as tankers and depot and repair ships.

Littoral and Constabulary Forces

The Indian Navy's littoral combat forces are built around corvettes that have surface and subsurface capabilities. The Project 25 Khukri class (Khukri, Kuthar, Kirpan, Khanjar) are 1,400-tonne corvettes designed by the Indian Navy's Directorate of Naval Design (DND). These vessels are a replacement for the ten Petya II class corvettes acquired from the former Soviet Union between 1969 and 1974. The follow-on Project 25 A Kora class (Kora, Kirch, Kulish and Karmukh) are equipped with anti-ship missile (ASM) packages of sixteen 3M-24 anti-ship missiles and can be deployed for saturation attacks on littoral targets. The 2,500 tonnes Project 28 (P28) ASW corvettes are for anti-submarine warfare (ASW) and four units were ordered in 2003. Reportedly, the vessels have shielding built with stealth technology that drastically reduces noise to prevent detection by enemy submarines and also facilitates prosecution of target submarine from a distance.[189] The vessels have been designed jointly by the Indian Navy's DGNDSSG (Directorate General Naval Design Surface Ship Group) and the ship builders, i.e. Garden Reach Shipbuilders and Engineers (GRSE). It is planned to build twelve units of this class.

The Indian inventory of small craft is of at least three origins, i.e. Russian, Israeli and Indian.[190] Among the combatants, a large number are equipped with surface-to-surface missiles. Both the Veer class (Russian Tarantul class) and Nirbheek class (Russian Pauk II class) carry missiles and torpedoes respectively. Goa Shipyard Limited has begun to build these vessels, but a large proportion of weapons, sensors and engineering systems continue to be imported from Russia. In 1998 and 1999, two Super Dovora MK II class fast patrol vessels were imported from Ramta, an Israeli company with a provision to build two in India. These vessels are primarily meant to provide coastal defence and therefore are deployed close to shore. The Sukanya class Offshore Patrol Vessels (OPV) (Sukanya, Subhadra, Suvarna, Savitiri, Sarayu, Sharada, and Sujata) are lightly armed platforms for defence and protection of offshore installations including patrolling in the EEZ.[191] Subhadra and Suvarna were customized to host a missile launch pad. In 2000 Sarayu was sold to the Sri Lankan Navy and renamed as SLNS Sayura. In March 2005, the Indian Navy placed orders for three naval offshore patrol vessels (NOPVs) at a cost of Rs.1,089 crores (US$236.74 million) to be built by the Goa Shipyard Limited (GSL). These vessels are designed for constabulary operations in Indian EEZ for patrol, surveillance and monitoring of sea lanes and defence of offshore oil installations. The ships are also fitted with a helicopter hangar to house one indigenous HAL-built Dhruv helicopter to assist in search and rescue and maritime surveillance.

Roles and Missions

The Indian Navy's roles and missions are closely linked to India's national interests. In broad terms, the Indian Navy's roles can be put into four different categories: (a) sea-based deterrence, (b) economic and energy security, (c) presence in areas of interest, and (d) multifaceted naval diplomacy.[192] As noted earlier, deterrence lies at the core of the Indian Navy's strategy and it should be able to deter any maritime challenge posed by littoral states individually or in concert with other regional states. It should safeguard territorial integrity and protect national interests. The naval capability should be such that it should raise the threshold of intervention or coercion by both littorals and extra-regional forces. As regards strategic nuclear deterrence, sea-based deterrence is critical to second strike capability. Also, the Indian Navy should be able to protect itself and take necessary precautions to clear nuclear-contaminated areas.

Naval presence is a traditional method of demonstrating capability to remind the local inhabitants of the effectiveness of the navy and the state that owns it. It also reflects the technological capability and is a reminder of national resolve. The Indian Navy should be able to underwrite regional stability, promote friendly ties with like-minded nations and provide timely response capability. India is highly dependent on shipping to transport energy resources from overseas suppliers. This includes import of crude products through tankers, transportation of offshore production to the mainland via tankers and the coastal movement of products. With nearly 90 per cent of India's oil coming by the sea route, it is inevitable that the SLOCs be protected. This security issue is magnified since most of the oil originates in the Persian Gulf that has remained plagued with political turbulence making the oil supply from the region its hostage. As noted in the previous chapter, closure of the Straits of Hormuz practically cuts off Gulf supplies to all countries in the Asia Pacific and part of the West, which is fed by pipelines. Similarly, the closure of the Straits of Malacca can seriously threaten the economies of Southeast Asia, China and Japan. The Indian Navy would be tasked to protect SLOCs and escort national shipping, vital cargoes and energy assets on the high seas as well as when they transit choke points. In its offensive construct, the Indian Navy should be able to engage in "commodity denial" to the enemy. The strategy is built on the argument that the Indian Navy should be able to interdict and deny critical resources that the adversary "needs badly and must be transported through the seas".

The discovery of offshore oil and gas in the Arabian Sea in 1974 and the Bay of Bengal in the 1990s resulted in additional roles for the Indian Navy. The most important oil and gas fields are located in the Arabian Sea some 200 nautical miles from Mumbai, comprising Bombay High, Heera Panna and South Bassein. The security of these offshore platforms is of considerable importance since they are vulnerable to accidents, sabotage and attacks. Any disruption in oil production would affect the economy and the replacement cost of each complex can be very high.[193]

Strategically, the Andaman and Nicobar and the Lakshadweep group of islands are of considerable significance and relevance to India's security. The islands lie astride the SLOCs through the Straits of Malacca and therefore occupy a commanding position for control of maritime traffic from the Indian Ocean to the Pacific Ocean and act as sentinels and a first line of defence. While there are strategic advantages, there are vulnerabilities too. This stems from their vast geographical separation from the mainland. They are prone to intrusion, illegal settlements, influx of refugee populations and even invasion. The islands are totally dependent on the mainland for all essential support. Given these geostrategic conditions, a local maritime contingency has direct security implications for India. Therefore, the Indian Navy should be able to defend and safeguard these island territories. Naval diplomacy is an important function of the Indian Navy. It should act as the ambassador of goodwill and build maritime bridges with like-minded states. This is discussed in detail in Chapter 5.

Defence Budget

The current economic boom in India has created euphoria and there is a strong belief that India will be among the top economies in Asia and can be the second leader after China to lead the Asian economic boom. With an expected annual growth rate of 8 per cent, it is highest in Asia after China which has been experiencing growth rates of over more than 9 per cent. The Indian leadership has been supportive of building a strong and a modern military to safeguard national interests, to serve as a deterrent and be a force to reckon with commensurate with the size and interests. During the Indian Military Commanders conference in 2005, Prime Minister Manmohan Singh assured the Commanders that the government could allocate about 3 per cent of India's GDP for its defence needs if the economy grows at 8 per cent annually.[194] India's defence budget has averaged between 2.3 and 2.6 per cent of GDP for almost a decade and has been insufficient for modernization and new acquisitions of military hardware required to be relevant to changing times.

It will be useful to locate India's defence expenditure in the overall context of India's grand strategic vision *vis-à-vis* her military capability and fiscal resources. In the past, the defence modernization had been stagnating with weapons systems completing their design and/or useful operational life finishing without replacement. At a time when India's growing economic prowess and beyond-region strategic vision are well acknowledged, India is spending the kind of money that could give her desirable dividends in achieving her strategic ambitions.

A closer look at India's defence expenditure suggests some trends. The government allocated Rs.105,600 crores (US$22.96 billion), a hike of over

10 per cent 2007–08 allocation of Rs.96,000 crores (US$20.87).[195] The allocation for 2006–07 was pegged at Rs.89,000 crores (US$19.3 billion), Rs.6,000 crores (US$1.3 billion) more than the 2005–06 budgetary allocations.[196] As percentage of GDP, the defence budget for 2007–08 is below 2 per cent as compared to Pakistan's 5 per cent and more than 10 per cent in the case of China. Trend analyses for the past fifteen years suggest that China's defence budget has been witnessing a real term increase of 10 to 11 per cent per annum and similar figures for Pakistan that has witnessed about 13 per cent increase annually. India's defence spending has seldom crossed 3 per cent of its GDP, and hovered around 2.5 to 2.6 per cent for the past decade.

The primary argument for an increase in defence budget is based on the fact that India has an active border with Pakistan and the two countries have fought three major wars in the last sixty years or so. Similarly, India has to maintain deployments along the India-China border despite the fact that the two sides signed a bilateral treaty on Maintenance of Peace and Tranquillity along the Line of Actual Control on the India-China border in 1993. There are regional factors too that prevent disengagement of militaries along the India-China border. These are: (a) Sino-Pakistan nuclear and missile cooperation, (b) China's military agreements with several South Asian countries, and (c) Chinese military surveillance and monitoring facilities in Myanmar. Besides, the PLA intrusions into the Indian Territory are now more frequent in Arunachal Pradesh, in the northeast of India (China claims 90,000 square kilometres that comprise the complete state of Arunachal Pradesh) and this is an issue of grave concern.[197] For instance in 2007, 140 intrusions by the PLA into the Indian Territory were reported.[198] The Indian Army is also engaged in internal security responsibilities in Kashmir and northeast India. Unlike India, China and Pakistan have been spending relatively larger sums for national defence. The upgradation and modernization is another reason for the increased defence spending.[199]

Indigenous military infrastructure is still very rudimentary when compared with western standards and there is a huge gap between India's domestic production efforts and weapons requirements, resulting in a situation where almost 70 per cent of actual requirements are met through imports. India's investment in military R&D had never crossed 7 per cent throughout history.[200] Insufficient funding in military R&D efforts has impacted negatively on India's indigenous production efforts, among other reasons.

CONCLUSION

The evolving force structures of the PLA Navy and the Indian Navy pivot on high technology platforms, nuclear-capable submarines to support the strategic triad and doctrinal and operational advancements. These capabilities are significant for guarding ocean frontiers against colonial-imperial forces, securing maritime interests, protecting littoral hubs that form nodes in the global supply chain, safeguarding critical sea lines of communications and exercising influence in the region.

The PLA Navy is quantitatively superior but witnessing qualitative changes through import substitution for immediate needs. Russian and Western technologies are being incorporated in new warship-building projects and new acquisitions from Russia are on the anvil to build a strong and capable navy to undertake missions to safeguard Chinese maritime interests and emerge as a major maritime power capable of influencing the regional security environment.

Similarly, the Indian Navy is building sophisticated platforms to respond to different crisis in "waters far away from home" and the need for building a combat-capable fleet ready to sail in harm's way to conduct combat operations anytime, anywhere, with maximum effectiveness and minimum risk and with utmost rapidity is urgent. Securing control/influence in the Indian Ocean is India's primary strategic objective. This strategic thinking is based on long-range naval operations and exercising influences around the strategic choke points of the Straits of Hormuz and the Straits of Malacca. Also, any maritime contingency that impacts on Indian security interests in the sea space off the Horn of Africa, South Indian Ocean and Pacific Ocean will be the responsibility of the Indian Navy.

With growing security interests beyond their immediate areas, China and India have enhanced their military capability. These capabilities have arisen partly due to the strategic vision of the political leadership and partly due to enhanced fiscal resources resulting from economic liberalization and globalization of the economy. In the above contexts, both India and China have set strategic targets to boost their respective naval power and substantial resources in terms of budgets are being augmented to build navies with regional power projection capabilities but remain short of being termed as blue water navies.

Notes

1. It is estimated that beginning with the Opium Wars till the founding of the People's Republic in 1949, China was invaded from the littorals more than

470 times. For more details see Srikanth Kondapalli, *China's Naval Power* (New Delhi: Knowledge World, 2001), p. xix. Before that, in 1592 and 1597, the Japanese attempted to conquer the Ming empire but were repulsed. In 1894, in an amphibious operation, Japan dislodged Qing troops in Korea. In the same year, the Chinese Peiyang fleet was annihilated at the Yalu river in the Yellow Sea; again, a year later in 1895, the Chinese naval base of Weihaiwei was attacked by the Japanese; these successive defeats resulted in China ceding Taiwan under the Treaty of Shimonoseki. The European naval powers entrenched into China's littorals through the 1840–41 Opium Wars, the French forced China to open ports to trade and the Chinese Navy was defeated at Fuzhao in 1884. For more details see Peter Howarth, *China's Rising Sea Power: The PLA Navy's Submarine Challenge* (New York: Routledge, 2006), pp. 15–16. Also see Andrew S. Erickson and Andrew R. Wilson, "China's Aircraft Carrier Dilemma", in *China's Future Nuclear Submarine Force*, edited by Andrew S. Erickson, Lyle J. Goldstein, William S. Murray, and Andrew R. Wilson (Annapolis: Naval Institute Press, 2007), p. 245.

2. In November 1510, a Portuguese fleet of twenty-three ships and 2,000 men under Albuquerque occupied Goa notwithstanding a strong resistance by the Sultan of Bijapur. After an occupation of nearly 450 years, they were finally defeated in a military operation undertaken by the Indian military in December 1961. The British established the East India Company (1600–1873) as a trading enterprise that later set up trading posts in Masulipatam, Surat, Madras, Calcutta, and Bombay, all coastal industrial hubs. The British victory in the Battle of Plassey was the springboard for the colonization of the subcontinent till 1947. The French established colonies in India in 1664 and Pondicherry, coastal town in Tamil Nadu, was acquired by France in 1674. It changed hands (the Dutch and the British occupied it for short periods) but was restored back to France who relinquished it to India in 1956.

3. "No Longer at Sea: Smooth Sailing for Indian Navy", *Times of India*, 3 December 2003.

4. For more details see, Thomas J. Torda, "The First Struggle for the Taiwan Strait: The October 1949 Communist-Nationalist Battle of Quemoy Island and Its Enduring Significance", available at <http://thomastorda.com/First%20Struggle%20for%20the%20Taiwan%20Strait%20(UPDATED%20112607).doc> (accessed 8 January 2008).

5. Pakistan Navy Historical Section, *Story of Pakistan Navy, 1947–1972* (Islamabad: Elite Publishers, 1991), pp. 228–29.

6. K.R. Singh, *Navies of South Asia* (New Delhi: Rupa Co., 2002), p. 63.

7. *Indian Maritime Doctrine (INBR 8)* (New Delhi: Integrated Headquarters, Ministry of Defence (Navy), 2004), p. 95; also see Andrew S. Erickson and Lyle J. Goldstein, "China's Future Nuclear Submarine Force: Insights from Chinese Writings", in *China's Future Nuclear Submarine Force*, p. 193.

8. Ibid., pp. 73–89.
9. These include 25,000 naval air force, 8,000–10,000 marines that can be increased to 28,000, and another 28,000 for coastal defence. Cited in *Jane's Fighting Ships 2007–08*, p. 115.
10. These include 7,500 officers, 5,000 naval airmen, and 2,000 marines called Marcos. Cited in *Jane's Fighting Ships 2007–08*, p. 311. There are plans to increase the Marcos force to 4,000. See "India to Increase Special Forces", *Pakistan Times*, 21 April 2008.
11. Michael S. Lindberg, *Geographical Impact on Coastal Defence Navies: The Entwining of Force Structure, Technology and Operational Environment* (London: Macmillan Press Ltd., 1998), p. 42.
12. Richmond M. Lloyd, "Strategy and Force Planning Framework", in *Strategy and Force Planning* (Newport: Naval War College Press, 1997), p. 2.
13. For a detailed discussion on strategy and force structuring see Henry C. Bartlett, G. Paul Holman, Jr., and Timothy E. Somes, "The Art of Strategy and Force Planning", *Naval War College Review* 48, no. 2 (Spring 1995): 114–26.
14. Ibid.
15. Cited in Bernard D. Cole, *The Great Wall at Sea: China's Navy Enters the Twenty-first Century* (Annapolis: Naval Institute Press, 2001), p. 9.
16. David Lague, "China Airs Ambitions to Beef Up Naval Power", *International Herald Tribune*, 28 December 2006, available at <http://www.iht.com/articles/2006/12/28/news/china.php> (accessed 23 January 2007).
17. Alexander C. Huang, "The Chinese Navy's Offshore Active Defence Strategy: Conceptualization and Implications", *Naval War College Review* 47, no. 3 (Summer 1994): 7.
18. David G. Muller, Jr., *China as a Maritime Power* (Colorado: Westview Press, 1983), p. 15. In September 1949, Mao was quoted as saying, "We will not only have a powerful army but also a powerful navy and a powerful air force." The navy was expected to be capable of defending territorial seas and preventing any aggression.
19. Ibid. Mao named Xiao Jingguang (a long-term political ally and an army officer) as the navy chief. Also see Huang, "The China Navy's Offshore Active Defence Strategy", p. 8.
20. Muller, *China as a Maritime Power*, pp. 8–9. By December 1948, the communists were able to cut off the naval base at Qingdao but the nationalists were still able to transport more than 600,000 military personnel as well as two million civilians to Taiwan. Chiang Kai-Shek himself was transported on board a destroyer.
21. Bruce A. Elleman, "The Nationalists' Blockade of PRC", in *Naval Blockades and Seapower: Strategies and Counter Strategies, 1805–2005*, edited by Bruce A. Elleman and S.C.M. Paine (London: Routledge, 2006), p. 218.
22. Bruce L. Swanson, *Eighth Voyage of the Dragon: A History of China's Quest for Seapower* (Annapolis: Naval Institute Press, 1982), p. 21.

23. Huang, "The Chinese Navy's Offshore Active Defence Strategy, Conceptualization and Implications", p. 17.
24. Ibid., p. 18.
25. Ibid.
26. Muller, *China as a Maritime Power*, p. 12.
27. It had 175 captured Buffalo Landing Vehicle, Tracked (LVT), 20 ex-U.S. Navy LST, 13 ex-U.S. LSM, 15 Landing Ship Infantry (LSIL) Types and 10 imported Soviet T-4 LCM. For more details see Xinhui, "A Look at People's Liberation Army Amphibious Sealift Assets", available at <http://www.china-defense.com/naval/plaas/plaas_1.html> (accessed 23 March 2008).
28. Lewis and Xue Litai, *China's Strategic Seapower: The Politics of Force Modernisation in the Nuclear Age* (Stanford: Stanford University Press, 1994), pp. 231–32.
29. Andrei Chang, "China's Nuclear Warhead Stockpile Rising", *UPI Asia online*, 7 April 2008, available at <http://www.upiasiaonline.com/Security/2008/04/05/chinas_nuclear_warhead_stockpile_rising/7074/> (accessed 30 April 2008).
30. See *Worldwide Submarine Challenges*, Office of Naval Intelligence, February 1997, p. 18
31. For an excellent history of the development of Chinese nuclear submarines, see Lewis and Xue Litai, *China's Strategic Seapower.*
32. David Lague, "Chinese Submarine Fleet is Growing: Analyst Says", *New York Times*, 25 February 2008; also see "China: Recent Security Developments", prepared statement of Richard P. Lawless, Deputy Under Secretary of Defense for Asian and Pacific Security Affairs before the House Armed Services Committee, 13 June 2007. It was noted that the sea-based deterrent with the JL-2 submarine-launched ballistic missile (SLBM) aboard the Type-094 or JIN-class SSBN will bring greater range, mobility, accuracy, and survivability to China's strategic forces, capable of striking many areas of the world including continental United States. Also see Dawai Xia, "Details Emerge of China's Jin SSBN", *Jane's Navy International* 112, issue 9 (November 2007): 4.
33. Chang, "China Nuclear Warhead Stockpile Rising".
34. *Jane's Fighting Ships 2007–08*, p. 116.
35. Ibid., p. 117. The first submarine of this class was launched in 1968 and took about ten years for its final trials. The Chinese built five such submarines (four by 1989 and the fifth in 1990).
36. Richard D. Fisher, Jr., "China Accelerates Navy Building", *China Brief* 3, issue 15, available at <http://www.jamestown.org/publications_details.php?volume_id=19&issue_id=680&article_id=4757> (accessed 8 March 2007).
37. Richard D. Fisher, Jr., " The Impact of Foreign Technology on Chin's Submarine Force and Operations", in *China's Future Nuclear Submarine Force*, p. 142.
38. "Chinese Navy Takes Delivery of New Destroyer", *NAVINT* 12 (1 and 2) (15 January 2000): 1. Also see *Jane's Fighting Ships 2007–08*, p. 123.

39. Bill Gertz, "Russia Readies Deadly New Cruise Missile Warship for China", *Washington Times*, 13 July 2000.
40. For more details on the PLA Navy destroyers and frigates, see *Jane's Fighting Ships 2007–08*, pp. 123–34.
41. Howarth, *China's Rising Sea Power: The PLA Navy's Submarine Challenge*, pp. 15–16.
42. Ibid., p. 3.
43. *China's Navy 2007*, Office of Naval Intelligence, p. 30, available at <http://www.fas.org/irp/agency/oni/chinanavy2007.pdf> (accessed 30 June 2008).
44. Jing-Dong Yuan, "China's Defence Modernization: Implications for Asia-Pacific Security", *Contemporary Southeast Asia* 17, no. 1 (June 1995): 70.
45. Paul Holtom, "The Beginning of the End for Deliveries of Russian Major Conventional Weapons to China", *RIA Novosti*, 31 March 2008.
46. Ibid. Also see Fisher, "The Impact of Foreign Technology on China's Submarine Force and Operations", p. 142.
47. "Song Class Patrol Submarine", available at <http://www.military-today.com/navy/song_class.htm> (accessed 31 March 2008).
48. Andrew S. Erickson and Lyle J. Goldstein, "China's Future Nuclear Submarine Force", *Naval War College Review* 60, no. 1 (Winter 2007): 55.
49. Howarth, *China Rising Sea Power*, p. 17.
50. *Jane's Fighting Ships 2007–08*, p. 135.
51. *Jane's All the World's Aircraft 1996–97*, p. 427.
52. "Y-8 Maritime Patrol Aircraft", available at <http://www.sinodefence.com/airforce/specialaircraft/y8mpa.asp> (accessed 12 March 2008).
53. Lester J. Gesteland, "China Naval Experts Ponder Need For Aircraft Carrier", at the website of China Online at <http://www.chinaonline.com/industry/aviation/Archive/Secure/1999/december/c9120104.asp>, cited in Vijay Sakhuja, "Dragon's Dragonfly: The Chinese Aircraft Carrier", *Strategic Analysis* 24, no. 7 (October 2001): 1378–79.
54. "Scrap Value: Buyers of an Unfinished Ukrainian Carrier Have China Ties", *Far Eastern Economic Review*, 9 April 1998, p. 20.
55. You Xu and You Ji, "In Search of Blue Water Power: The PLA Navy's Maritime Strategy in the 1990s", *The Pacific Review* 4, issue 2 (1991): 137–49.
56. Xia Jun, "An Interview with the Naval Air Force Commander of the South Sea Fleet", *Jianchun Zhishi* (June 1988), cited in Jun Zhan, "China Goes to the Blue Waters: The Navy, Seapower Mentality and the South China Sea", *Journal of Strategic Studies* 17, no. 3 (September 1994): 201.
57. Ronald O'Rourke, "China Naval Modernization: Implications for U.S. Navy Capabilities — Background and Issues for Congress", *CRS Report for Congress*, 4 February 2008, p. 18.
58. You Xu and You Ji, "In Search of Blue Water Power", p. 12
59. O'Rourke, "China Naval Modernization", p. 19.
60. Ibid.

61. Andrew S. Erickson, "China's Military Modernization and its Impact on the United States and the Asia-Pacific", Testimony before the U.S.-China Economic and Security Review Commission, 29 March 2007.
62. *Jane's Fighting Ships 2007–08*, p. 122.
63. "China to Buy Su-33 Carrier-Based Fighters from Russia?", 17 November 2006, available at <http://www.defenseindustrydaily.com/china-to-buy-su33-carrierbased-fighters-from-russia-02806/> (accessed 10 January 2007).
64. Sakhuja, "Dragon's Dragonfly: The Chinese Aircraft Carrier", pp. 1378–79.
65. Prasun K. Sengupta, "Dual Tasking Ships", *Force* (May 2007): 20–21.
66. *Jane's Fighting Ships 2007–08*, p. 147.
67. Prasun K. Sengupta, "China Commences Building a Helicopter Landing Deck", *Force* (November 2006). Also see Richard Scott and Jonathon Weng, "China Launches Type 071 LPD", *Jane's Navy International* 112, issue 2 (March 2007). M. Hanif Ismail, "Multi Role Support Vessels: New Key in Small Navy Operations", *Asian Defence Journal* (December 2007): 33.
68. Xinhui, "A Look at People's Liberation Army Amphibious Sealift Assets", available at <http://www.china-defense.com/naval/plaas/plaas_1.html> (accessed 15 March 2008). See also *Jane's Fighting Ships 2007–08*, pp. 138–41.
69. Charles R. Smith, "Chinese Navy Prepares to Invade Taiwan", available at <http://archive.newsmax.com/archives/articles/2001/7/9/171703.shtml> (accessed 15 March 2008).
70. Yihong Chang, "The PLA Strengthens Its Amphibious Capability", *China Brief* 2, issue 9 (25 April 2002), available at <http://www.jamestown.org/china_brief/article.php?articleid=2373049> (accessed 30 June 2008). Also see the website of China Academy of Aerospace Aerodynamics (CAAA) at <http://www.bia701.com/html/e_01_gsc.htm> (accessed 30 June 2008).
71. John C.K. Daly, "Can the Dragon Swim? The Naval Balance in the Taiwan Strait", *China Brief* 4, issue 2 (20 January 2004), available at <http://www.jamestown.org/publications_details.php?volume_id=395&issue_id=2901&article_id=23477> (accessed 23 March 2008).
72. Xinhui, "A Look at People's Liberation Army Amphibious Sealift Assets".
73. Ibid.
74. Thomas M. Kane, *Chinese Grand Strategy and Maritime Power* (London: Frank Cass, 2002), p. 91.
75. Vijay Sakhuja, "Peace Mission 2005: Reverberations in India", 3 September 2005, available at <http://www.ipcs.org/> (accessed 5 January 2007).
76. "Military Power of the People's Republic of China 2006", Annual Report to Congress, Office of the Secretary of Defense, U.S. Department of Defense, 2006.
77. *Jane's Fighting Ships 2007–08*, pp. 137–38.
78. Ibid.
79. Andrew Erickson, Lyle J. Goldstein, and William Murray, "China's Undersea Sentries", *Undersea Warfare* 9, no. 2 (Winter 2007), available at <http://www.navy.mil/navydata/cno/n87/usw/issue_33/china.html> (accessed 5 May 2008).

80. Ibid.
81. Rich Chang, "Air Force plans to buy Jets that need Shorter Runway", *Taipei Times*, 23 January 2006.
82. See Jin Liangxiang, "Energy First: China and the Middle East", *Middle East Quarterly* (Spring 2005). Also see Phar Kim Beng, "China Mulls Oil Pipelines in Myanmar, Thailand", *Asia Times*, available at <http://www.atimes.com/atimes/China/FI23Ad09.html> (accessed 24 July 2007).
83. Wenran Jiang, "China's Growing Energy Relations with the Middle East", *China Brief* 7, issue 14 (11 July 2007), available at <http://www.jamestown.org/china_brief/article.php?articleid=2373542> (accessed 30 November 2007).
84. Gabriel Collins, "An Oil Armada? The Commercial and Strategic Significance of China's Growing Tanker Fleet", in *Asia Looks Seaward: Power and Maritime Strategy*, edited by Toshi Yoshihara and James R. Holmes (Westport, Connecticut: Praeger Security International, 2008), pp. 111–24.
85. Ian J. Storey, "China's 'Malacca Dilemma'", *China Brief* 6, issue 8 (12 April 2006), available at <http://jamestown.org/images/pdf/cb_006_008.pdf> (accessed 14 November 2007).
86. Ibid.
87. Cited in Mokhzani Zubir and Mohd Nizam Basiron, "The Straits of Malacca: The Rise of China, America's Intentions and the Dilemma of the Littoral States", available at <http://www.mima.gov.my/mima/htmls/papers/pdf/mokhzani/mz-mnb.pdf> (accessed 14 November 2007).
88. Andrei Chang, "China's Fuel Oil Reserves", 21 December 2007; "China Starts Filling Strategic Oil Reserve", available at <http://www.chinadaily.com.cn/china/2006 10/06/content_702330.htm> (accessed 8 October 2006); Joseph E. Lin, "Filling of China's Strategic Oil Reserves Apparently Delayed", *China Brief* 7, issue 14, available at <http://www.jamestown.org/china_brief/article.php?articleid=2373537> (accessed 15 August 2007).
89. General Pervez Musharraf, President of Pakistan, Address at the ground-breaking ceremony of Gwadar Deep-Sea Port, Gwadar, 22 March 2002; also see Vijay Sakhuja, "Sino-Pakistan Maritime Initiatives", Article no. 730 (10 April 2002), available at <http://www.ipcs.org/> (accessed 23 March 2007).
90. Chong Pin Lin, "The Military Balance in the Taiwan Straits", *The China Quarterly* 146 (June 1996): 578.
91. "Background Information on China's Recent Military Threats Against Taiwan", Department of Planning, Government of the People's Republic of China, March 2007.
92. "Interview: Chen Confident of 2008 DPP Victory", *Taipei Times*, 3 March 2007.
93. "Taiwan to Upgrade to Tien Kung-2 SAM", available at <http://www.missilethreat.com/archives/id.49/subject_detail.asp> (accessed 30 March 2007).
94. Author's discussions with Taiwanese military officers during the annual military exercise "Han Kuang" in July 2006.

95. Harold J. Kearsley, "An Analysis of the Military Threats Across the Taiwan Strait: Fact or Fiction", *Comparative Strategy* 19, no. 2 (April–June 2000): 112.
96. Erickson, Goldstein, and Murray, "China's Undersea Sentries".
97. Yang Lei, "China's Marine Economy Tops RMB 1.7 Trillion", Chinese Government's official website at <http://english.gov.cn/2006-05/11/content_278052.htm> (accessed 14 February 2007).
98. Chong, "The Military Balance in the Taiwan Straits", p. 580.
99. Andrei Chang, "China's Fuel Oil Reserves".
100. For a detailed discussion on the dynamics of Taiwan's defence budget see Justin Logan and Ted Galen Carpenter, "Taiwan's Defense Budget: How Taipei's Free Riding Risks War", Policy Analysis no. 600 (13 September 2007), available at <http://www.cato.org/pubs/pas/PA600.pdf> (accessed 15 November 2007).
101. Paul H.B. Godwin, "From Continent to Periphery: PLA Doctrine, Strategy and Capabilities Towards 2000", *The China Quarterly* 146 (June 1996): 475.
102. Ibid. For sonars see James C. Bussert, "Chinese Naval Sonar Evolves from Foreign Influences", *Signal* (December 2002): 57–60. Also see *Jane's Fighting Ships 1996–97*, pp. 114–17.
103. Tai Ming Cheung, "The Growth of Chinese Naval Power", Pacific Strategic Paper (Singapore: Institute of Southeast Asian Studies, 1990), p. 19.
104. Bussert, "Chinese Naval Sonar Evolves from Foreign Influences", pp. 57–60. Also see *Jane's Fighting Ships 1996–97*, pp. 114–17 and *Jane's Fighting Ships 2007–08*, p. 120.
105. O'Rourke, "China Naval Modernization", pp. 15–16.
106. David Shambaugh, "China's Military in Transition: Politics, Professionalism, Procurement and Power Projection", *The China Quarterly* 146 (June 1996): 291.
107. *Military Balance 2007–08* (London: International Institute for Strategic Studies, 2008), pp. 369–70.
108. Peng Guangqian, "Defence Spending in Tune with Economic Growth", *China Daily*, 15 March 2006, available at <http://www.chinadaily.com.cn/english/doc/2006-03/15/content_540670.htm> (accessed 10 February 2007).
109. Ibid.
110. Lee Spears and Zhao Yidi, "China to Raise 2008 Military Budget by a Record 19.4%", available at <http://www.bloomberg.com/apps/news?pid=20601080&sid=a36iAaScSAFQ&refer=asia> (accessed 27 June 2008).
111. Martin Walker, "China Boosts Defense Spending Another 15 Percent", available at <http://www.sinodaily.com/reports/Walkers_World_Chinas_Big_Arms_Budget.html> (accessed 27 June 2008).
112. Lee and Zhao, "China to Raise 2008 Military Budget by a Record 19.4%".
113. "China says Strong Military is Central to Modernization", *Channel News Asia*, 5 March 2008.

114. Rear Admiral Satyindra Singh, *Blueprint to Bluewater: The Indian Navy 1951–65* (New Delhi: Lancer International, 1992), p. 32. The division was effected based on the recommendations of the Armed Forces Reconstitution Committee (AFRC).
115. Satyindra Singh, *Under Two Ensigns* (New Delhi: Lancer International, 1989), pp. 35–36.
116. Arun Prakash, "India's Quest for an Indigenous Aircraft Carrier", in *From the Crow's Nest* (New Delhi: Lancer Publishers, 2007), pp. 130–31.
117. Singh, *Under Two Ensigns*, p. 1.
118. Pranab Mukherjee, External Affairs Minister, "International Relations and Maritime Affairs: Strategic Imperatives", Lecture delivered at the annual Admiral A.K. Chatterjee Memorial Lecture Series, 30 June 2007.
119. Combined Commanders Conference is an annual event in which the political leadership addresses the top military officers of the Indian Army, Indian Navy and Indian Air Force.
120. "Shrug off the Cold War, this is a New World", *Indian Express*, 7 November 2003.
121. "India Challenges China in South China Sea", *Stratfor.com*, 26 April 2000, available at <http://www.stratfor.com/>.
122. Cited in *Freedom to Use the Seas: India's Maritime Military Strategy* (New Delhi: Integrated Headquarters, Ministry of Defence (Navy), 2007), p. iii.
123. Commodore R.S. Vasan, "Mile Stones in Growth of Indian Navy: Strategic Dimensions and their Relevance in the IOR", available at <http://www.saag.org/papers13/paper1270.html> (accessed 5 November 2007).
124. Admiral Arun Prakash, "At Sea about Naval History", *Sunday Tribune*, 2 September 2007.
125. Speech by Admiral Arun Prakash, Chief of Naval Staff and Chairman Chiefs of Staff Committee at the Institute for Defence Studies and Analyses (IDSA) Fortieth Anniversary commemorative seminar on 1 September 2005, titled "Emerging India: Security and Foreign Policy Perspectives".
126. David Scott, "India's Drive for a Blue Water Navy", *Journal of Military and Strategic Studies* 10, issue 2 (Winter 2007–08): 5.
127. "Changing Tides in the Indian Ocean", *Jane's Navy International* (November 1997): 39.
128. Sanjay J. Singh, "India's Maritime Strategy for the 90s", *USI Journal* (July–September 1990): 352–54.
129. In the ZPC, the navy should have the ability to execute sea denial using its sea-based assets and shore-based aircraft. The coast guard units must also be included in tactical plans. In the second zone, i.e. ZMC, stretching 500 kilometres from shore to 1,000 kilometres into the high seas, the Indian Navy must have the capacity as well as capability to exercise sea denial. In the ZMC, the Indian Navy should be able to engage long-range maritime. The forces that need to be deployed should include: submarines, long-range maritime

patrol aircraft and shore-based strike aircraft. Operations in this zone should be supported by intelligence, over-the-horizon targeting and surveillance. In the outer zone, i.e. ZSC, nuclear submarine, aircraft carrier supported by oil tankers and long-range maritime patrol aircraft should be deployed.

130. *Strategic Defence Review: The Maritime Dimension, A Naval Vision* (New Delhi: Naval Headquarters, 1998), pp. 33–35.
131. *Freedom to Use the Seas: India's Maritime Military Strategy* (New Delhi: Integrated Headquarters Ministry of Defence (Navy), 2007), pp. 59–60.
132. Sureesh Mehta, "The Immediate Need is to Augment and Upgrade Our Capacity for Sustained and Long-Range Airborne Surveillance", *Force* (December 2007): 18–19.
133. Ajit K. Dubey, "On the Watch", *Force* (March 2007): 59.
134. "Indian Navy — Today and Tomorrow", an interview with Chief of Naval Staff Admiral Sureesh Mehta, *Journal of Indian Ocean Studies* 15, no. 1 (April 2007): 1–11.
135. *Freedom to Use the Seas: India's Maritime Military Strategy*, p. 9.
136. Singh, *Navies of South Asia*, pp. 50–51.
137. In December 2003, Admiral Madhvendra Singh, Chief of Naval Staff was quoted as saying that the Indian Navy was moving towards a true blue-water capacity and needed a strength of at least 200 ships, including three aircraft carriers, about twenty frigates and destroyers each and the requisite number of support and auxiliary craft.
138. Sureesh Mehta, "The Immediate Need is to Augment and Upgrade Our Capacity for Sustained and Long-Range Airborne Surveillance", *Force* (December 2007): 18–20.
139. P. Jaitly, "Modernising the Indian Navy: Imperatives and Strategy", *SP's Naval Forces* (March 2007): 11–12; also see Pravin Sawhney and Ghazala Wahab, "Indian Navy Sails in Blue Waters", *Force* (December 2006): 26.
140. "Indian Navy will have Nuclear Capability in Future Says Admiral Sureesh Mehta", 10 May 2008, available at <http://www.thaindian.com/newsportal/world-news/indian-navy-will-have-nuclear-capability-in-future-says-admiral-sureesh-mehta_10047165.html> (accessed 30 June 2008).
141. Ibid.
142. Sureesh Mehta, "Indian Navy Fleet to Grow to 160-Plus by 2022", available at <http://www.thaindian.com/newsportal/business/indian-navy-fleet-to-grow-to-160-plus-by-2022_10081924.html> (accessed 10 August 2008).
143. Vijay Sakhuja, "Sea Based Deterrence and Indian Security", *Strategic Analysis* 25, issue 1 (April 2001): 30.
144. Arun Prakash, "The Missing Leg of the Triad", *Force* (September 2007): 28–29.
145. Sandeep Unnithan, "The Secret Nuke Sub Deal", available at <http://intellibriefs.blogspot.com/2007/08/india-secret-nuke-sub-deal.html> (accessed 25 June 2008).

146. The submarine was of 670 A Skat series, Charlie class by NATO classification, 4,800 tonnes and fitted with eight Ameist SS-N-7 Starbright anti-ship missiles with a range of 120 kilometres and capable of carrying nuclear warheads.
147. See "Need to Keep a High Priority on Indian Nuclear Submarine Project", at the website of India Policy at <http://wwww.indiapolicy.org/lists/india-policy/2000/march/msg00013.html>, cited in Sakhuja, "Sea Based Deterrence and Indian Security"; Arun Prakash, "The Missing Leg of the Triad", *Force* (September 2007): 30.
148. Wade Boese, "India Test-Launches Submarine Missile", *Arms Control Today*, 1 April 2008.
149. Devarshi Upadhyay, "India on a Nuclear Super-Highway", available at <http://www.merinews.com/catFull.jsp?articleID=124552> (accessed 15 July 2007).
150. "India has acquired 'state-of-the-art' Submarine-Launched Ballistic Missile Capability: DRDO", 13 May 2008, available at <http://www.domain-b.com> (accessed 30 June 2008).
151. Hemant Kumar, "Coming: India-make N-sub", available at <http://www.newindpress.com/NewsItems.asp?ID=IEQ20080410225004&Page=Q&Title=ORISSA&Topic=0> (accessed 10 May 2008).
152. "India to float Global Tenders for Six Conventional Submarines", *Times of India*, 9 May 2008.
153. Ilya Kramnik, "Reincarnation of Chakra", available at <http://en.rian.ru/analysis/20080708/113522621.html> (accessed 14 July 2008). Also see Thomas Neilsen, "Despite Three Years Leasing of Charlie-Class Submarine: Indian Submarine-Reactor will be no Blueprint", available at <http://www.bellona.org/english_import_area/international/russia/navy/northern_fleet/vessels/9515> (accessed 15 July 2008); "Russian-Made Nuke Powered Submarine Akula Set to join Indian Navy Next Year", *Press Trust of India*, 10 August 2008; "Akula Class N-Powered Sub to be Used for Crew Training", *Sindh Today*, 9 August 2008.
154. "Russia to Resume Tests of Troubled Nerpa Nuclear Submarine", *Pravda*, 13 May 2009.
155. Rajat Pandit, "Army Officer to Head Nuclear Command", *Times of India*, 26 August 2008.
156. Prakash, *From the Crow's Nest*, p. 130.
157. Author's discussions with retired and serving Indian Navy officers.
158. *Naval Aviation: A World History* (New Delhi: Birla Institute of Scientific Research, 1985), pp. 115–17.
159. Pushpinder Singh, *Fly Navy: An Illustrated History of Indian Naval Aviation* (New Delhi: Society of Aerospace Studies, 2006), p. 35. Also see "The Aircraft Carrier is Central to Our Concept of Operations", *Force* (December 2007): 22–24.
160. Prakash, *From the Crow's Nest*, pp. 130–31.
161. Mihir K. Roy, "Continental Versus Maritime Strategy: A Requiem", *USI Journal* (1989).

162. Sandeep Dikshit, "Centre Admits to Problems in Naval Deals", *The Hindu*, 17 April 2008. Also see Prakash, *From the Crow's Nest*, pp. 134–37.
163. "Capability-Driven: An Update on Indian Naval Modernisation", *Vayu Aerospace and Defence Review* (VI/2007): 31.
164. Arun Prakash, "Time for a Rethink", *Force* (August 2007): 8–9.
165. "Gates Butters Up India for U.S. Guns", *Business Week*, 26 February 2008.
166. "Indian Navy To Order Another Aircraft Carrier", 9 May 2008, available at <http://wwwnewspostindia.com> (accessed 2 June 2008).
167. *Jane's Fighting Ships 2007–08*, p. 316.
168. Mazumdar Mrityunjoy, "A Comparison of Delhi & Sovremenny Destroyers", available at <http://www.bharat-rakshak.com/NAVY/Articles/Article04.html> (accessed 24 March 2008).
169. Arunkumar Bhatt, "A Lethal Combination of Stealth and Strength", *The Hindu*, 1 April 2006.
170. *Jane's Fighting Ships 2007–08*, p. 299.
171. Ibid.
172. Ibid.
173. Admiral A.K. Chatterji, *Indian Navy's Submarine Arm* (New Delhi: Birla Institute, 1982), p. 62. Also see Admiral Sureesh Mehta, "We have Reasons to Believe Intelligence Flow from U.S. to Pakistan has Switched off", *Force* (January 2008): 58; Rahul Roy-Chaudhury, "The Chinese Navy and Indian Security", *Indian Defence Review* 1 (January 1994): 134.
174. *Jane's Fighting Ships 2001–02*, pp. 292–93.
175. For more details see <http://www.bharat-rakshak.com/NAVY/Sindhugosh.html> (accessed 7 March 2007).
176. *Jane's Fighting Ships 2007–08*, p. 312.
177. Arun Kumar Bhatt, "Scorpene Construction Work Begins in Mumbai", *The Hindu*, 24 May 2007.
178. "India To Float Global Tenders For Six Conventional Submarines", *Times of India*, 9 May 2008.
179. "Ruling the Seas", *Force* (December 2006): 38–39.
180. Naresh Chand, "UAVs for the Indian Navy", *SP's Naval Forces* 3, no. 1 (2008): 6–7.
181. Sawhney and Wahab, "Indian Navy Sails in Blue Waters", *Force* (December 2006): 26.
182. "India's Navy Holding Maritime Patrol Aircraft Competition (updated)", available at <http://www.defenseindustrydaily.com/indias-navy-holding-maritime-patrol-aircraft-competition-updated-01991/> (accessed 24 May 2008). Also see Sanjay Shrivastav, "Talks to Acquire Maritime Reconnaissance Aircraft on: Admiral", available at <http://mynews.in/fullstory.aspx?storyid=4014> (accessed 24 May 2008).
183. Prasun K. Sengupta, "At Take-off Point", *Force* (March 2007): 56–57.
184. Ajit K. Dubey, "On the Watch", *Force* (March 2007): 58–60.

185. Vishnu Makhijani, "P8I Aircraft Will Give Indian Navy Maritime Patrol Edge: Boeing", available at <http://www.indiaenews.com/america/20080515/118152.htm> (accessed 30 June 2008).
186. Atul Bhardwaj, "Cruise Missiles and the Changing Naval Strategy", *Journal of Indian Ocean Studies* 9, no. 3 (December 2001).
187. See "Sea-Launched Missile Dhanush Test-Fired", *Hindustan Times*, 1 September 2001.
188. "BrahMos Test Launch Successful", *The Statesman*, 5 March 2008; also see "Sea-based BrahMos Missile Hits Ground Target in Test Launch", *RIA Novosti*, 5 March 2008.
189. *Jane's Fighting Ships 2007–08*, p. 325.
190. *Jane's Fighting Ships 2007–08*, pp. 328–29.
191. Ibid., p. 329.
192. *Strategic Defence Review*, pp. 34–35; *Indian Maritime Doctrine (INBR 8)* (New Delhi: Integrated Headquarters, Ministry of Defence (Navy), 2004), pp. 101–3.
193. For instance an Indian Oil and Natural Gas Corporation (ONGC)-owned oil platform in the Mumbai High North (MHN) caught fire resulting in a major disruption of domestic crude oil supply. The platform, capable of producing 100,000 barrels of oil per day, has been damaged and it took nearly a year to restore operations.
194. Press Information Bureau, Press Release, Prime Minister's Office, "PM Addresses Combined Commanders' Conference", 20 October 2005, available at <http://pib.nic.in/release/release.asp?relid=12801> (accessed 20 January 2006).
195. Huma Siddiqui, "Defence Gets Richer But Poorer Than Neighbours", *Financial Express*, 2 March 2008.
196. "Shopping at Hand, Defence Allocation Jumps by Rs 6,000 Crore", *Indian Express*, 1 March 2006.
197. "Intrusion of Chinese Army into Indian Territory", Lok Sabha Unstarred Question no. 5984, answered on 4 May 2005. In June 2003, a PLA patrol allegedly intruded into the Asafila area of the Upper Subansari district of Arunachal Pradesh and stayed there for nearly a day. Again in 2008, just prior to Prime Minister Manmohan Singh's visit to China, External Affairs Minister Pranab Mukherjee was quoted as saying that "sometimes the PLA does intrude on its territory but the issues are addressed through established mechanisms". Ashis Sinha, "Communication Breakdown Caused Chinese Military Intrusion Deep into Arunachal Pradesh", 17 May 2005, available at <http://www.indiadaily.com/editorial/2752.asp> (accessed 30 June 2008); "China does intrude into India, admits India", *Indian Express*, 12 January 2008; Pushpita Das, "India Has to be Wary of Chinese Intrusions", *IDSA Strategic Comments*, 19 October 2007.
198. "Multiple Chinese Intrusions into India Met with Weak Response", 21 November 2007, available at <http://www.East-Asia-Intel.com> (accessed 22 November 2007).

199. While presenting the annual budget 2008–09, the Indian Finance Minister assured that additional resources would not be a constraint if they were needed for purchasing military hardware and capital outlay for 2008–09 was Rs.48,007 crore, a hike of almost 23.3 per cent over the 2007–08 outlay of Rs.37,705 crore.
200. Deba R. Mohanty, "Defence Budget: Hard Choices Ahead for India", Article no. 38, 6 June 2005, available at <http://www.sspconline.org/article> (accessed 30 June 2007).

4

ECONOMICS AND MARITIME POWER

Economics and maritime power constitute the core of a state's role and stake in the current global order driven by globalization. The emergence of maritime power as the vanguard of globalization has reinforced the criticality of maritime infrastructure to countries that are increasingly reliant on the medium of sea for economic interdependence, growth and prosperity. Significantly, maritime power is the keel of economic globalization as it facilitates economic growth and investments in the maritime domain.

The economic dimension of maritime power pivots on the state's ability to sustain a vast merchant marine built around civilian shipping assets, port infrastructure to transact large volume of trade, ability to build ships to conduct maritime trade and the availability of a quality human resource that shapes and conducts maritime business. Economics and maritime power also provide for technology development and inflow of investments since these are primary determinants that ensure a sustained and continuous growth of maritime commerce. In its economic topography, maritime power has interlinked the littoral and the hinterland through various ports and industrial centres such as the Special Economic Zones. The transportation network built around roads, rail and inland waterways facilitate long-haul bulk and containerized cargo traffic thus creating a seamless supply chain connecting the hinterland to the littoral.

Economics and maritime power is also built on the maritime-technological-industrial capacity that pivots on technological sophistication, infrastructure based on information technology, and modern systems and processes for conduct of maritime commerce. In the contemporary global maritime-based trading, these capabilities gain greater credence, particularly when the system is built around "just in time" cargo that provides for sustained manufacturing of goods. Information technology is vital to the efficient functioning of maritime enterprises and its operations depend heavily on the integrity of information infrastructure in a highly competitive globalized trading system.

Economics and maritime power deal with marine resources, both living and non-living, that abound in the EEZ of the state. The marine domain is a very important source of food security to the state and needs to be guarded against exploitation by other states that tend to overfish and encroach into others' EEZ. Preservation of the marine resources is also critical for the continued replenishment of the fishing economy of the state that constitutes a substantial slice of resources. Similarly, hydrocarbon constitutes a critical marine resource for the state's economic power. This resource has already moved out to the offshore domain and is being exploited to provide robust energy security. Likewise, deep seabed minerals are the next repository of resources and will aid the engine of maritime growth in the future.

Interestingly, maritime power is also the Achilles heel of globalization due to the risks and vulnerabilities in the supply chains that could result from disruption, natural and manmade, at sea, in the littorals and ashore. The disruptions could emerge from wars, competition and unforeseen contingencies arising from regime changes in the supplier countries that may employ denial measures to pursue their respective regime agendas. There is also the possibility of non-state actors seizing the sources of supplies and disrupting the supply chain with adverse consequences.

Taking a long-term view of the potential of the maritime sector and its significant contribution to economic growth, China and India have developed varying capacities and capabilities for building their maritime economic power and are on the verge of a new revolution of an emergent globalized maritime trading-transportation system that will be the vanguard of their economic development. Special Economic Zones have mushroomed along the coastline since the late 1970s and early 1980s in China and in the 1990s in India and these are the hubs of industrial and manufacturing activity. The impacts of globalization are evident in China and India and the economy is becoming further integrated into the global trade system.

This chapter examines the economic dimension of the maritime power of China and India and argues that both countries have invested in building a modern maritime industry to emerge into major maritime powers. This is supported by significant investments in the development of maritime infrastructure and exploitation of offshore marine resources. The chapter is divided into two main sections; the first section examines China's thrust in maritime infrastructure development. It highlights the economic boom experienced by the coastal provinces and discusses Chinese maritime infrastructure development strategy in shipbuilding, shipping, ports, fishing, offshore organic resources and the investments made in the development of human capital. Likewise, the second section examines India's economic ingredients of maritime power and undertakes an exhaustive analysis of its constituents.

CHINA: MARITIME ECONOMIC POLICY

In China, the maritime economy has witnessed impressive investment and development that has contributed significantly to national growth. It has played a leading role in the past, and the new thrust is on sustainable exploitation of marine resources, both living and non-living. The long coastline has facilitated the development of marine economy and nearly 40 per cent of the population, 50 per cent of cities, 70 per cent of GDP, 84 per cent of foreign direct investment and export products are generated within 200 kilometres of coast that corresponds to a little less than 30 per cent of China's landmass.[1]

In 1996, China announced "Ocean Agenda 21" that envisaged a development strategy for marine programmes and was considered a policy of the Chinese Government to rationally develop and utilize marine resources, protect the marine environment and sustainable utilization of marine resources.[2] In 1998, the Chinese Government published a White Paper on its maritime economy titled "Development of China's Marine Programs".[3] The White Paper, the first of its kind since 1949, identifies twenty different sectors of China's marine economy including shipbuilding, shipping, ports and harbours, inland waterways, fish industry, offshore minerals and salt industry, offshore oil and gas resources, seabed minerals and marine leisure industry. Several high-tech marine industries have been set up in the coastal areas that are engaged in exploitation of seawater, sea energy and seabed resources resulting in a comprehensive development of the national economy.

The White Paper notes that the Chinese maritime economy grew at 17 per cent annually in the 1980s, and 20 per cent in the 1990s. In 2006, the output of major marine industries witnessed a high growth that resulted in 4 per cent increase in the country's GDP[4] and the marine economy contributed Yuan 2.09 trillion (US$272 billion) equivalent to 10.01 per cent of the national GDP. The State Oceanic Administration (SOA) announced that the output value of marine industries, including fishing, transport, oil and gas exploitation, tourism and shipbuilding, increased by 13.97 per cent year-on-year, and the growth rate was 3.3 percentage points higher than that of the national economy. The coastal provinces have contributed substantially to the overall national GDP and the marine sector growth has been impressive growing at nearly 17 per cent. The marine sector has also generated greater employment opportunities for people, i.e. in 2006 the sector employment figures were pegged at 29.6 million people, 1.8 million more than 2005, and 31.5 million people in 2007, an increase of 1.9 million over 2006.[5] These maritime economic indicators point to the fact that China has developed a sophisticated strategy to build its maritime power.[6] Resources from the seas and oceans are contributing to national strength in terms of economic growth and play an important role in developing an export-oriented economy. Most of the coastal provinces are engaged in sustainable development and exploitation of marine resources.

Shipbuilding

Beginning with the economic reforms in China, the shipbuilding sector has been restructured and expanded to meet the growing global and domestic demand for cheap merchant ships. Successive political leadership has consistently supported investment in shipbuilding infrastructure to be self-reliant and competitive in the global market. China's shipbuilding industry entered the international market in the 1980s and in 1986, China had 523 shipyards, 160 specialized factories, 540,000 employees and 80 research institutes.[7] These have grown over the years to more than 1,250 shipbuilding and ship repairing enterprises, including 285 state-owned enterprises, 857 collective businesses and 78 foreign-funded ventures. Over the years, China has developed a highly sophisticated shipbuilding infrastructure that competes with traditional shipbuilding giants such as South Korea (35 per cent) and Japan (30 per cent) that control 65 per cent of the world shipbuilding capacity.[8] China continues to be the third largest shipbuilding country (23 per cent market share),[9] a position it has held for the past decade.

During the 1990s, Chinese shipbuilding output grew from 1.2 million tonnes gross registered tonnage (grt) in 1992 to 4.48 million tonnes grt in 1999 and the order values totalled US$1.8 billion.[10] During the Tenth Five-Year Plan period (2000–05), the shipbuilding industry witnessed an average annual growth rate of 29 per cent and China quadrupled capacity from 3.5 million to 12 million deadweight tonnage (dwt).[11] Shipbuilding is one of the important components of the Eleventh Five-Year Plan (2006–10) and the Chinese State Council has announced a long-term development plan for the sector that envisages a share of approximately 25 per cent of the world's total output by 2010.[12] Also, China's increasing need for energy, raw materials and markets to sustain economic growth has further stimulated the shipbuilding industry to meet the demands of domestic shipping companies which are engaged in expanding their fleets.

There are several reasons for an upsurge in Chinese shipbuilding capacity and its popularity among international buyers. Geographical advantages of an expansive coastline, plentiful and cheap labour, and a domestic ancillary industry and engineering skills have all contributed to China's rise as an international ship purchase destination. Another important factor responsible for this sudden interest in Chinese shipbuilding is the relative cost of shipbuilding.[13] Based on one dollar/hour/labour, the cost of construction is much less compared to Japan and Korea and this distinctive advantage is the catalyst for large orders.[14]

While Chinese shipyards carve out a major share in the international market, there are several challenges for the industry to be competitive against Japan and South Korea, the global shipbuilding giants. According to Zhang Xiangmu, an official from the Commission of Science, Technology and Industry for National Defense (COSTIND), "China still lags far behind the top shipbuilding countries in many ship functions, in structural design and technology. It is leagues behind the other players in many key technologies, with no domestic brands to provide support products for exported ocean ships."[15]

The Chinese Government announced key result areas (KRA) for the national shipbuilding industry which include: (a) world-class technological sophistication, (b) annual production of 17 million deadweight tonnes (dwt) of ships, (c) 1,100 units of diesel engines annually, totalling 4.5 million kw to meet domestic demand, and (d) indigenously produce more than 60 per cent of ship equipment.[16] In order to achieve the KRAs, the shipyards have augmented their capacity to build a variety of vessels for the international market and nearly 70 per cent of the ships now being built in 861 Chinese shipyards are for export.

The Chinese Government closely followed global market trends in shipbuilding and restructured the industry. In April 1995, the Chinese Ministry of Civil Affairs established the China Association of the National Shipbuilding Industry (CANSI), a non-profit organization with 530 member enterprises and organizations of shipbuilders, ship repair agencies, marine equipment manufacturers, R&D institutions, specialized universities and schools and other similar enterprises engaged in shipbuilding activity.[17] The COSTIND oversees the activities of CANSI that accounts for more than 90 per cent of new shipbuilding output from China. As part of restructuring, in 1999, the China State Shipbuilding Corporation (CSSC), which controls key shipyards, was divided into two entities. The CSSC is responsible for shipyards in northern China, while the China Shipbuilding Industry Corporation (CSIC) manages shipyards in the southern part of the country.[18] The CSSC had planned to increase its annual output to 2.5 million tonnes grt in 2005 to become one of the top five shipbuilding groups. Similar trends prevailed for the CSIC.[19] Although CSSC and CSIC are the leaders of the Chinese shipbuilding industry, there are nearly 3,000 private small and medium shipyards that contribute to Chinese shipbuilding capacity. These are located in coastal provinces such as Zhejiang (84), Jiangsu (79) and Shandong (50) and account for 53.3 per cent of China's total ship output, 51 per cent of total ship sales and provide nearly 65 per cent of the jobs in the country's shipbuilding industry.[20]

Economic liberalization of the economy and availability of funds have turned the Chinese shipyards into efficient enterprises capable of building vessels to owner specifications. New technologies have been inducted, and management techniques are being sharpened to build ships on time. Chinese shipyards also support the warship needs of the Chinese Navy and meet the demands of foreign naval shipbuilding.[21] The shipyards possess the capacity and capability to build various kinds of war vessels including submarines and other specialist craft for the PLA Navy and for export to international customers in Asia, Africa and the Middle East. The naval shipbuilding is briefly discussed in Chapter 3.

Shipping Industry

The Chinese shipping industry has emerged as the engine of economic growth and symbol of the growing economic power of China. Chinese flagged vessels play an important role in both domestic and international trade and transport more than 90 per cent of its seaborne trade. The fleet has a variety of vessels that include bulk carriers, oil tankers, LNG and gas carriers, container vessels, Ro/Ro ships and passenger liners. In the 1960s, China's merchant fleet comprised less than thirty ships.[22] Beginning in 1961, China established its national shipping company COSCO of twenty-five ships with a carrying capacity of some 200,000 tonnes annually. In 1965, Chinese flagged vessels carried only 2.33 million tonnes of the total trade volume of 17.54 million tonnes, representing a market share of only 13 per cent. The shipping industry remained sluggish and in 1978, the Chinese flagged fleet totalled approximately fifty vessels with annual carrying capacity of some 36 million tonnes. During this period, China relied on foreign hulls for international trade that hampered national growth with a severe impact on the national economy.

Over the next decade, the merchant fleet expanded and by 1985 China had established eleven shipping offices in foreign countries through joint ventures. By then, Chinese shipyards had begun to manufacture ships but these were not sufficient to meet the demand of domestic shipping. In 1986 China ranked ninth in world shipping with more than 600 ships and a total tonnage of 16 million.[23] During the 1990s, Chinese shipping made significant progress and by 2002, China's merchant fleet expanded to 37 million dwt including tonnages under the flag of convenience.

In China, the shipping industry is an integral part of economic growth. The manufacturing industry pivots on assured and timely supply of resources and carriage of finished goods to international markets, the bulk of which is carried in the hulls of merchant vessels. Being the world's biggest importer of a variety of metallic ores, second-largest oil importer and the third-largest exporter of finished goods, the Chinese shipping industry has come to play an important role in China's economic growth.

The Chinese oil and gas tanker fleet has been in great demand. As China's economy grows, its need for energy has increased correspondingly; China became a net importer of oil in 1993 and since then has been importing large proportions of its needs from the Persian Gulf, Latin America, Africa and Southeast Asia. It imported 163.17 million tonnes in 2007, 12.4 per cent higher than in 2006[24] and this figure is likely to witness a continued increase to sustain the growing economy. In 2004, foreign-flagged vessels had carried 90 per cent of the Chinese crude imports and the balance 10 per cent of imports were transported by the domestic fleet with a carrying capacity of only 5.2 million tonnes of crude.[25] The domestic oil companies perforce had to charter foreign-flagged vessels to transport most of the imports. In 2008, 40 per cent of the Chinese-controlled fleet were registered in China, of which 19.4 million dwt were of oil tankers.[26] The Chinese Government is concerned about the vulnerability of energy supply chains arising due to political uncertainties in the Persian Gulf and is seriously thinking of energy transportation security. The multi-pronged strategy envisages mobilization of the domestic fleet to transport crude, building new vessels and building strategic oil reserves. The plans envisage a Chinese-flagged tanker fleet that should be able to transport 60 to 70 per cent of national demand by 2020.[27]

Similarly, Chinese bulk shipping has witnessed great changes. The Chinese demand for iron ore, coal and grain has resulted in the growth of bulk vessels. For instance, China's need for iron ore has placed increasing pressure on bulk shipping. China was projected to import 400 million metric tonnes in 2007[28] and this would necessitate chartering nearly 70 per cent of the internationally available 6,000 ships that carry dry bulk to transport iron ore to China which is sourced from Australia, Brazil and India.[29] Although China has large reserves of coal, it is of poor quality, forcing China to import large quantities from Australia. Currently, China's coal production capacity is 2.35 billion tonnes, with 800 million tonnes of capacity under development.[30] While domestic coal production can meet the demand, the poor transport network can add to vulnerabilities, bringing additional responsibilities on coastal shipping. Similarly, China imports soybeans in bulk.[31] Container vessels are in the forefront of the Chinese export industry. China's container fleet has witnessed impressive growth and being the top producer of shipping containers, the Chinese container fleet is making great progress.

Ports

Development of transportation infrastructure is complex, time-consuming, and expensive. It is dependent on several inter-modal nodes built around rail and road systems that connect sources of raw materials to industrial centres and in turn to the ports and harbours. These nodes are spread over a wide area of geography and connecting them is a daunting challenge. In China, the bulk of the sources of raw materials are located in the hinterland and the industrial infrastructure is located in the coastal provinces thus necessitating a robust and well developed land and sea transportation network. As one of the world's largest growing economies, China is engaged in expanding transportation infrastructure both on land and along the coast to meet the ever-growing demand by the industrial centres for raw materials and transportation of finished goods.

In China there are two types of ports: seaports that dot the long coastline and inland ports that lie astride the rivers and waterways. There are more than 460 seaports and about 26 of these are major ports that handle nearly 86 per cent of the cargo coming in/moving out of China.[32] There are about 2,000 river ports controlled mainly by local municipalities. The 2004 government statistics note that China has 1,430 ports with a combined throughput of 4.17 billion tonnes that service a fleet of 210,000 ships used for ocean shipping.[33]

Since independence, China has invested in developing maritime infrastructure to facilitate trade. In 1949, Chinese ports handled 14.4 million tonnes of cargo through 223 berths; in 1979, berth capacity was augmented to 311 berths that handled 198 million tonnes of cargo.[34] Port development and augmentation of berths continued to be high on the agenda, and in 1996, Chinese ports handled 1,155 million tonnes of cargo, six times the 1979 throughput.

During the Eighth (1991–95) and the Ninth (1995–2000) Five-Year Plans, China invested large fiscal resources to remove bottlenecks in maritime transport infrastructure. Greater attention was given to meet the ever-increasing demand for deep-water berths, specialized wharves for a variety of cargo, including containers, bulk-handling equipment and oil and gas bunkering equipment, and infrastructure modernization to enhance trade.

The container port throughput increased from 2.2 million twenty-foot equivalent units (TEUs) in 1991 to 8.1 million TEUs in 1996.[35] In 2002, China invested RMB13 billion in seaport development and RMB315 billion on infrastructure facilities that resulted in an additional 24 large and medium-sized berths, including 19 deep-water berths, resulting in an increase in throughput of 65 million tonnes and 1,960,000 TEUs[36] and the ports handled 2.68 billion tonnes of goods and 37 million TEUs.[37] In 2007 (January to August), the Chinese ports, performance continued to be impressive and the cargo output was 3.447 billion tonnes, up 15.7 per cent compared to 2006 and the containers' throughput was pegged at 71.9706 million TEU.[38]

In recent years, the port capacity has improved significantly encompassing upgraded infrastructure, new port projects, enhancement and enlargement of the existing berth and quay capacity, modernization of cargo-handling equipment and removing bottlenecks thus reducing turnaround time. Besides, tools of information technology have been harnessed and freight is handled by using computer technology resulting in high efficiency in the clearance of freight. The port facilities improvement is focused on meeting the demands of international trade as well as domestic transportation of critical items such as oil, coal, and other raw materials and for the export of finished goods.

One of the greatest success stories of China's economic growth has been the development of container ports and international container shipping. Needless to say, large infrastructure projects such as ports require immense financial capital. China approached several financial agencies such as the World Bank, Asian Development Bank, and Japanese Overseas Corporation Fund, including developed countries, for aid to build new ports and augment the existing port facilities to meet the growing shipping traffic. For instance,

Japan provided aid (yen loans) to build/expand sixty large-sized berths capable of hosting ships of more than 10,000 grt.[39] The aid, totalling 272.6 billion yen, was utilized for the following projects:

(a) Qinhuangdao Port Expansion Project (67.4 billion yen)
(b) Qingdao Port Expansion Project (59.7 billion yen)
(c) Huanghua Port Construction Project (15.4 billion yen)
(d) Shenzhen Dapeng Bay Yantian Port First Phase Construction Project (14.7 billion yen)
(e) Dalian Port Dayao Bay First Phase Construction Project (6.7 billion yen)

Beginning with the economic reforms, foreign investment too has been pouring into China. Significantly, the port sector was the first to receive foreign investment and between 1979–2001, container ports witnessed investment of Yuan 25.3 billion (US$3.3 billion) in foreign capital.[40] The Chinese Government is confident of sustained economic growth and is encouraging foreign capital into the port infrastructure development industry, resulting in a high foreign investor confidence. Another vehicle for fund-raising is the domestic and overseas infrastructure bond.

Besides, overseas Chinese money is another source for funding. Since the 1980s, the economic reforms have encouraged local governments to adopt a new philosophy of self-reliance. It aims at following the dictum "using road to sustain road, using port to sustain port, using bridge to sustain bridge", meaning that they would raise funds locally to sustain growth and development.[41]

Some ports in China are of international standard and can compete with ports in the United States and Europe and occupy top positions in the Asian port sector. For instance, the Yangshan Port can match up to Singapore and Rotterdam; Qingdao's handling of ore exceeds that of Rotterdam; Zhanjiang Port is three times larger in area compared to the port of Rotterdam; the combined throughput of Ningbo and Zhoushan ports makes it the world's fourth port after Shanghai, Singapore and Rotterdam.[42] Interestingly, the world's top twenty container shipping companies have established offices in China.[43] Among all the ports in China, the port of Shanghai has emerged as a major global container hub port. It developed a sister relationship with the port of Rotterdam, a major container shipping hub port in Europe. Shanghai's container throughput exceeds that of Rotterdam.

At another level, China has been actively engaged in gaining control of operations at several important ports in Latin America. This initiative helps China to have direct access to raw materials. For instance, Chinese enterprises, both private and government, control the operations of Buenos Aires Container Terminal in Argentina, the Panama Ports Company, Cristobal and Balboa ports on either sides of the Panama Canal, Ensenada International Terminal at the international port of Manzanillo, operations in Veracruz, Mexico, and two ports in the Bahamas; similarly, Fujian province has a cross-Pacific shipping route with Latin America, linking the ports of Hong Kong, Xiamen, Qingdao and Shanghai with Manzanillo (Mexico), Buenaventura (Colombia), Guayaquil (Ecuador), Callao (Peru), Iquique, Valparaiso and Lirquen (all in Chile). All this helps secure China's access to Brazilian iron ore, Argentinean soybeans and Venezuelan oil.[44]

The Chinese Government is committed to invest and develop the port sector and plans envisage increasing the port throughput to five billion tonnes by 2010. Also, the government has drawn out a national plan for coastal ports that foresee five coastal port clusters, located in the Bohai Rim, the Yangtze River Delta, the southeastern coast, the Pearl River Delta and the southwestern coast to serve the economic development of the hinterland. In the coming years, China's port development will focus on the construction of coal, petroleum, ore berths, and deepwater channels to accommodate large ships. Besides, growing energy demands will call for larger capacity docks and feeder ports.

Fishing Industry

China accounts for nearly twenty-two per cent of the world population and is expected to settle at 1.49 billion people in 2025, followed by a gentle decline to 1.48 billion in 2050.[45] Being the most populous country of the world, there are global concerns about its food security and the quantity that it may have to import in the event of a crisis in its agricultural production. Lester R. Brown, President of the World Watch Institute, in his book titled *Who Will Feed China: A Wake Up Call for Small Planet*, warned that a rise in Chinese food demand would result in grain shortages and a rise in food prices.[46] Although China maintained agricultural trade surpluses during the last decade, it imported nearly 17 per cent of the globally traded wheat, 25 per cent of fertilizer, and 28 per cent of soybean oil, and exported about 10 per cent of agricultural commodities.[47] In 2000, the Chinese demand for grain was 450 million metric tonnes that will increase to 513 million metric tonnes in 2010 and 594 million metric tonnes by 2020.[48]

There have been concerns that large Chinese imports of food grain would adversely impact the global food situation, resulting in higher prices. The Chinese Government has dismissed these concerns and is confident that it can meet the growing demand and feed its people. According to the White Paper titled *The Grain Issue in China*, China has favourable and rich water resources to meet its requirements of food and will be no threat to the world food market.[49] As noted earlier, China is endowed with vast seas, large inland waters and suitable climatic conditions for the growth of aquatic life. In that context, fishery in China has a promising future and is an important sector of China's national economy.

Since 1990, China has emerged as the top producer of fish, surpassing the catches of Russia, Japan and Taiwan. In 1999, the fish production in China was estimated to be 40 million tonnes, accounting for 30 per cent of the world total.[50] Over the last two decades or so, Chinese fisheries production has grown many times over. The industry has evolved into a powerful industrial system consisting of aquaculture, sea-based fishing, processing, marketing, fishing vessels, shipbuilding, ports, science and technology and fisheries management. It forms an important part of China's maritime power and contributes towards economic development.

The Chinese Government adopted liberal policies and encouraged both domestic and foreign investments in the fisheries sector.[51] These policies permitted fishermen to sell their products anywhere and compete in the international market. Besides, the Bureau of Fisheries under the Ministry of Agriculture supports the development of strategies and policies to increase output. The development in the fisheries industry has correspondingly provided impetus to shipbuilding and the ship repair industry, including manufacture of powerful diesel engines, spare parts and fishing accessories. The industry has been constantly engaged in Research and Development. The Chinese Academy of Fishery Science (CAFS) is the lead agency with twenty-one related institutions. There are 5,362 seafood processing enterprises including 732 state-owned institutes associated with fisheries.[52]

Distant water fishing is a relatively new industry for China but it is actively exploring opportunities for exploitation of fishery resources on the high seas. It is also engaged in joint ventures for the rational utilization of marine resources. Importantly, the domestic shipbuilding industry has developed the capability to build ocean-going fishing vessels. These have on board arrangements for processing and canning, for both domestic and international markets.

Inland Waterways

China is endowed with 5,800 rivers of which fifteen are more than 1,000 kilometres long and twelve lakes with an area greater than 1,000 square kilometres[53] and there are several navigable rivers such as the Yangtze, Pearl, Heilongjiang, Huaihe, Qiantang, Minjiang and the Huangpu. Since ancient times, these river systems have been an important mode of transport for a huge country like China and even today, the significance of the inland waterway systems have not declined.

According to the World Bank, China's decentralization policy in 1985 had a positive impact on the inland waterways transport organizations/operations and the policy encouraged independent project implementation and operations, financial independence, an autonomous personnel policy and handling tariffs with the provincial or local governments.[54] Consequently, the inland waterway transport operations have progressively moved from "fully state-controlled operations" to a combination of "state-controlled-corporatized" and financially independent operations. There is an increasing private sector participation in planning, infrastructure, fleet and port operations that has acted as a catalyst for improvements in China's maritime transport system and contributed extensively to its maritime economy.

In the past, lack of funds had led to the deterioration of the inland waterway system that resulted in a reduction of the navigable passage from 172,000 kilometres in the 1960s to 148,400 kilometres in the 1970s. However, since the 1990s, the navigable waterways have increased to 109,700 kilometres and 110,200 kilometres in 1993.[55] In 2005, the length of navigable inland waterways in China totalled 123,000 kilometres and there were 1,300 inland ports with 30,944 berths and among these, 187 berths could handle vessels of more than 10,000 tonnes.

The inland waterway network accounts for nearly 29 per cent of the total length of all rivers in China[56] and is mainly concentrated in the Yangtze River, the Pearl River and the Huaihe Water basins. Of the total navigable river length, only 8,631 kilometres, i.e. 7 per cent, are suitable for vessels of more than 1,000 tonnes and 15,328 kilometres, i.e. 12 per cent, are suitable for navigation by vessels of more than 500 tonnes. In 2005, the net volume and turnover of cargoes transported touched 1.49 billion tonnes and 363.5 billion tonnes/kilometres respectively, and the number and turnover of passengers thereof totalled 126 million and 3.14 billion persons/kilometres respectively. The aggregated volume of cargoes and number of passengers handled by inland ports were 1.845 billion tonnes and 129 million person respectively.

In April 2007, the Chinese State Council approved the national plan for the development of additional high-grade inland waterways totalling 19,000 kilometres (14,300 kilometres of grade-three and above, and 4,800 kilometres grade-four) and spending of nearly 50 per cent of the Yuan 40 billion

(US$5.15 billion) to upgrade inland waterways during the Eleventh Five-Year Plan (2006–10), double that of the previous Five-Year Plan (2000–05).[57] The plan jointly developed by the National Development and Reform Commission and the Ministry of Communications envisages development of a network of waterways comprising the arteries of the Yangtze River, West River, Grand Canal, the Pearl River Delta, and twenty-eight major ports.

The 6,300-kilometres long Yangtze River is China's longest and the third longest river in the world. In terms of inland waterway shipping capacity, it has surpassed the Mississippi and the Rhine as the world's top transport river system. The Three Gorges Dam project is being developed on the Yangtze River and the provincial areas of Shanghai, Chongqing, Sichuan, Yunnan, Hunan, Hubei, Jiangxi, Anhui and Jiangsu that lie astride the river that contribute more than 41 per cent of the country's gross domestic product. In 2006, the Yangtze River handled 80 per cent of the iron ore, 72 per cent of the crude oil, and 83 per cent of the coal produced by enterprises along the river, totalling 990 million tonnes, and this figure is expected to grow to 1.3 billion tonnes by the year 2010.[58]

The 5,464-kilometre Yellow River is the second longest river in China and drains into the Yellow Sea. Lanzhou, Baotou, Zhengzhou, and Jinan are important trading centres that lie astride it. Similarly, the Pearl River has a navigable waterway of nearly 18,000 kilometres, accounting for approximately 13.5 per cent of China's total navigable waterways. The inland waterway is important because of its large container-handling volume and facilitates Hong Kong and Guangdong's economic cooperation. The future development of the Pearl River lies in the Xijiang River waterway and Hongshui river waterway to provide an inland waterway connecting with the sea for south-west areas such as Yunnan, Guizhou and Guangxi, resulting in a more than 30 per cent rise in the transportation ability of inland waterways in the Pearl River Delta.[59]

China is systematically engaged in developing high-class inland waterways that can handle vessels of more than 1,000 tonnes and these are efforts to standardize vessels for inland waterways. The plans envision a national inland waterway and port network system that could be the core of a comprehensive transportation system and this would increase the current capacity by 40 per cent by 2010, and double in 2020.

Marine Tourism and Leisure Industry

For an ancient civilization, tourism is a natural growth industry. China has attempted to showcase the Great Wall of China, one of the seven wonders of the world, the Terracotta Warriors at Xian and several other ancient civilization monuments and tourist sites from its long and chequered history of invasions and occupations, including periods of maritime glory and eminence. Also, geography and topography have contributed immensely to the growth of tourism in China. The long coastline, island territories with pristine beaches and natural scenic beauty have resulted in several marine tourist sites that have now been expanded with recreational sites to include water sports, marine resorts and sub-sea recreation. Soon after independence, China established the International Travel Service in 1954 with fourteen branches in major cities, including the coastal cities of Guangzhou and Shanghai and the State Tourism Administration of China was formally established by 1964.[60]

China's national tourism policy is driven by the thoughts of Deng Xiaoping who had devoted great attention to the development of tourism in China. The Chinese Party Literature Research Center of the CPC Central Committee and China National Tourism Administration (CNTA) published a book titled *Deng Xiaoping on Tourism* that provides guidelines for the development of tourism in China and the methods to achieve top tourist country status.[61] The CNTA is the nodal agency in China on issues relating to tourism and has sixteen overseas representative offices. It sets out guidelines, policies and plans for tourism development in China and is supported by (a) CNTA Logistics Center, (b) CNTA Information Center, (c) China Tourism Association, (d) China Tourism News, (e) China Travel and Tourism Press, and (f) China Tourism Management Institute.[62]

In 1998, nearly 63.48 million tourists visited China, thirty-five times more than in 1978, contributing nearly US$12.6 billion, forty-eight times more than in 1978.[63] The trend continued and by 2005, the inbound tourists volume increased by more than sixty times compared to 1978 to touch 120 million tourists per year and generated revenue of US$29.3 billion per year, more than a hundred times increase compared to 1978. According to the World Tourism Organization, China was originally expected to overtake France as the number one tourism destination in 2020 but would now achieve the first rank in six years, i.e. 2014.[64] Further, in 2007, revenue from the tourism industry in China was expected to touch US$78 billion, i.e. 2.5 per cent of GDP, and US$277 billion by 2017.[65] The tourism industry is expected to grow at 10.4 per cent in the coming decade, and this could result in the development of the hotel industry as well.[66] The phenomenal growth of the tourism industry and the revenue thereof has been a direct result of reforms and the opening-up process in China. Besides, domestic tourism has also witnessed impressive growth.

The burgeoning marine tourism industry in China is built along the 14,000-kilometres long coastline that is home to more than 160 bays and more than 1,500 tourism-related,[67] scenic and recreational sites. The coastal states have developed more than 300 marine parks and recreational zones, with a variety of marine leisure features such as marinas, water sport parks, and beach sports centres. There are also 90,000 lakes that are home to yachting and sailing clubs and some spectacular marine tourism sites.[68] China has also invested in Marine Nature Reserves (MNR). In 1963, the Snake Island Protected Area in the Bohai Sea was established and by 1998 there were fifty-nine MNRs covering a total area of 12,900 square kilometres.[69] These are home to a variety of birds and marine species that protect coastal ecosystems, conserve marine biodiversity, help sustainable fisheries and also facilitate marine ecosystem tourism. Significantly, China is actively engaged in the activities of the UNEP's (United Nations Environment Programme) programme called Coordinating Body on the Seas of East Asia (COBSEA) to manage and prevent serious impacts of marine litter on the marine environment in the region.[70] It is also engaged in Partnerships in Environmental Management for the Seas of East Asia (PEMSEA) that aims to work in partnership towards the sustainable development, use and management of coastal and marine resources. During 1989–99, the Xiamen Municipal Government invested 350 million RMB to restore polluted lagoons into marine tourism centres.[71]

Several marine tourism centres have emerged along the coast. For instance, Sanya, on Yalong Bay at the southern end of Hainan Island is like a Hawaii of the East. Sanya is popular with domestic and foreign visitors and in 2006 it recorded nearly 16 million Chinese tourists and half a million foreign tourists.[72] Likewise, Qingdao, a coastal city overlooking the Yellow Sea, is a popular tourist site. It is home to the Oceanic Science and Technology Hall, the Maritime Produce Museum, Qingdao Aquarium, and the Navy Museum and these are closely related to the seas and oceans.[73] The Qingdao Aquarium, one of the oldest, has a unique architecture and hosts Yellow Sea marine life and the Navy Museum has artefacts of the early Chinese Navy. Besides, Qingdao sponsors the annual Ocean Festival every July and aims to develop the maritime economy and industry. Also, Qingdao was the venue for the 2008 Summer Olympics sailing events.

Theme parks too have caught the attention of tourism developers in China but without much success. In Shenzhen, the decommissioned Russian aircraft carrier Minsk was converted into a tourist attraction. Run by a private company, it ran into losses and the platform was put up for auction with a reserve price of 128 million yuan (US$16 million).[74] There were plans to sink the vessel off Hong Kong in the hope that the sunken platform would rejuvenate underwater life and help growth of native corals.

The marine leisure industry in China is still in its infancy. It is expected to grow at a rapid pace and could touch US$10 billion over the next decade as wealthier Chinese look for marine recreations.[75] China hosts the annual China International Boat Show in Shanghai that attracts large numbers of exhibitors and visitors, but there is negligible private boat ownership in China and there are no leisure marinas. At the manufacturing level, however, Chinese companies produce a variety of marine leisure products equipment such as power and sail boats, yachts, and assorted accessories including clothing. The Chinese companies enjoy an edge over their western counterparts due to low labour costs and the quality of products is continuously improving.

Following real estate and automobiles, luxury boats are now considered the new status symbol of wealth but acquiring such boats attracts 27 per cent in tax and duty and there are several bureaucratic hurdles resulting in low boat ownership. Besides, the marine leisure industry is also plagued with security limitations. The Chinese military imposes several security restrictions on commercial activity at waterfronts including marina developments.[76] Notwithstanding that, pleasure boating is fast catching up in China and the Chinese Government is developing the Starbay Yacht Club built by the Grand Leisure Marina Development Company of Shanghai. When completed, it will have eighty slips with a total capacity for 270 yachts.[77] The Beijing 2008 Olympic Games in China resulted in development of marinas for the water sports and sailing activities. Also, luxury marina complex were developed for the World Expo 2010 held at Shanghai's Oriental Pearl Tower.[78]

Seabed Resources

Economic reforms and opening up of markets resulted in an enormous requirement for energy and raw materials in China. During the last decade, China's demand for metals has grown from 10 per cent to around 25 per cent and copper, aluminium, zinc, lead and steel[79] consumption witnessed a steady increase. China began to explore international markets to fulfil its needs and also began to look towards the seabed to meet the demand.

In April 2001, China announced the "National Program on Mineral Resources", and in January 2003,[80] it announced "China's Programme of Action for Sustainable Development in the Early 21st Century".[81] As part of sustainable development, the Chinese national minerals policy notes that there are more than 170 different mineral resources found in China and among these, 158 are proven. There are nearly 18,000 production areas of mineral resources and more than 7,000 of these are either big or medium-sized. The policy notes that maritime areas under Chinese jurisdiction are rich in mineral resources and the government is committed to undertaking research and development of mineral resources from the seabed as well as to actively participate in research, prospecting and exploitation of seabed mineral resources elsewhere under the United Nations.

Since 1972, China has been actively engaged in the formulation of the international seabed resource exploitation regime under the UN. At that time, it did not possess the technological capability to exploit seabed resources, but by the late 1970s, it was actively engaged in exploration of the seabed. During the 1980s, it dispatched two ships — Xiangyanghong 16 and Xiangyanghong 9 — on three voyages to undertake surveys of the seabed following which, on 5 March 1991, China registered with the UN as a Pioneer Investor of deep-seabed exploitation.[82] After several surveys, China was granted 300,000 square kilometres in the Clarion-Clipperton area in the Pacific Ocean. Soon thereafter, on 4 April 1991, the China Ocean Mineral Resources R&D Association (COMRA) was established.[83] The COMRA is the highest body in China for deep-seabed exploration and exploitation activities as well as the nodal agency for coordinating China's interaction with the International Seabed Authority (ISA). Since its registration as a Pioneer Investor with ISA, China has made significant progress in seabed exploration and exploitation. During 1990–95, it undertook five voyages, trained foreign scientists, established a database of minerals in its area, and in accordance with the Law of the Sea Convention, relinquished 30 per cent of the allotted investor area.

The successes of the past explorations period led to a more aggressive seabed exploration activity by China during 1995–2000. In 1998, China undertook nine voyages and deployed robots for exploration. The tenth voyage in March 1999 by Ocean I, led to the establishment of 75,000 square kilometres in the international seabed with exclusive rights for resources exploitation with China. It is estimated that China can produce annually three million tonnes of dry nodules and these can be exploited for the next twenty years. During 2000–05, China signed a contract with ISA for a survey of thermal fluid deposits and gas hydrates and began developing a manned submarine vessel capable of operating at depths below 6,000 metres in the deep sea. China has also developed a track underwater vehicle called pilot-miner for mining polymetallic nodule on the seabed. During trials in a lake, it was able to lift nodules to the supporting ship, thus proving that China is technologically ready for exploitation of the deep-seabed polymetallic nodule.

China has also been actively engaged in deep oceanic science research including deep ocean ridge science. In 2005–06, China dispatched research vessel Dayang 1 on an around-the-world oceanographic expedition visiting the Pacific Ocean, the Atlantic Ocean and the Indian Ocean, hoping to explore the abundant energy resources in the ocean and study marine life as well as to undertake a survey of undersea ridges for active hot vents.[84] The expedition, funded by COMRA, engaged in explorations 2,600 metres below sealevel for undersea sulfide deposits formed by hydrothermal vents that have an abundance of copper, zinc, gold, and other minerals. The expedition showcased Chinese technological sophistication in underwater technology and the competence of Chinese scientists.

As far as hydrocarbons are concerned, soon after independence in 1949, China began to invest in offshore oil in the South China Sea. By 1965, the offshore exploration began in Bohai Bay and during 1966–72 four fixed drilling platforms, fourteen wells and three oil-bearing structures were set up.[85] As part of reforms, in 1982 the Chinese State Council established the China National Offshore Oil Corporation (CNOOC) to develop the Chinese offshore oil industry and also explore partnerships with international players. In 2006, CNOOC's yearly oil production was more than 40 million tonnes (oil equivalent). The long-term development plans envisage an ambitious expansion to produce 100 million tonnes of oil and gas by 2010. The thrust areas are the South China Sea, Bohai Bay, seas of Senkaku Islands and East China Seas.

Chinese Seafarers

Like its economy, China's seafaring labour has witnessed extraordinary expansion and emerged as a dominating workforce. The Chinese seafarers man both domestic (coastal and ocean-going) and international shipping. Significantly, the Chinese seafarers have not been immune to globalization and are common sight on board foreign-flag vessels and have earned themselves a reputation of being a human capital to reckon with. The current estimates point to the fact that the global seafaring labour market is led by the Philippines followed by China.

According to the Chinese Maritime Authority, in 1989, there were 280,000 Chinese seafarers employed on board merchant vessels and among these, about 20,000 were engaged in ocean-going shipping.[86] By 1998, the Chinese seafaring force was pegged at approximately 330,000, out of which nearly one quarter, i.e. 80,000 were employed on board ocean-going vessels and among these, nearly 4,000 were serving on foreign-flag vessels.[87] In

2001, the Chinese Ministry of Communication estimated 500,000 seafarers in China with 340,000 working on board domestic shipping vessels and 160,000 engaged in foreign-going ships.[88] Of these, some 40,000 Chinese seafarers were in employment in foreign-flag vessels.

The ten-fold increase in Chinese seafarers employed on board foreign-flag vessels has been a result of the Chinese Government's aggressive strategy to promote Chinese seafarers in the international labour market. China established the Coordination Council for Overseas Seamen Employment of China (CCOSEC) with the primary aim of raising the profile of the Chinese seafaring labour force for employment on board foreign-flag ships and sent out delegations to Europe on promotional tours who tried to convince perspective employers by noting that the Chinese seafarers "having received the best training", "demonstrating a strong sense of discipline", "reasonably priced" and that therefore "there exists a great potential (for China) to supply a greater number of seafarers to world fleets".[89] Chinese seafarers began to man foreign vessels around 1979 and at that time the Chinese state-owned enterprises were the primary source of seafarers for domestic and international shipping companies. Interestingly, the state control over domestic shipping was so great that the authorities appointed a political commissar on board all Chinese-flagged vessels.[90]

Chinese seafarers too have benefited from the economic growth. The unprecedented expansion of the domestic shipping fleet has acted as a catalyst for the overall growth of its seafaring labour. The China Ocean Shipping Company (COSCO) and the China Shipping Group (CSG) are the largest shipping companies in China and are also the largest employers of Chinese seafaring labour. Both have their own manning arm: COSCOMAN (COSCO Manning Cooperation Inc.) for COSCO and for CSG, it is MASES (China Marine & Seamen Service Corp). COSCOMAN, being older and larger, has a monopoly and was the primary source of supply of manpower. Between 1979 and 1998, it enjoyed nearly 60 per cent of the market, employing some 150,000 Chinese seafarers for supply to its own fleet as well as for foreign shipowners and operators.[91] Currently, COSCOMAN has a seafaring labour force of 42,000 seafarers: 26,000 (60 per cent) for COSCO fleet and 16,000 (38 per cent) with foreign shipowners. Among these, at any point in time, there would be 18,000 (43 per cent) on board vessels, consisting of 10,000 on COSCO ships and 8,000 on foreign-owned vessels.

Unlike COSCOMAN, MASES is a more recent enterprise and between 1988 and 1998, it had nearly 40,000 seafarers with a market share of 16 per cent. It has some 20,000 seafarers, of which 4,000 are employed on foreign-flagged vessels that are supplied to some eighty international shipping companies from twenty countries in Asia, Europe and North Americas, providing seamen of various ranks for all types of vessels. Besides, several private agencies have now mushroomed in China and emerged as suppliers of merchant marine labour force, both for the domestic and international market.

China has invested significantly in marine education and training infrastructure and Chinese seafarers have proved to be technically competent. There are nearly 4,000 maritime education specialists and 60 per cent of these have both teaching and maritime qualifications.[92] Besides, China has established seven higher education institutions that have a maritime department and prominent among these are the Dalian and Shanghai Maritime Universities. There are also eighteen intermediate schools and forty-three specialized training institutions that support maritime training infrastructure and nearly 5,000 students graduate with maritime expertise annually.

China established the Maritime Safety Administration (MSA), a quality control organization that is tasked to ensure high standards of education and training, curriculum and examination system. Under the Ministry of Communications, an overseeing agency monitors the general quality of education in universities and schools. There is greater stress on the teaching of English to ensure that the Chinese seafarers are internationally competitive and nearly 20 per cent of courses are conducted in English. This is so because in the past lack of English language communication skills had been a barrier for integrating Chinese seafarers into the international market. This is being overcome through English language education and training.[93]

Besides, the MSA is also responsible for issuing the seagoing certificate (ISO 97). This certificate is a prerequisite for a seafarer to sail on a Chinese-flagged vessel and foreigners, holding a certificate from another authority approved under the IMO White List, can work on Chinese-registered vessels but with a prior approval of the MSA. All manning agencies for recruitment to foreign-flagged vessels must seek authorization from the Ministry of Foreign Trade and Economic Cooperation (MOFTEC).

In 1989, China established the China Coordination Council for Overseas Seamen Employment (COSE) under the China International Contractors' Association (CHINCA) to regulate the quota of Chinese seamen that can be employed by foreign companies. The Chinese Government has approved 40,000 seafarers to fifty-four companies with vessels on registers based in Greece, Hong Kong (China), Japan, North America, Norway, Singapore, Taiwan and the Republic of Korea. A legal and voluntary trade organization composed of corporations and enterprises engaging in the activities of providing overseas seafarer. The Chinese seafaring labour is in high demand globally and some estimates point that the supply of Chinese seafarers to foreign ships will rise to 60,000 by the year 2010, of whom 32,000 will hold officer qualifications.[94]

INDIA: NATIONAL MARITIME POLICY

The Ministry of Shipping under the Government of India announced a draft maritime policy designed to exploit the full potential of India's maritime geography, sea-based wealth and seafaring human resource to develop a thriving maritime economy in an environmentally sustainable manner. The National Maritime Policy (NMP)[95] sets out guidelines for harnessing the marine potential of the country and the National Maritime Development Programme (NMDP)[96] offers a detailed action plan for the marine sector to develop and augment capacity to sustain economic growth. The Policy is comprehensive and facilitates public-private partnership, enhances quality of service based on competition, and formulates favourable fiscal policies to achieve the above objectives. The NMDP harmonizes itself with the NMP and identifies sectors, projects, and schemes that merit investment to support the vision and strategy laid down in the NMP.

The NMDP highlights the need for investment in infrastructure development, additional shipping tonnage and capacity building through proactive initiatives, projects, and long-term plans for the shipping sector. The salient features of the plan include (a) tonnage acquisition, (b) maritime training, (c) coastal shipping, (d) port development, (e) navigational aids (f) shipbuilding, and (g) inland water transport.

The plan visualizes development of about 111 shipping projects an investment of Rs.44,535 crore (US$9.68 billion) over two phases stretching over 2006–07 and 2014–15.[97] Under tonnage acquisition, during the Tenth Plan, the Shipping Corporation of India plans to spend Rs.8,000 (US$1.74 billion) crores to acquire additional ships (thirty-nine vessels totalling 2.06 million grt), and under the Eleventh Plan to invest Rs.7,000 crore (US$1.52 billion) to acquire thirty-seven vessels of 1.44 million grt, thus expanding the existing tonnage to 4.0 million grt comprising ninety-six vessels.[98] The plans envisage investment in coastal shipping to enhance domestic trade by establishing two schemes: (a) establishment of a Coastal Shipping Development Fund (CSDF) for soft lending for acquisition of coastal vessels and (b) the Centrally Sponsored Scheme (CSS) for development of coastal shipping infrastructure. As regards maritime training, there is budgetary support to establish one university and acquisition of two training vessels.

The new infrastructure will enhance maritime education, training and research. The training ship will be multi-disciplinary and provide a holistic training to cover a variety of tradesmen.

The NMDP notes that by 2013–14, traffic at major ports in India will be 705.84 million tonnes thus necessitating raising the capacity of ports to around 917.59 million tonnes.[99] Consequently, the government plans to augment existing facilities as well as to develop new ports. The port infrastructure development has been categorized under five broad heads: (a) construction of jetties, berths etc., (b) procurement, replacement or upgrading of port equipment, (c) deepening of channels, (d) projects related to port connectivity, and (e) other related schemes. The total investment envisaged for the above projects is estimated at Rs.55,803.73 crores (US$12.13 billion), to be raised through budgetary support, port's own internal resources, private sector investment and from other agencies such as the Ministry of Railway, National Highway Authority of India (NHAI), etc.

The policy acknowledges the fact that shipbuilding is critical to the development of maritime infrastructure and investments in the shipbuilding sector act as a catalyst to national growth. Consequently, the focus is on modernization, enhancement of existing capacity, research in design and building of ships for both domestic and international customers. For that, the government plans to invest Rs.7,195 crore (US$1.56 billion) in the shipbuilding sector, to be raised through budgetary support from the government, internal resources of the shipyards, through private sector and other sources.

The Inland Waterway Transport (IWT) infrastructure is still in its infancy and the government plans to harness the potential of the large river systems in India. Given that the rail and road infrastructure is being modernized and IWT is still under development and its commercial viability is still to be ascertained, private participation is likely to be low. Bearing in mind that the government has entrusted the states to take responsibility for the development of IWT infrastructure.

Shipbuilding

The Indian shipbuilding industry is quite small and constitutes a miniscule percentage of the global shipbuilding market. Some of the shipyards in India are as old as 200 years, but a majority of them are public sector enterprises and in the past remained plagued with inefficiency, high cost of construction, irregular delivery schedules as well as low quality, and thus cannot match international standards. As a result, India could not adopt market-oriented policies and strategies in shipbuilding and take advantage of its low labour costs. Consequently, 90 per cent of all Indian-owned and Indian-flagged vessels were foreign-built.[100]

However, over the past few years, led by private shipbuilders, India is emerging as an important player in the offshore segment of shipbuilding. For instance in 2002, the Indian yards had orders worth Rs.1,500 crore (US$32.61 million) and this figure has witnessed a tenfold increase with an order book pegged at 220 ships worth an estimated Rs.15,000 crore (US$3.26 billion).[101] It is estimated that by 2020 India's share in global shipbuilding could be around 15 per cent, or US$22 billion (Rs.88,000 crore) from the current figure of just about 0.4 per cent. The government plans to establish two shipbuilding yards, one each on the east and the west coasts, to meet the burgeoning demand of both the domestic and international industry.[102]

This upsurge and interest in the shipbuilding industry is essentially driven by the government policies that have created favourable conditions for foreign investment to modernize and augment the capacity of the public sector shipyards. In that context, the government is planning to develop two sites on the eastern and western coasts to build two international quality shipyards as well as strengthen the National Ship Design Research Centre (NSDRC) to enhance its design and research capabilities.[103] Besides, availability of skilled and semi-skilled manpower, growth in technology and technical capabilities and a burgeoning ancillary industrial base have provided the impetus to the industry.

Currently, there are twenty-eight shipyards in the county capable of building coastal and ocean-going vessels for use by the domestic and foreign shipping industry and warships for the Indian Navy and the Coast Guard. Both public and private sectors administer these shipyards: seven of these are public-owned and managed by the Ministry of Defence (MoD) and the Ministry of Surface Transport (MoST). The Ministry of Defence administers the (a) Mazagon Dockyard Limited, Mumbai (MDL), (b) Garden Reach Shipbuilders and Engineers, Kolkata (GRSE), and (c) Goa Shipyard Limited, Goa (GSL). The Ministry of Surface Transport controls (a) Cochin Shipyard Limited, Kochi (CSL), (b) Hindustan Shipyard Limited, Vishakhapatnam (HSL), (c) Hooghly Dock & Port Engineers Limited, Kolkata, and (d) Rajabagan Dockyard Central Inland Water Transport Corporation, Kolkata. There are two shipyards that are under the control of the state governments of Gujarat and West Bengal: (a) Alcock & Ashdown Co. Ltd., Gujarat and (b) Shalimar Works Ltd., Kolkata, West Bengal.

The private sector too has been able to carve out a modest share in the Indian shipbuilding market but cannot boast of large infrastructure to match that of the public sector. Currently, there are nineteen shipyards in the private sector, of various sizes and capable of building small-to-medium vessels including fishing craft. The larger of these are (a) ABG Shipyard, (b) Bharti Shipyard, and (c) L&T Pipavav shipyard on the west coast of India is the new entrant into commercial shipbuilding. Privately owned, Pipavav Shipyard has the capacity to build Panamax bulk-carriers of 74,500 dwt tonnes and its order books in 2008 exceeded US$1 billion, ranking it the second largest builder of Panamax bulk-carriers behind the Japanese shipbuilder Oshima.[104]

The Indian Navy and the Coast Guard are the major customers of the public-owned MDL. The yard has constructed a variety of warships including submarines, destroyers, frigates, corvettes, patrol vessels, and auxiliaries.[105] INS Nilgiri, based on the British Leander class frigate design, was the first warship built by MDL and the success of this project encouraged the Indian Navy to place orders for follow-on vessels. The shipyard also has the distinction of building two Type 1500 Submarines based on a German design. Importantly, MDL has been the lead yard for building the first of the classes of several indigenously built naval vessels including seven 1,200 tonnes OPVs for the Indian Coast Guard that were designed, built and commissioned by MDL. MDL is now engaged in the construction of Scorpene class submarines (under technology transfer from France), P-17 and P-15 A class frigates.[106] Besides, MDL has also developed a wide range of products for the commercial sector including Offshore Supply Vessels (OSVs), harbour utility vessels/crafts such as tugs, dredgers, water tankers, and passenger-cum-cargo vessels. The shipyard has constructed an assortment of support vessels for the fishing industry. It has also supported the Oil and Natural Gas Commission's (ONGC) offshore exploration activities and built multi-point mooring systems and floating cranes.

Likewise, the Goa Shipyard Limited (GSL) has built several vessels for the Indian Navy. These include Advanced Offshore Patrol Vessels (2,200 tonne OPV), hydrographic survey vessels, and missile-equipped fast patrol vessels. The shipyard also undertakes repair of naval vessels, but only to the extent of hulls and fittings.[107] The Cochin Shipyard Limited, with ISO 9001 Certification for Shipbuilding is the biggest in India and has capacity to build and repair vessels up to 110,000 dwt and 125,000 dwt.[108] It has been selected to build the Indian Navy's Air Defence Ship (small aircraft carrier). Since 1952, the Hindustan Shipyard Limited has built 109 ships[109] and the shipyard also serves the repair/refit requirements of the Indian Navy. Garden

Reach Shipbuilders and Engineers, Kolkata, is a mirror image of MDL.[110] It has emerged as the follow-on yard for the naval vessels built at the MDL and has built several naval vessels that include missile corvettes, broad-width frigates, tankers and large-size landing vessels.

The three privately owned shipyards are ABG Shipyard, Bharti Shipyard and the L&T Shipyard. ABG Shipyard is larger and has modern facilities for shipbuilding and ship repair. It also has its own dry docks and its domestic client is the Coast Guard. Bharti Shipyard on the other hand is a small venture and essentially caters to the demands of the domestic market and is yet to build warships. Bharti Shipyard and ABG Shipyard have raised funds for their capital expansion from the stock market. The L&T Shipyard is a newcomer in the shipbuilding sector but has been closely associated with the DRDO (Defence Research Development Organisation) and Indian Navy for design, development and manufacture of systems and sub-systems for warships, helicopters and UAVs,[111] and will now be engaged in the construction of submarines for the Indian Navy. [112]

Shipping Industry

Indian shipping plays an important role in national economic development and in 2008 it ranked sixteenth in the world in terms of fleet ownership.[113] In 2006, the Indian fleet was 8.46 million gross registered tonnage (grt) and comprised 739 ships of which 236 vessels were engaged in international trade. The bulk of the Indian fleet consists of crude oil tankers (36.0 per cent), product tankers (19.7 per cent), LPG tankers (3.3 per cent) and bulk carriers (30.6 per cent). Besides, there are a variety of other vessels such as passenger-cum-cargo ships, offshore vessels, container ships, dry cargo ships and dredgers. The average age of the Indian fleet is seventeen years and nearly 380 vessels are over twenty-years-old.

The Indian shipping industry can be divided into four distinct categories, i.e. overseas shipping, coastal shipping, offshore support fleet, and inland transport. As their classification suggests, the overseas component transports cargo to different countries, the coastal component moves cargo among Indian ports, while the offshore fleet ferries men and material to offshore oil installations of the Oil and Natural Gas Corporation (ONGC), and the inland water transport includes natural modes such as navigable rivers and artificial modes such as canals.

Since independence, the Indian shipping fleet has grown slowly but consistently. At the time of independence it was pegged at 192,000 tonnes grt comprising fifty-nine ships and by the beginning of the Seventh Plan

(1985–89), the Indian fleet had increased to 630,000 tonnes grt with 438 ships. For the next eight years, the shipping fleet did not increase much and stayed below the 500-ship mark. Although in 2006, the Indian merchant fleet strength increased substantially to 756 vessels comprising 8.57 million tonnes,[114] it never met the planned target. Notwithstanding these trends in the growth of the Indian shipping fleet and the increase in the tonnage, the share of Indian ships in the carriage of the country's overseas trade has been consistently declining from 31.5 per cent in 1999–2000 to 13.7 per cent in 2004–05. This inadequacy in the national fleet is a major problem and the country is becoming highly dependent on foreign-flag vessels, resulting in higher freight payments in the carriage of maritime trade.

The Indian Government acknowledges the contribution of the shipping industry in the overall national growth strategy, and the declining share of the national fleet in the country's overall maritime trade. It has taken several initiatives to develop the shipping sector and increase self-reliance. The draft maritime policy for the maritime sector notes that the shipping sector needs a focused policy support through a variety of initiatives such as simplification of procedures, cargo support to promote national shipping, as well as to encourage 100 per cent foreign direct investments.[115] For instance, Non-Resident Indians (NRI) can invest 100 per cent in shipping with full repatriation benefits and there exists an automatic approval for Foreign Direct Investment up to 74 per cent in shipping by other entities.[116] The Department of Shipping announced that a National Shipping Policy to provide fiscal, financial, administrative and legislative measures for growth and development of shipping in India was being prepared. To that extent, the Tenth Five-Year Plan (2002–07) aims to increase the strength of the Indian fleet, and create a favourable environment for raising finances from the capital market by way of external borrowings.[117]

As regards coastal shipping, it is an efficient mode of transport creating trade linkages between India's west coast and the east coast, including the offshore islands of Lakshadweep and Andaman and Nicobar. The NMP indicated the government's intention to encourage and develop coastal shipping and raise its share in the movement of inland cargo from 7 per cent to around 15 per cent by 2025.[118] The NMDP notes that India's freight transport system carries approximately 1,000 billion tonne-kilometres, the bulk of which move by the road (60–65 per cent), and rail system (30–32 per cent) and only about 6–7 per cent by coastal shipping.[119] The NMDP has acknowledged the need to augment coastal shipping, given that the Indian economy is expected to grow at about 8 to 9 per cent and the freight transport demand is likely to grow to 2,000 billion tonne-kilometres in the next eight to ten years. This would reduce the density of freight on road and rail and develop coastal shipping. According to the NMDP it is planned to divert at least 5 per cent cargo moved by railroad to merchant shipping in the next ten years.

In the past few years, the Indian shipping companies have performed remarkably well with the buoyant freight market conditions and in 2007 the operational earnings and total income of five major Indian shipping companies (Shipping Corporation of India, Great Eastern Shipping Co., Essar Shipping, Varun Shipping, and West Asia Maritime) that represent about 67 per cent of the total Indian tonnage has increased from Rs.70.6444 billion (US$1.56 billion) to Rs.84,0062 billion (US$1.83 billion).[120]

Ports

India's coastline is dotted with twelve major ports and 187 non-major ports.[121] Nearly 97 per cent of the country's foreign trade by volume and 75 per cent by value is carried on board merchant vessels, and therefore the seaports play an important role in the national economy. At the time of independence in 1947, there were four major ports. These were located at Mumbai (Bombay), Calcutta (Kolkata), Madras (Chennai) and Cochin (Kochi).[122] Kandla in Gujarat was developed to offset the transfer of Karachi to Pakistan in 1947 and was declared a major port in 1955. In 1962, after the liberation of Goa, the Indian Government declared Marmugao Port (developed by the Portuguese) as a major port. In 1966, Paradeep, on the eastern coast, and years later, New Mangalore and Tuticorin, were added to the list of major ports. The Jawaharlal Nehru Port at Nhava Sheva, Mumbai, on the west coast, was commissioned in 1989 and raised the number of major ports to twelve. Of the total 190 ports, only twenty-six can service ocean-going vessels and loading/unloading operations are carried out at alongside facilities. Single-buoy moorings (SBM) cater for liquid (like oil) and bulk traffic in mid-stream barges carrying pellets and cement. Some minor ports are capable of carrying out operations during the fair season only.

Post independence, the development of major Indian ports was taken up in a planned manner and in recent years, mechanization and modernization of cargo-handling facilities at ports have been high on the agenda with emphasis on the development of dedicated infrastructure. The deepening of ports to receive larger vessels is yet another priority area. Most major ports in India offer a combination of some bulk terminals, limited specialized container terminals and a conventional general cargo berth. There has been a steady growth in the volume of traffic handled at the ports since the 1990s and over the years major ports have witnessed a steady increase in the capacity to receive deep-draught vessels.

At the major ports, the ship turn-round and waiting time is high and much below the generally accepted international standard and performance of regional ports. Another drawback with regard to the performance of Indian ports is the lack of modernization. Although the Indian economy has been growing at an average 5 to 6 per cent during the last decade, port infrastructure has not been able to keep pace with the growing demands of cargo movement. The Indian Government has supported Indian ports to compete in the international market by resorting to commercialization, liberalization, privatization and modernization of existing major ports. Several areas have been identified for private sector participation that include cargo handling, maintenance of berths and port equipment.

Fisheries

Though endowed with a long coastline and seas rich in marine living resources, fisheries development in India has been a slow process due to lack of coherent policies and lack of investment by the government. As a result, Indian fishermen did not engage in deep-sea fishing, and could not compete in the international market. However, in recent years the government has adopted proactive policies that resulted in growth in the fisheries sector and currently India ranks third[123] in the world in marine fish production and second largest producer of farmed fish followed by the Philippines, Indonesia, Japan, Vietnam, Thailand, South Korea, Bangladesh and Chile.[124] China holds the number-one position and its production of farmed fish is five times more than that of India. Marine products have become one of the important items in India's export earning and this is illustrated by the fact that from 20,000 tonnes of fish catch valued at Rs.2 crores (US$435,000) in 1950–51, the Indian fish industry has registered a record of 612,641 tonnes of catch valued at Rs.8363.53 crore (US$1,852.93 million) during 2006–07.[125]

In India, fisheries, aquaculture and the associated industry provide livelihood to more than 14 million people including 6 million fishermen and fish farmers and 4,000 villages who support this activity and the industry contributes approximately 1 per cent of the total GDP and 5.3 per cent of the GDP from the agriculture sector.[126] The Indian marine fishery activities are carried across the 8,118 kilometres of coastline, 2.02 million square kilometres of EEZ, 17,000 kilometres of rivers and canals, 2.02 million hectares of reservoirs and 2.86 million hectares of tanks and ponds.[127] Further, there is potential to increase the current production levels both in the EEZ and inland waters and it is estimated that in the EEZ the catch levels can be raised from 2.94 million metric tonnes to 3.37 million, with scope to raise it to 3.93 million metric tonnes intensifying the trapping operations in offshore and deep-sea grounds making use of the modern technologies and techniques. Similarly, fish production levels from the inland waters can be improved from 3.46 million metric tonnes to 4.5 million metric tonnes. Overall, India has the potential to increase production levels from 6.4 million metric tonnes to 8.4 million metric tonnes.

In the early years, the markets for Indian marine products were largely confined to neighbouring countries in South Asia and Southeast Asia, but with improvements in technology in the cold storage and canning industry, Indian exports found a place in Western, European and Asian markets, particularly in the United States, Japan, China, and several countries in Southeast Asia and the Middle East. The export trade is completely in the hands of the private sector.

The Marine Fish Policy 2004[128] acknowledges that initiatives are required not only for making marine fisheries sustainable and responsible, but also globally competitive so that Indian producers stand to gain in international markets. The Policy notes that these objectives can be achieved through an integrated approach to marine and inland fisheries and aquaculture, taking into account the need for responsible and sustainable fisheries. Fishery is a state subject and as such the primary responsibility for development rests with the state governments. The major thrust in fisheries development has been focused on optimizing production and productivity, augmenting export of fishery products, generating employment and improving welfare of fishermen and their socio-economic status. Interestingly, fish catch along the west coast accounts for more than 60 per cent of the total catch (Maharashtra and Gujarat 33.50 per cent, and Kerala, Karnataka and Goa 34.60 per cent) and the east coast (Andhra Pradesh, Tamil Nadu and Pondicherry 21.80 per cent and West Bengal and Orissa 10.10 per cent) combined production is less than that of Maharashtra and Gujarat.[129]

Inland production, including farming, is now catching up with production and is likely to overtake marine capture fisheries in the coming years. Inland aquaculture and brackish-water aquaculture had emerged as a major fish producing system in India and intensive shrimp farming become very common in India. However, it suffered a setback due to a ban imposed by the Supreme Court of India in response to a petition filed by environmentalists pleading that shrimp farming had created environmental damage.[130]

The Indian fishing industry and the associated infrastructure is growing rapidly and there have also been some noteworthy infrastructure developments. There are 6 major and 59 minor fishing harbours and 189 Fish Landing Centres (FLC); the fishing fleet comprises 181,000 traditional non-motorized craft, 45,000 motorized traditional craft, 54,000 mechanized craft (bottom trawlers and purse seiners) and 180 deep-sea fishing vessels. Nearly a million people engage in fish-catching and 0.8 million in post-harvest operations.[131] To support the fish industry, a large number of scientists, technocrats and other categories of personnel are involved in research, education, technology development and administration in marine fisheries.

Plans have been approved for the development of more fishery harbours and Fish Landing Centres and a number of cold storage, ice plants and cold chains have also been established.[132] The government is committed to future fisheries development to include enhancing fish production, generating employment, improving socio-economic conditions of fishers, increasing marine products for export, and increasing per capita availability of fish. Under the Centrally Sponsored Schemes (CSS) for the development of infrastructure of marine fisheries the Government of India has announced several schemes for (a) development of inland fisheries and aquaculture, (b) development of marine fisheries, infrastructure and post-harvest operations, (c) national scheme on welfare of fishermen, (d) fisheries training and extension, and (e) strengthening of database and information networking for the fisheries sector.[133]

Seabed Resources

India's interest in seabed minerals can be traced back to the early 1980s after the Indian Government established the Department of Ocean Development (DOD), a nodal agency responsible for policy-coordination, promotion of research and overall development in the ocean sector. In 1981, a programme for exploration of polymetallic nodules was initiated and a cruise for exploration of these nodules was undertaken in the Indian Ocean. In the initial stages, the DOD and the National Institute of Oceanography (NIO), Goa, identified an area of four million square kilometres and subsequent survey efforts led to the demarcation of 300,000 square kilometres, which was divided into two areas of equal estimated commercial value.[134] In 1984, India filed claim for the mine site in the Central Indian Ocean with the Preparatory Commission (PREPCOM) and after prolonged negotiations and deliberations, India was registered by PREPCOM and an area of 150,000 square kilometres was allotted in 1987, and India was granted the Pioneer Investor status. Detailed sampling was undertaken at 2,500 locations and total resources have been estimated at 607 million metric tonnes.[135] India also operates a modern research ship named Sagar Kanya.

In 1982 India announced its Ocean Policy Statement (OPS) and acknowledged the economic and industrial wealth of the oceans. It set up infrastructure for ocean resources development including institutions such as the National Institute Oceanography (NIO), ocean management and research centres in institutes of excellence like IITs and Annamalai University to focus on the scientific, geographic, marine and economic features of the India Ocean.[136] India also commenced R&D on the extractive metallurgy of polymetallic nodules at a number laboratories such as the Regional Research Laboratory (Bhubaneswar), the National Metallurgical Laboratory (Jamshedpur), the Hindustan Zinc Limited (Udaipur), Indian Rare Earths Ltd., Kerala State Minerals Corporation, and the Hindustan Copper Limited (Khetri). The Indian west coast extending from Kanyakumari to the Gujarat Coast is rich in mineral deposits and has large deposits of ilmenite, rutile, zircon and monazite and varying proportions of magnetite and garnet.[137] The region near Kollam District (earlier Quilon) is rich in associations of ilmenite, sillimanite, zircon, rutile, and monazite, leucoxene, garnet, kyanite and ferromagnesian minerals.[138] Similarly, there are heavy mineral deposits on the east coast off Tamil Nadu, Andhra Pradesh and Orissa. As technology advances and the importance and value of sea-based minerals increases, these resources will be extensively exploited.

As regards hydrocarbons, the ONGC and Oil India are responsible for surveys of hydrocarbons offshore. The rising demand for energy resources has led to aggressive surveys in the EEZ and also in the river estuaries on both the east and west coast to locate new oil and gas fields. The offshore production of oil and gas has however been declining due to low reservoir pressure.[139] For instance, the crude oil production from offshore declined from 20,635,000 tonnes in 2000–01 to 16,925,000 tonnes in 2006–07. Similarly, the natural gas production declined from 21,752 million cubic metres in 2000–01 to 16,925 million cubic metres in 2006–07.[140]

India has seven geologically defined offshore regions (Cambay/Mumbai basin, Cauvery basin, Krishna-Godavari basin, Kutch basin, Mahanadi and west Bengal basin, Andaman and Nicobar Islands basin, and Kerala basin), but only three produce oil and gas.[141] In 1998, the Indian Government announced the New Exploration Licensing Policy (NELP) to boost hydrocarbon exploration in the country. The initiative acted as a catalyst and several offshore gas finds were discovered in the deep waters off India's east coast and there were major finds onshore in Rajasthan in West India. The industry response to the

NELP was encouraging and so far seven rounds have been announced. Under NELP VI, the Indian Government opened 164 blocks of which 103 blocks are offshore in deep and shallow waters,[142] and NELP VII is likely to offer more than 60 exploration blocks, comprising 30 onshore blocks, 15 shallow-water blocks and 15 deep and ultra-deep water blocks in both the east and west coast offshore areas.[143] In 2000, India published a long-term energy policy document titled India Hydrocarbon Vision-2025[144] making the Indian energy sector globally competitive. The document noted that by 2025, petroleum product demand in India would quadruple to nearly 370 million tonnes per annum.

In India, the Oil and Natural Gas Corporation (ONGC) is the leader in oil exploration and production (E&P) and its production for 2006–07 crude oil was pegged at 26.05 million tonness, accounting for nearly 80 per cent of the domestic production.[145] The ONGC Videsh Limited (OVL), the wholly-owned subsidiary of Oil and Natural Gas Corporation Ltd. is engaged in exploration and production overseas and has acquired oil equity and participation in several projects in more than a dozen countries. For instance, OVL has a 20 per cent stake in Sakhalin-I fields in East Russia providing the country with 2.4 million tonnes of crude per annum.[146]

Inland Waterways

Nature has endowed India with several inland water bodies such as rivers, lakes, canals, backwaters and creeks. There are perennial rivers that originate in the Himalayas, non-perennial rain-fed rivers in the Deccan plateau, and western coastal rivers fed by catchment areas and rivers of western India that drain into the Rann of Kutch. Overall, the Indian inland water system network comprises approximately 10,000 kilometres of rivers and more than 4,000 kilometres in canals. However, the total length stated to be suitable for navigation by mechanized craft is limited to 4,500 kilometres.[147]

In 1986, the central government constituted the Inland Waterways Authority of India (IWAI), vide IWAI Act 1985, with a specific aim to develop and regulate the inland waterways for commercial purposes. Since then, IWAI has been functioning as a nodal agency to administer and develop the inland water transport system and it is also the advisory body for the purposes of shipping and navigation.[148] The government is investing in developing inland waterway transport to provide an efficient, flexible and cost-effective network of transportation. In some regions, these operations are structured and operated by both public and private enterprises, but there also exists unorganized movements by country boats of assorted capacity that operate in various rivers and canals. Currently, IWAI operations are limited to a few stretches in the Ganga-Bhagirathi-Hooghly rivers, the Brahmaputra, the Barak River, the rivers in Goa, the backwaters in Kerala, inland waters in Mumbai and the deltaic regions of the Godavari-Krishna Rivers.

The government has declared three National Waterways: National Waterway 1 (NW-1) is a river transportation system that connects the river Ganga from Allahabad to Haldia, covering a distance of about 1,620 kilometres transiting through the states of Uttar Pradesh, Bihar, Jharkhand and West Bengal. The river suffers from high sedimentation and is prone to large fluctuations in water level during summer and monsoon seasons that can be as much as ten metres and above. During non-monsoon periods, there are several shallow areas and the depths can be as low as two metres that result in low traffic. The primary commodities moved along this route are cement, rice, wood, logs, petroleum oil lubricants, fly ash, pulses and general cargo.

National Waterway 2 (NW-2) runs along the river Brahmaputra from Sadiya to Dhubri, running a length of about 891 kilometres to form the National Highway No. 2. At Dhubri, the river enters Bangladesh and both India and Bangladesh have signed a protocol on inland water transit and trade. NW-2 also suffers from heavy sedimentation and experiences large variations in water levels during monsoons and summers. Like NW-1, there remain problems for navigation preventing larger vessels to transit through the river. Cement, jute, forest products, building material, fertilizer, petro-coke, food grains, coal, machinery and general cargo are transported on this highway. National Waterway 3 (NW-3) is a 205-kilometre long tidal canal system in South India along the west coast from Kottapuram to Kollam. Sulphur, rock phosphate, liquefied ammonia gas, furnace oil and concentrated petroleum products are transported on it.

The central government has encouraged states to optimally utilize the natural geography and build up the IWT sector. It has offered a subsidy under the Vessel Building Subsidy Scheme payable to the entrepreneurs for construction of inland vessels built in India for operation in national waterways, Sundarban and Indo-Bangladesh protocol routes.

The government has also encouraged joint ventures in IWT projects that can be executed as Build Operate and Transfer (BOT) projects. A National Inland Navigation Institute (NINI) has been set up at Patna and since 2004 the Institute conducts training courses in IWT, hydrographic survey, river engineering, river terminal development, transport economics, etc. Notwithstanding these initiatives, the growth in the inland water transport system has been very slow compared to the road transport system. The

Indian IWT system suffers from several problems such as high silting of rivers, shallow depths during summers, poor dredging, narrow width of rivers and poor navigation aids due to bank erosion. Several new and potential waterways are under consideration and the government policies encourage greater participation of the private sector in fleet development and operation resulting in improved productivity.

Marine Leisure Industry

India's long coastline is endowed with pristine beaches and island territories. There are mangrove forests, nesting sites for sea turtles, sea grass beds, coral reefs and the adjacent seas are home to a variety of fish and mammals. However, Indian policy-makers never envisioned marine tourism as an engine for the growth of the national economy. In 1982, a national policy on tourism was presented to the Indian parliament; it never succeeded due to the closed nature of the Indian economy and restrictive licensing policy that was devoid of private and foreign participation. However, by 2001, the Indian Government had acknowledged tourism as an engine of economic growth and set out the 2002 National Tourism Policy.[149] It envisioned that tourism could act as an economic multiplier with direct benefits in employment opportunities and economic development. The policy also stressed the need to develop tourism in an environmentally sustainable manner.

The 2002 National Tourism Policy highlights and outlines various stakeholders and seeks to develop the tourism industry within the framework of "Government-led, private-sector-driven and community-welfare oriented". Under the policy, the government is committed to construct basic tourism infrastructure and provide regulatory mechanisms, and the private sector to revitalize and invigorate the industry while safeguarding social and economic advancement of the local communities and facilitating growth towards a fair social order. Overall, the policy seeks to "position tourism as a major engine of economic growth".[150]

The policy seeks to develop India's eastern and western coastal areas by encouraging tourism resorts on long-term leases and at preferential terms by the private sector. These are to be developed along the Goa, Kerala, and north Karnataka coast due to their easy air connectivity. The government is developing Kochi in Kerala and the Andaman and Nicobar Islands in the Bay of Bengal as international cruise destinations. Besides, the policy also seeks to develop river-based tourism in the Ganges and Brahmaputra rivers. It is hoped that the policy seeks to project India's image in its international tourism industry.

Ironically, much of the marine tourism industry has developed along India's west coast, particularly around Goa along the Konkan belt and Kerala along the Malabar Coast. Goa is a tourist paradise and often referred to as the "Pearl of the Orient". It has emerged as an important revenue earner for the state government and registers some 12 per cent of total foreign tourists arriving in India. Its popularity is best represented by the fact that 75 per cent of the total direct charter traffic in India arrives in Goa and this is a direct result of its international air connectivity.

Similarly, Kerala in South India is also a popular destination among international tourists visiting India. The region is known for its beaches, picturesque backwaters, canals, and lagoons that are lined with coconut palms and ferns. It boasts a highly developed aqua tourism industry and has witnessed a major increase in tourist arrivals. The abundant marine life in the backwaters provides fishing tours, pleasure houseboat cruises, and canoe rides in the backwaters. However, development of marinas is a recent initiative. For instance, the Kerala Tourism Development Corporation (KTDC) began development of a fully-fledged marina in March 2008 to house around fifty yachts at Bolgatty Island in Kochi. Interestingly, it will also be the world's only marina with a golf course. According to experts, "The market for boats and luxury yachts is just about taking off in India, and besides Kochi, Mumbai-Goa coastlines to get a marina each from the government soon."[151]

The Andaman and Nicobar Islands in the Bay of Bengal have one of the finest marine biodiversity and an excellent tourism potential,[152] but the Indian Government, under pressure from the environmentalists and security establishment has been reluctant to open the islands to tourism. The islands are closer to Southeast Asian tourism resorts like Phuket in Thailand and Langkawi in Malaysia but have remained closed to international cruise liners that frequent the area. The government has plans to open only a few islands and develop resorts and promote islands as an international cruise destination.[153] Like the Andaman and Nicobar Islands, the Lakshadweep Islands have remained insulated to tourism primarily due to security and controlled development reasons. Tourists are permitted to visit Bangaram Island and it has very limited infrastructure in terms of accommodation and facilities but offers one of the finest underwater marine life for scuba divers. The island is connected to the mainland at Kochi and a ship serves as transport for tourists and hotel supplies while the bulk of the workforce is indigenous to the island.

Cruise tourism in India has been a neglected and overlooked industry. Also, there is a scarcity of accurate information and whatever is available is inadequate and poorly collated with a result that India has not been a popular cruise destination among the cruise line industry. Significantly, most cruise liners bypass India either to Southeast Asia or the Middle East. The Indian tourism industry is conscious of its inadequacies in terms of infrastructure and has begun to develop it. Several cruise terminals are under development along the west and east coasts, and cruise tourism is expected to emerge as an important component of India's international tourism industry. This will facilitate the domestic hospitality industry that is also developing infrastructure and services to support port city excursions and domestic tourism.

"Water sports" is an emerging leisure and entertainment industry in India. Several facilities have sprung up along the waterfronts both in the eastern and western seaboards that offer sailing, windsurfing, boating, water scooter rides, parasailing and jet skiing and their popularity is fast catching up. Most of the seafront tourist resorts and hotels too have now begun to offer these facilities. In 1991, the Ministry of Tourism, Government of India established the National Institute of Water Sports (NIWS) at Caranzalem in Panjim, Goa to provide training to paramilitary and police forces including interested public in a variety of water sports.[154] It offers certification training in Lifesaving Techniques and Powerboat Handling that is essential for running water sports facilities in India. Besides, NWIS also offers consultancy in technical and management of such facilities.

India can emerge as a popular marine tourism destination and the government is investing in its infrastructure.

Ship Recycling Industry

India holds the top rank in ship recycling followed by Pakistan and Bangladesh and the annual turnover of the industry is about Rs.10,000 crore (US$2.17 billion).[155] Ship recycling in India is carried out at ten locations along the coast: Alang and Sachana in Gujarat, Tadri and Maipe in Karnataka, Baypore, Kochi and Azhical in Kerala, Vishakhapatnam in Andhra Pradesh, and Valinokan and Tuticorin in Tamil Nadu. Ship breaking yards in Alang began operations in 1983 and the yard recycles about 50 per cent of the decommissioned vessels in the world. There are 173 plots and ten of these are exclusively for VLCCs.[156] Till January 2005, 4,035 vessels amounting to 30.05 million metric tonnes had been beached.

The yards at Alang had invited controversy about working and living conditions of workers and the impact of the ship recycling industry on the environment.[157] The breaking of the fifty-year-old decommissioned French aircraft carrier FNS Clemenceau, offers an interesting case study in this regard. The vessel carrying 27,000 tonnes of steel scrap, some 500 tonnes of hazardous and toxic materials including asbestos had long been in search of a scrap yard and had been denied entry by several European countries. It found a customer in India and the ship left France on 31 December 2005, while Greenpeace and local NGOs attempted to stop the vessel through protests. On 16 January 2006, the Supreme Court of India denied entry to FNS Clemenceau in India's territorial waters until 13 February 2006 pending a decision whether the ship was to be allowed in the country for breaking.[158] On 16 February 2006, French President Jacques Chirac, prior to visiting India on a state visit, recalled the ship back to France.[159] Jacques Chirac's announcement came after France's highest administrative court ordered the ship's transfer to be called off in response to legal action by Greenpeace and three anti-asbestos groups.

Indian Seafaring Labour

The wave of globalization, expanding international maritime trade and growth in shipping has resulted in extraordinary expansion of the Indian marine workforce. The Indian seafarers dominate the domestic shipping industry and constitute a sizable proportion in the international shipping market.[160] Also, the high education, quality training and English fluency further adds to the huge demand. Maritime training in India dates back to 1910 when a ratings training institute was started by Ismail Yusuf, the then proprietor of Bombay Steam Navigation Company at Worli, Mumbai.[161] In 1927, officers training was started and since then maritime training has kept pace with the changing needs of the global shipping industry.

There are nearly 130 government-owned and private training institutes that offer training to the Indian seafaring workforce.[162] These include four training establishments in the public sector and 124 in the private sector, capable of producing 11,164 seafarers (4,575 officers and 6,589 ratings) annually.[163] According to data maintained by the Indian National Database of Seafarers (INDoS), an agency under the Directorate General of Shipping, a total of 146,245 seafarers are registered and it is estimated that Indian-flagged ships employ some 30,000 to 32,000 seafarers while 52,000 to 54,000 are serving on board foreign-flagged ships.[164]

In India, the Directorate General of Shipping (DG Shipping) under the Ministry of Shipping is the central agency entrusted with the implementation of national shipping policy relating to development, safety, security and training of the Indian shipping industry and the human resource related with the industry. The Lal Bahadur Shastri College of Advanced Maritime Studies and Research at Mumbai, Training Ship Chanakya at New Mumbai, and Maritime Engineering and Research Institutes at Kolkata and Mumbai are under the control of the DG Shipping and placed within the domain of the Indian Institute of Maritime Studies (IIMS).

The Indian Institute of Maritime Studies (IIMS) is a forerunner to the National Maritime University and is ISO-9001-2000 certified. It is one of the many premier marine training institutions in India that offers pre-sea level, degree programmes in nautical science and maritime sciences, and marine engineering. At post-sea level the institute offers all training programmes stipulated by the DG Shipping and the International Maritime Organisation and some 8,000 Marine Engineer Officers and 8,500 Nautical Officers have been trained.[165] In October 1991, the government established the Committee on Maritime Education and Training (CMET) to monitor the performance of government-run training institutes and the CMET recommended setting up an autonomous body.

In March 2007, the Indian Government introduced the Indian Maritime University Bill 2007 to establish a national level university to facilitate and promote maritime studies and research focusing on marine science and technology and marine environment.[166] The main university is planned at Chennai in Tamil Nadu and campuses in Mumbai, Kolkata, and Visakhapatnam, with a provision for additional campuses in other states. The existing government training institutes, currently under the Indian Institutes of Maritime Studies (IIMS), Mumbai and the National Institute of Port Management (NIPM), Chennai, will together form five campuses of the proposed IMU. Shipping companies such as the Shipping Corporation of India (SCI), a public sector undertaking, and Tolani, a private shipping company, have set up their own training institutes. Some foreign shipping companies too are engaged in promoting maritime training in India.

The Indian Government also adopted an aggressive strategy to promote the Indian seafarers workforce. The Ministry of Shipping established a team comprising representatives from FOSMA, MASSA, IIMS and seafarers representatives to market Indian seafarers. The current strategy aims to showcase the strengths of Indian seafarers to foreign shipowners, ship managers and manning agents as potential customers.[167] At the management level, in 2001, there were nearly 200 ship-management companies of various sizes operating out of India and a majority of these were of foreign origin,[168] including the globally acknowledged ship management companies recruiting seafarers such as Univan, Wallem, Barbers, V Ships and Fleet Ship Management.

The growth in the global shipping market has led to a severe shortage of trained manpower. In 2005, the worldwide shortage of officers was pegged at around 10,000 officers and in 2007 the shortage in the Indian industry was reported to be around 900 officers.[169] The burgeoning demand for trained and skilled manpower in India has resulted in a shortage of marine officers pegged at 10,000 in 2007–08 and expected to touch 27,000 in 2015.[170] In order to overcome the anticipated shortage, the training institutes under the IIMS have increased intake of trainees from 5,140 in 2005–06 to 6,299 in 2006–07. Significantly, the placement record of all the Pre-Sea Institutes under the IIMS has been successful. Also, the training infrastructure has been upgraded to meet the technology available in modern ships.

In India, the shortage is also due to the fact that most Indian seafarers prefer employment on foreign-flag vessels since the tonnage of the Indian-owned fleet is limited and foreign companies pay better. Also, Indian seafarers working on Indian ships do not enjoy favourable income-tax benefits as enjoyed by those Indian seafarers working on foreign flagships. The acute shortage of trained seafarers has adversely impacted the expansion plans of Indian shipping companies. This forced the Indian Government to allow foreign seafarers to work on Indian-flagged vessels. Also, the shipping department was considering imposing conditions on Indian seafarers trained on Indian ships: they should work for domestic companies for three years and any seafarer trained by an Indian ship should get permission from the trainer for joining a foreign ship.

CONCLUSION

In summary, this chapter has attempted to highlight the Chinese and Indian commitment to build maritime infrastructure including human resource. Chinese shipyards have made significant progress, are competitive and have the capacity to challenge shipbuilding giants in Japan and South Korea. The Chinese Government is conscious of the fact that if the Chinese economy is to grow, it must modernize port infrastructure to support the economy. Likewise, Chinese-flagged shipping has shown significant progress. Although the average age of national shipping is high, China's reputation is high in the international shipping world. The Chinese Government has adopted liberal policies and encouraged both domestic and foreign investment in the fisheries sector and these policies have brought about a boom in Chinese companies who now sell their products anywhere and compete in the international market. Developments in the fisheries industry have correspondingly provided an impetus to the shipbuilding and ship repair industry. It has also resulted in the growth of fishing ports and consequently in fish catch.

Unlike China, the Indian shipbuilding industry lags far behind international standards. It does not produce cheap ships and therefore remains largely insulated from the present boom in shipbuilding. Similarly, the productivity of Indian ports is poor due to lack of modern cargo-handling equipment, and high turnaround time and poor management techniques add to its woes. Indian shipping has also not made any noteworthy progress, and the bulk of Indian exports are carried on board foreign ships, resulting in revenue loss. The shipping fleet is aged and is not competitive in the international market. The only silver lining is that the fishing industry has progressed well and has adopted modern fishing techniques. Given the size of the Indian EEZ, its fish catch is below its capability. However, current Indian policies are facilitating development of infrastructure and the leadership is conscious of the fact that if India is to sustain its current growth rate of nearly 8 per cent, it must invest in maritime infrastructure.

Finally, China and India have witnessed a sea change in their maritime strategic thinking, and there is an appreciation of the importance of maritime infrastructure, offshore resources and the need to exploit these critical resources on a sustained basis. Both countries are pursuing the pathways of building maritime power in this multifaceted maritime economic activity. In evidence are developments in maritime infrastructure, shipyards, shipping, ports, interlinking highways and inland waterways, and an effective exploitation of offshore marine organic, mineral and hydrocarbon resources and paving the way for the globalization process.

Notes

1. Yang Lei, "China's Marine Economy Tops RMB 1.7 Trillion", available at <http://english.gov.cn/2006-05/11/content_278052.htm> (accessed 30 June 2006).
2. Li Rongxia, "Marine Economy: New Economic Growth Point", *Beijing Review*, 10 November, 6 December 1998.
3. "White Paper on China's Marine Development Programme", Information Office of the State Council, the People's Republic of China, November 1998.
4. Lei, "China's Marine Economy Tops RMB 1.7 Trillion".
5. Sun Xiaohua, "Value of Marine Industries Grows 15% in 2007", *China Daily*, 16 February 2008.
6. Haiqing Li, "China's Sustainable Ocean and Coastal Development Strategy in 21st Century", available at <http://www.iwlearn.net/abt_iwlearn/events/iwc2002/26sept/welcome_plenary/lhaiqing_iwckeynotespeech.ppt> (accessed 20 March 2005).
7. Government of the People's Republic of China, *China's Shipbuilding Industry in Progress* (Beijing: New Star, 1991), pp. 4–5.

8. Jasmine Yap, "China Shipbuilders Steam Ahead", *International Herald Tribune*, 22 March 2005.
9. "Shipbuilding Tonnage Up 30% in 2007", *Xinhua*, 2 March 2008.
10. See "The Shipbuilding Market in 1999", available at <http://www.brs-paris.com/annual/newbuilding-a/shipbuilding3-a.html> (accessed 13 December 2000).
11. "China Maps Out Ambitious Goal for Shipbuilding Industry", *Xinhua*, 25 September 2006.
12. Jiang Yuxia, "China's Ship Industry Strives for No. 1 Spot", *China Daily*, 14 February 2007.
13. Cited in Vijay Sakhuja, "Maritime Power of People's Republic of China: The Economic Dimension", *Strategic Analysis* XXVI, no. 11 (February 2001). For instance, the cost of production of a VLCC in the more competitive Japanese shipyards is about US$90 million while in China it is pegged at about US$60 to 70 million.
14. Yap, "China Shipbuilders Steam Ahead".
15. Wu Qiang, "China Maps Out Ambitious Goal for Shipbuilding Industry", *Peoples Daily Online*, 25 September 2006.
16. Ibid.
17. Details of China Association of the National Shipbuilding Industry (CANSI), available at <http://www.chinaship.cn/cansi/introduction.htm> (accessed 30 September 2006).
18. "Shipping and Shipbuilding Markets 2000", *Barry Rogliano Salles Annual Report*, available at <eww.brs-paris.com> (accessed 20 January 2002).
19. See "China's Shipbuilding Industry Projects Growth", available at <http://www.marinedigest.com/JulyVT3.html> (accessed 15 July 2003).
20. "Chinese Shipbuilders also ready to sail to Bright Horizon", *China Economic Net*, available at <http://en-1.ce.cn/Industries/Transport/200608/23/t20060823_8254506.shtml> (accessed 25 June 2008).
21. For instance, China has built a variety of warships for Pakistan and Thailand and supplied several vessels to developing countries in South Asia and Africa.
22. Gao Weijie, "Development Strategy of Chinese Shipping Company under the Multilateral Framework of WTO", available at <http://www.cosco.com/en/pic/forum/654923323232.pdf> (accessed 24 June 2007).
23. "China Maritime Shipping", available at <http://www.photius.com/countries/china/economy/china_economy_maritime_shipping.html> (accessed 28 June 2007).
24. "China's Crude Oil Imports Hit New Record in 2007: Customs", available at <http://www.energy-daily.com/reports/Chinas_crude_oil_imports_hit_new_record_in_2007_customs_999.html> (accessed 26 January 2008).
25. "China to Increase Oil-Supply Security", *Beijing Times*, 9 January 2004.
26. "Review of Maritime Transport, 2008", United Nations Conference on Trade and Development (UNCTAD), United Nations, p. 40.

27. Gabriel Collins, "An Oil Armada? The Commercial and Strategic Significance of China's Growing Tanker Fleet", in *Asia Looks Seaward: Power and Maritime Strategy*, edited by Toshi Yoshihara and James R. Holmes (Westport, Connecticut: Praeger Security International, 2008), p. 113.
28. "Chinese Iron Ore Demand Could Trigger a Shortage", available at <http://www.purchasing.com/article/CA6458614.html> (accessed 14 July 2007).
29. Michael Bush, "Hop On Board Another China Growth Play", available at <http://moneycentral.msn.com/content/P133913.asp> (accessed 15 July 2007).
30. "China to See 2.5-Bln-Ton Coal Demand in 2007", *Xinhua*, 28 December 2006.
31. "Rise in Soya Bean Imports Threatens China's Cooking Oil Producers", *People's Daily*, 24 July 2006.
32. Kim Jraiw, "Annex I to the Asian Development Bank and an Integrated Transport System", Infrastructure Division, East and Central Asia Department, Asian Development Bank.
33. "China to Raise Port Throughput to 5 Bln Tons by 2010, Minister", *Xinhua*, 2 November 2005.
34. Peter Y.C. Ng, "Container Shipping in China — A Perspective View", The Hong Kong Centre for Transport and Logistics, <http://www.hkctl.vtc.edu.hk/hkctl/servlet/ctlGetFile?file=/hkctl/public/m/m_china_contship.html> (accessed 11 July 2007).
35. See the website of the World Bank at <http://www.worldbank.org.cn?england constant/479i1216824.html> (accessed 30 September 2007).
36. Hong Kong Trade Development Council, "Key Ports' Throughput Improves", available at <http://www.tdctrade.com/report/indprof/indprof_030506.htm> (accessed 30 June 2007).
37. "China's Ports Post 22% Growth", *The Hindu*, 14 August 2006.
38. "China Port Industry Report Reveals Cargo Output to be 3.447 Billion Tons", available at <http://www.pr-inside.com/china-port-industry-report-reveals-cargo-r676369.htm> (accessed 21 July 2008).
39. "Overview of Official Development Assistance (ODA) to China", Ministry of Foreign Affairs, Government of Japan, 2005, available at <http://www.mofa.go.jp/policy/oda/region/e_asia/china/index.html> (accessed 14 June 2007).
40. Xin Dingding, "Foreign Investment Boosts Port Industry", *China Daily*, 22 June 2007.
41. Rebecca E. Sundstorm, "China's Port Facilities and Maritime Infrastructure: Bo Hai Rim Port Development Strategies for the 21st Century", Nan Huai Chin Scholarship Paper, Spring 1999.
42. Peter J. Peverelli, "Port of Rotterdam in Chinese Eyes", paper presented at the International China World conference, "Made in China vs. Made by Chinese: Global Identities of Chinese Business", Centre for Contemporary Chinese Studies, Durham University, 19–20 March 2007, available at <http://www.

dur.ac.uk/resources/china.studies/PeverelliPaperDurham.pdf> (accessed 20 June 2007).
43. "China to Raise Port Throughput to 5 bln Tons by 2010, Minister", *Xinhua*, 2 November 2005.
44. "Looking Ahead: Strong Growth for Asia Pacific Ports", Report by Fusion Consulting, Singapore.
45. Gerhard K. Heilig, "Can China Feed Itself? A System of Evaluation of Policy Options", available at <http://www.iiasa.ac.at/Research/LUC/ChinaFood/index_s.htm> (accessed 21 June 2007).
46. Lester R. Brown, *Who Will Feed China? Wake-Up Call for a Small Planet* (Washington: Worldwatch Institute, 1996).
47. Colin A. Carter and Scott Rozelle, "Will China's Agricultural Trade Reflect Its Comparative Advantage?", *China's Food and Agriculture: Issues for the 21st Century*, Agricultural Information Bulletin no. 775, Market and Trade Economics Division, Economic Research Service, U.S. Department of Agriculture, available at <http://www.ers.usda.gov/publications/aib775/aib775k.pdf> (accessed 20 June 2007).
48. "Growth in China's Grain Imports an Opportunity for Exporting Countries, Not a Threat to World Food Supply, Says New Report", available at <http://www.ifpri.org/pressrel/021297.HTM> (accessed 25 June 2007).
49. Information Office of the State Council, People's Republic of China, "White Paper on the Grain Issue in China", November 1998.
50. "China Fisheries", available at <http://www.lib.noaa.gov/china/> (accessed 26 August 2007).
51. Information Office of the State Council, People's Republic of China, "The Development of China's Marine Programs", May 1998.
52. "Chinese Academy of Fishery Science (CAFS)", available at <http://www.lib.noaa.gov/china/archi/headquaters.htm> (accessed 20 June 2008).
53. "Report No. PIC5433, China–Second Inland Waterways Project", World Bank, available at <http://www-wds.worldbank.org/external/default/WDSContentServer/IW3P/IB/1997/09/05/000009265_3971229184944/Rendered/INDEX/multi0page.txt> (accessed 22 June 2007).
54. Ibid.
55. Also see "China Inland Waterways II, IWW Transport Sector Development Strategy Study", World Bank, available at <http://www.worldbank.org/html/fpd/transport/ports/_tor/iwtchina.pdf> (accessed 12 June 2007).
56. Letain Pan, "National Plan for Inland Waterways and Ports", available at <http://www.China.org.cn.> (accessed 20 July 2007).
57. Xiao Xin, "Boosting Inland Water Transport", *China Daily*, 6 July 2007.
58. Ling Zhu, "Nation to Modernize Yangtze River Waterway", *Xinhua*, 21 November 2006.
59. Zhang Chunxian, "Construct a Perfect Road and Waterway Network in Pan-Pearl River Delta Region", available at <http://www.newsgd.com/specials/

panprdforum/centralgovtsupport/200406020058.htm> (accessed 10 August 2007). Also see Marion Chyun-Yang Wang, "Greater China: Powerhouse of East Asian Regional Cooperation", available at <http://www.dur.ac.uk/chinese.politics/papers%20conference%20Brussels/Wang%20Marion%20paper.pdf> (accessed 10 July 2008).
60. "Tourism in China", available at <http://www.asianinfo.org/asianinfo/china/pro-tourism.htm> (accessed 21 August 2007).
61. Letian Pan, "Tourism Policy", available at <http://english.gov.cn/2005-08/19/content_24810.htm> (accessed 20 August 2007).
62. "China National Tourism Administration(CNTA)", available at <http://en.cnta.gov.cn/lyen/index.asp> (accessed 20 August 2007).
63. "China Rings up US$219 bln from Inbound Tourism Since 1978", *Xinhua*, 22 July 2006.
64. "China Heading for Top Spot in World Tourism Ranking", *AFP*, 2 July 2007.
65. Ibid.
66. Michael Verikios, "China's Tourism Industry Keeps Growing Fast", available at <http://www.traveldailynews.com/pages/show_page/16872> (accessed 20 June 2007).
67. Information Office of the State Council, People's Republic of China, "The Development of China's Marine Programs", July 1998.
68. "Maine's Boat Builders to be Highlight of Trip to China", available at <http://www.econdevmaine.com/announcements/details.asp?PressID=72> (accessed 30 September 2007).
69. Zou Keyuan, "Management of Marine Nature Reserves in China: A Legal Perspective", EAI Working Paper no. 86 (Singapore: East Asia Institute, January 2002), p. 2.
70. For more details see, "COBSEA", available at <http://www.cobsea.org/Other/NOWPAP%20partnership.html> (accssed 25 February 2009).
71. "Yuangdang Lagoon Cleanup", available at <http://pemsea.org/sites/china-xiamen> (accessed 25 February 2009).
72. Edward Cody, "China's Little-known Tropical Resort", *Washington Post*, 22 July 2007.
73. Li Xia, "Qingdao: An Oceanic City", *China Today*, September 2002, available at <http://www.chinatoday.com.cn/English/e2002/e20029/qingdao.htm> (accessed 30 September 2007).
74. "China Plans to Make Russian Aircraft Carrier into Artificial Reef", available at <http://diving-industry.com/news> (accessed 25 June 2007).
75. "Maine's Boat Builders to be Highlight of Trip to China", available at <http://www.econdevmaine.com/announcements/details.asp?PressID=72> (accessed 30 September 2007).
76. "Boating World Growth Big — But Wait For China", *Sail-World*, 18 January 2006.

77. "China Votes for Its Favourite Luxury Items", 9 February 2007, available at <http://www.hoayachting.com/news.php> (accessed 30 November 2007).
78. China Market Overview, "China Business Report", available at <http://www.ibinews.com/ibinews/mkt_info/country_reports/mkt_info_china.htm> (accessed 30 September 2007).
79. "More of Everything", *The Economist*, 14 September 2006.
80. "China's Policy on Mineral Resources", Information Office of the State Council, the People's Republic of China, December 2003, available at <http://www.chinamining.org/Investment/2006-08-04/1154674314d441.html> (accessed 20 December 2007).
81. "Program of Action for Sustainable Development in China in the Early 21st Century", National Development and Reform Commission (NDRC), available at <http://en.ndrc.gov.cn/newsrelease/t20070205_115702.htm> (accessed 30 June 2007).
82. "Marine Mineral Resources: Scientific Advances and Economic Perspectives", United Nations Division for Ocean Affairs and the Law of the Sea, Office of Legal Affairs, International Seabed Authority, p. 9, available at <http://www.isa.org.jm/files/documents/EN/Pubs/ISA-Daolos.pdf> (accessed 23 June 2007).
83. "China Ocean Mineral Resources R & D Association (COMRA)", available at <http://www.comra.org/english/eindex.html> (accessed 30 June 2007).
84. "Science Ship Returns After 300 Days At Sea", available at <http://news.xinhuanet.com/english/2006-01/23/content_4087324.htm> (accessed 26 June 2007). Also see "A Ridge Too Slow?", available at <http://www.whoi.edu/oceanus/viewArticle.do?id=26106> (accessed 26 June 2007).
85. For more details see, "China National Offshore Oil Corporation (CNOOC)", available at <http://www.cnooc.com.cn/yyww/gsjj/default.shtml> (accessed 25 February 2009).
86. International Labour Organization, "Report on an ILO Investigation into the Living and Working Conditions of Seafarers in the Asia/Pacific Region", Regional Maritime Conference in the Asia/Pacific Region, Singapore, 2002, available at <http://www-ilo-mirror.cornell.edu/public/english/dialogue/sector/techmeet/rmcap02/rmcap-r2.pdf> (accessed 30 June 2007).
87. "Chinese Seafarers: Value for Money or Cheap Labour", available at <http://www.sirc.cf.ac.uk/pdf/ChinSea.pdf> (accessed 24 July 2007).
88. Leggate and McConville, op. cit., p. 10.
89. "Chinese Seafarers: Value for Money or Cheap Labour", op. cit.
90. Seafarers International Research Centre, Annual Report 2000, available at <http://www.sirc.cf.ac.uk/pdf/Annual%20Report%202000.pdf> (accessed 26 June 2007).
91. "Chinese Seafarers: Value for Money or Cheap Labour", op. cit.
92. "Report on an ILO Investigation into the Living and Working Conditions of Seafarers in the Asia/Pacific Region", p. 10.

93. Ibid., p. 12.
94. Ibid.
95. "Draft Policy for Maritime Sector (Ports, Shipping and Inland Water Transport)", Ministry of Shipping, Government of India, 9 August 2004.
96. "National Maritime Development Programme (NMDP)", Ministry of Shipping, Road Transport and Highways, Government of India, 2006.
97. "National Maritime Development Programme (NMDP)", pp. 21–31.
98. Ibid.
99. Ibid., p. 31.
100. Author's discussions with shipyard officials from MDL, Mumbai, GRSE, Kolkata and HSL, Vishakhapatnam. Also see Madhu Chittora, "India has lost Competitive Edge in Shipbuilding", available at <http://www.projectsmonitor.com/detailnews.asp?newsid=9474> (accessed 12 August 2008).
101. P. Manoj, "Shipbuilding Firms Lobby Hard for Subsidy Extension", available at <http://www.livemint.com/2007/07/06003103/Shipbuilding-firms-lobby-hard.html?d=1> (accessed 10 July 2007).
102. "More Greenfield Projects for Navy: Mehta", *Business Standard*, 9 May 2008.
103. The investment of Rs.7,195 crore have been earmarked for these projects, out of which Rs.3,235 crore would be met through budgetary support from the government, Rs.960 crore from the internal resources of the PSUs and Rs.3,000 crore will come from the private sector and other sources.
104. "Ship Building Industry Needs Govt Help", available at <http://www.moneycontrol.com/india/news/pressnews/pipavavshipyardshipbuilding/shipbuildingindustryneedsgovthelp/market/stocks/article/334707> (accessed 20 May 2008).
105. See the company profile of Mazagon Dock Limited, Mumbai at the website of Mazagon Dock Limited at <http://www.mazagondock.gov.in/ship_building/introduction.htm> (accessed 20 January 2008). Also see India section in *Jane's Fighting Ships 2007–08*, pp. 311–37.
106. Vice Admiral S.K.K. Krishnan, "Building Warships is Not Purely a Shipyard Activity Alone", *Force* (December 2007): 30–31.
107. See the company profile of Goa Shipyard Limited at the website of Goa Shipyard Limited at <http://www.goashipyard.co.in/index.asp> (accessed 28 August 2007).
108. See the company profile of Cochin Shipyard Limited at the website of Cochin Shipyard Limited at <http://cochinshipyard.com/> (accessed 28 August 2007).
109. See the company profile of Hindustan Shipyard Limited at the website of Hindustan Shipyard Limited at <http://www.hsl.nic.in/> (accessed 28 August 2007).
110. See the company profile of Garden Reach Shipbuilders and Engineers, Kolkata at <http://www.grse.nic.in/choice.htm> (accessed 28 August 2007).
111. G. Srinivasan, "L&T Looks for Tie-Up with Israeli Cos in Defence and Water Treatment", *The Hindu*, 15 August 2007.

112. Shiv Kumar, "Private Players Play Big in Defence Sector", *The Tribune*, 23 July 2007.
113. "Review of Maritime Transport, 2008", United Nations Conference on Trade and Development (UNCTAD), United Nations, p. 39.
114. Ibid., p. 75.
115. Draft Policy for Maritime Sector (ports, shipping and inland water transport), Ministry of Shipping, Government of India, 9 August 2004.
116. "Shipping Policy Highlights", available at <http://www.shipping.nic.in/index2.asp?slid=308&sublinkid=186> (accessed 24 September 2007).
117. Annual Report 2006–07, Ministry of Surface Transport, Government of India.
118. Draft Policy for Maritime Sector (ports, shipping and inland water transport), p. 32.
119. "National Maritime Development Programme (NMDP)", p. 7.
120. "Income of Indian Shipping Companies Showing Increasing Trends", *Press Bureau of India*, 22 August 2007. This information was presented by the Minister for Shipping, Road Transport and Highways in a written reply in the Lok Sabha.
121. Annual Report 2006–07, Ministry of Surface Transport.
122. Animesh Ray, *Maritime India: Ports and Shipping* (Calcutta: Pearl Publishers, 1993), pp. 87–94.
123. Sandip Das, "Climate Change to Adversely Impact Global Fish Production", *Financial Express*, 28 February 2008.
124. K. Venkiteswaran, "India Second Largest Producer of Farmed Fish", *The Hindu*, 4 February 2007.
125. See the website of Marine Product Export Development Authority, Government of India at <http://www.mpeda.com/> (accessed 31 August 2007).
126. Anjani Kumar, P.K. Joshi, and Pratap S. Birthal, "Fisheries Sector in India: An Overview of Performance, Policies and Programmes", in *A Profile of People, Technologies and Policies in Fisheries Sector in India*, edited by Anjani Kumar, Pradeep K. Katiha, and P.K. Joshi (Delhi: Chandu Press, 2004), p. 2.
127. Arun Shivnath Ninawe, "Food Security from Sea: Policy and Economic Measures", UNITAR Hiroshima Office for Asia and the Pacific, Series on Sea and Human Security Training Workshop on Food Security, 26–30 September 2005, Hiroshima, Japan.
128. "Marine Fishing Policy 2004", Department of Animal Husbandry and Dairying, Ministry of Agriculture, Government of India, available at <http://www.dahd.nic.in/fishpolicy.htm> (accessed 24 May 2007).
129. K. Gopakumar, "Marine Fishery Resources of India's Exclusive Economic Zone: Exploitation, Utilization, Policies and Problems", *Maritime Affairs* 3, no. 1 (Summer 2007): 138.
130. "Campaign Against Shrimp Industries", *Advocacy Update*, available at the website of National Centre for Advocacy Studies (NCAS), Pune at <http://

www.ncasindia.org/archives/advocacy_update/au_11.doc>. The Supreme Court of India on 11 December 1996 noted that shrimp farms caused serious environmental damage and ruled that by 31 March 1997 all shrimp farms operating within the Coastal Regulation Zone (CRZ), within the 500 metres of the coast, be demolished.

131. "Economic Survey of India 2006–07", Government of India, pp. 166–67.
132. Report on "Stakeholder Consultation on Fishing Harbour and Landing Centres Management", Government of Tamil Nadu, United Nations Team for Tsunami Recovery Support and Marine Products Export Development Authority.
133. "Fisheries Sector Occupies An Important Place", available at <http://dahd.nic.in/fish/fisheries.htm> (accessed 22 May 2007).
134. S.Z. Qasim and R.R. Nair, eds., *From the First Nodule to the First Mine Site: An Account of the Polymetallic Nodule Project* (New Delhi: Department of Ocean Development, 1988), p. 56.
135. Vice Admiral G.M. Hiranandani, *Transition to Eminence* (New Delhi: Naval Headquarters, 2005), pp. 33–35.
136. S.Z. Qasim, "Minerals of the Deep Seabed", *Journal of Indian Ocean Studies* 9, no. 1 (April 2001): 93–99. Also see S.Z. Qasim, "History and Development of Ocean Science in India II", *Journal of Indian Ocean Studies* 2, no. 3 (July 1995): 199–208.
137. G.S. Roonwal, "Marine Mineral Potential of India and South Africa: A Comparison", *Journal of Indian Ocean Studies* 2, no. 1 (November 1997): 15.
138. G.S. Roonwal, "Mineral Resources of the Indian Ocean", Occasional Paper no. 4, Society of Indian Ocean Studies, New Delhi, pp. 1–59.
139. N.K. Mitra, "Advanced Technology & Spirited Workforce led to Successes at Western Offshore", *Oil Asia Journal* (May–June 2007): 13.
140. Annual Report 2006–07, Ministry of Petroleum and Natural Gas, Government of India, p. 157.
141. "Energy Files: India", available at <http://www.energyfiles.com/asiapac/india.html> (accessed 22 May 2007).
142. Partha Pritam Basistha, "Offshore Drilling to provide Shipping with New Dimensions", *Oil Asia Journal* (March–April 2007): 11.
143. Piyush Pandey, "OIL Ropes in BG to Bid for NELP VII Deepwater Blocks", *Economic Times*, 11 December 2007.
144. "India Hydrocarbon Vision 2025", available at <http://www.petrodril.com/hydrocarbon.htm> (accessed 25 June 2007).
145. T.S. Subramanian, "Energy Giant", *Frontline* 25, issue 05 (1–14 March 2008).
146. "Deora to Press for Stake in Sakhalin-III project", *The Hindu*, 25 January 2007.
147. Santanu Sanyal, "Is Ganga Losing Navigability?", *The Hindu*, 22 January 2001.

148. Annual Report 2004–05, Inland Waterways Authority of India (IWAI), Department of Shipping, Ministry of Shipping, Road Transport and Highways, Government of India, p. 7.
149. "National Tourism Policy 2002", Department of Tourism, Ministry of Tourism and Culture, Government of India.
150. Ibid., p. 6.
151. Priyanka Joshi, "Kochi Set to Have India's First Marina", *Business Standard*, 5 March 2008.
152. N. Rajavel, *Tourism in Andaman and Nicobar Islands* (New Delhi: Manas Publications, 1998), p. 17.
153. Vijay Sakhuja, "Andamans-Phuket link", *Sahara Times*, 11 September 2005.
154. "National Institute of Watersports", Ministry of Tourism, Government of India, available at <http://niws.nic.in/> (accessed 23 March 2008).
155. Ticy V. Thomas, "Ship Recycling Industry in India: Legal Implications", *Maritime Affairs* 2, no. 1 (Summer 2006): 55.
156. For more details see shipbreaking at <http://www.greenpeaceweb.org/shipbreak/india.asp> (accessed 28 November 2007).
157. The daily wages of workers vary between Rs.60 and 100. In contrast, the labour cost in the shipbreaking business in the United States could be something between US$40 and US$45 per hour.
158. "French Toxic Ship not to Enter India Till Feb 13", *Hindustan Times*, 16 January 2006.
159. "More Fighting over the Scraps", BIMCO Bulletin no. 2, 2006, available at <http://www.bimco.org/Members%20Area/News/Issues/2007/01/Recycling/BB2006_02_More_fighting_over_the_scraps.aspx> (accessed 7 January 2007).
160. "T.R. Baalu Calls for Early Report on Updation of Equipment of Maritime Studies", Press Release by Ministry of Shipping, Road Transport and Highways, Government of India, 18 May 2007.
161. "A Survey of Maritime Education in India", available at <http://www.imaritime.com/backoffice/published_files/Maritime_education_in_india.pdf> (accessed 31 March 2008).
162. Dev Dutt, "Ports & Shipping: Ferrying in the Future", available at <http://www.projectsmonitor.com/detailnews.asp?newsid=7736> (accessed 28 February 2008).
163. "National Maritime Development Programme (NMDP)", p. 46.
164. "Supreme Court to Rule on Missing Ship Jupiter-6", *Times of India*, 17 July 2007; P. Manoj, "Age Limit Hiked in bid to attract Rural Youth to Merchant Navy", available at <http://www.livemint.com/2008/08/18001647/Age-limit-hiked-in-bid-to-attr.html> (accessed 19 August 2008).
165. "T.R. Baalu calls for Early Report on Updation of Equipment of Maritime Studies", Press Release by Ministry of Shipping, Road Transport, Government of India, 18 May 2007.

166. "Maritime University Bill Introduced", *The Hindu*, 14 March 2007.
167. P. Manoj, "Maritime Training Should Have More Elements", *The Hindu*, 10 May 2004.
168. Raja Simhan T.E., "Ship Management Agencies: A Smooth Sailing for Owners", *The Hindu*, 31 December 2001.
169. P.R. Sanjai, "Staff Crunch Halts Shippers Plans", *Business Standard*, 31 July 2007.
170. "Thiru Baalu Addresses AGBM of Indian Institute of Maritime Studies", *Press Bureau of India*, 10 March 2008.

5

POLITICAL COMPONENTS OF MARITIME POWER

Diplomacy is fundamental to states and critical for the conduct of international relations. It is exercised to further national interests, consolidate existing relationships, or to avert a crisis/conflict and can be invoked at any time across the spectrum of cordial-adverse relationship. There is a symbiotic relationship between the state and its navy since both operate in a partnership for furtherance of national interests. States have integrated diplomacy with their navies and have found this instrument of military power a useful means to exhibit goodwill, provide humanitarian assistance, showcase technological prowess, build alliances, and for the demonstration of coercive power. In that context, navies plan and train for the entire spectrum of diplomatic activities from coercion, presence, friendship missions and disaster relief operations.

Historically, seas and oceans have facilitated movement of people, cultures, ideas, religion, and trade resulting in growth of maritime enterprise. States have also transported state power, both coercive and benign, beyond national shores through the medium of the sea. Naval diplomacy has been in vogue and practice since ancient times and was exercised by the Greeks and Romans in the Mediterranean and Cholas in India, Srivijaya in Southeast Asia and by several dynasties in China in furtherance of national interests, be it to appease powerful kingdoms, enhance trade, safeguard sea lanes, and also in its coercive format of "gunboat" diplomacy. For instance, the Chola king Rajendra Choladeva I dispatched a powerful naval fleet to Southeast Asia targeted against Srivijaya kings ostensibly to protect own trade and maritime interests. As part of diplomacy, the Srivijaya kings had sent embassies to India and China with precious gifts for the rulers and also built Buddhist vihara (temples) in these kingdoms as goodwill gestures and also to seek protection against attack by powerful neighbours. In China, the Ming rulers dispatched naval fleets to establish trade links and in its coercive construct established influence in some countries in Southeast Asia and in the Indian Ocean. In the 21st century navies continue to be the vanguard of various political roles and missions that militaries perform during peacetime.

The political milieu of maritime power serves the state in several noteworthy dimensions. The navies possess a unique profile of being instruments that are most suitable for projecting power and influence in special dimensions over distant lands. They support operations in "aid to civil power", both in the national context and in multinational operations in the entire swath of sea space across the globe. Significantly, navies are not only undergoing transformation in terms of operations, doctrines and technologies, but are in the throes of transformation to meet both the previous and emerging political requirements of the states.

This chapter endeavours to examine the changing contexts of the political elements of maritime power in its transformational scope. These are premised on competitive and cooperative maritime strategies, joint and coordinated exercises and patrols and the diplomatic-strategic imperatives of leveraging naval power for strategic maritime purposes. Also under discussion is the political discourse that shapes maritime and naval operations, doctrines, and how the decision-making in China and India exploits the maritime power of the state to achieve political goals and objectives.

At the core of this chapter is a critical analysis of the political contexts of maritime power of China and India. The chapter highlights how the rising powers perceive and shape the political outlook of maritime power. It examines the Chinese writings, articulations and conduct of naval diplomacy. Its military posturing against Taiwan, frequent encounters with the U.S. Navy and occasional presence in Japanese waters provide an insight into Chinese understanding and employment of naval forces for national objectives. Beijing's engagement in multilateral confidence-building initiatives, particularly in the South China Sea and the Straits of Malacca, shows its commitment to building cordial relations with neighbours and upholding maritime order. Likewise, the chapter highlights the Indian writings on naval diplomacy and illustrates how this instrument of the state is being used in furtherance of foreign policy objectives. The Indian naval participation and contributions to preserving order at sea, participation in UN maritime peacekeeping operations and its initiatives to engage in multilateral confidence-building initiatives built around goodwill ship visits, joint naval exercises and humanitarian assistance operations are discussed to provide insights into the Indian use of its maritime forces in naval diplomacy.

THEORIES ON NAVY AS AN INSTRUMENT OF FOREIGN POLICY

It is useful to examine some of the existing theories propounded by strategists, practitioners and academics on how states use their navies as instruments of foreign policy. Edward Luttwak coined the term "naval suasion" to explain the ability of a nation to use naval power for political purposes.[1] Luttwak describes naval suasion as "latent" and "active"; latent naval suasion is representative of the deterrent and is based on the premise that the adversary would be prevented from attacking, and the naval deployment threatens to inflict unacceptable costs on an adversary and its ally if any. On the other hand, active suasion is deliberate, purposeful and meant to send out a signal of impending naval action. This can also be used to reassure an ally or a friendly state about the determination of support against the other adversary.

James Cable argues that gunboat diplomacy is "the use or the threat of limited naval force, other than an act of war, in order to secure advantage or to avert loss, either in furtherance of an international dispute or else against foreign nationals within the territory".[2] According to Cable, navies can be used in the coercive mode in at least four different ways. These are (a) definitive force, (b) peaceful force, (c) catalytic force, and (d) expressive force. These create "crucial psychological pressures" on the enemy thereby signalling intention. In diplomacy, the use of navies is best expressed in the view: "behind the gunboat are known to lurk a cruiser, and behind the cruiser a formidable battle fleet".[3]

In the post-1982 UNCLOS III ocean order, several disputes relating to nautical boundaries and sea territories have become apparent. At times states attempt to extend the UNCLOS III regime to islands and territories where ownership and sovereignty is under dispute, which results in an unstable security environment. To reinforce their claims, states engage in making declarations and pronouncements flavoured with nationalism thus making contested territories a potential arena for combat action. There is also the attraction and promise of resources (marine and hydrocarbons) that compels states to reinforce their claims. Notwithstanding the concerns that emerge from the new nautical regime under the 1982 UNCLOS III, there is enhanced interaction among navies and coast guards of neighbouring states. This is so due to the fact that navies and coast guards are deployed on patrol till the extremities of the EEZ, where there is a very high possibility of meeting neighbouring navies. These meetings could also happen when ships cross through the EEZ of another country. In essence, routine patrols and meetings at sea result in prospects for coordinated and joint patrols, which facilitates closer cooperation. However, unscheduled sightings, particularly when ships are engaged in surveillance, snooping, or illegal survey generate mistrust and alarm.

Further, the seas are being used for piracy, gunrunning, drug smuggling and sea-based terrorism that provide additional sources of interstate tensions, particularly when states have not formulated bilateral or multilateral agreements relating to "hot pursuit", extradition treaties and legal systems that prevent illegal activities at sea. Although states acknowledge the need for cooperative approaches to uphold maritime order, there is at times an absence of diplomatic mechanisms among states that results in tensions in bilateral relations with a high possibility of confrontation. It is in this context that naval diplomacy adds pressures on national political institutions to evolve cooperative arrangements with neighbouring states to preserve order at sea and also promote national interests.

It is a well-known fact that the political dimension of maritime power has well-girded diplomatic, military and policing roles[4] that are performed by the navies through combat, benign, and constabulary operations to support a state's domestic and foreign policy objectives. In times of a crisis escalation, naval task forces serve a substantive political directive of the motivations-intentions-capabilities that it could deploy against the adversary in a given situation. At another level, the use of navies to support international humanitarian efforts termed as "disaster diplomacy" has added a new dimension to naval roles. Humanitarian assistance operationalized through the navy is both symbolic as well as substantive and is the "soft power" of the state projected through this military instrument.

The new United States maritime strategy titled "A Cooperative Strategy for 21st Century Seapower" places humanitarian and economic functions at par with high-end naval warfare.[5] The U.S. naval role in this spectrum of "soft power" operations calls for the use of naval platforms to engage in peacetime civil-military coordinated roles and missions in diverse fields in civil construction, educational initiatives, medical public health services, community development programmes and environmental protection, etc. The strategy hopes to transform the coercive combat force of the navy with a soft touch that in this age of globalization, cooperative security and interdependence, could pave the way for transforming the role of militaries, particularly the navies, into agencies for civil development in foreign lands. Thus the political context of maritime power is a wide spectrum by which navies are being leveraged for power, influence, as well as in added dimensions to facilitate the national strategy of several states of winning "hearts and minds", particularly in the cases where adversarial relations have barred cooperative mechanisms for maritime interactions.

Given that navies aid the political establishments through a number of ways, and are significant instruments for the pursuit of grand strategy, several states are developing their naval capability to evolve into enduring and sustaining forces that have the potential and the advantage of being forward deployed and flexibly leveraged to accrue maximal political gain. Consequently, the naval doctrines of these navies are in the throes of transformation, pivoting on distant deployments, sustained operations and the ability to operate autonomously both in the coercive, benign and humanitarian roles. Importantly, these doctrinal changes provide the navy wih the political context of their operations. At the heart of these developments lies the fact that navies continue to provide states with the assurance to "remain" deployed during times of peace and conflict, in any region, thus conferring a substantial prestige[6] and sense of autonomy for the state.

Navies have also emerged as important platforms that deliver to the state and its marine domain the requisite custodial and constabulary functions. Good order at sea is a critical function for the navies particularly in the context of the prevalent age of asymmetric conflicts. The rise of asymmetric actors, their propensity to challenge state authority, and the ability to inflict unimaginable loss has imposed new roles for the navies. The navies are being called upon to develop operational capabilities to provide effective monitoring of the maritime domain in their respective EEZs. Round-the-clock monitoring of EEZs is indeed a daunting task and has serious implications for maritime trade and commerce that is critically dependent on safe port access and coastal passage, particularly when the coastal areas remain porous and illegal activities continue to thrive. There are several challenges for the navies that entail a substantial balance of their traditional operational roles focused on sea-control and sea-denial operations to micro-management of low-level asymmetric threats that would be premised on naval and air operations to contend with incidents of sea piracy, counterterrorism, anti-drug and gunrunning and illegal human smuggling.

The above tasks call for real-time intelligence of asymmetric actors in an otherwise opaque maritime environment. Given that round-the-clock surveillance is an overwhelming responsibility, naval constabulary missions call for convergence of naval forces of the littoral states and extra-regional powers even though they may not have a high degree of cordial political relations as well as operational capability, yet could cooperate to contend the transnational nature of maritime asymmetric threats. Significantly, the convergence accrued is functionalist in scope and facilitates political dialogue between the cooperating states. In operational terms, coordinated and joint operations provide for sustained maritime reconnaissance/surveillance of the maritime domain, enhanced interoperability resulting in sharing of intelligence for an improved maritime domain picture and appropriate tasking orders both in concert or independently.

Interoperability with diverse navies is a significant issue that fosters multilateral maritime cooperation and allows diverse naval platforms from different countries to function seamlessly as a single unit at the tactical and operational levels to work together to meet a shared objective, which results in synergy. Perhaps what is more significant is that interoperability facilitates joint service, multi-nation, and at times *ad hoc* coalitions that bring with them a variety of platforms, personnel, doctrines and operating procedures.

These lateral cooperative initiatives provide states with the ambient conditions to develop a broad and substantive agenda for building mutual trust and confidence, and in some cases translate into strategic partnerships. These initiatives are particularly significant for naval forces that operate in close proximity to each other when engaged in surveillance functions in their respective EEZs and are yet to develop such partnerships. In the regional context, states arrive at consensus on the nature and scope of issues and challenges that they have to contend with, and with political will, they build synergies in joint and coordinated naval patrols and exercises that are usually focused on a specific operational theme. At the same time, maritime strategic partnerships are also significant for the navies that are engaged in naval modernization and evolving new missions for interoperability.

The political dividends of these initiatives give the collaborating countries new dimensions of coalition-building of naval power that can be leveraged in times of crisis. It also serves to remind potential adversaries and rising challengers, both state and non-state, that the option of balancing and countering has powerful deterrent effect to any adventurous strategies of the challenger. Maritime strategic partnerships provide opportunities to develop technological interoperability in terms of technology transfers, development of defence industrial complex, and joint operations in different maritime environments. Regionalization of maritime strategy and its operationalization with the allies of the state has immense politico-strategic overtones in statecraft that have been argued and mandated by strategists such Sun Tzu and Kautilya. In essence, a navy represents a powerful force at sea and yet is a flexible force that can be deployed or withdrawn in short periods unlike land forces. The navy can be a symbol of goodwill and humanitarianism but at the same time, with bristling weapons and sensors, it serves as a compelling and powerful deterrent.[7]

CHINESE NAVAL DIPLOMACY

Successive White Papers titled *China's National Defense* published in 1998,[8] 2002,[9] 2004,[10] and 2006[11] note that China conducts military exchanges and cooperation with other countries on the basis of the Five Principles of Peaceful Coexistence. Towards that end, the White Papers illustrate that China's armed forces have developed extensive military contacts in several countries and these have resulted in bilateral exchanges resulting in joint exercises, high-level personnel engagements, academic studies, military education, armed forces administration, sports, and several other facets of military interactions. These military initiatives serve the Chinese foreign policy and have been instrumental in enhanced interactions and military cooperation between the Chinese armed forces and other military establishments in foreign countries. In that context, the 1998 paper highlights that the Chinese armed forces have "presented themselves before the world as a civilized force and a force of peace, a force which has made its due contributions to keeping regional peace and peace throughout the world".[12]

At the military-diplomatic level, by 2006 China had established military contacts with more than 150 countries and posted military attachés in 107 countries.[13] Likewise, eighty-five foreign military attaché offices were set up in China. High-level military delegations led by defence ministers, military commanders-in-chief, high-ranking officers and military delegations belonging to defence universities and military institutions also witnessed significant increases.[14] These interactions highlight the significance of military diplomacy in Chinese foreign policy and the PLA has made significant contributions to enhance bilateral and multilateral cooperation in defence and security fields.

Chinese military diplomacy has become more "active and pragmatic" and exchanges with big militaries like the United States, Russia, Japan and India have increased. Also interactions with the militaries of the neighbouring countries, particularly Southeast Asia and several developing countries[15] have further contributed to military confidence-building measures (CBM). China believes that CBMs are effective tools for maintaining stability and security and these connections have resulted in several security dialogues and improved military cooperation with several militaries in the Asia-Pacific region as well as with the United States and European countries. China has played an active role in regional security institutions and advocated regional-security dialogue and cooperation at different levels. It participates in both Track I and Track II dialogues, workshops and conferences. It has been active in the ASEAN Regional Forum (ARF), Conference on Interaction and Confidence-Building Measures in Asia (CICA), Shanghai Cooperation Organization (SCO), Council on Security Cooperation in Asia and Pacific Region (CSCAP), and the Northeast Asia Cooperation Dialogue (NEACD).[16]

China's contribution to UN peacekeeping operations has been regular and noteworthy.[17] The 1998 White Paper asserts: "As a permanent member of the UN Security Council, China has consistently engaged in efforts to maintain international peace and security. It cherishes and supports the role of the United Nations in keeping international peace and security under the guidance of the principles of the Charter of the United Nations."[18] During 1990–98, China sent 437 military observers in thirty-two groups to six UN peacekeeping operations and by 2006 the Chinese contribution to UN peacekeeping operations increased significantly to 1,487 military personnel serving in nine UN mission areas and the UN Department of Peacekeeping Operations.[19]

According to an observer, during the last two decades China has relied on diplomacy in the conduct of international relations and promoted cordial relations with its neighbours resulting in enhanced cooperation and expansion of trade.[20] There are a few articulations or writings in the public domain on the Chinese view of naval diplomacy and navies as instruments of foreign policy. In one such articulation, it is noted that a navy is unique in its role and serves as an important tool for pursuing foreign policy. Navies possess distinctive characteristics that are different from other armed forces, demonstrated by the fact that the force enjoys freedom of navigation on the high seas and can freely engage in limited operations outside the territorial waters of the opponent.[21] It has also been argued that the Chinese follow a two-pronged strategy that pivots on diplomatic dialogue aimed at threat reduction and is flavoured with accommodation; this is reflected in China's relations with competitors such as the United States, Japan, India and Vietnam; at another level, the Chinese can be extremely assertive particularly where issues of sovereignty and territory are at play.[22] For instance, China has threatened to use force if Taiwan were to declare independence, or any act by the claimants that threatens Chinese sovereign rights over the disputed islands and other features in the South China Sea.

China has often been targeted for lack of transparency in military matters, but the Chinese have defended themselves by noting that opaqueness contributes to deterrence.²³ In the past, the military opaqueness may have facilitated exposing the weak links in the Chinese military capability resulting in a lack of international military exposure, however in recent times the Chinese appear to be more transparent in their military activities and this is best showcased through the publications of the first White Paper on security in 1995 and the subsequent White Papers on national defence in 1998, 2002, 2004 and in 2006. Interestingly, the White Paper *China's National Defense 2006* even provides details of Chinese defence spending suggesting that the Chinese are making significant progress towards transparency in military matters. Frequent interactions with foreign navies through ship visits and joint exercises, and military dialogues such as the China-ASEAN dialogue have also contributed significantly to transparency in military matters.²⁴

During the last few decades, on several occasions, China has relied on its naval power as the currency for doing business in the Asia-Pacific region. It has used force, coercive diplomacy, and intimidation to safeguard its national interests. Notwithstanding this posturing, China has also engaged in confidence-building measures aimed at enhancing stability and security in the region. It has shown signs of resolving disputes in an amicable manner through political dialogue, bilateral and multilateral cooperation and through economic engagement. China uses diplomacy in all its forms, from coercive to benign, and these can be broadly divided into at least four categories: (a) naval posturing, (b) naval CBMs, (c) challenging disorder at sea, and (d) maritime support for international relief operations.

Naval Posturing

The Chinese claims to the Spratly Islands have conflicted with those of Brunei, Malaysia, the Philippines, Taiwan, and Vietnam. Chinese maps depict virtually the entire South China Sea encompassing the Spratly Islands and the Paracel Islands as their territory. Further, the Chinese view the presence of any economic or military activity in the South China Sea as an invasion of their territory. In 1974, China clashed with Vietnam and seized the Paracel Islands. In 1988, China took over several islands in the Spratly Islands in a two-day clash. The aggressive posture continued and China clashed with the Philippines over Mischief Reef in 1995 clearly showcasing its belligerent intent. The trend towards assertive jurisdiction continued unabated, and in 1996, the two sides were again engaged in a skirmish over the Scarborough Shoal, claimed by the Philippines.

The above incidents showcase Beijing's assertiveness with regard to its disputes with other claimants to the South China Sea. There are several reasons for this posturing. First, China does not hesitate to use force when it comes to issues of its sovereignty. Second, China can be quite assertive to protect marine resources such as hydrocarbons, fish and minerals that are available in the disputed South China Sea. Third, the strategic location of the islands serves as a base for protecting China's long and vulnerable sea lines of communications. Despite the exercise of such assertiveness by China, diplomacy to prevent the escalation of disputes has a prominent place in Chinese conduct of international relations as demonstrated by the 2002 Declaration on the Conduct of Parties in the South China Sea.

Although there has been no major confrontation between China and Taiwan after the Jinmen and Matsu crisis of 1953,[25] Beijing is concerned about Taiwan declaring independence and these concerns have been the singular reason that has led to the Taiwan Straits being declared as a major flashpoint.[26] In the late 1970s, China announced the "one China and two system" policy reflecting its intention to peaceful reunite Taiwan. Taiwan on its side renounced the use of force to fight back the mainland and what emerged was a series of cross-Straits initiatives such as the Straits Exchange Foundation (SEF) and the Association for Relations Across the Taiwan Straits (ARATS).[27] However, two significant events in Taiwan resulted in China shedding the peaceful process of reunification and adopting a belligerent stand and threatening to use force against Taiwan if it declared independence. First, in 1995, Lee Teng-Hui, Taiwan's President, decided to visit Cornell University, his alma mater in the United States. China reacted sharply against the United States for its show of support for Taiwan in granting the visa to President Lee and violating the one China policy.[28] China threatened to take military action against Taiwan and conducted military exercises in the Taiwan Straits, also referred to as the "Taiwan Strait crisis" involving intimidation and a display of force. It also aimed to deter Taiwan for declaring independence. What finally emerged was a higher degree of Chinese animosity towards Taiwan and it continued to adopt a belligerent stand on the unification process. Second, on 18 July 1995, China conducted missile tests in waters about ninety miles northeast of Taipei. Six CSS-6/M-9 missiles (short-range ballistic missiles) were fired. Soon thereafter, in August 1995, about twenty PLA Navy ships and forty PLA Air Force planes carried out joint exercises in the same area and conducted missile and artillery firing. These exercises continued later into the year, and in November 1995, as legislative elections approached in Taiwan, the PLA held large-scale naval and amphibious exercises off Dongshan Island, opposite Taiwan. These were followed by major military exercises in March 1996.

Since then, bilateral relations remained tense. In 2000, after Chen Shui-bian, the Democratic Progress Party candidate, came to power, the relationship became more adversarial and official contacts between China and Taiwan under the SEF and ARATS were severed. The "anti-separation law" (ASL), enacted in 2005, clearly spells out that China could attack Taiwan if the latter announced independence and in that context China has, along its southeast coast, deployed more than a thousand missiles targeted against Taiwan[29] and the number of missiles deployed is increasing at about 100 to 120 missiles annually. Added to that, the PLA Navy has the capability to deploy nearly fifty submarines that can execute a naval blockade on Taiwan. In his New Year address in 2008, Chen Shui-bian, the Taiwanese President, noted that "Over the past seven-plus years, the number of tactical ballistic missiles deployed by China on its side of the Taiwan Strait has increased from 200 in 2000 to today's 1,328, by our accounting."[30] Further, between 2020 and 2035, China should be able to build a three-to-one advantage in total combat capabilities over Taiwan.

As far as Japan is concerned, repeated aggression from 1894 to 1945 led to a bitter sense of national humiliation and personal suffering among the Chinese. In 1992, China declared the Senkaku Islands as part of its offshore island territories.[31] In 1996, it began to undertake oil exploration activities that prompted Japan to respond by dispatching its coast guard vessels.[32] Since then, the seas around the Senkaku Islands have witnessed PLA naval activity and Chinese naval vessels routinely monitor Japanese activity.[33]

There have been several provocative attempts by the PLA Navy in Japanese waters. For instance, in November 2004, two PLA Navy vessels including a nuclear submarine were sighted in Japanese waters in a possible attempt to flex naval muscles.[34] In September 2005, the Japanese in the vicinity of a disputed undersea exploration site sighted five PLA Navy ships including a destroyer and two frigates. In May 2007, the PLA Navy flotilla transited very close through the waters off Okinawa. In September 2007, the Japanese and Chinese military aircraft were engaged in a stand-off in the air space over the disputed Chunxiao gas field, known as Shirakaba in Japanese, in the East China Sea.[35]

As far as the South China Sea is concerned, in 1992 China announced an oil exploration concession to the U.S. Crestone Company and occupied Da Lac Reef.[36] This was followed by the deployment of three Romeo-class conventional submarines to patrol the area that aroused alarms among the ASEAN states, which had just called for the non-use of force in resolving the Spratly Islands dispute as part of the Manila Declaration on the South

China Sea.³⁷ Over a period of time, China has built basic, but limited naval facilities and infrastructure on some of the islands in the South China Sea. These include satellite monitoring and communication infrastructure, gun and missile emplacements, and helicopter landing sites. Some PLA Navy vessels under the South Sea Fleet are dedicated to operations in the South China Sea and in the absence of berthing facilities in the islands, most of the naval vessels have to use the sheltered anchorages for operational turnaround, rest and recuperation. During bad weather and the cyclonic period, these forces return to the mainland and their tasks shift to satellites, shore-based reconnaissance and patrol aircraft and UAVs. In this context, Chinese naval facilities at Woody Island merit attention. Reportedly, China has built a 2,600-metre runway on the island that can handle most of its fighter aircraft.³⁸ The island is known to have a large sophisticated military garrison with electronic and satellite monitoring facilities, oil tanks and logistic support infrastructure. The shore-based missiles, possible the C 801 variety, are deployed and are capable of hitting both military and civilian ships.

Goodwill Ship Visits

Like any other navy, the PLA Navy endorses the fact that goodwill visits by navy ships is an important tool available to states to further national interests and showcase military technological prowess. It is argued that goodwill visits demonstrate China's achievements in economic, scientific and defence fields and its rising status in the international community.³⁹ Also, these naval exchanges, referred to, as "handshaking between oceans", are the most suitable means of promoting international military contact as well as to contribute to transparency.

The Chinese naval interactions with foreign navies have been built around high-level exchanges by PLA Navy chiefs, goodwill visits to foreign ports, and participation in international fleet reviews, maritime-related defence exhibitions, international maritime symposiums/conferences and joint exercises. These exchanges showcased the PLA Navy's keenness to promote goodwill and dispel fears among regional navies. Also, these exchanges have provided the PLA Navy with an opportunity to exercise with advanced navies such as the U.S. Navy, British Royal Navy, French Navy, Spanish Navy, Russian Navy, Indian Navy and several other medium and small navies. For instance, during the Sino-British naval exercises in waters off the United Kingdom, Rear Admiral Su Zhiqian, Commander of the PLA naval task group and Deputy Commander of the South China

Sea Fleet, noted that the joint Sino-British naval exercises have expanded diplomatic interactions and "promoted the constant deepening of our army's military relations" resulting in "pragmatic exchanges and cooperation" that would have "positive political and military significance".[40]

These visits also help the PLA Navy to familiarize itself with the trends in naval technology to improve its own knowledge and understand the changing nature of naval warfare. At the same time these visit have showcased to the international naval community the PLA Navy's technological sophistication. On their side, the PLA Navy has hosted several foreign ships, clearly reflecting the growing bilateral relationship with other navies and strengthening navy-to-navy contacts. During the 1980s, the PLA Navy's two-ship task group (a destroyer and tanker) undertook two overseas voyages and called at ports in South Asia (Karachi, Pakistan, Colombo, Sri Lanka and Chittagong, Bangladesh).[41] The group did not call at any Indian port since relations between the two countries were still cold and normalization only began after 1988. The second voyage to Hawaii was undertaken by the PLA Navy's training ship Zhenghe in March 1989.[42]

In the 1990s, there was a significant surge in Chinese naval overseas voyages from two to ten that witnessed port calls by the PLA Navy ships in East Asia (Russia, North Korea), Southeast Asia (Indonesia, Thailand Malaysia, and the Philippines), South Asia (Bangladesh, Pakistan, Sri Lanka and India), Latin America (Mexico, Peru and Chile), Africa (Tanzania and South Africa), and the United States (San Diego and Hawaii), thus covering the Indian and Pacific Oceans.[43] Significantly, the destroyers (Luhu and Luda class) were the lead ships of the group and were escorted by a tanker. These voyages enabled China to build military contacts in different countries across the globe and showcased their naval capability and the ability to operate far from homeports. In all, the PLA Navy task groups called at ports in nearly twenty countries; beginning 2000 till 2007, the PLA Navy undertook foreign voyages on an annual basis and also to ports in Europe comprising thirteen voyages and calling at ports in thirty-seven countries. Like the earlier voyages, these too have been led by the destroyers and frigates (Luhai and Luhu class destroyers and Jiangwei class frigates) and often escorted by a tanker. On its side, in the 1980s, the PLA Navy was host to 23 foreign ships from 14 countries, 30 ships from 17 countries during the 1990s and 25 warships had called at Chinese ports up until August 2006. Thus the PLA Navy has benefitted from its ships calling at foreign ports and also by hosting foreign vessels in Chinese ports.

Naval Confidence-building Measures

During the Cold War, U.S. and Soviet maritime superiority was clearly visible at sea. Both forces sailed close to each other and there were many "close quarter" situations at sea that resulted in several accidents involving ships, submarines and aircraft. The U.S. and Soviet domination went unchallenged and the PLA Navy had not encountered these forces, and thus did not feel the necessity of developing any kind of naval confidence-building measures with these navies. Besides, the PLA Navy ships' "area of operations" was limited to its territorial waters and close to its shores. It rarely sailed out on long deployments far into the sea and was quite content with the then existing state of affairs. However, a series of incidents involving China and the United States resulted in bilateral confidence-building measures at sea.

In July 1993, the Chinese flagged container ship *Yinhe*, suspected of carrying banned chemicals to Iran was stopped at sea but not boarded.[44] The Chinese had vehemently denied that the vessel carried illegal or contraband cargo but it was refused entry to a number of ports in the Persian Gulf. After inspections by the Chinese and Saudi inspectors, the vessel was allowed to proceed to its original destination. The Chinese Government accused the United States of violating international law, freedom of innocent passage and conduct of legitimate international trade.

A year later, on 27 October 1994, the PLA Navy and the U.S. Navy were involved in an incident involving the *USS Kitty Hawk*, the U.S. Navy aircraft carrier and a nuclear-powered submarine in the Yellow Sea (some 100 nautical miles west of Kyushu, Japan).[45] After the U.S. battle group departed Yokosuka naval base in Japan, a Chinese Han class nuclear submarine had been shadowing the carrier. U.S. Navy S3 anti-submarine aircraft from the carrier spotted the submarine some 450 nautical miles from the carrier and the Chinese dispatched fighter aircraft to intercept U.S. planes. No shots were fired, there was no communication between the two forces and the cat-and-mouse game continued till the submarine closed to twenty-one nautical miles from the carrier and finally returned to base.[46] Reportedly, a U.S. military attaché in Beijing was cautioned by the Chinese that if such a confrontation takes place again, the Chinese would not hesitate to shoot.[47] The 1994 *USS Kitty Hawk*-PLA Navy Han incident forced both navies to develop a mutual arrangement for maritime contingencies to avoid misunderstandings, inadvertent tensions and work towards common communication procedures.

In reaction to the 1995–96 Chinese saber ratting and missile firings to intimidate Taiwan, the United States dispatched two carrier battle groups, i.e. *USS Independence* and *USS Nimitz* along with their escorts comprising sixteen vessels, as a "show of force".[48] The Chinese leaders were surprised by the strong U.S. reaction and the military exercises targeted against Taiwan were scaled down. But it was almost two years after the Taiwan Strait crisis that the Military Maritime Consultative Agreement (MMCA) was discussed.[49] In January 1998, China and the United States signed the "Agreement Between the Ministry of National Defence of the PRC and the Department of Defense of the USA on Establishing a Consultation Mechanism to Strengthen Military Maritime Safety".[50] Between 1996 and 1997 there was a series of talks and visits that were initiated by the U.S. side under the leadership of the then Commander of the U.S. Pacific Fleet Admiral Joseph Prueher. The U.S. Defense Secretary William Cohen and China's Defence Minister General Chi Haotian finally signed the agreement on 19 January 1998. The agreement aimed to increase understanding and reduce the chances of miscalculation between the respective naval and air forces.[51]

The MMCA is the first ever agreement on confidence-building measures between the maritime forces of China and the United States. The agreement paved the way for establishing a forum of dialogue on maritime communication issues and it was decided to hold these meeting on a regular basis to enhance mutual trust and encourage cooperation between the two navies.[52] Among the issues discussed were the techniques and procedures for communications at sea between ships and aircraft. This was especially important because U.S. naval officers had rarely communicated with Chinese ships or aircraft at sea. Since 1997, China and the U.S. have held seven annual meetings, twelve working groups meetings and one special meeting on consultation mechanisms on strengthening maritime military safety.[53] The mechanism has played an important role in enhancing mutual understanding and trust, promoting China-U.S. maritime military safety, and deepening exchanges and cooperation between the two navies.

Notwithstanding the provisos of the MMCA, the PLA Navy continued to challenge the U.S. Navy ships and aircraft. In one of the more serious stand-offs between the United States and China, a U.S. Navy EP-3 spy plane collided with one of the fighters of the PLA Navy.[54] The Chinese naval fighter aircraft crashed, and its pilot was missing and presumed dead. The U.S. plane suffered major damage and was forced to land at an airbase at Hainan, China. After several diplomatic parlays, the Chinese Government, out of humanitarian consideration, decided to let the U.S. crew go, but detained the aircraft.

In 2006, the *USS Kitty Hawk* was once again at the centre of attention when a Chinese Song class diesel submarine penetrated the carrier defences.[55] The submarine surfaced close to the aircraft carrier, which surprisingly was not operating its anti-submarine warfare (ASW) equipment and there were no ASW aircraft in the air to warn the carrirer about the lurking Chinese submarine. What perhaps merits greater attention is the fact that the Chinese conventional submarine had penetrated the aircarft carrier underwater defence screen and surprised it, clearly exposing the vulnerability of large platforms like the aircarft carriers. Significantly, the incident highlighted chinks in the MMCA and raised questions about Chinese intentions and commitment to uphold bilateral agreements such as the MMCA.

The Chinese can be quite unpredictable in developing naval CBMs. For instance, in 2007, China rejected a U.S. request for the frigate USS *Reuben James* permission to enter Hong Kong harbour for New Year's Eve. It also refused permission to U.S. minesweepers to enter Hong Kong for a halt when the vessels were encountering inclement weather at sea. In another instance, China refused the USS *Kitty Hawk* a scheduled visit to Hong Kong during Thanksgiving holidays but did a volte-face later and announced that the carrier could dock in Hong Kong. The official spokesperson stated, "We have already decided to allow the USS *Kitty Hawk* aircraft carrier group to stay in Hong Kong for rest and reorganization during Thanksgiving. It is based completely on humanitarianism."[56]

The Chinese refusal to allow the USS *Kitty Hawk* was particularly worrisome to the United States as the two sides had agreed to establish a hotline to prevent misunderstandings that could lead to conflict. Reportedly, these successive refusals were linked to a series of U.S. actions involving the honouring of the Dalai Lama and the proposed military sales to Taiwan that included upgrade of the Raytheon Patriot air and missile defence system, refurbished P-3 Corion maritime patrol aircraft and diesel submarines.[57] Any attempt by the United States to augment Taiwan's military capability is of serious concern to China and Beijing has conveyed its apprehensions to the United States on several occasions.

Notwithstanding these differences and mistrust, in February 2008, China and the United States signed an agreement to set up a DTL (defence telephone link) for quick communication in times of crisis.[58] The two sides also agreed to share archives to facilitate finding the remains of U.S. military personnel missing in the 1950–53 Korean War. Besides being a naval CBM, the DTL will also facilitate quick decision-making to defuse a crisis between the two sides. For the United States, this is significant because decision-making during crisis in China is slow as a number of civilian and military departments must be consulted before anyone can take decisions on behalf of the Chinese Government.[59] For instance, during the EP 3 incident in 2001, it took a long time to secure the release of the crew. Although it took more than two years to negotiate the DTL, the initiative is symbolic and in the perspective of Admiral Timothy Keating, Commander, U.S. military forces in Asia and the Pacific, "We really don't need a hotline for better communications, technically. There's a broader point, meaning it will give us a better sense of communications even if it won't make it any easier or harder to communicate."[60]

Like the United States, Japan too is concerned about Chinese intentions of upholding bilateral naval confidence-building measures. On its side, Beijing remains suspicious of long-term Japanese security policies, the U.S.-Japan security alliance and its territorial disputes over Senkaku Islands whose waters are rich in energy and other marine resources. Of particular concern to China is the growth of the Japanese military capability and how Japan would react to China's rise. Several historical and political obstacles preclude maritime CBMs between the two sides, but in recent times, there have been several initiatives to build better relations between the two navies. For instance, in August 2007, China and Japan agreed to establish a crisis hotline and commence naval ship visits.[61] The hotline gains greater significance in the light of the fact that a PLA Navy submarine surfaced in Japanese waters in 2004 much to the discomfort of the Japanese. Although bilateral ship visits were planned in May 2002, several political issues prevented military exchange between the two sides. Nearly half a decade later, in November 2007, a PLA Navy ship visited Tokyo. The Japanese Defence Minister Shigeru Ishiba noted, "The two countries should strengthen defence communications in the future to eliminate misunderstanding and build up a relationship in which different opinions could be thoroughly discussed … Japan's SDF warship is to pay visit to China following the PLA Navy warship's Japan visit."[62]

China and India fought a bitter war in 1962 in the Himalayas. After restoration of diplomatic relations, naval contacts were established in 1994, marked by the visit of PLA Navy training ship Zheng He to Mumbai. This was followed by a successful reciprocal goodwill visit in 1995 by a flotilla of two Indian naval vessels to Shanghai. In 2000, the Indian Navy transited through the South China Sea and announced exercises in the area. This Indian plan was perceived by China as a direct challenge since it considers the entire South China Sea as its waters. Observers pointed out that the Chinese are in the habit of "making noise over an issue because they don't want their basic views to be ignored by the international community. Subsequently, though, they work out practical solutions."[63] In February 2001, China declined to participate in the Indian Navy International Fleet Review (IFR), "bridges of friendship" to commemorate India's fifty years of independence. Chinese protests over Indian naval manoeuvres in the South China Sea may have been one of the reasons. Close on its heels, in May 2001, two Chinese naval vessels, with an Admiral embarked on board, visited Karachi in connection with the Fiftieth Anniversary celebrations of Pakistan-China relations, clearly sending out a signal to India that its relations with Pakistan are more important. In that context, Rear Admiral Zhang Yan, Deputy Commander North Sea Fleet, noted that Pakistan and China were great neighbours and that their friendship was time-tested.[64]

After decades of animosity, China has found in Russia a great friend. China's interest in Russia is showcased by the fact that the latter has emerged as a major source of military equipment for the PLA. The gradual Sino-Russian reconciliation, closer interaction under the Shanghai Cooperation Organization (SCO), the six-nation grouping involving Central Asian Republics, China and Russia, has paved the way for bilateral cooperation involving naval exercises. For instance, the Peace Mission 2005 naval exercise had three purposes. From Beijing's and Moscow's perspectives, the manoeuvres signalled to the United States its new military competitors in the Western Pacific; individually, for the Chinese it was a display of force targeted against Taiwan, and for Russia it displayed its military-industrial complex to the Chinese, who are looking for modern military hardware in the absence of other sources of military hardware in the West.[65]

At the functional-operational level, China is a member of the ISMERLO (International Submarine Escape and Rescue Liaison Office).[66] Established in 2004, the ISMERLO is a submarine-operating nations' organization that helps coordinate international submarine rescue by providing assistance.

Preserving Order at Sea

Chinese ports have generally remained free of piracy but seas around China have witnessed several pirate attacks in the South China Sea and East China Sea. During 1992–94, the sea areas bound by the triangle Hong Kong-Luzon-Hainan Island (HLH) had been notified as hot spots of sea piracy. Interestingly, the attacks in this area were referred to as "quasi-military" and the Chinese officials were suspected of being responsible for such activities.[67] Also, there were several attacks on Russian- and Japanese-flagged vessels in the East China Sea that prompted Russia to deploy its naval forces to protect shipping. Japan and China established hotlines between their Coast Guards which resulted in a significant decline in piracy-related attacks in the area. Notwithstanding that, China was under international pressure for not taking legal action against culprits and providing safe haven for pirates and captured vessels.[68] Protest by the International Maritime Bureau (IMB) and the Baltic and International Maritime Council (BIMCO) prompted China to establish the

Customs Administrative and Public Security Department for anti-smuggling operations. Since then, Chinese waters have generally remained free of piracy as the hot spots had shifted elsewhere, particularly in the Straits of Malacca.

In recent times, China has been proactive in supporting international efforts to enhance the safety and security of maritime traffic in the Straits of Malacca. It is estimated that nearly 60 per cent of Chinese crude is sourced from the Middle East[69] and given the growing demands this figure is sure to rise beyond 70 per cent in the near future,[70] the bulk of which would naturally transit through the Straits of Malacca. In that context, China is an important stakeholder in the safety and security issues in the Southeast Asian region, particularly in the Straits of Malacca. As part of its diplomatic initiatives, China offered assistance to improve the safety and security of merchant traffic transiting the Straits of Malacca.[71] For instance, in 2004, China expressed willingness to provide assistance to the Strait littorals to fight transnational crimes, protect the marine environment and help improve safety and security for the transiting traffic. In 2005, it reiterated its stand of supporting the littoral states in enhancing safety and security in the Strait. After the 2005 meeting, China offered to finance the project on replacement of navigational aids damaged during the 2004 Indian Ocean Tsunami and the estimated cost for the project is pegged at US$276,000.

China's assistance during natural disasters abroad has been quite significant and it has provided assistance to the affected countries during the earthquake in Pakistan and Hurricane Katrina in the United States.[72] However, China's response to the 2004 Indian Ocean Tsunami disaster prompted severe criticism due to the small amount of donations for the tsunami-affected countries[73] clearly reflecting the limitations of a rising power. Perhaps what was more discomforting to China was its exclusion from the core group comprising the United States, Australia, and India as these countries quickly deployed their warships for relief efforts. The PLA Navy, Asia's largest navy in numerical terms, was conspicuously absent in international relief efforts and this inadequacy reflected poorly on China's naval diplomacy, exposed its weakness to undertake distant water sustained operations, as well as its lack of experience in working with multinational forces. For instance, it was noted that the Japanese dispatched a JMSDF vessel thus demonstrating their great power status; the United States deployed its carrier task force, and the Indian Navy was in the vanguard of the disaster relief operations.[74] Notwithstanding that, China offered material and financial support but in some quarters it was believed that the Chinese assistance was "motivated not by concern for the tsunami victims, but rather by economic and political considerations".[75] Be that as it may, it was important for Beijing to contribute to a multinational relief effort. The Chinese do acknowledge the fact that the armed forces are required to engage in non-traditional military operations such as national reconstruction, disaster relief and rebuilding.

INDIAN NAVAL DIPLOMACY

One of the important roles of the Indian Navy is to engage in naval diplomacy to support India's foreign policy objectives. Since its inception, the Indian Navy has been actively engaged in furthering national foreign policy objectives, facilitating closer relations with several countries across the globe and building "maritime bridges" with like-minded states. It has participated in international fleet reviews, rendered relief during disasters, conducted joint exercises and anti-piracy patrols, provided waterfront security to states and developed institutional linkages with several navies aimed at building confidence and trust.

Currently, India is an active member of several international and regional arrangements for maritime cooperation at both government and non-government levels. It is signatory to the UNCLOS III, member of Indian Ocean Rim-Association for Regional Cooperation (IOR-ARC), ASEAN Regional Forum (ARF), East Asia Summit (EAS), Association for Bangladesh-India-Myanmar-Sri Lanka-Thailand Economic Cooperation (BIMST-EC), South Asia Association for Regional Cooperation (SAARC), Council for Security Cooperation in Asia Pacific (CSCAP), as an observer in the Western Pacific Naval Symposium (WPNS)[76] and Regional Cooperation Agreement on Combating Piracy and Armed Robbery Against Ships in Asia (ReCAAP). India also participates in several maritime security-related events including defence exhibitions, seminars, symposia, and conferences at both Track I and II levels such as the International Maritime Defence Exhibitions (IMDEX) in the Persian Gulf and Southeast Asia, Langkawi International Maritime and Aerospace Exhibition (LIMA), International Seapower Symposium in the United States, and Shangri-La Dialogue in Singapore. At another level, the Indian Navy hosts events such as MILAN, Indian Ocean Naval Symposia (IONS), International Fleet Reviews (IFR), symposia, seminars and conferences as part of its engagement in naval diplomacy.

During the last two decades, the Indian Navy has been proactive in support of national foreign policy objectives evidenced in its involvement in UN sponsored activities to support international commitments, significant participation in joint naval exercises aimed at a cooperative approach to maritime security, interoperability with diverse navies, building trust and confidence, frequent flag-showing missions reflecting technological prowess, assistance during natural disasters showcasing the soft power of the nation, and preserving order at sea, thus contributing to international efforts aimed at enhancing maritime safety and security. These initiatives are a pointer towards the Indian Navy's capacity and capability to further national interests. In that context, participation by power projection platforms like aircraft carriers, destroyers, submarines and frigates in the above roles and missions have added to India's prestige and provided the opportunity to showcase India's resolve to safeguard maritime interests and also to project Indian naval technological capability.

The Indian Navy's perspectives on the political dimensions of maritime power can be understood through a variety of documents, articulations, pronouncements, initiatives and activities. The *Strategic Defence Review* (SDR) defines naval diplomacy as "the use of naval force as a diplomatic instrument in support of foreign policy and is designed to influence the adversary in peace time and in all situations short of full hostility".[77] The application of naval diplomacy is to be achieved in three distinct ways: (a) presence, (b) preventive and precautionary diplomacy, and (c) pre-emptive diplomacy. The SDR notes that one of the traditional ways of signifying naval presence is through port calls aimed at building friendship, showcasing technological prowess, and at the same time sending a message of the effectiveness of the navy and the state that owns it; however, these visits are not intended to represent threat of force, instead, the ships act as goodwill ambassadors to create a favourable impression. At the other end of the spectrum, the SDR observes that a customized naval force, under specific rules of engagement, poised for national objectives serves preventive diplomacy. Such deployments influence the adversary in the initial stage of a crisis by positioning naval forces and carrying out offensive manoeuvres and this demonstration contributes to crisis prevention.

The Indian Maritime Doctrine (IMD) stipulates the missions envisioned for the Indian Navy: (a) Military, (b) Diplomatic, (c) Constabulary, and (d) Benign.[78] Essentially, these missions are based on the triangle of "uses of the navy" propounded by Ken Booth (Diplomatic Role, Military Role and Policing Role) and slightly modified by Eric Grove (Diplomatic Role, Military Role and Constabulary Role).[79] The Indian Navy has further expanded the triangle to a "pyramid of roles" with the Indian Navy at the apex and the Military Role, the Diplomatic Role, the Constabulary or Policing Role and the Benign Role forming the base.[80]

Under the diplomatic role, the Indian Navy is to act as an instrument of national foreign policy, build maritime partnerships, contribute to UN peacekeeping operations, and develop capabilities for interoperability with multinational forces. Under the military component, the Indian Navy is required to provide conventional and strategic nuclear deterrence, deter intervention by extra-regional powers, and exercise sea control in designated areas of the Arabian Sea and the Bay of Bengal. The navy must also guard India's mercantile marine and seaborne trade, both during peace and war, and provide security to India's coastline, island territories, and offshore assets from seaborne threats. The navy should also be able to project power, land the army in areas of interest, and be able to provide second- strike nuclear capability in the event of a nuclear conflict.

The benign roles for the Indian Navy include its participation and contribution to both international and domestic Humanitarian Assistance and Disaster Relief (HADR), search and rescue (SAR), pollution control, diving assistance, salvage operations, and hydrographical support. The doctrine reinforces the traditional naval thinking that the navies are the only instruments of state that are flexible forces and can be legally deployed in the entire spectrum of conflict from peace to war and across the entire swath of the oceans. Also, the navy is a powerful instrument endowed with deterrence and mobility and the doctrine sees the Indian Navy play a key role in shaping India's destiny in the emergent world order.

In the Indian context, strategists, practitioners and academics have studied and articulated their views on naval diplomacy. An Indian naval legal expert notes that navies are important tools for foreign policy management without the actual use of force[81] and naval diplomacy is guided by three factors: (a) strong political will to deploy warships to achieve foreign policy objectives, (b) the right types of warships, and (c) an opportunity to deploy. It is argued that states employ their navies to achieve foreign policy objectives and also to demonstrate strength to coerce, to compel, abstaining from doing any act, supportive role, influence-building or symbolic tasks. The new nautical regime under UNCLOS III has also affected naval diplomacy,[82] since the extension of territorial waters out to twelve nautical miles and an EEZ of 200 nautical miles at sea where states enjoy sovereign rights. It is argued that there are three ways in which UNCLOS III will impact naval diplomacy. First, naval diplomacy will become more assertive because "legal and psycho-legal boundaries would offer states a chance to send clear diplomatic signals". Secondly, the existing EEZ regime under UNCLOS III has resulted in 40 per cent of the world's ocean being brought under national jurisdiction and could lead to the downfall of naval diplomacy. It is important to bear in mind that warships and merchant ships enjoy the status of neutrality in the EEZs and therefore naval diplomacy will continue to be effective since the nautical regime does not hamper coercive/demonstrative military manoeuvres. Further, UNCLOS III will not be able to prevent naval influence involving goodwill visits and humanitarian operations.

Successive Indian naval leadership has consistently aired views on the role of the Indian Navy as an instrument of foreign policy and these have been reflected in the Indian Navy's deployment patterns. In 1992, an Indian naval task group comprising INS Kuthar (corvette), INS Deepak (tanker) and INS Cheetah (amphibious ship) participated in the humanitarian relief operations in support of the war-stricken and famine-affected people of Somalia, under Operation Restore Hope, a United States-led coalition initiative, and mandated by the UN.[83] The Indian Navy deployed its second task group comprising INS Ganga (frigate), INS Godavri (frigate) and INS Shakti (tanker) in the naval presence role in support of the de-induction of Indian Army units from Kismayu and Mogadishu. During their deployment, the naval units spent 347 ship days maintaining vigil along the Somali coast and ports. In essence, the Indian Navy switched its role from its humanitarian mission to a coercive format showcasing the flexibility of the force that can be deployed across a wide spectrum of activities.

The Indian Navy played a significant role in support of international disaster relief operations in the aftermath of the 26 December 2004 Tsunami tidal waves that hit the shores of eleven Indian Ocean littoral countries, namely Bangladesh, Burma, India, Indonesia, Kenya, Malaysia, Maldives, Somalia, Sri Lanka, Tanzania and Thailand. More than thirty naval ships and two-dozen aircraft and helicopters were deployed in support of rescue and relief missions both at home and abroad.[84] India was part of the core group of four countries alongside the United States, Japan and Australia to coordinate aid efforts in the affected areas. The international community acknowledged India's capability and it registered its presence in the tsunami-affected region as a compassionate power capable of helping its neighbours even when its own shores are troubled.

The Indian Navy's disaster relief efforts have exhibited its disaster response strategy and showcased its capability to assist any regional country during disaster crisis. For instance, in 2007, four Indian Navy ships transported 5,000 tonnes of rice in response to the devastation caused by Cyclone Sidr in Bangladesh.[85] Similarly, Indian Navy ships were mobilized to transport relief materials to Myanmar after the devastating Cyclone Nargis hit it in May 2008.[86]

Joint naval exercises too have been significant to the Indian Navy to promote maritime cooperation and these have contributed to a greater understanding with foreign navies, developed trust and contributed to transparency and an understanding of each others' rules of engagement, operating procedures, and communication plans and aircraft operations. Between 1989 and 2000, the Indian Navy conducted nearly fifty joint naval exercises, both institutionalized and Passage Exercises (PASSEX) with at least twenty countries.[87] Significant among these have been the institutionalized interaction with the navies of the United States, France, Russia, the United Kingdom, Singapore, Sri Lanka, and Indonesia. Besides, the Indian Navy has also conducted PASSEX with visiting warships from Germany, Mauritius, the Seychelles and Japan. In essence, the navy has established itself as a force with which both advanced and coastal navies are able to conduct joint naval exercises, clearly showcasing its adaptability to conduct business with navies of different levels of capabilities and sophistication.

Since 1995, the Indian Navy has also been hosting "Milan" meetings at Port Blair in the Andaman and Nicobar Islands in the Bay of Bengal. "Milan" in Hindi means "confluence" and these biennial meetings are aimed at fostering closer cooperation among navies of countries in the extended neighbourhood of the Southeast and as far as Australia.[88] In 2001, the Indian Navy hosted the International Fleet Review (IFR), the first of its kind since 1953 and addressing the gathering of naval ships from twenty-three countries the Indian Prime Minister noted that the Indian Navy "plays a crucial role in India's cooperation with other countries, especially those that share maritime borders. Active cooperation between navies is a must in [these] times of sea piracy, gunrunning and drug menace, which are all part of international terrorism."[89] It was also noted that institutionalized arrangements facilitate "bridges of friendship" which was the theme of the fleet review.

Expanding on the MILAN, in February 2008, the Indian Navy hosted the Indian Ocean Naval Symposium (IONS–2008) at New Delhi.[90] Naval delegations from twenty-nine countries of the Indian Ocean participated in the symposium followed by a two-day conclave for the naval chiefs of the participating countries. The symposium "Contemporary Trans-National Challenges: International Maritime Connectivities", served as a platform to address maritime-related security concerns and explore solutions without extra-regional assistance, clearly reflecting a shift from competitive to collective security paradigm. As the name of the initiative suggests, delegations from Indian Ocean states Eritrea, Brazil, the Seychelles, Kuwait, Qatar, Mauritius, Madagascar, Myanmar, Oman, Sri Lanka, the United Arab Emirates, Kenya, Djibouti, Egypt, Mozambique, South Africa, Sudan, Tanzania, Malaysia, Maldives, Indonesia, Australia, Thailand and France attended the seminar. Addressing the delegates at the Symposium, the Indian Prime Minister stated that the "need for cooperation among navies of the region in preventing such global crimes is therefore of paramount importance". Expressing similar sentiments, the Defence Minister noted that dialogue and cooperation between countries promotes regional peace and stability and promotes mutual understanding and enhances transparency. Though ambitious, the IONS seeks to enhance a regional understanding of maritime security issues confronting Indian Ocean countries, building regional capacity and enhancing stability. For this to be achieved, the IONS proposes the establishment of a variety of consultative and cooperative mechanisms designed to address and mitigate regional maritime security challenges through naval exercises, information-sharing and regional capacity-building.

The cooperative maritime initiatives by the Indian Navy with regional and extra-regional navies has enabled exchanges on operational issues involving sharing of doctrinal expertise, exchange of transformational experiences, imbibing of "best-practices", interoperability, and Maritime Domain Awareness through a variety of information-sharing mechanisms.[91] However, these maritime interactions are "predicated on step-by-step processes" that would result in building capacity among the smaller littoral states resulting in self-confidence. At the institutional level, in September 2005, the Indian Navy established the Directorate of Foreign Cooperation (DFC), a nodal agency under the direct supervision of the Assistant Chief of the Naval Staff (Foreign Cooperation and Intelligence), a two-star Admiral, for planning and execution of missions in support of the navy's diplomatic role in close coordination with the Ministry of External Affairs.[92]

Since the 1990s, India has been nurturing an ascendant operation maritime profile. It has established bilateral engagements with the United States, Russia, France, the United Kingdom, Israel, Japan and several countries in the Southeast Asian region. Codenamed Malabar, the Indo-U.S. naval exercises were conceptualized in 1992 to mark the beginning of a new relationship between India and the United States,[93] and fourteen such naval exercises have taken place in the past. In the beginning these exercises were rudimentary and these have progressively improved in content and complexity with participation by several complex platforms such as aircraft carriers, nuclear submarines and long-range maritime patrol aircraft.[94] The exercises paved the way for greater understanding between the naval forces and helped to develop a broad framework for operating together in support of non-military operations such as anti-piracy, safety of sea lanes and anti-drug and gunrunning patrols. The 1998 Indian nuclear tests abruptly ended cooperation between the two navies, but bilateral exercises were resumed and the cooperation got a boost with the Indian Navy dispatching a naval helicopter to *USS Hewitt* to carry out the medical evacuation of a U.S. navy sailor.[95]

Similarly, the Indian Navy has developed institutional naval interaction with the French Navy through the Varuna series of naval exercises, Indra series with the Russian Navy, Simbex series with the Republic of Singapore Navy, Konkan series with the British Royal Navy and several exercises with the Japanese Navy and the Coast Guard. As part of South-South cooperation, i.e. India, Brazil and South Africa (IBSA), the Indian Navy has institutionalized interaction with the navies of South Africa and Brazil. The interaction envisages joint naval exercises codenamed IBSAMAR (IBSA Maritime) that seek increased interoperability and enhanced understanding and cooperation among the navies and the first such exercise was conducted off South African waters in May 2008.[96] As far as the Indian Navy is concerned, the bilateral interaction has been limited to port calls and rudimentary naval exercises that have not seen any significant improvement in their content since their beginning in the 1990s.

The Indian Ministry of Defence Annual Report 2006–07 notes that the Indian Navy has employed interoperability as an important tool for naval confidence-building and several navies are eager to exercise with the Indian Navy.[97] These bilateral exercises assist in developing skills for joint operations to address problems related to maritime order and in establishing professional relationships with other navies. Interoperability has also facilitated institutionalized naval interactions with the United States, Russia, France, the United Kingdom, Oman, Sri Lanka and Singapore and coordinated patrols continue with Indonesia and Thailand. What is perhaps more significant in these interactions is the factor of interoperability that has facilitated such naval interactions.

At the functional-operational level, during Malabar 07-2, the Indian Navy showcased its capability to be interoperable with the most advanced navy, i.e. the United States Navy.[98] For instance, Indian ships used NATO standards "MTP" document for communication frequencies, technical terminology, command structures and were even fitted with special U.S. equipment to connect to its Centrix satellite-based system that enabled the exchange of audio, video and data between the participating ships. Perhaps the most significant interoperability among naval forces was displayed when an Indian Sea Harrier fighter "buddy refuelled" from an F-18 Super Hornet. Similarly, the opportunity to operate with a sophisticated underwater platform such as the nuclear submarine (*USS Chicago*) during the exercise was a unique example of interoperability.

Commenting on the Malabar 07-2, Vice Admiral William Crowder, Commander of U.S. Seventh Fleet, noted, "These are the sort of things that require really high-end skills. There is no other exercise available to develop such capabilities."[99] According to Rear Admiral Nigel Coates, Commander Australian Fleet, "Exercise Malabar is a great training opportunity and is advantageous to the readiness and professional development of the participating navies."[100] Commenting on the multinational exercises, Vice Admiral Yoji Koda, Commander of the Japan Maritime Self Defence Force (JMSDF) "Internationally, Navies understand each other", and "We are flexible enough to learn the different ways from the international navies and it is easy for us to become friends on humanitarian issues."[101] From an Indian naval perspective, "The smoothness of operations was incredible. We understand each other's way of communication and to some extent have got an insight to the thinking each side does."[102]

In the immediate neighbourhood, Sri Lanka has been an important arena for Indian naval diplomacy. Beginning in 1971, Indian Navy ships operated off Sri Lanka to blockade any supply of arms, and ammunitions/stores for the militant group Janatha Vimukti Perumuna (JVP). This was in response to a Sri Lankan request that India provide naval vessels to carry out patrolling in waters in South Sri Lanka and prevent gunrunning/incursions by the militant groups.[103] In 1988, the Indian Navy executed Operation Pawan in waters around Sri Lanka, particularly Palk Bay, in pursuance of a request made by the Sri Lankan Government to counter the LTTE (Tamil Tigers).[104] In August 2008, the Indian Navy deployed its vessels off Colombo, outside Sri Lankan territorial waters, to provide waterside security to the SAARC summit against a possible attack by the LTTE.[105]

The Indian Navy has also been effectively deployed for safeguarding the sovereignty of smaller nations.[106] On 3 November 1988, two trawlers carrying 150 PLOTE (People's Liberation Organization of Tamil Eelam) mercenaries landed in the Maldives[107] and overpowered the Maldivian Militia using rockets and machine guns and attacked the President's residence. The Maldivian Government sent out calls asking for India's assistance, Operation Cactus was launched and Indian Navy warships later captured the fleeing mercenaries.

Unlike Sri Lanka and the Maldives, India and Pakistan do not enjoy cordial relations and the two sides have fought four wars. There is a strong animosity and the militaries are forward deployed and maintain an eyeball-to-eyeball contact on their land borders. Both the Indian Navy and the Pakistan Navy meet each other frequently at sea and engage in frequent shadowing and buzzing of each other force's reminiscent of the Cold War in which the U.S. and Soviet naval forces had engaged.[108] These incidents continue unabated to date with few diplomatic protests from either side. During one such incident two MiG 21 aircraft of the Indian Air Force shot down a Pakistan Navy Atlantique maritime reconnaissance aircraft that had intruded into

Indian airspace. A 1991 agreement clearly spells out that aircraft will not fly within ten kilometres of each other's airspace,[109] and the failure to abide by the agreement resulted in loss of life as well as a maritime asset.

Although India and Pakistan have made positive declaratory statements to serve conciliatory purposes,[110] these statements have failed to generate trust and confidence. Besides, there is a dispute with regard to the maritime boundary in the Sir Creek area.[111] Despite several meetings of experts from both sides, the boundary dispute continues and Coast Guards of the two countries have often intruded into each other's EEZ to exercise control. In recent times, the two agencies have established "hot lines" to prevent incidents at sea.[112] Under the circumstances, the bilateral naval relationship between India and Pakistan is uncertain and volatile.

As far as naval coercion is concerned, Indian experiences present a mixed bag of successes and failures. In the past, on two different occasions, the Indian Navy was a victim of coercive diplomacy. First, in 1965 during the Indo-Pakistani war, Indonesia dispatched a submarine to Pakistan to deter India and also threatened to open another war front in the Andaman and Nicobar Islands.[113] President Soekarno of Indonesia noted that an attack on Pakistan was like an attack on Indonesia and agreed to provide whatever Pakistan needed for its war effort against India. The Indonesian naval chief was of the view that the Andaman and Nicobar Islands were an extension of Sumatra and even enquired if Pakistan wanted Indonesia to take over. The Indonesian Navy began to patrol around the islands and also dispatched a submarine and missile boats to Pakistan.

In the second incident, the United States dispatched the Seventh Fleet, comprising the aircraft carrier *USS Enterprise*, and its escorts towards the Bay of Bengal, ostensibly to deter India against Pakistan during the 1971 Indo-Pakistan conflict. It is believed that the motive of this display of force was "to ensure the protection of U.S. interests in the area".[114] No Indian naval vessel encountered the U.S. Seventh Fleet. While another observer notes that the presence of the U.S. carrier task force could divert Indian attention and weaken India's blockade of "East Pakistan" ports, divert the Indian aircraft carrier Vikrant from its military mission and force India to keep planes on defence alert, thus reducing offensive operations against Pakistani ground forces.[115]

In the "compelling" format, in 2001 the Indian Navy reinforced the Western Fleet at Mumbai with naval assets from the Eastern Fleet headquartered at Vishakhapatnam to force Pakistan to vacate the Kargil sector in North India occupied by the Pakistan Army. The build-up was also aimed at imposing a naval blockade of the Karachi port. The Indian fleet conducted offensive manoeuvres in the Arabian Sea resulting in the Pakistani naval fleet operating very close to its coast. A Pakistani commentator interpreted this to mean that the Indian Navy was preparing to enforce a "quarantine or blockade of the coastline" and prevent the supply of oil from the Persian Gulf.[116] It is argued that this "was an important factor, which led to Pakistan's humiliating withdrawal from the heights of Kargil and the Indian Navy played its part in convincing the Pakistani military leadership of the futility of prolonging the Kargil conflict".[117]

Preserving maritime order and safety of sea lanes is one of the missions of the Indian Navy. The Indian Defence Minister A.K. Antony, speaking at an interactive session at the Pravasi Bharatiya Divas 2007, pointed out that "... Another key foreign policy related issue is security of shipping and sea lanes", in the Arabian Sea from the oil producing countries of the Gulf. He also noted, "... The Indian Ocean is home to the busiest sea lanes, with an estimated $1,800 billion of merchandise trade passing through the region ... Thus, India has the potential and the capability to be a significant maritime player. I would even venture to say that the Indian Ocean could, in fact, be India's New Silk Route."[118]

Under a joint operation, in November 1999, the Indian Navy and the Coast Guard captured the hijacked MV *Alondra Rainbow*, a 7,000-tonne Panama-registered vessel, belonging to Japanese owners. Following an alert from the Piracy Reporting Centre in Kuala Lumpur, the Indian maritime forces were mobilised and secured the vessel to its owners.[119] In 2002, after the terrorist attacks in the United States, the Indian Navy provided naval security cover to U.S.-flagged high-value vessels including nuclear submarines through the Straits of Malacca that was plagued with pirates and possible terrorists.[120] Under Operation Sagittarius, Indian naval ships Sharda and Sukanya escorted twenty-four U.S. vessels between 2 April and 16 September 2002.

As noted earlier, more than 97 per cent of India's trade by volume and 75 per cent by value is seaborne and following the "direction of trade", nearly 50 per cent of Indian trade transits through the Straits of Malacca. As regards energy requirements, 67 per cent of India's need is sourced from the Persian Gulf and 17 per cent from West Africa. There is very little that is sourced from the Southeast Asian countries. However, in December 2006, the first consignment of crude oil from Yuzhno-Sakhalinsk, Sakhalin I, Russia, has resulted in a new source of energy for India.[121] The ships carrying this oil would cover a route of more than 5,700 nautical miles transiting through the Pacific, South China Sea and Straits of Malacca to Indian ports. In that context, the safety and security of the Straits of Malacca is extremely vital for India's economic growth and prosperity.

At the political level, the leadership has consistently offered to provide assistance to the Straits littorals. In July 2004, while attending the ASEAN Plus Three meetings and the ASEAN Regional Forum (ARF) in Jakarta, India's External Affairs Minister Mr Natwar Singh observed that India was ready to provide security in the Straits of Malacca and stressed that it was in India's national interest to ensure that the Straits remained a crime-free sea lane. It was noted, "From our side it is affirmative ... details can be worked out but in principal yes ... We are neighbours. Nicobar Island and the northern part of Sumatra are only 80 miles apart."[122]

Similar sentiments were expressed in 2007. At the Fourteenth Annual ASEAN Regional Forum (ARF) meeting, Pranab Mukherjee, India's External Affairs Minister, said: "India will design and conduct a training module on maritime security, specifically for the ARF member states, with themes of anti-piracy, search-and-rescue [missions], offshore and port security, anti-smuggling and narcotics control and anti-poaching operations." The nucleus of the module would be "capacity-building" and related aspects of maritime security. At the functional-operational levels, the Indian Navy has expressed readiness to undertake anti-piracy patrols in the Straits of Malacca provided a specific request was received from Southeast Asian countries.[123]

Meanwhile, India has been engaged in bilateral naval cooperation with several Southeast Asian countries with the primary aim of addressing problems related to maritime disorder. This has resulted in naval exercises, common operating procedures, search and rescue at sea and protection of the marine environment. These issues are discussed in greater details in Chapter 7.

Indian response to multilateral naval and maritime initiatives such as the Proliferation Security Initiative (PSI), 1000 Ship Navy (TSN), International Ship and Port Security Code (ISPS) and Container Security Initiative (CSI) conceptualized for the monitoring, surveillance, regulatory and safety mechanisms at sea presents a mixed bag of support and rejection. During Colin Powell's visit to India in March 2004, the United States had suggested that India join the PSI. India has debated the issue of joining the Initiative but stayed away from any active participation. Legality of the Initiative, legitimacy of international weapons trade and freedom of the seas are some of the issues that concern New Delhi. In his 2007 guidelines, Admiral Mike Mullen, Chief of Naval Operations, U.S. Navy announced that the "1,000 ship navy" (TSN)[124] as a concept had "resonated well" among leaders of several maritime forces. The concept *per se* is in line with the existing Indo-U.S. maritime cooperation primed on the Malabar series of naval exercises and consolidates Indo-U.S. naval cooperation, but the Indian Government noted that it could not be part of any alliance. Addressing the Lok Sabha, Pranab Mukherjee, India's Foreign Minister noted that India was party to two United Nations' conventions on crimes on high seas and as such had not considered joining any other network and large maritime crimes take place when ships are on the high seas, endangering their safety and security, but such crimes are always tackled through UN conventions.[125]

However, India has supported the International Ship and Port Security (ISPS) Code and adopted as an amendment to the International Convention for the Safety of Life at Sea (SOLAS) 1974 on 12 December 2002, under The Merchant Shipping (Amendment) Bill, 2004 that further amends the Merchant Shipping Act, 1958 and the Indian Ports Act, 1908.[126] As regards the Container Security Initiative (CSI), India has supported the initiative and taken measures to secure the ports by installing equipment to scan incoming and outgoing containers that may be used by non-state actors and terrorists for illegal activates.

CONCLUSION

Navies are flexible forces and can be deployed or withdrawn in short periods unlike land forces. They take pride in their right of free passage and enjoy a high degree of flexibility, mobility and visibility. These attributes are unique in nature, primarily due to the medium in which the navies operate, i.e. the sea. Further, the shape, size, and war-fighting capabilities of a navy are three important determinants for use as instruments of foreign policy. Importantly, naval diplomacy is a term that has found an important place in the lexicon of theory and practice of international relations.

The chapter has attempted to explain the utility of the navy as a political instrument of power. It has examined the understanding and conduct of naval diplomacy of Chinese and Indian strategists, naval planners and practitioners. The empirical evidence clearly illustrates that both India and China have used navies as political instruments to influence events in their respective areas of interest. These have been achieved through actual deployment, presence and threat of use of naval force. Their navies have also served as instruments for building confidence and trust as well as to preserve order at sea. Finally, for China and India, any aspiration to emerge as an independent regional power, among other initiatives, would be achieved through a robust build-up of power at sea.

Notes

1. Edward Luttwak, *The Political Uses of Seapower* (Baltimore, M.D.: John Hopkins University Press, 1974), p. 7.
2. James Cable, *Gunboat Diplomacy 1919–1991* (London: Macmillan, 1994), p. 14.
3. L.W. Martin, "The Use of Naval Forces in Peacetime", *Naval War College Review* (January/February 1985).
4. Ken Booth, *Navies and Foreign Policy* (London: Croom Helm, 1977), pp. 15–16.
5. Ann Scott Tyson, "New Maritime Strategy to Focus on 'Soft Power'", *Washington Post*, 17 October 2007.
6. For instance, Captain Xu Qi of the PLA Navy notes that naval vessels are symbols of state power and authority that act as mobile territory and navigate freely on the high seas. For more details see Andrew S. Erickson and Andrew R. Wilson, "China's Aircraft Carrier Dilemma", in *China's Future Nuclear Submarine Force*, edited by Andrew S. Erickson, Lyle J. Goldstein, William S. Murray, and Andrew R. Wilson (Annapolis: Naval Institute Press, 2007), p. 245.
7. David L. Stern, "A Ukrainian Port with a Heavy Russian Accent", *International Herald Tribune*, 25 August 2008.
8. Information Office of the State Council, the People's Republic of China, *China's National Defense 1998*, Beijing, available at <http://www.china.org.cn/e-white/5/index.htm> (accessed 10 January 2006).
9. Information Office of the State Council, the People's Republic of China, *China's National Defense 2002*, Beijing, available at <http://www.china.org.cn/e-white/20021209/index.htm> (accessed 10 January 2006).
10. Information Office of the State Council, the People's Republic of China, *China's National Defense 2004*, Beijing, available at <http://china.org.cn/english/2004/Dec/116032.htm> (accessed 10 January 2006).
11. Information Office of the State Council, the People's Republic of China, *China's National Defense 2006*, Beijing, available at <http://www1.china.org.cn/english/Books&Magazines/194419.htm> (accessed 30 June 2006).
12. See "International Security Cooperation", White Paper on China's National Defence, available at <http://www.china.org.cn/e-white/5/5.4.htm> (accessed 20 June 2007); "Cohen Signs, Hails Deal in China Pact Could Thwart Miscalculation", *Washington Times*, 19 January 1998; also see "Sino-US Armies Advance Ties", *Beijing Review*, 16–22 February 1998.
13. *China's National Defense 2006*, p. 37.
14. "New Era for China's Military Diplomacy", available at <http://english.peopledaily.com.cn/200211/06/eng20021106_106369.shtml> (accessed 10 January 2008).
15. "Military Diplomacy Helps China's Peaceful Development", *Xinhua*, 29 December 2005.

16. *China's National Defense 2002*, p. 32.
17. These are: United Nations Truce Supervision Organization (UNTSO) in the Middle East, United Nations Iraq-Kuwait Observation Mission (UNIKOM), United Nations Transitional Authority in Cambodia (UNTAC), United Nations Mission for the Referendum in Western Sahara (MINURSO), United Nations Operation in Mozambique (ONUMOZ) and United Nations Observer Mission in Liberia (UNOMIL). In 1992, a 800-men engineer unit was sent to Cambodia as part of the UNTAC peacekeeping operations. There are thirty-two Chinese military observers serving with UNTSO, UNIKOM and MINURSO.
18. See "International Security Cooperation", White Paper on China's National Defence, 2006, available at <http://www.china.org.cn/e-white/5/5.4.htm> (accessed 20 June 2007).
19. *China's National Defense 2006*, p. 38. These include 92 military observers and staff officers, 175 engineering troops and 43 medical personnel in Congo (Kinshasa); 275 engineering troops, 240 transportation troops and 43 medical personnel in Liberia; 275 engineering troops, 100 transportation troops and 60 medical personnel in Sudan; and 182 engineering troops in Lebanon. China also has a total of 180 peacekeeping police officers in Liberia, Kosovo, Haiti and Sudan.
20. Liu Huaqiu, "China's Foreign Policy", 1 December 1997, available at the website of the Chinese Embassy, Washington, D.C. at <http://www.china-embassy.org> (accessed 20 May 2008).
21. Cited in Geoffrey Till, "The Navies of the Asia Pacific in a Revolutionary Age", in *Maritime Security and Cooperation in Asia Pacific: Towards the 21st Century*, edited by Dalchoong Kim, Seo-Hang Lee, and Jin-Hyun Park (Seoul: Dooilnet, 2000), p. 31.
22. Srikanth Kondapalli, *China's Naval Power* (New Delhi: Knowledge World, 2001), p. 205.
23. Kurt Campbell and Richard Weitz, "The Limits of U.S.-China Military Cooperation: Lessons from 1995–1999", *The Washington Quarterly* 29, no. 1 (Winter 2005): 169–86.
24. A China-ASEAN dialogue on "Military Modernization and Mutual Trust Building" was held in Beijing in March 2008 at which twenty-five senior military experts from China and ASEAN countries participated. Li Xiaokun, "Defense Program No Threat to Others", *China Daily*, 12 March 2008.
25. In December 1952, the Communists carried out raids on the heavily fortified nationalist-held islands of Jinmen and Matsu and these attacks continued into 1953. For a detailed account on the incident, see David G. Muller, Jr., *China as a Maritime Power* (Colorado: Westview Press, 1983), p. 23.
26. Allen S. Whiting, "The PLA and China's Threat Perceptions", *The China Quarterly* 146 (June 1994): 603. In July 1995, China fired surface-to-surface missiles that fell eighty nautical miles northeast of Taipei and southeast of

Kaohsiung. These were accompanied by amphibious exercises involving the PLA Navy, Air Force and Army.

27. "One-China Principle: Historical Facts about 'One-China' Consensus", Commentary on 1992 cross-Straits Consensus, The Taiwan Affairs Office of the State Council, Taipei.
28. For a good analysis of the events see Andrew Scobell, "Show of Force: Chinese Soldiers, Statesmen, and the 1995–1996 Taiwan Strait Crisis", *Political Science Quarterly* 115, no. 2 (Summer 2000): 227–46.
29. "Background Information on China's Recent Military Threats Against Taiwan", Department of Planning, Government of the People's Republic of China, March 2007.
30. "Taiwan President Raps China Over Missile Build-up", available at <http://www.spacewar.com/reports/Taiwan_president_raps_China_over_missile_build-up_999.html> (accessed 20 January 2008).
31. Clive Schofield, "Island Disputes in East Asia Escalate", *Jane's Intelligence Review* (November 1996): 519–21.
32. Ibid.
33. Robert G. Sutter, "The PLA, Japan's Defense Posture, and the Outlook for China-Japan Relations", in *Shaping China's Security Environment: The Role of the People's Liberation Army*, edited by Andrew Scobell and Larry M. Wortzel (Pennsylvania: Strategic Studies Institute, October 2006), p. 182.
34. Ellis Joffe, "China's Military Buildup: Beyond Taiwan?", in *Shaping China's Security Environment*, pp. 42–43.
35. Tsuyoshi Nojima, "China's Sudden Show of Force Sent SDF Jets Scrambling", *Asahi Shimbun*, available at <http://www.asahi.com/english/Herald-asahi/TKY200801020031.html> (accessed 15 February 2008).
36. Scott Snyder, "The South China Sea Dispute: Prospects for Preventive Diplomacy", Special Report, United States Institute of Peace, available at the website of Chinese Foreign Policy Net at <http://www.stanford.edu/~fravel/chinafp/scs.htm> (accessed 10 January 2008).
37. Ibid.
38. David G. Wiencek, "South China Sea Flashpoint", available at <http://www.jamestown.org.> (accessed 30 June 2006).
39. "PLA Fleet Starts First Round-the-World Voyage", People's Daily Online, available at <http://english.peopledaily.com.cn/200205/15/eng20020515_95767.shtml>.
40. Jon Rosamond, "China Completes Joint Exercise with UK Aircraft Carrier", *Jane's Navy International* 112, issue 8 (October 2007): 6.
41. Srikanth Kondapalli, "Exchanging Concerns", *Sainik Samachar* 52, no. 13 (1–15 July 2005).
42. *China's Navy 2007*, Office of Naval Intelligence, p. 114, available at <http://www.fas.org/irp/agency/oni/chinanavy2007.pdf> (accessed 5 January 2008).

43. For a detailed account of the PLA Navy's overseas visits to foreign ports see, "People's Liberation Navy — Foreign Policy", available at <http://www.globalsecurity.org/military/world/china/plan-fp.htm> (accessed 5 January 2008).
44. Mayuka Yamazaki, "Origin, Developments and Prospects for the Proliferation Security Initiative", Institute for the Study of Diplomacy, Edmund A. Walsh School of Foreign Service, Georgetown University, 2006, p. 15, available at <http://isd.georgetown.edu/JFD_2006_PSA_Yamazaki.pdf> (accessed 10 January 2008).
45. Bernard D. Cole, "Beijing's Strategy of Sea Denial", *China Brief* 6, issue 23, available at <http://www.jamestown.org/single/?no_cache=1&tx_ttnews%5Btt_news%5D=32259> (accessed 14 March 2007). Also see Lieutenant Commander Ulysses O. Zalamea, "Eagles and Dragons at Sea: The Inevitable Collision Between the United States and China", *Naval War College Review* 41, no. 4 (Autumn 1996): 62.
46. James C. Bussert, "China Taps Many Resources for Coastal Defence", *Signal* (November 2002): 29–32. Also see "US-China Confidence-Building More Important than Detargeting", available at <http://www.nyu.edu/globalbeat/pubs/ib39.html> (accessed 23 March 2006).
47. Cited in Campbell and Weitz, "The Limits of U.S.-China Military Cooperation: Lessons from 1995–1999", pp. 169–86.
48. Chris Rahman, "Ballistic Missile in China's Anti-Taiwan Strategy", in *Naval Blockades and Seapower: Strategies and Counter Strategies, 1805–2005*, edited by Bruce A. Elleman and S.C.M. Paine (London: Routledge, 2006), p. 218.
49. "Sino-US Armies Advance Ties", *Beijing Review*, 16–22 February 1998.
50. The text of the agreement is available at the website of the Federation of American Scientists at <http://www.fas.org/nuke/control/sea/text/us-china98.htm> (accessed 23 March 2006).
51. See "The Military Maritime Consultative Agreement", *U.S. Naval Institute Proceedings* (August 1999).
52. The first annual MMCA meeting in July 1998 established a timeline and goals for two subsequent working group meetings that were completed in the summer of 1999. In late 1998, the first working group meeting was held in San Diego to implement the charter established by Secretary Cohen and General Chi Hotian.
53. Yan Liang, "China, U.S. Navy Officers Meet on Maritime Military Safety Consultation Mechanism", 27 February 2008, available at <http://english.cri.cn/2946/2008/02/27/1321@327345.htm> (accessed 20 March 2008).
54. "U.S.-China Airplane Collision Believed to be Accidental", see the transcript on the incident available at <http://transcripts.cnn.com/TRANSCRIPTS/0104/01/sm.17.html> (accessed 30 June 2006).
55. John J. Tkacik, Jr., "China's Quest for a Superpower Military", Asian Studies Center Backgrounder 2036, The Heritage Foundation, 17 May 2007.

56. Daniel Schearf, "China Quiet About Delay of US Navy's Planned Thanksgiving Hong Kong Port Call", 22 November 2007, available at <http://www.voanews.com/english/archive/2007-11/2007-11-22-voa6.cfm?CFID=272103146&CFTOKEN=56190008> (accessed 15 December 2008).
57. "China Blocked U.S. Navy From Hong Kong Harbor in 3rd Incident", *Fox News*, 30 November 2007, available at <http://www.foxnews.com/story/0,2933,314222,00.html> (accessed 15 December 2008).
58. "China and U.S. Sign Accord on Defense Hotline", *Reuters*, 29 February 2008. Also see "China, US Establish Military Hotline", *Asian Defence Journal* (December 2007): 1.
59. Gordon G. Chang, "Miscomprehending China", *Daily Standard*, 5 March 2008.
60. Richard Halloran, "China Beefing up Military Brains", *Taipei Times*, 9 March 2008.
61. "Japan, China Agree To Ease Military Tensions", *Taipei Times*, 31 August 2007.
62. "Japanese DM: Chinese Warship's Visit to Japan Conducive to Building Mutual Trust", *Xinhua*, 26 November 2007.
63. Josy Joseph, "Navy Hails Successful South China Sea Visit", available at <www.rediff.com/news/2000/oct/17spec.htm> (accessed 30 June 2003).
64. "Chinese Admiral Lauds Pakistan Foreign Policy", *Dawn*, 21 May 2001.
65. Vijay Sakhuja, "Peace Mission 2005: Reverberations in India", available at <http://www.ipcs.org/kashmirLevel3.jsp?action=showView&kValue=1832&subCatID=null&mod=null> (accessed 30 June 2007).
66. Lyle Goldstein and William Murray, "International Submarine Rescue: A Constructive Role for China?", *Asia Policy* 5 (January 2008): 167–83.
67. Stanley B. Weeks, "Sea Lines of Communication (SLOC) Security and Access", Working Paper, Institute of Global Conflict and Cooperation, February 1998.
68. ICC International Maritime Bureau, "Piracy and Armed Robbery Against Ships", Report for the Period 1 January–31 December 1998, p. 2.
69. See Jin Liangxiang, "Energy First: China and the Middle East", *Middle East Quarterly* (Spring 2005). Also see Phar Kim Beng, "China Mulls Oil Pipelines in Myanmar, Thailand", *Asia Times*, available at <http://www.atimes.com/atimes/China/FI23Ad09.html> (accessed 24 July 2007).
70. Wenran Jiang, "China's Growing Energy Relations with the Middle East", *China Brief* 7, issue 14 (11 July 2007), available at <http://www.jamestown.org/china_brief/article.php?articleid=2373542> (accessed 30 November 2007).
71. For a detailed account of Chinese initiatives see Hasjim Djalal, "The Role of the Users for the Enhancement of the Safety and the Protection of the Strait of Malacca and Singapore in Relation with UNCLOS 1982", paper presented at the Symposium on the Enhancement of Safety of Navigation and

the Environment Protection of the Straits of Malacca and Singapore, Kuala Lumpur, 13–14 March 2007.
72. "Military Diplomacy Helps China's Peaceful Development", *Xinhua*, 29 December 2005.
73. Soeren Kern, "The Geopolitics of Tsunami Relief", Análisis ARI 8/2005, Real Instituto Elcano, available at <http://www.realinstitutoelcano.org/analisis/666.asp> (accessed 14 February 2008). The Politburo had initially announced US$2.6 million as aid but soon raised it to US$63 million after Taiwan pledged US$50 million and this figure was further raised to US$83 million when Japan increased aid from US$30 million to US$500 million. Also see Srikanth Kondapalli, "Tsunami and China: Relief with Chinese Characteristics", available at <http://www.niaslinc.dk/gateway_to_asia/Asia_insights/China%20%20Tsunami.doc> (accessed 14 February 2008).
74. See Andrew S. Erickson and Andrew R. Wilson, "China's Aircraft Carrier Dilemma", in *China's Future Nuclear Submarine Force*, edited by Andrew S. Erickson, Lyle J. Goldstein, William S. Murray, and Andrew R. Wilson (Annapolis: Naval Institute Press, 2007), p. 245.
75. John Chan, "China's Tsunami Aid: Political Interests Not Humanitarian Concerns", 18 January 2005, available at <http://www.niaslinc.dk/gateway_to_asia/Asia_insights/China%20%20Tsunami.doc> (accessed 15 June 2006).
76. Annual Report 2006–07, Ministry of Defence, Government of India, p. 33.
77. *Strategic Defence Review: The Maritime Dimension, A Naval Vision* (New Delhi: Naval Headquarters, 1998), p. 27.
78. *Indian Maritime Doctrine (INBR 8)* (New Delhi: Integrated Headquarters, Ministry of Defence (Navy), 2004), pp. 100–3.
79. "Gathering the Instruments", *Leadmark: The Navy's Strategy for 2020*, available at <http://www.navy.dnd.ca/leadmark/doc/parts1to8_e.asp> (accessed 20 May 2008).
80. "Indian Navy: Today and Tomorrow", an interview with Chief of Naval Staff Admiral Sureesh Mehta, *Journal of Indian Ocean Studies* 15, no. 1 (April 2007): 1–11.
81. Lieutenant Commander B.M. Dimri, "Naval Diplomacy and UNCLOS III", *Strategic Analysis* (April 1994): 55.
82. Ibid., p. 70.
83. "UN Peacekeeping", available at <http://www.indiannavy.nic.in-UNPeacekeeping-Somalia> (accessed 15 January 2007).
84. *Operation Madad* (Andhra Pradesh and Tamil Nadu coast, India), *Operation Sea Waves* (Andaman and Nicobar Islands, India), *Operation Castor* (Maldives), *Operation Rainbow* (Sri Lanka), and *Operation Gambhir* (Indonesia). On 26 December 2004, the Indian Navy deployed 19 ships, 4 aircraft, and 11 helicopters which rushed to the Maldives, Sri Lanka and Tamil Nadu, and Andaman and Nicobar Islands. The Indian Navy also deployed its hydrographic survey teams and underwater clearing crews to operationalize Sri Lankan ports

and harbours that were hit by the tsunami. The harbours in Galle, Trincomalee and Colombo were surveyed and the maps handed over to the Sri Lankan authorities. Also, Indian naval diving crews cleared several ports rendered non-operational due to sunken/aground boats and debris.

85. "Bangladesh Relief Operations, Indian Navy", Press Information Bureau, Government of India, 13 December 2007.
86. "India Sends Relief Ships To Cyclone-Hit Myanmar", *Times of India*, 6 May 2008.
87. Various Annual Reports 1988–89 to 2001–2002, Ministry of Defence, Government of India.
88. Vijay Sakhuja, "Naval Diplomacy: Indian Initiatives", *Indian Defence Review* 6, no. 1 (July–August 2003).
89. See "PM Calls For Institutionalisation of Co-operation Between Navies" at the website of Rediff at <http://rediff.com/news/2001/feb/18fleet.htm> (accessed 31 March 2001).
90. "Indian Ocean Naval Symposium (IONS)", available at <http://indiannavy.nic.in/ion.htm> (accessed 31 March 2008).
91. Pradeep Chauhan, "Indian Naval Foreign Cooperation Endeavours", *Journal of Indian Ocean Studies* 15, no. 2 (August 2007): 225–41.
92. "Indian Navy: Today and Tomorrow", an interview with Chief of Naval Staff Admiral Sureesh Mehta, *Journal of Indian Ocean Studies* 15, no. 1 (April 2007): 1–11.
93. Assistant Secretary of Defense for International Security Affairs Henry Rowen visited India in 1990 and General Claude Kickleighter offered a proposal to increase military-to-military cooperation in 1991. A Joint Services Committee was set up at New Delhi. An Indo-U.S. Naval Steering Committee was established in 1992 at New Delhi to chart out naval cooperation involving naval personnel exchanges, joint exercises and information sharing.
94. The U.S. Navy fielded a P-3C Orion maritime patrol aircraft and the nuclear-powered submarine Birmingham. The Indian Navy deployed the conventional German-built submarine, Shankush.
95. For more details see the transcript of Admiral Dennis C. Blair, Commander in Chief U.S. Pacific Command interview with *Times of India*, 25 October 2001.
96. L.A. Benjamin, "Exercise IBSAMAR 1: Maritime Camaraderie Across Three Continents", available at <http://www.navy.mil.za/> (accessed 2 June 2008).
97. Annual Report 2006–07, Ministry of Defence, Government of India, p. 31.
98. Manu Pubby, "What the Navy Learnt From Malabar", *Indian Express*, 9 September 2007.
99. Ibid.
100. Ibid.
101. "Australia Participates in Joint Maritime Exercise", available at <http://www.navy.gov.au/news/australia_participates_in_joint_maritime_exercise>.

102. Pubby, "What the Navy Learnt From Malabar".
103. Dimri, "Naval Diplomacy and UNCLOS III", p. 67.
104. Palk Bay is frequently used by the LTTE for carrying out strikes against the Sri Lankan naval forces and to keep the arms' supply lines open at sea. The LTTE also hires several small vessels to transport arms, ammunition, stores, and logistics to sustain its forces. These vessels are suspected to originate from India, some Southeast Asian countries and transit through the Bay of Bengal.
105. "India to dispatch three warships to shield PM during SAARC meet in Lanka", available at <http://www2.irna.ir/en/news/view/menu-234/0807163047110522.htm> (accessed 28 July 2008).
106. Also see Second Lieutenant Scott A. Cuomo, "US and Indian Navies Close Again", *U.S. Naval Institute Proceedings* (February 2002): 41.
107. See "Operation Cactus" at the website of Bharat Rakshak at <http://www.bharat-rakshak.com/CONFLICTS/Operation cactus.html> (accessed 9 January 2007).
108. "Buzzing Fleets in the High Seas", *Asian Defence Journal* (October 1999): 34.
109. See "Agreement between Pakistan and India on Advance Notice of Military Exercises, Manoeuvres and Troop Movements" signed between Shaharyar M. Khan and Muchkund Dubey, dated 6 April 1991, at New Delhi, available at the website of Henry L. Stimson Centre, Washington D.C., at <http://www.stimson.org/southasia/?sn=sa20020109216> (accessed 24 March 2007).
110. P.R. Chari, "Declaratory Statements and Confidence Building in South Asia", in *Declaratory Diplomacy: Rhetorical Initiatives and Confidence Building*, edited by Michael Krepon, Jenny S. Drezin, and Michael Newbill (Washington, D.C: Henry L. Stimson Centre, April 1999), p. 89.
111. Rahul Roy-Chaudhary, *India's Maritime Security* (New Delhi: Knowledge World, 2000), pp. 55–60.
112. "Hotline Between CG and Pak's MSA Almost Finalized", *Press Trust of India*, 28 July 2004.
113. Pakistan Navy Historical Section, *Story of Pakistan Navy, 1947–1972* (Islamabad: Elite Publishers, 1991), pp. 228–29.
114. Ashley J. Tellis, "Securing the Barracks", in *The Modern Indian Navy and the Indian Ocean*, edited by Robert H. Bruce (Perth: Curtin University of Technology, 1989), p. 13. Also see B. Dismukis and J. McConnell, *Soviet Naval Diplomacy* (New York: Pergamon Press, 1990).
115. Robert Jackson, *South Asian Crisis, India-Pakistan-Bangladesh* (London: Chatto & Windus, 1975), p. 231.
116. Cited in P.K. Ghosh, "Revisiting Gunboat Diplomacy: An Instrument of Threat or Use of Limited Naval Force", *Strategic Analysis* (February 2001): 2014.
117. Gurmeet Kanwal, "Pakistan's Military Defeat", in *Kargil 1999: Pakistan's Fourth War for Kashmir*, edited by Jasjit Singh (New Delhi: Knowledge World, 1999), p. 220.

118. "India's Defence Imports to Touch $35 Bn by 2026: Antony", available at <http://news.indiamart.com/news-analysis/india-s-defence-impo-14556.html> (accessed 17 January 2007).
119. Prabhakaran Paleri, *Role of the Coast Guard in the Maritime Security of India* (New Delhi: Knowledge World, 2007), p. 147. Also see Vijay Sakhuja, "Maritime Order and Piracy", *Strategic Analysis* 24, issue 5 (August 2000).
120. Arun Prakash, *From the Crow's Nest* (New Delhi: Lancer Publishers, 2007), p. 173.
121. T.S. Subramanian, "Sakhalin Success", *Frontline* 23, issue 26 (30 December 2006–12 January 2007).
122. "India Ready to Protect Malacca Strait: Natwar Singh", 1 July 2004, available at <http://www.rediff.com>.
123. Vijay Sakhuja, "Challenging Pirates in Malacca Straits", Article no. 6, 20 September 2004, available at <http://www.sspconline.org/article_details.asp?artid=art5> (accessed 30 June 2007).
124. The "1,000 ship navy" concept aims to build a network of navies built on "partnership" that will work together to create a force capable of "standing watch over all the seas".
125. "US Thousand Ship Navy Programme", Question no. 5802, Lok Sabha Debates, New Delhi.
126. Bill no. 108 of 2004, available at <http://www.prsindia.org/docs/bills/11712 65268/1171265268_The_Merchant_Shipping_Bill_2004.pdf> (accessed 24 May 2008).

6

TECHNO-MILITARY DIMENSION OF ASIAN MARITIME POWER

Asia has captured the transformational momentum in the techno-military dimension of maritime power with assent on information technology. Revolution in Military Affairs (RMA) driven by information technology leading to military transformation is evident in the emerging order of battle of several Asian navies including China, India, Japan, Korea and Singapore. The other Asian navies are still technologically inferior and this deficiency is evident in the imageries of their naval orders of battle. Significantly, the new maritime/naval platforms being inducted by China, India, Indonesia, Singapore, Malaysia and Thailand are both technology-centric and technology-intensive and these navies are engaged in exploiting the benefits of the information revolution and developing their technological strengths. Among these countries, there is evidence of zestful desire and visible quest in China and India to achieve technological proficiency and translate the same into operational competence and for exercising strategic autonomy.

There are several causal factors that shape the ongoing RMA in China and India. First and foremost, great emphasis is being placed on the techno-military dimension of maritime power that is considered vital for guarding the ocean frontiers. As noted earlier, ocean frontiers had remained vulnerable leading to subjugation by the colonial-imperial forces. Second, the objective is to build credible maritime military capability to dominate regional affairs and assemble significant maritime power to deter any challenger. Also of significance is the safety of maritime trade and securing the littoral hubs that form important nodes in the global supply chain. Third, industrial and technological development is considered critical for development of a military industrial complex to build and support a modern military force. Fourth, China and India are conscious of the fact that there exist several political, economic and technological constraints on importing technology and it is critical to develop an indigenous technological industrial base as well as train human resources for the full spectrum of civil-military applications. Fifth, the socio-cultural and behavioural factors have also been a driver for the growth of RMA in the two countries, particularly China.[1] Last but not the least, there are civilizational factors that drive the RMA in China and India. Both Sun Tzu and Kautilya (also known as Chanakya) were great proponents and advocates of information. Their thoughts on information are reflected in the great classics *Art of War* (Bingfa) and *Arthashastra* (science of politics)[2] and are evident in the RMA philosophy in China and India.

In recent times, high technology growth in China and India has been quite impressive with strong assents on expansion of the existing defence industrial infrastructure. Further, globalization and the opening up of the military industrial complex has led to home-grown technologies. Also evident is the synergy with select-import substitution from Russia, Israel and other European defence industries that have paved the way for the two states to develop their indigenous technological strengths. However the scope of these remains limited because the ability to translate these technologies into large-scale assembly production is still limited.

In the case of China and India, "hybridization" of platforms based on imported sensors and weapons, is yet another avenue of technology enrichment. These Asian powers have often combined the rugged Soviet/Russian military hardware with both indigenous and western systems to enhance the combat and operational efficiency of their navies. These endeavours have added teeth to the offensive capabilities of their naval forces and provided momentum for conduct of sustained operations. However, China and India must contend with a technologically superior United States-led military-industrial power that has the technological lead over the developing world. The ability of this group to effectively stifle the technological growth trajectory of China and India through sanctions presents a major dilemma. Importantly, bitter experience of technology denial in the past has necessitated a surge in the technology-building momentum in China and India.

The Persian Gulf War (1991), the war in Bosnia (1992–95), the military action in Kosovo (1999), the United States-led War on Terror (2001) and the War on Iraq (2003) experiences encouraged both China and India to invest in information warfare and build a military with smart technologies.

Importantly, the 1991 Gulf War showcased a new military strategy based on technology that came to represent a new era in strategy formulation in China and India. The technological inputs into this war had a far-reaching impact on the concept of future wars, and these militaries began to reorient their tactical military doctrines to deal with information-technology based tactics. The operational synergy among various arms of the military revealed that China and India had to introduce a process of transformation of the military, pivoting on informational technology that may not be as grandiose as the United States-Europe-led West, but would be able to appropriately address the future challenges. The quest for technological autonomy is quite evident in China and India and these Asian powers are investing substantial fiscal and human resources to sustain the momentum of ongoing military transformation. Also, there are concerns in China and India that the United States-led West would not hesitate to take punitive actions against powers that develop long-range capabilities and begin to dominate regional security matters.

Towards that end, the chapter examines the concept of the Revolution in Military Affairs (RMA) and its relevance for the maritime power of India and China. It traces the military-technological revolution, and the challenges posed by RMA and the complexity of demands on tactical commanders to network with their forces at sea and shore. The chapter highlights RMA-related strategic thought among national leaders, practitioners and strategists and the level of attainment of the RMA in the Indian and Chinese navies. Finally, the chapter argues that the RMA in the Chinese and Indian naval context is still evolving, and the trend lines point to a greater commitment by the respective institutions towards making their forces network-centric.

CHANGE IN THE NATURE OF WARFARE

The nature of warfare is under transformation due to the advances made in information and communication technologies, and trends indicate that in future states will seek to take advantage of these technologies to overpower and overwhelm the enemy by dominating the C4I2SR (command, control, communications, computers, intelligence, interoperability, surveillance and reconnaissance) capability. To achieve this, the navies across the globe are shifting from platform-centric to network-centric warfare that pivots on complex integration of platforms at sea, in the air, underwater, ashore and even in the outer space. This is a distinct departure from the conventional deployments in which platforms operated independently in far-flung battle groups and this dispersion of units presented daunting challenges for tactical commanders to network the formations into a cohesive and networked force for conduct of operations across a large swath of sea space.

At another level, it has been argued that the growth in information technology and the concurrent growth in computer networks and hardware have pegged nations in three tiers based on their "economic modes of production".[3] These tiers are dependent on the techno-industrial capability of states and their ability to harness the benefits of information technology. The bottom tier comprises states that are dependent on natural resources for their economic growth. The middle tier states rely on their industrial infrastructure for prosperity, while the top tier is home to states that harness information technology to boost their economy. It is evident that the ability of states to harness information technology is an important factor in national growth and an effective tool for boosting the economy.

Analysts note that a military revolution occurs when there is a significant change in operational concepts and organizational structure that leads to a major transformation in the conduct of military operations in any conflict.[4] Historically, there have been several revolutions in the military that have shaped its development and conduct of warfare. The ongoing revolution in military affairs centred on information technology is a part of a continuous process of advancement in technology that shaped the previous revolutions and revolutionized the conduct of warfare. Beginning in the 5th century, the horseback saddle equipped with stirrups provided the cavalry soldier with a secure footing and stability that was skillfully exploited by the heavily armed knights in Europe and the Mongols in the Steppes. In the 12th century, the longbow, probably developed in Wales, enhanced the range, accuracy and power of attack of the land forces. Infantry warfare underwent another transformation during the 14th century when Swiss peasants adopted the Greek Phalanx formation (a compact square formation of soldiers) and used the pikes and longbows with devastating effect. In the 15th century, artillery cannon was the most potent weapon for lobbing heavy projectiles across fortified castles and was effective during sieges, both in defence and in offence. Soon thereafter, in the 16th century, cannons came to be carried on board ships but they had limitations since these were very heavy and the ships were not designed to withstand the recoil. Although the guns were useful, the gunpowder was quite dangerous for stowage on board ship due to problems of fire and there was no special compartment on board to serve as ammunition magazine. It was also feared that fire during the shots could endanger the ship itself. This led to transformations in ship design and gun ports were built for broadside fire.

Several industrial and agricultural advances in the 18th century resulted in easy availability of larger numbers of human resource and these could be mobilized for war and thus began the era of modern war based on large armies. In the 19th century, momentous advancements in transportation due to rail and rapid communications through telegraph brought about a transformation in warfare. Further, there were significant developments in weaponry that resulted in greater accuracy. By the late 19th century, shipbuilders began using iron for cladding their vessels and later used mild steel for building the entire ship that could now be used to ram the enemy vessels. Also, technological advances in design, shipbuilding and propulsion resulted in larger and stronger ships, propelled by steam engines that were capable of carrying large calibre guns. The 20th century witnessed seminal industrial-technological developments resulting in advances in warfare such as the internal combustion engine and the military triad built around the tank, aircraft and radio. These developments transformed the nature of warfare that till date continues to be significant in any conventional war. Also, development of nuclear weapons and their delivery systems came to impact warfare in the 20th century.

The 21st century too is witnessing yet another technological transformation led by information technology. The battle space is transparent and real-time dissemination of information is facilitated by seamless connectivity among platforms and operators resulting in instant communications through computers and rapid dissemination of information and intelligence. Significantly, this has resulted in the expansion of communication space, compression of time, enhanced situational awareness and quick decision-making to prosecute enemy's centres of gravity and above all, a greater transparency overcoming decades of opaque battle space. It is noted that in the naval domain, RMA is not new and can be traced back to 1957 when the Canada-United Kingdom-United States (CANUKUS) Naval Data Transmission Working Group had ratified the technical standards for the exchange of data.[5]

In evidence is a rapid rise in information and communication technologies such as satellites, terrestrial communication highways, digital networks and complex integrating systems to transport large volumes of information across the globe in short time. The militaries have been quick to exploit information technologies and harness these knowledge-based information systems to attain their respective strategic and tactical aims. Information technology is closely and inextricably linked to the concept of information warfare. In simple terms, information warfare is the means to deny, exploit, corrupt or destroy the information infrastructure (command, control and decision-making apparatus and systems) of an adversary while protecting oneself.⁶ Its application as a destructive force against enemy computers and networks that support infrastructure such as government, military, power grid, communications, financial, and transportation systems is now a reality. For the military, information technology plays an important role in the conduct of warfare and military planners conceptualize information warfare as a prerequisite to the successful conduct of any operations, be it covert or overt.⁷ The aim is to use information superiority to attack enemy command and control structures, networks, and systems, thus gaining battle-space superiority and winning the war through asymmetry.

In recent times, there has been a dramatic application of information technologies in warfare, particularly during 1991 Operation Desert Shield/ Desert Storm, Operation Enduring Freedom (OEF) in 2001 and Operation Iraqi Freedom (OIF) in 2003. In these military operations, information technologies were extensively employed to support combat operations as well as to blind enemy forces to the extent that they were rendered incapable. Interestingly, the 1991 Persian Gulf War had a major impact on the thinking of military planners and the lessons of the war encouraged several nations (both developed and developing) to invest in information warfare and build a military equipped with smart technologies and intelligent weapons. Operation Desert Shield/Desert Storm represented a new era in strategy formulation, i.e. the technological inputs into this war had a far-reaching impact on the concept of future wars, and militaries began to reorient their tactical doctrines by incorporating information technology for conduct of operations.

During the 2003 Operation Iraqi Freedom, the awesome power of the technology was once again in operation. The United States attempted to prosecute the war on the theory of "shock and awe"⁸ and the aim was to shock the Iraqis into defeat rather than killing them indiscriminately. On declaration of hostilities, hundreds of armoured units and aircraft surged into Iraq in a blitzkrieg while hundreds of cruise missiles were launched from ships and submarines, fighter aircraft fired bunker-buster missiles and electronic bombs (E-bombs) thus disrupting communications. In simple terms, the "shock and awe" was aimed to shatter Iraq's will to fight, thus achieving victory without many casualties. The air and missile strikes were indeed so dramatic in effect and precise in targeting the regime's leadership and military infrastructure with few civilian casualties that the enemy's decision-makers had no choice but to surrender.

The war witnessed unprecedented use of ordnance and during the first two weeks of war some 14,000 precision-guided bombs were dropped and more than 750 Tomahawk cruise missiles had been fired.⁹ These were guided to targets by laser-homing devices supported by pre-positioned Special Forces troops, GPS, other satellites and designation devices. Of greater significance is that information technologies facilitated real-time conduct of operations.

REVOLUTION IN MARITIME AFFAIRS

Dramatic changes brought about by information technology have impacted maritime forces too. Within this wider debate on Revolution in Military Affairs (RMA) there is a "Revolution in Maritime Affairs" currently in progress.[10] The technological changes have revolutionized naval platforms, war fighting, communications and military supply chains. These developments have transformed the purpose of maritime forces that can now project maritime power with much more confidence and a greater guarantee across the littorals into the heartland.

The modern maritime battle space is dotted with an assortment of platforms engaged in multifarious tasks, resulting in a complex operational milieu that poses a major challenge for tactical commanders to conduct and control naval operations. There are also immense demands to network forces at sea, platforms in the air and space and command authorities ashore. In such a situation, information technology is critical to modern warfare techniques and vital for a sophisticated C4I2SR network. The network facilitates sharing large volumes of information among different platforms that form the nodes of the network.[11] Significantly, effective exploitation of information technology can result in some very cost-effective successes in a short time without even exposing humans to combat. From an operational perspective, early enemy detection, accurate identification, quick decision-making and timely engagements have become possible through creation of complex networks among sensors, command and control units and weapons that can now be fired from stand-off ranges. It also supports interoperability that is fast emerging as critical for multifaceted and multidimensional platforms. This new architecture in operational concepts is now referred to as network-centric warfare (NCW).

The U.S. Navy defines NCW as "military operations that exploit information and networking technology to integrate widely dispersed human decision-makers, situational and targeting sensors, and forces and weapons to highly adaptive, comprehensive systems to achieve unprecedented mission effectiveness".[12] The *Indian Naval Doctrine for Information Warfare* (INDIW) notes that "Network Centric Operations enable exchange of information amongst a large number of heterogeneous nodes in a network" and "is crucial for gaining competitive edge in a naval warfare by generating information and exploiting information superiority".[13] China has conceptualized the concept of Integrated Network-Electronic Warfare (INEW).[14] According to General Dai Qingmin, Head of the Fourth Department of the General Staff, INEW serves as an information operations theory with Chinese characteristics that envisages amalgamation of "electronic warfare and computer network warfare measures to disrupt the normal operation of enemy battlefield information systems" while shielding its own, thus obtaining information superiority. This definition is quite similar to the U.S. definition of Information Operations.

Given the various perceptions, understanding and conduct of modern military operations, the primary goal of NCW is to network assorted and dispersed platforms for an effective decision-making to prosecute operations. These networks facilitate sharing battle space pictures amongst various network nodes and also integrate with the tactical commander's strategic and tactical goals to facilitate unity of effort in the battlefield. Also, the level and success of these networks has a direct bearing on naval operations and missions, therefore it has become very important on the part of naval forces to undertake tactical, organizational and operational changes in their force structures and tactical doctrines that would enable optimal use and exploitation of the information being exchanged among different nodes in the network.

While information technology is a great facilitator, a big challenge confronting tactical commanders is the process of information management. It is true that excessive information may lead to "information overload", but modern information systems are designed to facilitate military commanders with the optimal information for action. At another level, tactical commanders have to contend with protecting their own information systems and insulate them against disruption by the enemy. These attacks would emerge through electronic warfare, cyber warfare and psychological warfare and these are inherently information technology-intensive. The primary aim is to outwit the adversaries and prevent exposure of one's own networks and systems to an enemy's offensive information warfare.

There are several parameters to determine a nation's keenness and capacity to absorb RMA.[15] These include: (a) threat perceptions, (b) the force structure's stage of development, (c) sophistication of indigenous defence science and technology, (d) local defence industries, and (e) the closeness of alliance with major military and technological powers. These variables help create a hierarchy to rank nations based on their absorption capabilities. The share of the defence budget for the RMA is another important indicator of a military's march towards the RMA.

CHINA'S ATTEMPTS AT INFORMATION REVOLUTION

During the last two decades, China has undertaken several transformational initiatives that have resulted in a sophisticated information and communication infrastructure.[16] Likewise, several reforms in the field of science and technology have provided the impetus for commercializing information technology. As a result of these initiatives, China has integrated information technology with commerce, banking, and transport, and augmented computer-based air, rail, sea and power nets. The Chinese also believe that "knowledge is a tradable commodity and is increasingly going to cost more if imported; hence it is necessary to develop indigenous capabilities with market incentives."[17] Consequently, China has made considerable progress in the field of software and hardware-related infrastructure and services. The old communication networks have been upgraded to modern information highways that are used by a variety of customers including the government, provincial authorities and private agencies. These networks assist in governance, economy, trade, social development, education and the security agencies, including the military establishment.

In China, information highways and networks, based on fibre-optic trunk lines, are spread over several provinces and cities that facilitate contact among federal government offices, provincial capitals and municipalities that fall directly under the government. Beside, the domestic Internet provides for exchange of scientific, technical and management data. The thrust of the Chinese Government is to harness information technology for the development of a web of intricate networks and in that context, in 1993 China established three networks (a) Golden Bridge, the National Public Economic Information Communications Network, (b) Golden Custom that connects all foreign trading enterprises, and (c) Golden Card for a uniform card-issuing system for electronic currency flows.[18] At another level, China established a web of intricate networks that connects the "Three Golden Networks", i.e. Public Communication Network, Economic Infrastructure Network and China Education and Research Network.[19] It is evident that great strides have been made by the Chinese Government to build information networks to enable governance, commerce, education and infrastructure development.

The Chinese Government plans to build a countrywide intranet called China Wide Web that would facilitate greater usage of the Internet by both government and civil institutions and organizations, encourage people to use e-mails, and this will help augment the development of domestic commuter and related service industries. As of January 2008, in China, there were 0.21 billion Internet users, 11.93 million domain names, 1.006 million CN websites, 0.135 billion IP addresses and an ever-increasing international bandwidth.[20] Importantly, China is second only to the United States with a gap of five million users. Great strides have been made by the Chinese Government to build information networks to enable governance, commerce, banking, education and infrastructure development. Although this is a welcome sign, the Chinese Government remains uneasy about the fact that such an access to the World Wide Web can be a source of social problems too. The World Wide Web can act as a powerful tool to challenge state authority in terms of human rights, pornography, espionage, anti-government propaganda and even independence of Taiwan.[21] For instance, the publicity of the Tiananmen Square incident looms large in the minds of the Chinese political leadership. Further, the use of a mobile phone in 1999 by Wang Lingyun (the mother of the leader of the 1989 Beijing protests) to speak to the commemoration rally in Hong Kong was indeed worrisome to the Chinese authorities.[22] These incidents clearly showcase that the Chinese are worried about the liberal use of the Internet. As a result of these developments, the Chinese Government is indisposed towards "information pluralism".[23]

Interestingly, information and communication technology has both empowered and undermined the Chinese state.[24] It has facilitated more nationalism among Chinese people to suit the policy objectives of the central government, but on the flip side, it has presented a unique dilemma for the government: whether to be in command of information resources or allow information technologies to shape the Chinese society. To that extent, Chinese concerns are genuine and the government has built several intrusive devices and systems to prevent misuse of the Internet. It is widely believed that the government censors the Net and closely monitors the users and has promulgated strict regulations for Internet users and service providers.

Notwithstanding the sensitivities to the intrusive nature of the World Wide Web, the Chinese have taken note of the global developments in information technology and are engaged in harnessing the benefits that accrue from information technology.[25] The China Information Technology Report notes that major sectors driving IT growth are telecom, finance, government, energy, education and transport, and several government initiatives are likely to boost the domestic IT market from US$51 billion in 2005 to around US$104 billion in 2010.[26]

CHINA AND REVOLUTION IN MILITARY AFFAIRS

While China remains committed to socio-economic development it has successfully integrated the national economy with the global economy supported by a robust IT infrastructure. Similarly, its security strategy has also witnessed significant advances wherein information technology acts as a catalyst and a force multiplier for national security. Information technology has entered into every facet of Chinese military activity that includes war fighting, battle space information management, administration, personnel management, military logistics and supply chains. In evidence is a qualitative improvement in the Chinese war fighting doctrines and practices reflected in the choice of weapons and sensors currently available on board PLA Navy ships, submarines and aircraft. Significantly, the Chinese have demonstrated an ability to absorb various information warfare concepts, strategies and practices that have mesmerized both the political masters and defence establishment.

In China, Shen Weiguang, a PLA combatant can be credited with the genesis of the study of information warfare through his book *Information Warfare*, extracts of which were later published in the *Liberation Army Daily* published in 1985.[27] Major General Wang is acknowledged as the founder of Chinese information warfare conceptualization and was also instrumental in defining several terms associated with this discipline.[28] But it was not until the 1991 Gulf War that the role and lethality of information technology in warfare came to impact on Chinese military leadership who were obviously impressed by the performance of the U.S. military in destroying Iraqi military hardware that was largely of Soviet/Russian origin. The Chinese military closely observed the technological superiority of the United States-led coalition forces, the role of information warfare in a modern battlefield, and studied the lessons of Operation Desert Storm. Similarly, Operation Enduring Freedom and Operation Iraqi Freedom came to impact on the Chinese information warfare strategic thinking.

Chinese scholars engaged in research on the role of information warfare in a modern battlefield and began to articulate their views through papers, conferences and journals. Much of their attention was focused on the role of satellites, network-centric warfare, electronic systems, precision-attack systems and technologies, minimal role for combatants and other technologies that could provide the force commander with a comprehensive battle space picture. The thrust of their study focused on satellite-based reconnaissance and positioning systems, stealth platforms, the role of AWACS, aircraft carriers, long-range precision-guided munitions. In order to understand global trends in warfare, the Chinese military establishment subscribes to several foreign military journals including *Jane's Defence Weekly, Aviation Week, U.S. Naval Institute Proceedings, Parameters*, including military literature originating in France, Germany and Russia.[29]

Over the last decade and a half, Chinese scholars, analysts and military officers have published a large body of strategic literature on RMA and warfare in the 21st century and several major information warfare research centres began to mushroom. For instance, the Academy of Military Sciences is the primary IW research centre in China, the Strategy Research Centre engages in developing IW strategies, integrating IW into overall military doctrine, as well as identifying the military hardware for IW.[30] The Centre is also associated with the Society for International Information Technologies. China also established the PLA Academy of Electronic Technology, the China National Research Centre for Intelligence Computing Systems and the COSTIND University of Electronic Science and Technology at Chengdu. Also, the PLA began to study the applications of information technology in tactical doctrines and war-fighting techniques, including the need for guided missiles, electronic warfare equipment including electronic jamming and secure tactical communications. What emerged was *Unrestricted Warfare*, published by two senior PLA colonels who advocated both conventional and unconventional warfare against an enemy's social, economic, and political activities indiscriminately.[31]

The PLA Academy of Military Sciences text, the *Science of Military Strategy* (2000) notes "war is not only a military struggle, but also a comprehensive contest on fronts of politics, economy, diplomacy, and law."[32] Perhaps what merits attention is the fact that Chinese scholars, strategists and practitioners are convinced that knowledge and information are central to any future warfare and this conviction further reinforces their understanding and practice of Sun Tzu's philosophy that they have imbibed in the conduct of military affairs.

Hacker warfare appears to be an important subject in Chinese military thinking and is practised as part of asymmetric warfare. There have been several instances of hacker attacks by "hacktivists" based in Taiwan and China on each other. Although the details of such attacks on the Chinese establishments are not publicly available, there were as many as 250,000 cyber attacks on Taiwanese establishments between 1996 and 2000.[33] Both sides appear to be prepared for hacker warfare. Chinese authorities believe that it is important to develop high-quality hackers and Internet warriors, both among the civil and military establishments.[34] In recent times, the Chinese "hacktivists" have focused their attention towards the United States and countries in Europe. For instance, in 2007, the PLA was suspected of having hacked into several government offices that focus on defence and foreign policy-related issues in the United States, the United Kingdom and Germany.[35] During the EP 3 incident in 2001, both the Chinese and U.S. hackers had engaged in hacker warfare that resulted in defacing hundreds of websites in both countries.[36] Likewise, China has been active in scanning and mapping Indian government computer systems such as the NIC (National Infomatics Centre) to gain access into the National Security Council and the Ministry of External Affairs. Once penetrated, these networks are prone to disruption during a conflict.[37]

On its own side, China remains worried about international groups capable of defacing Chinese websites. For instance, the Chinese Government was concerned about possible attacks on Chinese computer systems during the Beijing Olympics and China's National Computer Network Emergency Response Technical Team (CNCERT) in its report noted that hackers with political motivations would target the 2008 Olympic Games and engage in attacks on Chinese websites and this could be a major network security situation for the government.[38] According to CNCERT, some one million computers in China have "trojan software" installed, much higher than in 2006, experiencing a net increase of more than 2,000 times primarily because of pirated software.

The Chinese have taken a keen interest in virus warfare and believe it is a powerful weapon that can destroy computer systems, network information highways and satellite communications. They even conceptualize dormant viruses that can be installed in a weapon system or an information network that can be activated at a time of one's choice. The military establishments are conscious of these hidden perils and have created security filters and tests on equipment.

REVOLUTION IN NAVAL AFFAIRS

Since the 1991 Gulf War, the PLA Navy has studied advances in information technology and its impact on naval operations. Chinese naval writings available in the public domain suggest that the Chinese naval officers are attentive to the changing nature of naval warfare and the complexity of information warfare tools. They are convinced that modern naval equipment poses immense challenges to traditional maritime strategy, sea-based operations, tactical doctrines, exploitation procedures and even organizational structures.

Chinese naval practitioners argue that the 21st century will witness revolutionary changes in naval platforms with assents on stealth features, hybrid propulsion for greater efficiency, and several new technologies such as micro-electric systems, infra-red devices, precision-guided munitions, satellite-based command, control, communication and intelligence, super-conductor technology/fibre optics and laser weapons will further contribute to the complexity of naval warfare and bring about a major transformation in maritime strategies, tactical doctrines and employment of ships in combat.[39] The transformation in naval ship design will feature improved protection and survivable capabilities, rapid mobility, expanded operational area and quick deployment/withdrawal. Also, these platforms will host smart electronic warfare equipment supported by satellites and capable of performing multiple functions such as detection, classification, and identification, resulting is greater transparency in the battlefield. There will also be significant transformation in over-the-horizon surveillance, target acquisition, designation and the destructive power of new and improved munitions will add new dimensions to the lethality of the platforms. There will also be greater need for multi-dimensional joint warfare.

At another level, there will be added demands for trained human resources that should be skilled to not only handle complex naval systems but be proficient in computer, information engineering and satellite technology. The gap between training and actual operation will have to be bridged through extensive use and training through simulators for an effective exploitation of the human resource.[40] In short, the PLA Navy is aware of the fact that the 21st century naval battle space is complex, dynamic and rapid. The new battle space encompasses outer space, the water surface, the underwater domain and the electromagnetic environment.

The 1991 Gulf War demonstrated the complexity of the naval battle space in which multiple platforms were integrated to achieve success. The lessons of the War and its implications for the RMA, space-based surveillance systems, and information technology contributed immensely to the Chinese assessment of future warfare. In the backdrop of the 1991 Gulf War, Chinese RMA strategists concluded that in the future naval vessels will have to be defended by a system of layered defence formations and stealth techniques. The concept of multi-layered defence means an all-round arrangement of surveillance, detection and weapon systems operating in close contact with each other. The target would be detected at long distances and attacked far from the fleet.[41] According to Yu Guoquan , Director of Department of Naval Equipment Technology and Warship Division, future warship designs will be technology-intensive and will offer more flexibility in terms of equipment facilitating multi-environment exploitation.[42] There would be several transformations in aircraft carriers including their design, size, capability, and technology and these platforms would continue to be a strategic tool available to the navies. For medium and small navies, the submarine will be the platform of choice due to its stealth, strike capabilities and low cost of nuclear propulsion. Motivated by RMA, the PLA Navy has begun restructuring its forces in terms of human resource and platforms. There are no indicators and trends to suggest that the naval human resource is being reduced, instead there is evidence to show that naval ships and submarines are being modernized and equipped with modern warfare tools to meet the growing demands and complexities of emerging warfare that has significant assents on information warfare.

It is not surprising to note that there is strong evidence of U.S. influence on the PLA Navy's strategic thought as well as on the understanding of revolution in military affairs. Significantly, Alvin Toffler, William Owens, and Martin Libicki are alluded to in PLA Navy writings on RMA. For instance, Professor Zhang Zhao Zhong, who served in the PLA Navy for three decades and was head of the Science and Technology Research Office, National Defense University, is perhaps the most celebrated writer in China on matters relating to military affairs, conflict with Taiwan, etc. He published three books titled *Who Will Win the Next War?* (Shei Hui Ying Xia Yi Zhanzheng?), *How Far is War From Us?* (Zhanzheng Li Women You Duoyuan?) and *Who is the Next Target?* (Xia Yige Mubiao Shi Shei?).[43] Among these, the first two provide a Chinese perspective on information warfare. In the book *Who Will Win the Next War?* Professor Zhang Zhao Zhong notes that militaries the world over are placing significant importance on technology-intensive weaponry and in the case of the United States, it is building a highly digitalized military force that is transforming itself to meet the requirements of the 21st century warfare. *How Far is War From Us?* deals with theories of information warfare, issues relating to C4I2SR, IW, digitalization of the battle space and the networked military platforms

In recent years, China's defence, science and technology sector is growing but it will still take at least two to three decades to come out of obsolescence to the technological sophistication levels of the West. For that to fructify, it will need to resort to import-substitution of technology, foreign collaboration, training domestic human resources and most importantly, large fiscal resources. As a result, the PLA has been engaged in an internal debate on "Build or Buy". Professor Zhang Zhao Zhong expounds that RMA has forced the PLA Navy to accept that "concepts drive platform decisions rather than the reverse". Zhang also notes that although commercial off-the-shelf technology (COTS) support interoperability, this could result in vulnerability due to the fact that the adversary is familiar with the exploitation parameters of such technologies.[44]

In 1986, China launched the National High Technology Research and Development Programme, also called the 863 Programme covering twenty fields, to ensure its competitiveness in the international market as well as to improve China's R&D competence in high-end technology development.[45] Under the 863 Programme, several disciplines were identified as priority areas and include biotechnology, information, automation, energy, advanced materials, marine, space and laser.

China's defence electronics industry has supported the modernization effort of the PLA Navy and several new ship-borne radars, electronic support systems, electronic counter-measure equipment and a variety of electronic intelligence systems have been fitted on board ships. The China National Electronic Import and Export Corporation, with four subsidiaries and twenty-nine branches, have emerged as a nodal agency for the manufacture of modern information warfare equipment.[46] Similarly, the China Precision Machinery Import and Export Corporation contributed immensely to the development of missiles for the Chinese Navy.[47]

Satellites

The White Paper titled "China's Space Activities" published in December 2003 notes that since ancient times the Chinese were the front runners in gunpowder rocketry and continue to strive for peaceful use of outer space.[48] China has made great advances in the space domain that is showcased by the growth and extensive application of space-based systems in social, political, security, and science and technology fields. During 1985 to 2000, China launched and put into orbit more than 600 satellites and is fast emerging as a global space power. It has also made great strides in the fields of multi-satellite launch with a single rocket, rockets with cryogenic fuel, strap-on rockets, launch of geo-stationary satellites and Telemetry Tracking and Command (TT&C) networks.

The Eleventh Five-Year Programme (2006–11) for National Economic and Social Development and The National Guideline for Medium- and Long-term Plans for Science and Technology Development (2006–20) spell out the long-term development goals for the Chinese space industry. The future space technology development programmes envisage manned space flight, lunar exploration, high-resolution earth observation, a new launch vehicle to put into orbit several telecommunication, navigation and remote-sensing satellites. These satellites have both civilian and military uses; in the civilian domain, the satellites are used for telecommunications and broadcasting, weather forecasting, marine survey, monitoring the marine environment and several other peaceful uses, and in the military domain, Chinese satellites can provide photographic and electronic intelligence.

It is a well-known fact that space-based capability is intrinsically dual-use in nature. Based on their resolution capability, they can perform civilian functions and can be exploited for military tasks including to improve the efficiency and effectiveness of both strategic and cruise missile systems. The first-generation Chinese imaging satellites did not have the capability to provide near real-time imagery and used film canisters that are dropped back to earth for processing.[49] The Chinese digital transmission technology and satellites can now provide high-resolution imagery for intelligence purposes. Advances have also been made in the field of synthetic aperture radar technologies to provide radar imagery and these advances and enhanced capabilities enable China to have multiple uses in both civilian and military applications.

The military satellites are most suitable for electronic intelligence and reconnaissance, particularly to monitor potential military activity and vessel traffic in areas such as the Taiwan Strait and the South China Sea, thus enhancing greater situational awareness and providing early warning to impending dangers that are critcal for national security. China has established several tracking, telemetry and control (TT&C) systems on the mainland as well as on island territories in the South China Sea.[50] For instance, a maritime satellite communication earth station has been set up in Beijing to enhance communication links with ships and other naval vessels in the Pacific and the Indian Ocean Region. China is also believed to have signal monitoring facilities in Myanmar and Pakistan. China's first overseas Space Tracking and Control Station at Tarawa in the Republic of Kiribati, situated in the Pacific Ocean was equipped with the orbit survey satellite communication equipment.[51] It enabled China to widen the range of coverage of China's space tracking and control network and strengthen the space tracking and control capabilities. This facility, however, had to be dismantled due to domestic political conditions in Kiribati.[52]

The PLA relies on the U.S. GPS (global-positioning system)[53] and the Russian Glonass system. It is developing its own global positioning system centered on the Beidou series of satellites. Also called Compass Navigation Satellite System, the Beidou system comprises a constellation of thirty-five satellites, including five geo-stationary earth orbit satellites and thirty medium earth orbit satellites to cover the whole of China and surrounding areas including seas.[54] The Beidou 2 system, an advancement over the Beidou 1, can provide 0.5-metre accuracy compared to Beidou 1's ten-metre resolution. The primary aim of building an indigenous global positioning system is to reduce reliance on the U.S. Global Positioning System (GPS) that remains vulnerable to jamming.

China has also invested in the European Union's Galileo global positioning system.[55] Naturally, the United States viewed the Chinese partnership in the Galileo programme with great concern and believes that this initiative provides the PLA with an alternate to the GPS and could pose several military challenges to the United States. As noted earlier, for China, this can overcome the vulnerability of relying on the U.S. GPS, particularly during times of tension and crisis.

Several of the Chinese space initiatives are linked to military programmes. The ongoing exploration and research efforts point to the fact that the PLA is seriously examining the possibility of a conflict with the United States to seek control over outer space. Several counterspace systems such as the space-based "killer" satellites, kinetic-kill vehicles, ground-based lasers, and electronic jammers are under consideration.[56] Also of interest to China are the directed energy weapons and agile microsatellites that possess the ability to attack other space-based platforms. Chinese intentions with regard to counter-space operations has been demonstrated by the January 2007 anti-satellite test.[57] A rocket launched from the Xichang Launch Facility in Sichuan province destroyed a meteorological satellite in a low-earth orbit. The Chinese were quick to set international fears aside and noted that the test was not aimed at any country, but the test clearly demonstrated Chinese intentions in space and is a direct challenge to U.S. space superiority.

The PLA Navy plays a significant role in the Chinese space development programmes. Built under Project 718 and classified as maritime aerospace survey vessels (Long View), the Yuan Wang satellite-tracking ships host an impressive array of dish antennas, a variety of on board computers and electronics to track and control the spacecraft, as well as weather forecasting equipment.[58] The history of these types of vessels goes back to the mid-1960s when Premier Zhou Enlai suggested that China build its own fleet of ocean-going missile- and space-tracking vessels. In 1980, the vessels were deployed for the tests and recovery of the warhead of DF-5 and JL-1 missiles and tracking China's first geostationary communication satellite DFH-2. Since then, these vessels have been deployed for various space and missile tests. The current inventory includes five such vessels and these are deployed in the Pacific, the Indian Ocean and the Atlantic Ocean for TT&C operations involving satellites, missiles and space craft recovery. These vessels are also responsible for search and rescue missions.

The PLA Navy also operates major SIGINT stations located in Shanghai and on Hainan Island. The former covers the Yellow Sea and the East China Sea and the latter is responsible for monitoring electronic and signal traffic in the South China Sea and the Philippines.[59] Also, SIGINT monitoring facilities have been established on the Rocky Island and Woody Island in the Parcels and Mischief Reef in the Spratly group of islands responsible for monitoring electronic traffic in the South China Sea. The PLA Navy ships host a variety of electronic warfare systems including ECM and ESM equipment. Some of these are indigenously developed and some are based on Soviet/Russian designs. In order to monitor naval activity in the Pacific Ocean, China has established sky-wave based over-the-horizon radar stations and also set up networks of underwater sonars to monitor U.S. submarines.[60]

INDIA AND REVOLUTION IN MILITARY AFFAIRS

Critical need for industrial-technological infrastructure and a desire for self-sufficiency is the primary driver that has shaped the technological revolution in India. Since the 1990s, economic reform and liberalization processes have been underway to make Indian industry more competitive in the international market as well as to augment the domestic technological base for national technological developments. A series of initiatives have improved the performance of public sector and state-owned enterprises, and the private sector has been provided with incentives to support the technological revolution. The border conflicts with China and Pakistan have also been instrumental in developing self-sufficiency in military hardware and the growth of the computer and electronic industry.[61]

The Indian Government set up an electronics committee to devise a strategy to build a domestic technological infrastructure base and reduce dependence on imported technologies. The Department of Electronics, the Electronic Commission, Electronics Corporation of India Limited (ECIL) and Electronic Export Processing Zones further supported this initiative. By the 1980s, the government had announced new computer policies, software development and exports, and training of specialist manpower. Indian-owned companies were able to establish a large share in the domestic market.[62]

Since the 1990s, the Indian IT industry has been growing at an impressive pace and has received substantial support from the government. A series of measures was undertaken by the government that contributed to the growth of the IT industry in India which included the setting-up of a nodal ministry for IT and related issues and introduced several special bills in Parliament for the promotion and regulation of the IT sector. It set up a national venture capital fund and developed several software technological parks under the Department of Electronics (DoE).

The Indian military establishment has benefited from the growth in the IT industry. Both the army and navy have exploited the satellite-based telecommunication system and developed their own respective networks. The Indian Space Research Organisation (ISRO) and the Department of Space (DoS) have adopted policies to support networks to meet the demands of the military. Special emphasis has been given to the quality of electronic equipment, identification of reliable and diverse sources of supply, and training of manpower.[63]

At the policy-making level, the Ministry of Defence established the Directorate General for Information Warfare for formulating policy and guidelines for different facets of information warfare and monitoring its implementation in the army.[64] The government is also examining setting up a tri-service body that would coordinate with the Home Ministry and intelligence agencies for coordinated information warfare against external forces as well as against insurgent groups operating in the country.

REVOLUTION IN NAVAL AFFAIRS AND THE INDIAN NAVY

The Indian Navy is a technologically advanced force and global trends in Revolution in Naval Affairs (RNA) are impacting on its strategic thinking and force structure. There is widespread application of IT and related systems in tactical doctrines, operational deployments, logistic support systems and administrative functions. The Indian Navy has taken note of the developments in information warfare and has set in motion a series of initiatives towards a network-centric force that is focused on Network Centric Warfare (NCW) under which a number of programmes and projects are underway to understand and build a networked navy through optimum exploitation of information technology. The 2006–07 Ministry of Defence Annual Report notes that networking and e-enabled solutions are the two key thrust areas of the Indian Navy and several IT applications have been initiated across a wide spectrum of naval activities.[65] These initiatives can enhance the operational efficiency of the force through better resource planning and war-fighting capability. The Indian naval leadership too remains conscious of the emerging trends in naval warfare and has placed immense emphasis on high technology, changes in warfare, the necessity to re-evaluate the existing policies, strategies and doctrines, future needs of the force, development and acquisition of automated systems and networks to facilitate a joint and networked force.[66]

At the helm, naval planners have been evolving a comprehensive strategy to make the Indian Navy relevant in the 21st century. There is a visible emphasis on information technology, information warfare and NCW in their strategic thought and articulations. It is argued that electronic warfare has moved from the periphery of military planning to centrestage, but there still remain challenges of absorbing technical details.[67] The leadership envisions a knowledge-based Indian Navy where information technology is the driver, C4I2SR systems are the tools, and a technology-proficient human resource drives the transformation processes. The thrust is on developing seamless integrated networks at the operational levels to maximize combat power and facilitate networked and interoperable operations to meet the transformed battle space. Also, the shore-based segment of the Indian Navy is being networked, including logistical material, medical and human resources.[68] It is envisaged that real-time networking of units ashore and afloat is long and arduous and would be the major thrust area during the Eleventh and Twelfth Defence Plan periods.

At the conceptual level, the naval leadership notes that transformation not only involves creation of capabilities but also organization changes, war-fighting concepts, tactical doctrines and operating procedures.[69] At the heart of transformation thinking lies the willingness to constantly challenge old thinking and adapt to new concepts of operations that are currently based on seamless networks. Also, network-centric operations dictate changes in not only the weaponry, but also in the training of personnel, who are the end-users.

The *Indian Naval Doctrine for Information Warfare* (INDIW) spells out the Information Warfare (IW) strategy for the Indian Navy in the 21st century.[70] The doctrine highlights the transformation trends among several navies as a result of conclusions drawn from recent conflicts in terms of the relevance of technology as a tool for information superiority. The INDIW notes that with the advent of information technologies, a new paradigm of warfare has emerged but offers both opportunities and challenges that were not available to maritime forces in the past.[71] The doctrine encourages tactical commanders to understand the transformational trends and have a clear understanding of the complexities of information warfare. Besides, they must be proficient in handling, disseminating and exploiting the available information for conduct of operations successfully.

In the Indian context, the Indian Navy was perhaps the first among the fighting forces to imbibe NCW. It established information technology-enabled connectivity among its shore-based command centres, ships and other support establishments including logistic centres. The navy also conceptualized seamless integrated network architecture at the operational and support levels to exploit combat power and evolved information technology-based concepts that were in synergy with international practices to facilitate interoperability with international navies such as the United States, Britain, France and Japan. The overall approach was to make the Indian Navy relevant to international maritime operations that are conducted on common high-speed networks and to respond to international operations in cooperation with multinational forces to support international efforts in the event of emergencies and crisis.

In that context, the Indian Navy has been able to exploit its technological proficiency and translate the same into operational competence for interoperability with diverse navies that host varying levels of NCW capabilities. Interoperability has facilitated multi-nation joint exercises and *ad hoc* coalitions that bring with them a variety of platforms, personnel, doctrines and operating procedures. Modern-day naval operations involve a variety of platforms that function together in real time, and whose scale and scope can be localized or encompass a huge maritime space anywhere in the oceans. At the functional-operational level, the Malabar 07–2 conducted in 2007 in the Bay of Bengal showcased interoperability between the navies of the United States and India.[72]

Broadly, the Indian Navy's NCW development strategy envisages a shift from platform-centric navy to a network-centric navy, information technology-driven concepts of operation, entrenchment of information technology across all operational and support functions, development of a C4I grid among command posts both ashore and at sea, including joint command centres for integrated operations, continuous assessment of technology needs of the NCW operations, NCW education strategy, development of a technology culture amongst rank and file and collaboration with industry to meet future needs.

The Indian naval strategy seeks development of networks for seamless integration of sea, shore, air and space platforms so that decision-making is knowledge-based and on a real-time navy-wide basis at sea and ashore. This would be achieved through integration of sensors, weapons, decision-support apparatuses, communication/data link nodes, navigation aids, computer/processors, networking elements, integrating/interfacing devices. In that context, information technology is the facilitator of network-centric warfare for combat power.[73] The Indian Navy's concept of Network Centric Operations (NCO) pivots on integration of individual surface, subsurface and air platforms forming an overarching network connected through high-speed data links to provide a common picture of the battle space to commanders at sea and ashore. For instance, the leadership envisions a Fleet Commander with his forces near the Horn of Africa who can view the radar picture of a helicopter operation along the Indian coast or an aircraft flying at 10,000 feet, connected to a submarine to enable it to fire her missiles.[74]

Expounding on information warfare, the doctrine identifies key technologies that will be in the forefront of future warfare and will shape the battle space. These are (a) C4ISR (command, control, communication, computers, intelligence, surveillance, and reconnaissance) technologies and (b) precision-force technologies.[75] These technologies will have several strategic applications in future warfare and will have extensive application in the field of space, electromagnetic spectrum, micro-embedded technologies to penetrate enemy decision loops and weapon systems. At the heart of the doctrine lies the belief that information superiority can be the winning tool in a war[76] and in order to protect against enemy attack, force posture must be based on intensity of attack. Towards that end, the doctrine lists five stages: (a) Defensive Posture centred on information protection, (b) Offensive Posture emphasizes information denial, (c) Quantity Posture places emphasis on the primacy of information transport capability, (d) Quality Posture's main thrust is on efficient information management, and (e) Sponge Posture lays stress on attaining information dominance through innovative means and improvisations.[77]

The doctrine acknowledges the fact that RNA would result in major changes in doctrine, organization and force structure, but it raises an important question about the mindset of its users? It is easy to import an idea but to implement it is another challenge altogether. This demands change in thinking, creativity and innovations to exploit high technology. It calls for special training, education on the changing nature of warfare and a change in attitude towards the complexity of ongoing technology transformations. There will also be added demands on leadership at all levels. It will call for new command structures, dismantling or modification of existing set-ups and even the disbanding of middle-level management layers.[78]

The Indian Ministry of Defence Annual Report 2006–07 notes that networking and e-enabled solutions are two key thrust areas and the Indian Navy has initiated a large number of IT applications aimed at enhancing efficiency in the fields of maintenance, healthcare management, and human resource and material management that acts as a catalyst for resource planning and war-fighting capability.[79]

There are significant changes underway in combat operations by the Indian Navy, primarily driven by technology both within the force as well as with the U.S. Navy, British Royal Navy, French Navy, Japanese Navy and Singapore Navy that are technologically advanced and host hi-tech networked systems. At the hardware level, there is visible stress on long-range precision-guided munitions and intelligent/smart systems that can effectively destroy fixed and moving targets at long distances. The Indian Navy has been able to integrate diverse systems on board platforms as well as in tactical doctrines that are exhibited by the weaponry installed on Indian Navy ships. Existing low-technology platforms are upgraded with high-technology systems that are capable of performing multiple functions.

Networks, Systems and Training

In 1979, the Indian Navy formulated the first master plan for "computerization of the Navy" and a building block approach enabled it to evolve itself into a highly networked force compared to the army and the air force. There are more than 400 naval units (surface, underwater, air including support establishments ashore) connected through a complex network of LANs (Local Area Networks), WANs (Wide Area Networks) and MANs (Metropolitan Area Networks) facilitating a seamless connectivity across Indian Navy establishments and other organizations that are engaged in business with the navy.[80] The LANs, WANs and MANs are supported by a Navy Enterprise-Wide Network (NEWN), a flexible network and there are plans to build fibre-optic networks to connect thirty naval stations.[81]

The Sanchar Automatic Message Switching System (AMSS) is a tactical information-based network system that links all communication centres and Project ODOC networks in the various maritime operation centres to the War Room in New Delhi. The navy also plans to connect the National Command Authority, Naval War Room in New Delhi, Maritime Operations Centres, Fleet Operation Centres and Command Shelters into a computer-aided networked web for decision and support activities.[82]

There are several other systems such as the Computerized Action Information System (CAIS), Equipment Modular for Command and Control Applications (EMCCA), Saransh Submarine Combat System, Tactical Mission System for Advanced Light Helicopter (ALH), Tactical Data Links (LINK II, SADL), Tactical Decision Support Systems like TMS and ODOC, Trinetra Stand Alone and Network Security System, Integrated Logistic Management System (ILMS), Weapon Equipment Depot (WED)

Net, Computerization and Networking of Dockyards and several networks at the level of local administration.

While there have been some noteworthy investments in information systems to support RMA, there have been significant developments in training the human resource.[83] Acknowledging the fact that humans are the critical enabler to harness information technology for warfare, in 1998 the Indian Navy announced its IT policy and it was envisaged to develop a computer-literate force by 2002.[84] Several computer courses, at various levels, were introduced and engineer and electrical officers with M-Tech qualifications and sailors (engineer artificers) were encouraged to undertake information-technology education. The Naval Institute of Computer Applications (NICA), located in Mumbai, is the premier training centre for training Indian Navy personnel in information technology. At the grassroots level, from 2010 onwards, all new officers recruited would be engineers with B. Tech degrees.[85] Cadets at the Naval Academy (commissioned on 1 January 2009) are to be awarded B. Tech (Bachelors of Technology) degrees from the Jawaharlal Nehru University (JNU) in Delhi and endorsed by the All India Council for Technical Education (AICTE). The initiative is driven by the argument that the battles of the future would be technology-dominated and the focus will be on techno-savvy officers.[86]

Satellites

Space-based systems are an integral part of the Indian armed forces and provide critical information in the conduct of military operations. Satellite imagery for the Indian armed forces is provided through several "Space"-related agencies including the Indian Space Research Organisation (ISRO), and the Defence Imagery Processing and Analysis Centre (DIPAC).[87] The INDIW acknowledges the need to augment space-based sensors for NCW and the naval leadership has argued that satellites provide C4I network, facilitate NCW and enable the navy to gain battle space dominance and therefore projected its need for a dedicated satellite. In 2004, the Scientific Adviser to the Defence Minister stated that India was planning to launch a satellite for use by the military and the project was being developed jointly with the Defence Research and Development Organisation and Indian Space Research Organisation (ISRO)[88] and there were plans by ISRO to launch the first Technology Experiment Satellite-I (TES-I) from Sriharikota that came to be known as a precursor to the planned military satellite. The TES-I is capable of mapping and taking pictures of border areas and can beam one-metre high-resolution images of troop movements and armoured columns to earth stations in India. Its need was most felt for monitoring Pakistani military movements during the 2001 India-Pakistan military stand-off.

In 2003, the ISRO launched the RESOURCESAT-1 (IRS-P6), a highly sophisticated remote-sensing satellite with a resolution of nearly six metres.[89] On 5 May 2005, ISRO launched a 2.5-metre resolution CARTOSAT-1 satellite capable of taking pictures of an object from two different angles.[90] India is engaged in building a satellite-based maritime surveillance and reconnaissance system to facilitate a continuous watch on maritime developments in Indian areas of maritime interest[91] and in February 2008, the Chief of the Defence Research and Development Organisation (DRDO) announced that a blueprint for a satellite-based coastal surveillance system was under development.[92] The system built around a specially fabricated satellite (on the lines of the Oceansat of the Indian Space Research Organisation)[93] will be placed in the geostationary orbit and operational by 2012.

In 2004, it was announced that US$100 million had been allocated for launching a communication satellite for exclusive use by the Indian Navy. The satellite, to be launched by the Indian Space Research Organisation (ISRO), will enable Indian Navy ships, submarines and aircraft to be networked with each other and facilitate critical connectivity required for a networked force. This connectivity will provide a digital tactical battle space view of the dispersed fleet formations, aircraft locations and even submarine deployments. Besides, shore-based intelligence support will facilitate building a larger strategic picture. This should provide a quantum leap to the quality of tactical operations undertaken by the Indian Navy. In 2008, the naval leadership announced that there were plans for a space-based reconnaissance system to be used by the three services.[94] This will be critical for maritime domain-awareness and could also be shared with friendly navies that operate in the Indian Ocean and could contribute significantly to the Indian Navy's efforts at foreign cooperation.

The ISRO plans also include launching a military satellite CARTOSAT–2A (on a Polar Satellite Launch Vehicle) fitted with a range of cameras to provide advance imagery with a high spatial resolution that would give India the ability to monitor missile launches in the neighbourhood.[95] In addition, advanced reconnaissance and surveillance satellites are needed to provide India round-the-day monitoring capabilities. These include the Radar Imaging Satellite (FRISAT) that would carry C-band synthetic aperture radar with a spatial resolution of three to fifty metres with a ten to twenty-four kilometres swatch and the OCEANSAT-2 equipped with eight-band multi-spectral cameras that can monitor up to 1,420 kilometres of ocean space and track ships and submarines.

At the institution level, two important agencies support the Indian Navy's information networking; the Directorate of Information Technology (DIT) and the Information Warfare (IW) cell. The DIT is responsible for the implementation, operation and projection of information-based support infrastructure. It is the central agency that procures hardware for the navy.[96] The IW cell is the executive agency for the conduct of information warfare and is managed under the Assistant Chief of Naval Staff (Information Warfare and Operations). Information Warfare cells have also been constituted at the Command Headquarters to integrate information warfare as a part of naval plans. These cells coordinate all information and develop techniques relating to non-lethal operations. The doctrinal and policy issues relating to Information Warfare fall under the purview of the IW cell under the Naval Headquarters. It also undertakes collection, processing and dissemination of information for decision-making processes and measures to ensure security of information. As a nodal agency, it coordinates various information warfare tasks and provides administrative support to related agencies in terms of security of information and validation of doctrinal concepts.

Bharat Electronics Limited (BEL) in collaboration with the Indian Navy and Centre for Development of Telematics has produced the Combat Management System (CMS) for the C4I2SR requirements of the Indian Navy.[97] The Defence Electronics Research Laboratory (DLRL), a constituent lab under the Defence Research and Development Organisation (DRDO), and the Indian Navy have jointly developed the Sangraha system[98] that comprises a family of Electronic Warfare suites for different naval platforms capable of "intercepting, detecting and classifying pulsed, CW, PRF-agile, frequency-agile and chirp radars".[99] The system integrates the Electronic System Measures (ESM) and ECM suites of assorted platforms deployed in the air, sea, underwater and ashore. The system also incorporates integration of state-of-the-art technologies such as Multiple-Beam Phased array jammers meant to simultaneously handle multiple threats. Airborne platforms of the Indian Navy are being fitted with a variety of ESM systems. For instance, the Kite ESM system is installed on Kamov and Chetak helicopters, Eagle ESM systems on Dornier aircraft and Homi ESM on TU-142 aircraft. Similarly, subsurface forces and surface are equipped with ESM: the EKM Submarines are equipped with the Porpoise ESM system[100] and the Ellora system developed jointly by the Defence Electronic Research Laboratory of DRDO and Bharat Electronics Limited (BEL) has been installed on board INS Beas and P-17 class frigates will also be equipped with the same system.[101] Elllora is an offshoot of the Sangraha and can handle multiple threats five times faster than the servo-controlled jammers. Observers believe that the system is similar in appearance to the Shark MBAT developed by Israel's Rafael Advanced Defence Systems Limited, suggesting that it could be a transfer of technology by Israel or simply a generic design for such systems.

The Indian Navy's requirement for an Airborne Warning and Control System (AWACS) has been gathering momentum. The navy is seeking a medium-sized, twin turbofan-powered aircraft with Multi-role Electronic Scanned Array (MESA) radar capable of 360-degree coverage and simultaneous air and sea search and tracking of 3,000 targets including control of friendly-fighter aircraft.[102] The platform is being built by the DRDO is expected to cost Rs.1,800 crore (US$390 million) and will be ready for delivery in 2011.[103]

At the organizational level, the Indian Navy effectively executed several support systems such as the ILMS (Integrated Logistic Management System) and WMS (Works Management System). These systems integrate the Indian Navy's logistic centres with ships, naval repair centres, dockyards and shore-based organizations, including command headquarters.

Industry

A complex network requires a high level of system engineering, human skills, expertise and infrastructure. The Indian strategy aims to harness Commercial Off-the-Shelf Technology (COTS) and trained manpower available in the civil domain. In its efforts towards "self-reliance through indigenisation", the navy has relied heavily on its in-house capability in system engineering and software development; it has also tapped the resources of the highly talented Indian IT industry. For instance, the services of domestic Indian IT companies like Satyam Technologies and Tata Consultancy Services are being sought for developing software for the navy's in-house information warfare systems.[104] The Confederation of Indian Industry (CII) has acted as a catalyst to foster a long-term Indian Navy-Industry partnership that lays the grounds for joint working and co-development of naval systems and applications. These initiatives have led to strategic alliances with leading IT houses in terms of technology transfer as well as resource-sharing among personnel. For instance the Weapons and Electronic System Engineering Establishment (WESEE) of the Indian Navy and the Indian Institute of Technology at Kanpur (IIT, Kanpur) have collaborated for the engineering and development of Trinetra, an encryption code for naval communications, which is considered to be a major block cipher system.[105]

It is true that IT-intensive systems are expensive and have till date and in future will continue to be acquired by rich nations that have both a sophisticated domestic technological base and in the absence of such capability have fiscal resources to acquire from external sources. In the Indian context, the IT industry has evolved to be a world-class institution and Indian software specialists are in great demand globally. Interestingly, the IT industry contributes significantly towards the national economy.

There are no publicly available figures to determine the percentage of Indian military expenditure in the development of RMA-related technologies. However, some estimates suggest that India will need to spend Rs.6,000–7,000 crore (US$1.3–1.5 billion) to make the armed forces network-centric.[106] For the Indian Navy, the cost of inducting frontline technology could be around Rs.300–400 crore (US$65–87 million) to make the force network centric and the navy has so far expended nearly Rs.1,000 crore (US$217 million). The naval leadership has acknowledged that there will remain fiscal constraints and the force will have to be selective in its IT-related equipment induction programme and "we will have to pick and choose on what technology we need at what time".[107]

Foreign Collaborations

According to the Associated Chambers of Commerce and Industry of India (ASSOCHAM), the Indian domestic defence market under the private sector is expected to grow at nearly 30 per cent and could exceed US$700 million by 2010.[108] Currently, the Indian military establishment, particularly the Indian Navy, procures 70 per cent (by value) of the high-end military hardware from foreign sources since the public sector is ill-equipped to meet the needs of the navy due to lack of indigenous R&D, resulting in low quality and slow rate of supply. According to the Indian Navy Chief, Admiral Sureesh Mehta, the Indian Navy, in collaboration with a foreign partner, is developing a "path breaking" new generation of Unmanned Aerial Vehicle (UAV), designed like a helicopter for reconnaissance of spaces over land and sea for collection of intelligence and imageries to be transmitted back to shore.[109] Lockheed Martin is an important contender to meet all C4ISR requirements of the Indian armed forces, with an emphasis on Net Centric Operations.[110] Similarly, Boeing has established Boeing India, an integrated enterprise-wide office in India. Boeing has offered the P-8I, a derivative of the B-737-based P-8A Poseidon anti-submarine warfare aircraft under development for the U.S. Navy and has also bid for the Indian Air Force's requirement for 126 Multi-Role Combat Aircraft (MRCA).[111]

CONCLUSION

In sum, significant advances in economic, technological and education fields have provided the required impetus for China and India to pursue the RMA and improve military capabilities. In that context, both countries exhibited their capacity and capability to absorb and imbibe RMA in the strategic and tactical naval doctrines that is best reflected through their aggressive naval acquisition plans. Besides, the 1991 Gulf War acted as a catalyst in the transformation of the two navies.

The trends in naval acquisitions of both India and China reveal an interesting picture of naval weapons proliferation. Some of the acquisitions are defensive but others are certainly more offensive. These include power projection platforms like aircraft carrier, destroyers, submarines, modern surface combatants, and maritime aircraft (both fighters and reconnaissance). Trends also show that there has been a proliferation of missiles, advanced torpedoes, electronic warfare equipment, and radar systems as well as stealth technologies. The qualitative and quantitative nature of these acquisitions is highly flavoured with information technology.

Both India and China have the strategic potential to aggressively pursue and imbibe RMA in their strategic doctrines. Presently, there are no indications to suggest that the two navies have the technological capability to challenge either the U.S. or the Japanese navy. However, given their limitations, both continue to develop a hybrid navy based on imported and domestically-produced weapons ands sensors.

Notes

1. Bates Gill and Lonnie Henley, "China and the Revolution in Military Affairs", Strategic Studies Institute, Pennsylvania, 20 May 1996, pp. 20–24.
2. Giri Deshingkar, "Strategic Thinking in Ancient India and China: Kautilya and Sunzi", in *Across the Himalayan Gap: An Indian Quest for Understanding China*, edited by Tan Chung Tan (New Delhi: Gyan Publishing House, 1998); Roger Boesche, "Kautilya's 'Arthasastra' on War and Diplomacy in Ancient India", *The Journal of Military History* 67, no. 1 (January 2003): 36.
3. Alvin and Heidi Toffler, *War and Antiwar: Survival at the Dawn of the Century* (New York: Warner Books, 1993), p. 37.
4. Andrew F. Krepenevich, "Cavalry to Computer: The Pattern of Military Revolution", *The National Interest* (Fall 1994): 30, cited in A. Anand, *Information Technology: The Future Warfare Weapon* (New Delhi: Ocean Books, 2000), p. 37; also see Kapil Kak, "Revolution in Military Affairs: An Appraisal", *Strategic Analysis* 24, issue 1 (April 2000): 5–15.

5. Norman Friedman, *The Naval Institute Guide to World Naval Weapon Systems* (Annapolis, M.D.: Naval Institute Press, 2006), p. 34. Also see Robert Bud and Philip Gummett, eds., *Cold War, Hot Science: Applied Research in Britain's Defence Laboratories, 1945–1990* (London: NMSI Trading Ltd., 2002), p. 258.
6. Akshay Joshi, *Information Age and India* (Delhi: Knowledge World, 2001), p. 83.
7. Information Warfare Bulletin, *Infowar Navy*, Indian Navy, Naval Headquarters, New Delhi, March 1998.
8. "Iraq Faces Massive U.S. Missile Barrage", available at <http://www.cbsnews.com/stories/2003/01/24/eveningnews/main537928.shtml> (accessed 26 January 2003). A Pentagon official had noted, "There will not be a safe place in Baghdad" ... "The sheer size of this has never been seen before, never been contemplated before."
9. Stephen Budiansky, "Air War: Striking in Ways We Haven't Seen", *Washington Post*, 6 April 2003.
10. Geoffrey Till, "The Navies of the Asia Pacific in a Revolutionary Age", in *Maritime Security and Cooperation in Asia Pacific: Towards the 21st Century*, edited by Dalchoong Kim, Seo-Hang Lee, and Jin-Hyun Park (Seoul: Dooilnet 2000), p. 7.
11. P.T. Mitchell, "Small Navies and Network-centric Warfare", in *Military Transformation and Strategy: Revolutions in Military Affairs and Small States*, edited by Bernard Loo (New York: Routledge, 2008), p. 130.
12. Cited in Prem Chand, "Network-Centric Warfare: Some Fundamentals", *Air Power Journal* 2, no. 1 (Spring 2005).
13. *Indian Naval Doctrine for Information Warfare*, Information Warfare Cell, Naval Headquarters, New Delhi, 2001, p. 45.
14. Timothy L. Thomas, "Chinese and American Network Warfare", *Joint Forces Quarterly*, issue 38, p. 77.
15. Paul Dibb, "The Revolution in Military Affairs and Asian Security", *Survival* 39, no. 4 (Winter 1997–98): 93–116.
16. Qingxuan Meng and Li Mingzhi, "New Economy and ICT Development in China", Discussion Paper no. 2001/76, World Institute of Development Economics Research, September 2001, p. 2.
17. Major General Yashwant Deva, *Secure or Perish* (New Delhi: Ocean Books, 2000), p. 20.
18. For more details, see China Internet Network Information Center (CNNIC), available at <http://www.cnnic.net.cn/html/Dir/2003/12/12/2000.htm> (accessed 16 November 2007).
19. Janice M. Burn and Maris G. Martinson, "Information Technology Production and Application in Hong Kong and China: Progress, Policies and Prospects", in *Information Technology Diffusion in Asia Pacific: Perspectives on Policy, Electronic Commerce and Education*, edited by Felix B. Tan, P. Scott Corbett, and Yuk-Yong Wong (Hershey: Idea Group Publishing, 1999), p. 24.

20. For more details see, "CNNIC Released the 21st Statistical Survey Report on the Internet Development in China", China Internet Network Information Centre (CNNIC), the state network information centre of China, available at <http://www.cnnic.net.cn/en/index/0O/index.htm> (accessed 22 January 2008).
21. Joshi, *Information Age and India*, p. 19. Pro-democracy activists used dish antennas and video cassette players for sending messages across China.
22. Ibid., p. 37.
23. Burn and Martinson, "Information Technology Production and Application in Hong Kong and China", p. 25.
24. Shanti Kalathil, "Chinese Media and the Information Revolution", *Harvard Asia Quarterly* (Winter 2002).
25. Xiaodong Li, "The Internet Revolution in China: Current Situation and Future Outlook", in *Towards a Knowledge-based Economy: East Asia's Changing Industrial Geography*, edited by Seiichi Mariyama and Donna Vandenbrink (Singapore: Institute of Southeast Asian Studies, 2003), pp. 112–14.
26. "The China Information Technology Report", available at <http://www.wtexecutive.com/cms/content.jsp?id=com.tms.cms.section.Section_bookstore_chinait> (accessed 23 March 2008).
27. James C. Mulvenon, "The PLA and Information Warfare", in *The People's Liberation Army in the Information Age*, edited by James C. Mulvenon and Richard H. Yang (Santa Monica, C.A.: RAND, 1999), p. 177.
28. Toshi Yoshihara, "Chinese Information Warfare: A Phantom Menace or Emerging Threat?" (Pennsylvania: Strategic Studies Institute, November 2001), p. 11.
29. John Frankenstein, "China's Defence Industries: A New Course", in *The People's Liberation Army in the Information Age*, p. 200. Also see Toshi, *Chinese Information Warfare*, pp. 18–21.
30. Mulvenon, "The PLA and Information Warfare", pp. 175–86.
31. Qiao Liang and Wang Xiangsui, *Unrestricted Warfare* (Beijing: PLA Literature and Arts Publishing House, 1999).
32. Cited in "Military Power of the People's Republic of China 2007", Annual Report to Congress, Office of the Secretary of Defense, U.S. Department of Defense, p. 13.
33. "Suspected Chinese Hacker Attacks Target, MND", *Taipei Times*, 19 June 2006.
34. M. Ehsan Ahrari, "Chinese Prove to be Attentive Students of Information Warfare", *Jane's Intelligence Review* (October 1997): 473. Also see Deva, *Secure or Perish*, pp. 198–200.
35. Tom A. Peter, "Alleged Chinese Hacker Attack Stirs Fears of Digital Cold War", 7 September 2007, available at <http://www.csmonitor.com/2007/0906/p99s01-duts.html> (accessed 12 December 2007).
36. Sumner Lemon, "China Worries Hackers Will Strike During Beijing Olympics", 23 April 2008, <http://www.infoworld.com/article/08/04/24/China-worries-

hackers-will-strike-during-Beijing-Olympics_1.html> (accessed 30 June 2008).
37. Indrani Bagchi, "China Mounts Cyber Attacks on Indian Sites", *Times of India*, 5 May 2008.
38. Lemon, "China Worries Hackers Will Strike During Beijing Olympics".
39. Naval Captain Shen Zhongchang, Naval Lieutenant Commander Zhang Haiyin, and Naval Lieutenant Zhou Xinsheng, "21st Century Naval Warfare", in *Chinese Views of Future Warfare*, edited by Michael Pillsbury (Washington, D.C.: National Defence University Press, 1997), pp. 261–74.
40. Naval Captain Shen Zhongchang, Naval Lieutenant Commander Zhang Haiyin, and Naval Lieutenant Zhou Xinsheng, "The Military Revolution in Naval Warfare", in *Chinese Views of Future Warfare*, pp. 261–74.
41. See "Shuimian Jianchuan de fangyu" [Naval Ship Self Defence], *Xiandai Junshi* 15, no. 40 (August 1991): 21–24, cited in Srikant Kondapalli, *China's Naval Power* (New Delhi: Knowledge World, 2001), p. 83.
42. Ibid.
43. "Saber Rattling", *Beijing Scene* 6, issue 5 (12–18 November 2005).
44. Cited in Charles F. Hawkins, "The People's Liberation Army Looks to the Future", *Joint Force Quarterly* (Summer 2000): 11–16.
45. Jon Sigurdson, "China Becoming a Technological Superpower: A Narrow Window of Opportunity", Working Paper no. 194, June 2004, available at <http://swopec.hhs.se/eijswp/papers/eijswp0194.pdf> (accessed 23 September 2007).
46. Ibid., p. 109.
47. Ibid.
48. "China's Space Activities, A White Paper", Information Office of the State Council, the People's Republic of China, available at <http://www.spaceref.com/china/china.white.paper.nov.22.2000.html> (accessed 30 June 2007).
49. For more details see Phillip C. Saunders, "China's Future in Space: Implications for U.S. Security", available at <http://www.space.com/adastra/china_implications_0505.html> (accessed 20 September 2007).
50. For a detailed account of China's SIGINT, ELINT and IW facilities, locations, platforms and equipment see Manuel Cereijo, "La Nueva Cuba", 9 October 2006, available at <http://www.lanuevacuba.com/archivo/manuel-cereijo-125.htm> (accessed 11 June 2007).
51. Phillip Saunders, Jing-dong Yuan, Stephanie Lieggi, and Angela Deters, "China's Space Capabilities and the Strategic Logic of Anti-Satellite Weapons", available at <http://cns.miis.edu/pubs/week/020722.htm> (accessed 24 May 2008).
52. Bruce Gilley, "Pacific Outpost: China's Satellite Station in Kiribati has Military Purposes", *Far Eastern Economic Review*, 30 April 1998, pp. 26–27.
53. China imported its first GPS receivers in the 1980s and is currently a major GPS user.

54. "China to Launch 2 Satellites for Compass Navigation System", *Xinhua*, 14 November 2006.
55. "China Joins EU Space Program to Break US GPS Monopoly", *People's Daily*, 26 September 2003.
56. Martin E.B. France and Richard J. Adams, "The Chinese Threat to US Superiority", *High Frontier Journal* 1, no. 3 (Winter 2005): 17–22.
57. Stephanie C. Lieggi, "Space Arms Race: China's ASAT Test a Wake-up Call", available at <http://cns.miis.edu/pubs/week/070124.htm> (accessed 30 January 2007).
58. "Yuanwang Space Tracking Ships", available at <http://www.sinodefence.com/navy/research_survey/yuanwang.asp> (accessed 30 March 2008).
59. Manuel Cereijo, China and Cuba and Information Warfare (IW), Signals Intelligence (SIGINT), Electronic Warfare (EW) and Cyber-warfare, available at <http://www.amigospais-guaracabuya.org/oagmc207.php> (accessed 26 August 2007).
60. James Lyons, "LYONS: China's One World?", *Washington Times*, 24 August 2008.
61. Joshi, *Information Age and India*, p. 145.
62. Ibid.
63. Ibid., pp. 170–73.
64. Kushal Jeena, "India Sets up IW Directorate", *United Press of India*, 6 September 2007.
65. Annual Report 2006–07, Ministry of Defence, Government of India, p. 28.
66. Discussions at New Delhi with retired and serving Indian Navy officers.
67. Vice Admiral Sangram Singh Byce and Rajni Kant Tewari, *Maritime Electronic Warfare: Soft Kill Measures* (New Delhi: Anmaya Publishers, 2007), p. v.
68. Sureesh Mehta, "The Immediate Need is to Augment and Upgrade Our Capacity for Sustained and Long-Range Airborne Surveillance", *Force* (December 2007): 18–20.
69. Arun Prakash, "Transformational Technologies for Navy of the Future", in *From the Crow's Nest* (New Delhi: Lancer Publishers, 2007), p. 117.
70. *Indian Naval Doctrine for Information Warfare*.
71. Ibid., p. i.
72. For instance, Indian ships used NATO standards "MTP" document for communication frequencies, technical terminology, command structures and were even fitted with special U.S. equipment to connect to its Centrix satellite-based system that enabled the exchange of audio, video and data between the participating ships.
73. *Indian Naval Doctrine for Information Warfare*, p. 45.
74. Arun Prakash, "Aware and Secure", *Force* (June 2007): 4.
75. *Indian Naval Doctrine for Information Warfare*, p. 45.
76. Ibid., p. 2.

77. Ibid., pp. 4–5.
78. Ibid., pp. 13–14.
79. Annual Report 2006–07, Ministry of Defence, Government of India.
80. Prashant Bakshi, "Gearing For Information Warfare", *Indian Express*, 14 December 2000.
81. "CCEA Set to Release Rs.1,077 Crore for Defence Network", *Economic Times*, 17 April 2008.
82. *Indian Naval Doctrine for Information Warfare*, pp. 45–49.
83. Ibid., pp. 89–92.
84. Bakshi, "Gearing For Information Warfare".
85. Josy Joseph, "Navy to Recruit BTech Officers From 2010", *DNA*, 3 March 2008.
86. "Ezhimala Academy to Begin Training in 2009", *The Hindu*, 27 November 2007.
87. *Indian Naval Doctrine for Information Warfare*, pp. 33–34.
88. Fakir Chand, "India to launch military satellite soon: Aatre", available at <http://www.rediff.com/news/2002/aug/02fakir.htm> (accessed 23 October 2007).
89. "PSLV Launches RESOURCESAT-1 (IRS-P6)", available at <http://www.isro.org/pressrelease/Oct17_2003.htm> (accessed 30 June 2007).
90. "Earth Observation System", available at <http://www.isro.org/rep2006/EOS%20System.htm> (accessed 23 May 2006).
91. Annual Report 2006–07, Ministry of Defence, Government of India, p. 28.
92. M. Somasekhar, "DRDO Plans Satellite-Based Coastal Surveillance System", *The Hindu*, 6 February 2008.
93. Reports note that ISRO has developed a satellite-based system to help fishermen to send distress messages. Also, a responder is being installed on boats that follow their location and relays distress messages.
94. Sureesh Mehta, "The Immediate Need is to Augment and Upgrade Our Capacity for Sustained and Long-Range Airborne Surveillance", *Force* (December 2007): 18–20; also see "We Need to Press for Ariel and Satellite Surveillance", *Force* (December 2007): 26–27.
95. "Indian Military to get Hawk Eye in Sky", *Press Trust of India*, 10 June 2007. Also see Udayavani, "Dedicated Military Satellites set for Launch by India's ISRO", available at <http://www.idrw.org/2007/07/29/india_to_launch_dedicated_military_satellite.html> (accessed 26 December 2007).
96. *Indian Naval Doctrine for Information Warfare*, pp. 55–59.
97. "Capability-Driven: An Update on Indian Naval Modernisation", *Vayu Aerospace and Defence Review* (VI/2007): 36.
98. Annual Report 2005–06, Ministry of Defence, Government of India, p. 95.
99. H. Satish, "DLRL Firms Up Projects for Airborne Intelligence", *The Hindu*, 23 February 2008. Also see the website of DLRL at <http://www.drdo.org/labs/dlrl/areas.html> (accessed 2 March 2008).

100. "Sangraha for Indian Navy", *Frontier India Defence and Strategic News Service*, 5 May 2007.
101. "India's Ellora Shipborne ECM Revealed", *Defence Asia Review* 2, no. 2 (March–April 2008): 11.
102. Vivek Raghuvanshi, "India parlays IT expertise into a comprehensive ISR upgrade", *C4ISR Journal* (4 January 2008).
103. "AWACS Project to be Completed by 2011", *The Statesman*, 10 March 2008.
104. "More Greenfield Projects for Navy: Mehta", *Business Standard*, 9 May 2008.
105. Akshay Joshi, "A Holistic View of the Revolution in Military Affairs (RMA)", *Strategic Analysis* 22, no. 11 (February 1999).
106. "Network Centric Warfare", *Press Trust of India*, 21 December 2005, available at <http://www.iansa.org/regions/scasia/documents/ControlArmsIndia-Update-Nov-Dec2005.pdf> (accessed 30 June 2008).
107. Ibid.
108. "Defence Market to touch US$700mn by 2010: ASSOCHAM", *India Infoline News Service*, Mumbai, 11 February 2008, available at <http://www.indiainfoline.com/news/innernews.asp?storyId=58683&lmn=1> (accessed 20 February 2008).
109. "Indian Navy, HAL Developing Next-Generation Rotor-Wing UAV", available at <http://www.domain-b.com/aero/mil_avi/uav/20080212_rotor.html> (accessed 25 June 2008).
110. For more details see, "India", available at <http://www.lockheedmartin.com/asia_pacific/india/index.html> (accessed 30 June 2008).
111. Nick Cook, "All For One: Boeing in India", *Jane's Navy International*, 26 March 2008.

7

STRATEGIC TRANSACTIONS: CHINA, INDIA AND SOUTHEAST ASIA

The rise of Asian power and its transformed strategic profile in the 21st century is predicated on the robust restructuring and rejuvenation of several countries in the region. Among these, China and India have a long history of pre-eminence and are now embarking on the process of economic-industrial transformation reflected in trajectories of their phenomenal and sustained economic growth, socio-economic development, and strategic transformation. The two states have impressively progressed with the strong penchant of adapting their respective cultural and civilizational ethos that has resulted in a powerful and resilient capacity to absorb the western institutional processes and indices of national power. Significantly, these processes and indices have been gradually assimilated into their socio-cultural-political-strategic matrix.

The phenomenal rise of Asia in the 21st century has its foundations in "antiquity". China and India were the two great powers that were the richest and indeed most formidable powers[1] in ancient times, epitomized by their networks of politico-economic and strategic transactions in the neighbourhood in Southeast Asia and as far as Persia, the Eurasian landmass and the Mediterranean. China and India were the pre-eminent maritime powers in Asia that possessed mercantile and naval prowess, which was brought to bear on their respective strategic conduct. The early modern period witnessed the relative decline of the two states in comparison to the imperial-colonial powers of Europe that benefited immensely from the Industrial Revolution. China and India could not compete with the ingress of colonial and mercantile initiatives of the European powers that came from the sea, to the littoral and into the heartland that resulted in their gradual decline and eventual subjugation.

In the civilizational history of Asia, Southeast Asia made a seminal contribution and played a significant role in the prosperity of China and India facilitating movement of people, cultures, and religion otherwise constrained by difficult and challenging overland geography. Notwithstanding its distinctive geographical position as a gateway to the East and the West and its civilizational eminence, there is a tendency to understand Southeast Asia through the prism of Indian and Chinese civilizations. This was due to a wide and dominating prevalence of Indian and Chinese social, cultural, religious practices, and language, trade and even statecraft in the region. Ironically, Southeast Asia came to be known as "Greater India", "Farther India", and "Little China".[2]

In terms of global and regional connectivity, the ancient "Silk Route" stretching thousands of kilometres linking Asia with the Mediterranean had been established. Caravans loaded with luxury goods travelled across the Tarim Basin, Kashgar, Ferghana Valley, Persia, Syria, and beyond. But otherwise the intra-Asian land routes were underdeveloped due to the rugged mountainous terrain and vast deserts, and trade was conducted using animal transport such as mules and yaks that crossed to India through the high passes over the Pamir and Karakoram mountains. In the South, inhospitable dense tropical forests and the numerous river systems of the Irrawaddy, Salween, Menam, Mekong and Red River made overland transportation difficult.[3] A large amount of the intra-Asian trade came to be carried over the seas and comprised "high value-low-volume" goods such as silk, porcelain, spices, etc.

The sea has shaped the destiny of Asia in significant ways. Since ancient times, seas have fashioned geographical boundaries, political and economic interactions among states and also facilitated power projection beyond shores. Traders from China, India, Southeast Asia and Persia sailed through Asian waters and facilitated a flourishing maritime enterprise resulting in interdependence. Importantly, a sophisticated maritime trading system emerged in Asia that contributed to the growth of China, India and Southeast Asia. This Asian trading system was also linked through the Indian Ocean as far as the Mediterranean. In its coercive format, Asia witnessed its fair share of warfare and influence. The great fleets of King Rajendra I and Admiral Zheng He sailed through the Straits of Malacca projecting power, defeating challengers, and establishing spheres of influence. In fact, the sea has been a distinctive entity linking mainland Asia with the archipelagic Southeast Asia and therefore provides the geographical framework[4] for discussing the transactions among China, India and Southeast Asia.

The 21st century Asian power has strong historical roots in ancient maritime power built on the distinctive maritime geography, sea-based commerce, high dependence on the sea for growth and development, a seafaring population, glorious maritime traditions, and a penchant to use the sea for economic growth and prosperity. While China and India are now engaged in rediscovering their maritime prowess that reached its pinnacle several centuries ago, Southeast Asia remains critical to both the rising Asian powers to achieve their ancient maritime glory.[5] In evidence is China's engagement with Southeast Asia, reminiscent of ancient times, because of its crucial energy and trade routes running through the Straits of Malacca and the other Southeast Asian straits that continue to serve as maritime gateways to the Indian Ocean. China is concerned about the expanding maritime power and profile of other Asian powers including India and Japan and the United States that has superior maritime technological and operational capabilities in the region and considers itself as the "resident power"[6] in Asia. Similarly, India has been increasing its substantive and symbolic engagement with Southeast Asian states articulated through its "Look East" policy, yet evocative of its ancient maritime connections, expanded maritime trade, interactions pivoting on maritime contiguity and common understanding of security concerns. It seeks a greater role in Asia but has to contend with China, the other rising power in Asia. Its politico-economic engagements with several countries in the Asia-Pacific region are flourishing and maritime/naval engagements are on a higher trajectory. India's engagements, particularly in East Asia and the littorals of the South China Sea, also appear to convey unmistakable signals of its symbolic response to the Chinese maritime access and basing strategies in South Asia.

Southeast Asia is the convergent maritime hub of competing and cooperative maritime dynamics of the rising Asian maritime powers, i.e. China and India. The criticality of the sea lanes, the expanding forward presence of navies, and naval nuclear developments in China and India have their sensitivities in Southeast Asia. Also, of significance is the role of Japan and the United States, the pre-eminent maritime naval power engaged in the region through several bilateral alliances and arrangements that would provide the levers of stability/instability.

On their side, the littoral navies of Southeast Asia have engaged in force modernization and transformation of their navies and air forces.

These are driven by several factors such as overcoming years of technological obsolescence, building capabilities to secure and protect vital national interests, deterrence against the possible escalation of prevalent disputes, and a response to the competitive process of regional interactive arms procurement, including maintenance of equality among relatively friendly countries.[7] Southeast Asian naval modernization has resulted in enhanced interoperability with the maritime powers of Japan, China and India and other advanced navies of the United States, the United Kingdom and Australia through institutionalized naval interactions.

At another level, the terrorist attacks on *USS Cole* and *M V Limburg* have necessitated enhanced reconnaissance, surveillance and naval patrolling. The persistence of sea piracy, presence of terrorist groups capable of conducting maritime terrorism in the region, and other illegal activities such as drug smuggling, gunrunning and human trafficking in Southeast Asian waters exposes the vulnerabilities of the sea lanes that would have severe consequences for the global economy resulting in disruption of energy and trade flows. Given the critical nature of the geo-economic and geo-energy stakes in the region, these asymmetric challenges have the potential to complicate regional powers' relationships.

This chapter examines the impact of the rising maritime power profiles of China and India on the regional powers in Southeast Asia and how these interactions could evolve and the possible benign and negative consequences that could emerge. Given the strong historical interactions among China, India and Southeast Asia, the chapter begins by tracing the ancient maritime exchanges and impacts of these interactions on Southeast Asia. The chapter also argues that in their strategic conduct, China, India and Southeast Asia draw their political theory and statecraft from the respective schools of thought epitomized in the eras of their antiquity and golden flourish that had firm maritime foundations.

A PEEP INTO THE PAST

Since ancient times, China had engaged in widespread maritime activity and the Chinese annals of the 3rd century BC mention navigation on the high seas.[8] By the end of the BC period, the Han rulers had established commercial contacts with the states of the Nanhai and in the west with India to fulfill the high domestic demand for luxury goods particularly of the ruling elite.[9] By the late 2nd century AD, trading contacts between China and Southeast Asia were established and around the middle of the 3rd century AD through the city-state federation of Funan.[10] Funan ships that sailed to Bengal in

India were large in size and could carry up to 100 oarsmen and Indian-built ships also engaged in India-China trade[11] illustrating the fact that the two states were engaged with each other through maritime trade since ancient times. Also, Fa Hsien on his return journey travelled by the sea route in AD 413–14 and visited Sumatra.[12] This voyage encouraged other Chinese pilgrims to undertake similar voyages to India by the sea route through the Straits of Malacca. The Chinese monk I'sing visited Palembang en route to India in AD 671 and 695 and travelled by the sea route.[13]

While China continued to trade with Nanhai under the Tang dynasty, the trade had diversified from decorative goods like feathers, pearl and ivory to other products such as drugs, medicines and some kinds of spices. The base of Nanhai had also widened to include Persian and Arab traders thereby reaching "a new epoch of sea trading".[14] By AD 977, under the Sung dynasty, a Bureau of Licensed Trade was established and in that context it is important to point out that foreign trade was generating substantial revenue for the state.[15] Profits from maritime commerce encouraged China to send four missions under imperial seal in AD 987 to induce foreign trade under the promise of special import licences.[16] Perhaps the most significant development of the Sung period was the establishment of maritime administration offices called Superintendency of Merchant Shipping at several places. The Superintendency was responsible for control of merchants and merchandise including levy on imports, and supervision of merchants sailing overseas for trade. Besides, a massive maritime infrastructure programme was started that focused on shipbuilding, development of ports, widening of canals, dredging, and building storehouses which resulted in a "rise to power in the state of a powerful merchant class" as an influential group who began to manage government policies. Also, several foreign merchants, particularly the Arabs, came to live in China in the port towns and soon grew into powerful institutions and even assisted the government with loans and shipping.

Seafaring was at its peak during Emperor Gao Zong's (AD 1127–AD 1162) rule, and he is reported to have issued an edict that the profits from maritime commerce were quite large and if these were managed properly, there was no necessity to tax the people.[17] The Chinese overseas trade at that time comprised a variety of goods and of the 1,141 items of trade, 339 items were imported from Southeast Asia, India and the Middle East.[18] Arab vessels from the emporia in Arabia and the Persian Gulf shipped goods to Srivijaya ports in Southeast Asia from where these were transshipped to China.

The Sung Empire was under threat from the western and northern borders and the Song capital Hangzhou was considered susceptible to attack from the sea that resulted in development of a navy; between AD 1130 and AD 1237, the force levels jumped from 11 squadrons to 20 and from 3,000 to 52,000 conscripted men.[19] There were simultaneous developments in ship design and weaponry and the Emperor offered incentives for innovation. Warships were fitted with catapults, incendiary weapons and protective screens. A variety of ocean-going junks including logistic support craft were built. The Chinese began studying oceanic geography, created navigation charts, wind, tide and sea current tables, astronavigation guidelines, and even invented the floating compass.[20] These developments resulted in China emerging as a significant maritime power and by the 13th century, the Chinese had captured the bulk of the Indian Ocean trade. The Sung Navy was defeated at the hands of the Mongol King Kublai Khan who later attempted to occupy Japan on two different occasions in 1274 and 1281, but a strong storm came to the rescue of the Japanese resulting in the withdrawal of the Mongols.

By 1280, China was under the Mongols. They remained connected with Southeast Asia and allowed the existing maritime enterprises to continue business with Java and Srivijaya.[21] During 1328–98, under the first Ming dynasty ruler Zhu Yuanzang, several maritime trade restrictions were introduced that forbade private trade with countries in Southeast Asia. This was essentially to bring maritime trade under state monopoly and discourage competition, but this led to the smuggling of goods leading to loss of revenue.

China's maritime supremacy reached its zenith under Emperor Chengzu (1403), referred to by his reign-name Yongle. Under his leadership China built the largest navy of that period. Zheng He, the famous mariner from China led seven expeditions from 1405 to 1433 visiting Southeast Asia, India, the Persian Gulf and East Africa, engaging in diplomacy, projecting China's glory, establishing Confucian order and building trade relations through the tributary system.[22] These expeditions showcased China's maritime prowess of the times that was built around a fleet of more than 300 vessels of various types manned by a large crew.

INDIA

Sea finds a prominent place in ancient Indian discourse and documentation. The ancient Indian sculptures, cave paintings and coins also represent ships and boats. Archaeological discoveries at Lothal point to the fact that maritime trade had flourished as early as the 16th century BC in the Indus Valley civilization. The ancient shipbuilders in India had good knowledge of wood for building different types of ships that was derived from *Vriksha-Ayurveda,* or the science of Plant Life.[23] Similarly, *Yuktikalpataru*, a Sanskrit treatise of ancient times, lists important instructions for building river and sea-going vessels providing evidence that shipbuilding in India was highly advanced and that sea-going vessels were built for trade with distant lands. There are several references to maritime activity in the *Rig-veda*.[24] Thus both archaeological and literary evidence showcase the golden age of India's maritime prominence and are testimony to the burgeoning foreign trade that provided the impetus for the development of global connectivity and the ancient maritime power of India.

From the ancient to the contemporary, there have been several epochs of maritime glory in the Indian history. For over twenty centuries, several dynasties and rulers in India developed maritime power and engaged in international commerce including wars at sea. The Mauryas (321–184 BC) developed a sophisticated maritime trading system, the Andhra-Kushana period had trading links with Rome (200 BC–AD 250), the Gupta Empire had extensive maritime trading contacts in the 5th and 6th centuries. The Chalukyas and Cholas in South India developed maritime intercourse and trade relations in Southeast Asia. During the Mogul period, several rulers, including Akbar and Aurangzeb, built maritime enterprises. Significantly, India occupied a unique location as the primary supplier of luxury goods such as silk, precious stones, ivory, sandalwood, metals and even animals such as elephants. It emerged as the heart of the commercial world with extensive trade linkages with the ancient world of Phoenicians, Greeks, Egyptians, Romans, Persians, and Chinese and later with the Portuguese, Dutch, Spaniards, and English. Ships and traders from these countries frequented Indian ports on the Arabian Sea and the Bay of Bengal.

During the Mauryan period (321–184 BC) under Emperor Chandra Gupta Maurya, India developed a flourishing maritime enterprise that extended from the west to the east coast of India. According to Megasthenes, shipbuilding in India was patronized by the state and there were several shipyards engaged in the activity to meet the demands of both domestic and foreign customers.[25] With such extensive maritime activity, the Emperor established an organization of the Board of Admiralty and Naval Department as part of the state War Office. An elaborate account of its activities is provided in the most respected and important Sanskrit work of that period titled *Arthasastra*.[26] This *magnum opus* provides insights into the high level of proficiency in Indian shipping, level of knowledge of ocean navigation and seaborne trade in the BC period. The Naval Department was headed by the Superintendent of Ships who was responsible for the efficient conduct of maritime activity of the kingdom including shipbuilding, certification of vessels for seaworthiness, ensuring trained officers and crew, instructions for navigation on the oceans and port management. The process of levy and collection of dues from visiting ships and other users and prosecution of violators of harbour regulations and illegal possession of weapons showcases the sophistication in the conduct of maritime business in India. Under King Ashok the Great, India had trade links with Egypt under King Ptolemy who established a trading emporia at the city of Alexandria. Also, a Maritime Edict was issued under the king to the seafaring Nagas (pirates) to stop plundering. According to Vincent Smith, an elaborate regulatory system for conduct of maritime trade provides conclusive evidence that the Maurya Empire was engaged in maritime trade with distant states and a large number of traders visited the capital on business.[27]

Numismatic evidence shows that during the period AD 100–300, South Indian rulers had established commercial maritime links with Rome under Augustus and Antoninus. Several Roman coins have been discovered in South India, particularly on the Coromandel coast.[28] In AD 47, the discovery of the regularity of the monsoon winds in the Indian Ocean by Hippalus provided a boost to trans-Indian Ocean trade between Egypt and South India with the Malabar Coast experiencing intense maritime activity.[29] On the Coromandel coast, the Tamil heartland, several Roman traders established outposts for trade, particularly spices, which were traded in gold.[30]

The Tamils of the Coromandel coast had maritime trading links in Southeast Asia evidenced by the existence of merchant guilds and Indian settlements in several places in Southeast Asia including Burma, Thailand, Malaysia, Sumatra, Java, Cambodia and as far as China. The Chola were the pre-eminent power in South India having conquered a large territory as far as the Gangetic delta in the north, and peninsular India after defeating the Chera kings and conquering kingdoms in Sri Lanka.[31] In the east, Chola kings had established social, cultural, and political relations with Srivijaya rulers in Sumatra. Also, several Tamil mercantile guilds were established at several places in Southeast Asia including Nakhon Si Thammarat (Thailand),[32] and Barus (Sumatra, Indonesia)[33] which resulted in a sophisticated India-Southeast Asia trading system that extended as far as China.

But relations between the two kingdoms began to deteriorate. While there is no credible evidence to determine the cause of the dispute between Chola and Srivijaya rulers, historians tell us that unfavourable trade practices by Srivijaya rulers favouring China and commercial rivalry may have angered the Chola king Rajaraja I (AD 1012–44). It is also argued that the raid is a reflection of Chola compulsive expansion and maritime ambition to control the sea-lanes in Southeast Asia for undertaking the 1025 naval expedition against the Srivijaya rulers.[34] The Chola naval expeditionary capability was unprecedented and was demonstrated by naval attack at eleven different places in Southeast Asia. The naval expedition ordered by the Chola king Rajendra Choladeva I to Southeast Asia is mentioned in the inscription dated 1030–31 of the big temple of Tanjavur, in South India, and the places attacked have been subjected to historical geography; six can be found on the Malay peninsula, four in Sumatra, Manakkavaram has been identified as Nicobar Islands and two, i.e. *Valaippanduru* and *Mevilimbangam*, are unknown.[35]

The attack destroyed the Srivijaya domination of Southeast Asia but the Chola kings did not establish permanent political authority over any territory in Southeast Asia. However, relations were restored and the primacy of the Cholas continued. Later, the king of Kambujadesa (modern Cambodia) sent a chariot to the Chola king "probably to appease him" so that the Chola strategic interest did not extend beyond Malaysia. The Chola kings had also established cultural and trading links with China. At the political level, Chola kings sent embassies to China.[36] There were Brahmanical temples in Guangzhou in the middle of the 8th century. A bilingual Tamil-Chinese inscription of the year AD 1281 reports the dedication of a Siva statue in yet another Hindu temple at Quanzhou.

By the 11th century, under the Sung dynasty rulers, China was experiencing burgeoning foreign trade and emerged as an attractive market for trade in commodities such as porcelain, silk and spices. Like other merchants from Southeast Asia and Persia, Indian traders came to frequent Chinese ports. At the political level, the Cholas dispatched an embassy to China in AD 1015 that reached after AD 1150 days including a halt in Srivijaya for several months. It is observed that India and China continued to send embassies to each other's ports; the Yuan court dispatched sixteen embassies between 1272 and 1296, and eighteen embassies from India are recorded to have arrived at the Yuan court. By the 13th century a large South Indian merchant community had established themselves in China and for Chinese traders in South India.

SOUTHEAST ASIA

The burgeoning Asian maritime trade (China, Southeast Asia and India) linking Persia and the Mediterranean resulted in a number of *entrepôt* in Southeast Asia. The Bay of Bengal, Takuapa, Trang and Kedah on the west coast of Malaya emerged as trans-shipment points from where goods were carried through rugged territory across the peninsula to Chaiya, Ligor, and

Patani in the Bay of Bandon.[37] Ships bound for China would then set sail across the Gulf of Siam via the Funan port of Oc Eo to Canton. Interestingly, a "shuttle service" between India, through the Bay of Bengal to either side of the Malaya Peninsula onward to China had come into operation. Referring to serious threats and insecurity in the Straits of Malacca, John F. Cady tells us that this trade could avoid the squally weather and pirate-ridden seas of Southeast Asia.[38] Importantly, the challenges of tropical hinterland geography had not deterred the traders and the obstacles were not so formidable as compared to piracy in the Straits.

Sumatra in archipelagic Southeast Asia, strategically located astride the international trading route, emerged as a significant region and several ports along its coast mushroomed supporting international trade as well as being a transit point for ships engaged in east-west trade. During the last quarter of the 7th century, the Srivijaya kingdom with its capital at Palembang in Southeast Sumatra on the Musi River was a powerful kingdom with great maritime power, supported by burgeoning trade, a powerful navy and an ambitious political leadership. Palembang's geographic location close to the Sunda Strait endowed the Srivijaya rulers with a strategic geographical position to trade with both India and during monsoons with China as well as access the Java Sea and the Moluccas.[39]

Palembang was a sophisticated port and an important trading hub buzzing with commercial activity where foreign traders competed with each other and moneychangers facilitated transactions. The local merchants had a roaring business particularly in agricultural products like aloe wood and spices such as pepper, cloves, nutmeg, cardamom, etc. Besides, gold, silver, camphor, and other luxury items were also traded and these goods were in abundance. The state had a total monopoly over trading, it fixed prices for goods brought in and levied tolls on passing ships showcasing a complex system of maritime trade and business.

Palembang was also an important centre for ship repair, and provided stores and supplies needed by the ships engaged in east-west voyages. I'Sing, a Chinese pilgrim recorded that he travelled on a Persian vessel from China to Srivijaya and on a Srivijaya ship to India.[40] Significantly, Palembang also emerged as a centre for Buddhist learning and monks and priests heading to India by the sea route spent time in Palembang to learn the basics of Buddhism before visiting Nalanda, in India. Social, cultural, religious, political and economic relations between Srivijaya, China and India flourished and had strong foundations in maritime connectivity.

With Sunda Strait under its control, the Srivijaya leadership was determined to command the Straits of Malacca. As a pre-eminent maritime power in the region, it established itself in the northwest in the Malaya peninsula thus controlling the strategic waterway of the Straits of Malacca, a vital gateway connecting the Indian Ocean and China Sea. Significantly, in order to maintain a monopoly over the Indian and Chinese trade in the region, Srivijaya rulers conquered Kedah in Malaya to wipe out any competition.

The Jambi kingdom, further east of Palembang astride the Batang Hari River (known for its gold mines, and gold was a critical resource as a currency of trade), a rival power to Srivijaya, was also absorbed into the empire through conquest.[41] Several other smaller kingdoms in the region were also brought under Srivijaya control thus guaranteeing it a predominant position around the Straits of Malacca, the international trading route.[42] Srivijaya even put claims on Sri Lanka.[43]

Thus during the 7th and 10th centuries, the maritime supremacy of the Srivijaya kingdom over the trading routes between India and China through the Straits of Malacca was well established and it dominated regional affairs. Arab-Persian records highlight the supremacy of Srivijaya over the Straits of Malacca and peninsular Malaya and Sumatra. Kenneth Hall notes that Srivijaya kings developed a sophisticated network for trade, built on alliances and sharing profits from business rather than on direct coercion. The Srivijaya monarchs came to be acknowledged as powerful sources of regional political stability and were thus instrumental in enhancing international trade leading to economic linkages with other trading communities as far as Persia.

Between AD 695 and 742, Srivijaya rulers sent several emissaries with precious and rare gifts to China and in return obtained honorary titles from the Chinese ruler. Historians, tell us that in AD 990, when the Srivijaya ambassador in the Chinese court heard of the news of a conflict between his rulers and the king of Mataram, he sought their help. In essence, Srivijaya rulers skillfully employed diplomacy and secured protection against powerful neighbours. Similarly, Srivijaya supported Buddhism in India and a Buddhist monastery was built in India for pilgrims from Sumatra. The temple was named Chulamani Varmadeva Vihara and the upkeep of the Vihara was supported from the revenue of nearby villages.

In Southeast Asia, Srivijaya kings brought vast territories under their control through wars and conquest, dominated the east-west trade and maintained diplomatic contacts through regular movement of emissaries to both neighbouring and distant countries to encourage trade. These economic and diplomatic engagements led to interdependence and security linkages that were marshalled in times of crisis. However, in the subsequent years, political instability and loss of power in the region led to the decline of the Srivijaya empire. Some Srivijaya kings adopted repressive and unfavourable trade policies that led to mistrust and antagonism resulting in wars. These were perhaps the reasons for a near-total destruction of the great maritime power of Srivijaya.

Kenneth Hall tells us that the Chinese kings found the Srivijaya rulers "a perfect trading partner".[44] They facilitated the movement of goods to South China and serviced vessels transiting through the Straits of Malacca. Besides, the ports under the control of Srivijaya were favoured ports of call and provided layover for ships and crew waiting for favourable winds to resume their voyage. Significantly, the Srivijaya kingdom protected ships and crew against piracy prevalent along the international trade route through the Straits of Malacca. The Chinese acknowledged the power of the Srivijaya empire and granted it a "preferred trading status". It also meant that the ships that called at Srivijaya ports were given preferential treatment when visiting Chinese ports.

From the above, it is evident that the Chinese and Indian connection was critical to the prosperity of the Srivijaya empire, or for that matter any Southeast Asian ruler. But in latter years, China began to dominate trade in Southeast Asia resulting in the decline of regional power centres. The Srivijaya empire was a true maritime power based on its strategic location astride the international trade route, vibrant commerce, skilful diplomacy with assent on trade, and a highly developed port, shipping and shipbuilding infrastructure. The Empire also possessed substantive capacity and capability to ensure safety of maritime traffic against piracy.

The above discussions suggest that in ancient times, China, India and Southeast Asia were the Asian powers with assents on maritime trade and relied on a robust build-up of their navies. The ancient rulers and kings of the Chola empire in India, the Ming dynasty of China and Srivijaya empire exhibited a strong penchant for maritime power that had expeditionary roles factored in them even as they launched their mercantile trade criss-crossing Southeast Asia and the Indian Ocean. Above all, China, India and Southeast Asia were the pre-eminent Asian maritime powers in ancient times and they developed extensive political, economic and security relations, though these were not necessarily always peaceful and had their fair share of competition and cooperation.

STRATEGIC TRANSACTIONS: THE *SHIH*, THE *MANDALA* AND THE *NEGARA*

The contemporary Asian maritime engagements among China, India and Southeast Asia exhibit civilizational legacy in the operations of the state and political economy. Significantly, the sources of their contemporary political theory and statecraft are sourced to the respective ancient schools of thought epitomized in their golden ages. China had the profound influence of its renowned military strategist Sun-Tzu or Master Sun (circa 403–221 BC) through his seminal work *Sun-Tzu: The Art of Warfare (Sun-Tzu ping-fa)*, which provides an understanding of Sino statecraft and its historical dynamics of over 2,000 years through various dynasties and turbulences. Indian statecraft is influenced by *The Arthasasthra*, a classic, authored by the Indian strategic thinker Kautilya who was the royal court advisor to the ancient Indian emperor Chandragupta Maurya II. Southeast Asian statecraft is derived from the concept of *Mandala* an ancient Indian Hindu-Buddhist construct of religion and polity, adapted to the region as *Mandala* or *Negara*, through social, cultural and religious exchanges and influences from India.[45]

The *Shih*

Since ancient times, China has had an enduring interest in military thought. Its ancient philosophical literature is replete with discussions on matters "military" and is showcased through a variety of treatises dealing with warfare; to name a few: *Master Mo, Master Hsun, Master Kuan, Book of Lord Shang, Spring and Autumn of Master Lu* and *Master Huai Nan*.[46] At a fundamental level, Sun Tzu's military thought highlights the seriousness of war and exhibits distaste for warfare, but it does not dismiss the use of warfare particularly when social and political disorder (disorder originates from order) creates conditions necessitating the use of arms. Emphasizing the primacy of state, statecraft and stratagem, Sun Tzu states that it is vital to preserve the state without the use of force, and in that context, the master strategist notes, "To win a hundred victories in a hundred battles is not the highest excellence; the highest excellence is to subdue the enemy's army without fighting at all"[47] for which it is crucial to place complete reliance on stratagems in all statecraft.

Perhaps the most important idea in *Sun-Tzu: The Art of Warfare (Sun-Tzu ping-fa)*, is the concept of *Shih*. Although the Chinese characters for *Shih* have "multiple alternative meanings" it is based on Sun Tzu's "dialectic views and the philosophies of *Yin* and *Yang* and Daoism".[48] *Shih* translates as "strategic advantage" that should be manipulated to favourable disposition in the different conditions that prevail and exploited to obtain ascendancy. *Shih* can be applied to unique prevalent political and social conditions, and encompasses terrain, climate, moral disposition of the leadership, economic and material circumstances, and the military and its operating environment. *Shih* also includes abstractions and unquantifiable attributes such as morale, opportunity, and psychology. In statecraft, *Shih* seeks broader strategic factors such as political disposition, the strength of alliances and robustness of an opponent's politics. As regards its timeliness, *Shih* is at play across the entire spectrum of peace and conflict and must be nurtured and practised by both the political and the military leadership in their strategic thinking and skilfully employed to advantage at all times.

The Chinese political leadership has assiduously applied *Shih* to the development of China's comprehensive national power, pursuit of its strategy of "peaceful rise" and in its zestful quest of regional strategies employing a variety of stratagems. These can be discerned and gleaned through several Chinese articulations, formal declarations and practices in the conduct of international relations. In recent years, China has been an advocate of multipolarity, argued for expanded economic engagements, and suggested cooperative security, arms control and non-proliferation as effective means to reduce tensions. Notwithstanding that, China's global strategy pivots on a geo-centric construct of the Middle Kingdom that mandates balancing the "barbaric states" against one and another in concentric circles to offset their hegemonic power, intentions and capabilities against China.

At the military level, the leadership is well versed with the dialectics of Sun Tzu and epitomizes the concept of *Shih* in war and diplomacy through the famed four-character proverbs.[49] The Chinese military establishment craftily employs *Shih* to develop a favourable military situation to achieve political objectives. China views its strategic tradition as superior to that of the West and that it will help regain ancient glory. In essence, Chinese strategic culture places greater emphasis on strategy and stratagems that are often masked in deception and mystery in direct contrast to the Western discourse that adopts a direct approach built on the sinews of hard power showcased through the use of overwhelming force and technology that supports its strategy for "shock and awe" to mesmerize the enemy. In its salient essence, the ancient Chinese treatise rests on espousal of war and its political uses, i.e. the process of diplomacy.

The *Mandala*

Like the Sino statecraft, Indian statecraft finds its comprehensive theoretical expressions in the ancient Indian classic *The Arthasastra*. Ancient India was made up of several states ruled by different kings with varying sizes of territories under their control. The rulers witnessed highs and lows of competition and cooperation for political dominance and both smaller and weaker states vied to align with the dominant power. India was a civilizational power of global strategic significance pivoting on an abundance of natural resources including a burgeoning economy and several ancient economies including Rome, Greece, Persia, Southeast Asia and China had established trading links with India. The Indian emperor Chandragupta Maurya (317–293 BC) ruled the first united ancient India. With victories over the Nandas, having stopped the advancing Greek invaders who came after Alexander the Great, taking over Punjab and Sindh and concluding a treaty with Seleucus, the Mauryan Empire extended across the whole subcontinent barring South India. Chandragupta Maurya, his successor Bindusara (293–268 BC) and grandson Ashoka the Great (268–232 BC) were counselled on the conduct of state functions by Kautilya, the royal court advisor, the master strategist of ancient India and author of the famed Indian classic *The Arthasastra*. The word "Arthasasthra" has been translated as "science of politics". A.L. Basham termed it as "treatise on polity" and Heinrich Zimmer called it "timeless laws of politics, economy, diplomacy and war".[50] Like the Chinese classic *The Art of War* by Sun Tzu, "Arthasastra" provides significant insights into the Indian grand strategic thought that has served as a strategic legacy.

In statecraft, the *Arthasastra* conceptualizes a geostrategic and a geopolitical framework of interests, alliances and strategic conduct termed as the *Mandala*. *Mandala* is a construct in international relations that signifies the contiguity of region and defines the interests and relations of the state and in spatial terms *Mandala* denotes a zone. Schematically, *Mandala* is figurative of concentric circles, which define the relations of a state that lies at the core, with its immediate, intermediate and outer ring of countries.

A classic *Mandala* would thus appear as follows: "vijigisu", i.e. the king as the hub with states (both friends, enemies, medium and major powers) located in front, adjacent and the rear. The first concentric circle in the front is occupied by the enemy, followed by successive concentric zones under the influence of the friend, enemy's friend, friend's friend, and friend of the enemy's friend, in that order. In the rear, the rear-enemy, rear-friend, rear-enemy's friend and rear-friend's friend surround the "vijigisu". The adjacent zones are occupied by a medium power and a "paramount power". In all, the "vijigisu" has to contend with 4 states in its adjacent zones, 12 kings, 60 elements of sovereignty, and 72 elements of states.[51]

Kautilya offers a number of choices to the king to manage the relations of the state with the states of the *Mandala* that range from "just war doctrine" to employment of diplomatic tools such as treaties, alliances and neutrality. It is important to remember that the term "vijigisu" does not denote a conqueror in the military sense of conquest that seeks destruction of the adversary; it also reflects the soft power of the state by which other states submit to the glory of the king. However, for the above, the "vijigisu" will be driven by the disposition of the state, its sovereign, and the subjects including friends and enemies.

According to Kautilya, the state is the core actor that is surrounded by tiers of contending states who transact relations among themselves driven by the primacy of power and interests and attempt to maximize these with little room for moral principals and obligations. This has its parallel in China's Middle Kingdom construct that envisions that China is the core state surrounded by three heavens and the outer-lying states that are barbarian powers. Expounding his views on war, Kautilya argued that diplomacy is a "subtle act of war" and an important tool available to the state to weaken the enemy thus gaining advantage for ascendancy leading to ultimate subjugation. In essence, "Arthasashtra" is a treatise in political realism showcasing how the political world works with firm foundations in self-interests, strategic autonomy, and the dynamic nature of alliances.

The *Negara*

In ancient Southeast Asian statecraft, politics and religion were inseparable. Historical evidence from inscriptions point to the fact that religion was used to acquire political and economic gains and sometimes religion was manipulated beyond actual religious practice to obtain political ascendancy.[52] The Southeast Asian political rulers adapted the principles of Indian statecraft that had religious (Buddhism) and political (*Mandala*) connotations. There are some other corresponding terms to describe the Southeast Asian *Mandala* such as *Negara* (meaning "kingdom" in Sanskrit), particularly Java and Indonesia,[53] to represent the region within which the political ruler exercised his influence and the ruler draws the state inward toward the centre, and "galactic polity" in which the weak political entities drifted to the stronger.[54] Significantly, the *Mandala*, *Negara* and "galactic polity" clearly showcase the primacy of the Centre (Core) in a political system that radiated power, attracted the periphery and was dynamic in nature.

Different *Mandala* emerged in the history of Southeast Asia: "proto-*Mandala*" during the late BC period wherein the political power was linked to ancestors and animist spiritual beliefs; the "Siva-influenced *Mandala*" of the 5th–7th centuries in which the political leaders derived their power through meditation and were respected for their cosmic connections; the

"Imperial *Mandala*" emerged during the 9th–12th centuries, during which Southeast Asia was a maritime power at its highest glory pivoting on mercantile commerce and a burgeoning maritime economy. After Srivijaya, another Mandalic polity emerged at Melaka, yet another period of Southeast Asian maritime prowess, linked into a religious base through propagation of the faith.[55] It is noted that the Southeast Asian *Mandala* was of "Indian origin but of Southeast Asian persuasion"[56] and Rosita Dellios observes that Southeast Asian understanding of the *Mandala* was not in conformity with the traditional sense of a state as "a legal, territorial entity but displayed the cosmological characteristics of states of Hindu-Buddhist persuasion".

Several ancient Indian sutras, smritis, and shashtras have made significant contributions to ancient Southeast Asian political developments and statecraft. According to O.W. Wolters, Cambodian kings were "drunk in the ocean of Sastras" and were familiar with political organization in India.[57] For instance, a 12th-century Cham king claimed accession on the basis of his Sanskrit treatise on governance ostensibly similar to an Indian Sastra. Further, some Southeast Asian rulers appear to have adhered to the guiding principles of statecraft expounded in the Arthashastra. An 11th-century Javanese king, Erlangga, challenged his enemy by craftily employing the precepts of the Arthashastra. In the later period, in 1592, the Ayudhya king Naresvara, with great astuteness, proposed an alliance to help China beat Japanese pressure and defy Hideyoshi in Korea. Drawing from the precepts of the Arthashastra, King Naresvara considered China as his rearward friend and Japan as the "rearward enemy" that needed to be defeated.

From the above it is evident that in Southeast Asia the concept of *Mandala* and *Negara* came to prominence both in its sacred and political dimensions and provided the political leaders with an opportunity to claim a degree of divinity and political authority. It also came to be exercised in Southeast Asian statecraft. The different *Mandalas* did not accept each other on equal terms, were "divinely ruled and universal" and exercised autonomy. Although there were several *Mandalas*, the concept of "ekacchatra" (one umbrella sovereignty)[58] never emerged, partly due to the geographical separation among various *Mandalas* as well as their "historical experiences".

CONTEMPORARY MARITIME DIMENSIONS OF THE *SHIH*

China is vigorously building its maritime prowess that has strong and deep-rooted foundations in its historical pre-eminence showcased through the expansive and extensive voyages by the legendary mariner Zheng He. It has expanded its maritime horizons, is leveraging the tangible and intangible dimensions of maritime power towards attainment of comprehensive national power, has zestfully undertaken an unequivocal transformation of the navy to develop into a formidable force, and is craftily employing the force to exercise *Shih*. Its interests extend as far as the Indian Ocean in the west and East Pacific towards South America in its attempt to regain the ancient maritime glory attained during the Ming dynasty. As China builds its comprehensive national power, there is a significant build-up of the PLA to its full potential.[59]

In the 21st century, China has emerged as a major maritime power in Asia and has successfully synergized its strategic culture and skilfully employed *Shih* in the maritime domain to enhance its profile. It has developed strategic partnerships based on convergence of key issues to aggressively expand its interests and challenge hegemonic powers to regain its pivotal Middle Kingdom role in Asia. These partnerships have evolved into security dialogues on issues of common concern, access and basing arrangements, wide-ranging military exchanges and joint exercises, and high technology transfers.

China has adopted conciliatory postures with its peer rivals but it keeps the choices of "hard-balancing" should the competition become intense, particularly when it faces aggressive opposition to its rising power. It can then leverage relationships to challenge peer rivals to its power position, a critical element of *Shih* that envisages the need to "encircle and gradually attrite peer rivals".[60] In that context, China has dexterously cultivated brinkmanship states to support *Shih* and counter-challenge India in South Asia and the United States and Japan in East Asia.

China is efficiently navigating regional politics and has concluded boundary settlements with several countries. It has put into operation peace-making postures on unresolved borders and adeptly negotiated to the backburner disputes that can be settled in the future more on China's terms. These initiatives have resulted in military exchanges and joint exercises which provide China with favourable and peaceful settings to develop its comprehensive national power, a critical aspect of *Shih* that seeks a favourable situation to achieve political objectives. At another level, China has employed *Shih* to leverage a negotiating position for access and basing arrangements in return for infrastructure development, military-technical aid, and arms transfers with economic largesse. These strategic gains for China provide the means to secure access to markets and resources that are critical for its economic growth.

Strategic Partnerships

Rapprochement between China and Russia in the 1990s manifested in Sino-Russian strategic partnership at the Shanghai summit in April 1996 which culminated in the 2001 Treaty for Good Neighbourliness, Friendship and Cooperation.[61] Besides consolidating their relationship, the Treaty also supported the quest for a multipolar world apparently to balance U.S. hegemony emerging in the post-Cold War period.[62] The synergy also arises from the Chinese and Russian perception that the United States continues to deal with these states with a Cold War mentality. For instance, the RIMPAC (Rim of the Pacific) exercises, started in 1971, have China and Russia simulated as enemies. In recent times, these two countries have participated in RIMPAC as observers, but during the 2008 RIMPAC the two were excluded raising speculations that the exercises were targeted against China to contain it.[63]

China's close partnership with Russia has been quite evident in the maritime domain pivoting on naval exercises, acquisition of hardware and high-level exchanges. In 1999, the two regional giants conducted joint naval exercises involving the Russian Pacific Fleet and the PLA Navy's Eastern Fleet and the 2001 joint exercises allegedly included Russian strategic bombers simulating attacks on U.S. military assets in East Asia.[64] As a show of force, China and Russia conducted joint military exercises within the Peace Mission 2005 under the Shanghai Cooperation Organization (SCO), the six-nation security group, to challenge U.S. military presence in the Pacific Ocean and Central Asia.[65] Interestingly, the exercises were conducted off the East Russian coast-Shandong Peninsula in northeastern China and included a naval blockade and amphibious landings.[66] From the Chinese perspective, it signalled a show of force and its resolve to thwart any U.S. support to Taiwan in the event of intervention. Although the Peace Mission 2007 focused on counter-terrorism and was played out on land, it recognized the power that China and Russia exert in Central Asia.[67] These exercises provided China with the opportunity to affirm itself as a significant regional power.

The Sino-Russian partnership also provides China with significant leverages in terms of upgrading the defence production capacity and military modernization to challenge U.S. military superiority. Russia has been the primary supplier of military hardware to China.[68] It has provided critical technological assistance for the development of, among other hardware, strategic submarines, missile technology, fighter aircraft and naval systems. Some of these have resulted in indigenous designs with significant resemblance to Russian systems.[69] China is now seeking advanced weapons systems with provisions for joint production that will provide it with critical access to state-of-the-art military technologies and composite materials.[70] In essence, China is seeking to build enough naval power to challenge U.S. naval and air superiority in East Asia and intimidate Taiwan and Japan. This critical military ballast provides favourable conditions to play a pivotal role in Asia clearly showcasing the ancient Chinese strategy of employing *Shih*.

Rivals: India and Japan

The Chinese strategic calculus visualizes challenges to rivals to attain a power position. In Asia, China views India and Japan as its rivals,[71] which are significant economic and military powers that have the potential to challenge its rise to pre-eminence in Asia. China's primary geopolitical ambition is to build comprehensive national power to emerge as a "Pan-Asian power" and expand its influence in South Asia and across a larger swath of the Indian Ocean. Significantly, the Indian Ocean has figured prominently in the strategic thinking of ancient Chinese mariners for trade and also in the geostrategic calculus of the Sung and Ming emperors. After all, Zheng He's naval expeditions in the Indian Ocean had established Chinese suzerainty, spheres of political, economic and strategic influence. Given its critical needs for raw materials, markets and energy (sourced from Africa, the Persian Gulf, South Asia and Southeast Asia), China's maritime strategy nurtures and sustains robust relations with several navies in South Asia and the Indian Ocean littoral extending to the Middle East and Africa. These dynamics steer China's South Asia and Indian Ocean policy and strategies.

In South Asia, China has to contend with India which possesses significant maritime prowess showcased by its growing maritime trade and a powerful navy. In that context, Sino-Indian relations present a mixed bag of competition and cooperation that has wider political and security consequences given that both powers are experiencing extraordinary rates of economic growth resulting in higher outlays for military modernization. The boundary dispute in the Himalayas[72] is perhaps the most contentious issue. China's consummate diplomacy resulted in lowering tensions in bilateral relations on its own terms and it has craftily put the issue on the backburner and extracted the 1993 Border Peace and Tranquillity Agreement (BPTA) and the 1996 agreement on Confidence Building Measures in the Military Field.

Although both the militaries have pulled back to rear positions, the arrangement does not rule out peaceful settlement of the dispute since rivalry and competition persists.[73] Besides, China has an advantageous position both geographically and operationally because India has not been able to redeploy its troops to the western sector against Pakistan. Although both sides have exhibited reciprocity by playing down the Tibet and Sikkim issues, if China begins to aggressively pursue territorial claims against India, it can apply pressure on India at a time of its choosing.

The South Asia-Indian Ocean region is of critical importance to China's strategic calculations, a legacy that continues since ancient times. First, China's strategic intent is to ensure the safety and security of its trade and energy supply chains that transit through the Arabian Sea and the Bay of Bengal where the Indian Navy has effective presence and capability. Second, China needs connectivity for its western and southern regions that will result in land-based maritime access into the Indian Ocean, i.e. the Karakoram Highway linking China and Pakistan through Xinjiang onward to the Persian Gulf, and the "Irrawaddy Corridor" linking Kunming in Yunnan through the Irrawaddy in Myanmar to the Bay of Bengal. The latter gains significance given that China can transport gas from Myanmar's offshore platforms to Yunnan province in its Southeast. Essentially, these access corridors help China to partially overcome the vulnerability of its shipping through the Southeast Asian choke points, particularly the Straits of Malacca. Third, in spatial and strategic terms, access and basing arrangements in the Indian Ocean littorals, particularly in the Arabian Sea and the Bay of Bengal, ensure a strategic initiative of China to contain India in South Asia. China has provided financial and technological assistance to Pakistan and Myanmar in building maritime infrastructure such as ports, repair yards and warehouses that can be accessed by the PLA Navy to support its deployment in the Indian Ocean. Besides, these facilities also make possible surveillance and reconnaissance of Indian naval activity and monitor the Persian Gulf and Straits of Malacca maritime traffic.

Beijing has no doubt that India would oppose China's strategic surge and this prompted General Zhao Nanqi, former Director of the General Logistic Department of the PLA, to note that the Indian Ocean is not an Indian lake.[74] China has been able to challenge India in the South Asia-Indian Ocean region by leveraging Pakistan (all-weather ally), Bangladesh (consistently weak political regimes) and Myanmar (adversarial international relations and military rulers) as brinkmanship actors, assuring them of security, a critical necessity for the execution of *Shih*. China has systematically bolstered their capability through political, economic and military assistance. It is a signal assurance to the brinkmanship actors that Chinese power can challenge India's hegemony, prevailing influence, and naval power in the Indian Ocean region.

Japan is the second rival of China. There is a newfound confidence in Beijing about its economic potential and China is competing with the Japanese industrial and financial might. Further, the bilateral trade and Japanese investments in China have been increasing rapidly and acting as the key engine generating growth in China.[75] However, there are several issues that plague bilateral relations and range from historical mistrust, contentious issues such as war crimes, history textbooks, and visits to Yasukuni Shrine to foreign policy choices. It took more than ten years of consultation and talks to accomplish military exchanges between Japan and China that resulted in the PLA Navy ship visit to Tokyo in November 2007[76] and a JMSDF ship visit to China on a goodwill and humanitarian mission[77] clearly reflects the nature of military distrust.

China remains cognizant of the fact that Japan is fast turning to a "normal" state and the JMSDF is forward deployed with strong assents on distant-water operations well beyond the JMSDF mission responsibility of 1,000 nautical miles from Japan[78] through the Straits of Malacca as far as the Arabian Sea/Persian Gulf in support of the U.S.-led war on terror.[79] The JMSDF proactively participated in minesweeping operations in the Persian Gulf in 1991[80] and is currently engaged in support operations for U.S.-led coalition forces engaged in the war on terror. Japan had drawn out plans for a multinational anti-piracy patrol for the Straits of Malacca but strong protests and non-acceptance of the proposal by China resulted in Japan keeping the idea on hold.[81] Significantly, joint naval operations and forward deployment, once unthinkable, now appear to be increasingly accepted as part of national defence.

The JMSDF is technologically superior and has far-ranging capabilities as compared to the PLA Navy that is attempting to build capabilities for distant operations and emerge as a blue water navy. Although China has significant nuclear and missile capabilities, Japan has developed a potent anti-missile defence systems and is engaged in building, in collaboration with the United States, the Theatre Missile Defence (TMD) shield. For China, the TMD is a threat to regional security and stability.[82] From a Chinese perspective, it encourages remilitarization, building Japan's strategic capabilities and could be marshalled to protect Taiwan, which China considers as a challenge to its sovereignty.[83] Besides, the TMD will encourage other states to develop similar capabilities, could result in a regional arms race and undermine the regional balance of power. There also remains unresolved maritime dispute over the Senkaku Island that has witnessed military deployments and skirmishes.[84] Above all, China sees Japan as its competitor in Asia who has the potential to challenge its rise to Asian ascendancy either on its own potential and capability or in concert with its alliance partner the United States and the other Asian power, i.e. India. Likewise, the Japanese are concerned about Chinese naval intentions, and are keen to be part of any security architecture that can contain China and curtail Chinese maritime ambitions.

In East Asia, North Korea is an ardent supporter and the mainstay of China's *Shih* strategy. It is an important brinkmanship actor and has found favour among China's ruling elite. China has assisted Pyongyang's quest for nuclear and missile capability and supported the regime during times of international pressure consequent to its nuclear tests and the subsequent Six-Party talks. North Korea's nuclear and missile capability is significant to neutralize Japanese technological superiority[85] and defeat the Japanese missile defences.[86] This is representative of China's asymmetric strategy of using the North Korean nuclear/missile capability flavoured with brinkmanship, a clear reflection of *Shih*. Further, the Beijing-Pyongyang axis has also been an architect of nuclear-missile networks in Pakistan, Iran and Syria.

China's concerns about India and Japan also arise from their close relationship with the United States, the primary challenger to China's rise as a global power. The May 2007 joint statement by the United States and Japanese spoke about a "common strategic objective" of "continuing to build upon partnerships with India to advance areas of common interests and increase cooperation, recognising that India's continued growth is inextricably tied to the prosperity, freedom, and security of the region".[87] China's policy towards India has been one of eroding any possible India-U.S.-Japan alliance and to limit cooperative ventures between India and the United States, as it perceives such cooperation would be inimical to its interests.[88]

In May 2007, Beijing issued a démarche seeking an explanation from New Delhi, Washington, Tokyo, and Canberra on the purpose of holding a meeting in Manila, the Philippines.[89] The Chinese Foreign Ministry spokesman Qin Gang noted "China believes that to enhance mutual trust, expand cooperation for mutual benefit and remain win-win, being open and inclusive is the global trend",[90] obviously referring to the evolving alliance among the democratic partners. In that context, Sun Shihai, Deputy Director of the Institute of Asia Pacific Studies under the Chinese Academy of Social Sciences (CASS) noted, "The so-called democratic alliance is not good for Asia ... Any attempts to take China as a rival or contain China will not work."[91]

There is also an ideological disconnect between China and the two challengers who espouse democracy in the conduct of international relations. For instance, Japan ordered a withdrawal of the JMSDF vessels deployed in the Indian Ocean since 2001 to provide logistic support to coalition forces engaged in Operation Enduring Freedom-Maritime Interdiction Operation (OEF-MIO). The withdrawal was necessitated after the Japanese political leadership came under intense pressure from the main opposition Democratic Party that is currently supported by smaller allies and had vowed to vote against the extension of the Anti-Terrorism Special Measures Law because it lacks a UN mandate. Similarly, the Left parties in India had vigorously protested against the naval maneuvres involving the United States, Japan, Singapore and Australia claiming that the exercises had "dangerous implications" for national sovereignty and would provide the United States with much-needed strategic space in Indian areas of maritime interest and could curtail strategic autonomy. It was also feared that such naval interactions had the potential to result in several strategic predicaments for India, such as being part of the Israel-U.S. axis targeted against the Muslim world or the U.S.-Japan axis against China and these may not be in India's interests. In the case of Japan, the opposition parties were successful in forcing the government to recall ships (the mission has now been restored), but in the Indian case the government allowed the exercises to continue without taking cognizance of the opposition by the Left parties, clearly showcasing that different democracies behave differently.

Balancing the Primary Challenger

The United States is the primary challenger in Asia to China's global-regional strategy for its pre-eminence. China has responded to this challenge through the East Asia Initiative and the SCO that has kept the United States out of the dialogue. Notwithstanding that, it has to contend with the global superpower that enjoys significant economic strength, technological supremacy, and overwhelming military advantage. It also has allies and alliance partners such as Japan, South Korea, Australia, Singapore, Thailand and the Philippines with access and basing arrangements and forward deployed troops to project power with ease throughout East Asia as well as to ensure peace and stability in the Asia-Pacific region through which U.S. commercial maritime traffic transits.

The U.S. military presence in East Asia is discomforting to China. The planned relocation of some U.S. air and naval forces from Japan and South Korea to Guam has not reduced the conventional deterrence capabilities of the United States in the region. Instead, Guam has witnessed significant defence build-up including relocation of strategic submarines and bombers. The U.S. naval leadership has made it known that an important driver for military augmentation and build-up on Guam is a response to any tensions in the Taiwan Straits and to deter North Korea.[92] In 2004, China dispatched a Han class SSN to waters off Guam to monitor a joint exercise between the United States and Japan navies and it was detected.[93] Interestingly, on its return passage, the submarine intruded into Japanese waters, knowing fully well that it had been detected, clearly challenging U.S. and Japanese naval superiority in the region.

In the maritime domain, China faces several limitations and has weaknesses particularly in C4ISR systems,[94] long-range surveillance and targeting equipment for detecting and tracking ships at sea, integral anti-air and anti-submarine capability. Above all, the PLA Navy's ability to conduct sustained operations, both surface and air, in distant waters remains limited. The PLA Navy has not engaged in any naval combat after the military engagement in the South China Sea in 1974. At another level, it may face a deficit of trained and technologically savvy human resources to man and operate sophisticated platforms. These limit the PLA Navy's ability to project power in distant waters and China acknowledges this asymmetry *vis-à-vis* the United States with regard to the sophistication of U.S. military apparatus.

It has adopted the strategy of *shashaojian*, i.e. "defeating a superior enemy with an inferior force" that seeks to counter and neutralize high-end U.S. military-technology in a conventional conflict.[95] This strategy pivots on acquiring modern naval capabilities for air/space, surface and subsurface warfare designed to attack U.S. carrier groups with cruise and ballistic missiles fitted with a variety of warheads, high-speed torpedoes, sea mines and disrupting C4ISR systems using both "hard kill" and "soft kill" measures. China is working on new types of missiles capable of multiple warheads including an ability to dispense decoys. These are conventional weapons and China hopes to offer some challenge to Japan and the formidable naval power of the United States.

The biggest threat for China comes from the U.S. carrier groups. This perception arises from the fact that in the past the United States has relied on its aircraft carriers to intimidate China. China could engage the United States through the deployment of its subsurface force in protracted submarine warfare, which it believes would be able to challenge the will and motivation of the United States to intervene in a Taiwan crisis, thus raising the costs of intervention for the United States. At the operational-tactical level, China has challenged the U.S. carriers by deploying its fleet of submarines to shadow U.S. carrier groups and surfacing very close, clearly exposing the vulnerabilty of large platforms like the aircarft carriers. As noted in an earlier chapter, in 1994, a Han class SSN surfaced in close vicinity to the *USS Kitty Hawk* and in recent times, a Chinese Song class diesel submarine surfaced within weapons' range of the same carrier. Notwithstanding this, China has invested significantly in sea-based deterrence built around nuclear submarines.[96] The Jin class (Type 094) nuclear-powered ballistic missile submarine (SSBN) is armed with JL-2 nuclear-armed submarine-launched ballistic missiles with ranges of about 8,000 kilometres. When forward deployed, these missiles can hit U.S. territories in the Pacific Ocean and mainland United States. Similarly, the Shang class (Type 093) nuclear-powered attack submarine (SSN) can carry both anti-ship cruise missiles and land-attack cruise missiles and can inflict enormous damage to the U.S forces at sea.

Envelopment

For China, ancient trading connections and socio-cultural-diaspora linkages are the catalysts to successfully bring Southeast Asia into its embrace. Also, it has adopted "pacification strategies" to generate goodwill among its southern neighbours, notwithstanding the deep-rooted suspicions and its creeping assertiveness, particularly in the South China Sea. It has also offered allurement of economic cooperation and Free Trade Agreements (FTA) for accessing critical raw materials and removed some of the barriers to China's exports into the region.[97] At another level, multilateralism has been the Chinese stratagem to assiduously develop friendly relations in Southeast Asia and it has successfully softened the "neighbourhood" for its rising power.[98] China hopes to wean away regional powers from the major Asian powers as well as from the United States, a task that has its own dynamics.

Perhaps the biggest challenge for China has been to convince Southeast Asian nations of its peaceful rise and its military modernization given the fact that it has maritime boundary disputes with Vietnam, the Philippines and Malaysia in the South China Sea believed to contain significant oil and gas as well as living marine resources such as fish. China clashed with Vietnam and the Philippines over territorial disputes in the Paracels and Spratly Islands and has successfully been able to temporarily set aside contentious maritime boundary disputes for the joint development of resources in the South China Sea. It has supported confidence-building mechanisms and cooperative activities till the peaceful settlement of territorial and jurisdictional disputes by cleverly crafting the 2002 Declaration on the Conduct of Parties in the South China Sea.

For China, Southeast Asian maritime choke points are critical for safe and secure transit of its shipping, which carry critical raw materials, energy, and goods that sustain its superlative economic growth. China has adeptly engaged the Straits of Malacca littorals and offered assistance to improve the safety and security of merchant traffic transiting the Straits of Malacca. It also signed the Regional Cooperation Agreement on Combating Piracy and Armed Robbery Against Ships in Asia (ReCAAP) that aims to enhance multilateral cooperation among Asian countries. In essence, China is engaged in "charm offensive" to ally fears among Southeast Asian nations and put in practice the strategy of *Shih*.

Access and Resources

Expounding on nine different types of terrain, Sun Tzu, the master strategist noted that "alliances with the neighbouring states at strategically vital intersections" is critical for survival "but will perish if you fail".[99] China's current strategy is in congruence with Sun Tzu's thought, whereby it is strengthening the core, i.e. the Middle Kingdom with access and basing arrangements with several states astride maritime choke points. After all, maritime choke points are "strategically vital intersections" and "passes" at sea through which maritime traffic transits and which are most vulnerable to disruption, which necessitated articulation of the "Malacca Dilemma".

China has civilian access to several major global maritime gateways leveraged through concerted political, economic and diplomatic initiatives. China supported the development of Gwadar port in Pakistan in close vicinity to the Straits of Hormuz so that it could forward deploy PLA Navy assets in the event of a crisis as well as to monitor U.S. naval activity in the Persian Gulf. Its military sales, development of naval facilities and the establishment of electronic surveillance systems in Myanmar support its monitoring of merchant traffic through the Straits of Malacca. The development of Port Said astride the Suez Canal which connects the Mediterranean Sea and the Red Sea and facilitates a shorter route for oil traffic to Europe and the United States, provides it potential leverages to monitor U.S. and NATO naval assets transiting through the Canal. The Red Sea also gains salience from the fact that China has made significant investments in Sudan which is an important source to meet its energy needs. Similarly, port operations at Balboa and Cristobal that lie at the ends of the Panama Canal on the Atlantic and Pacific Oceans offer monitoring of U.S. naval movements. Commercial operation of ports in Argentina, Mexico and Bahamas are clear indicators of how China obtains strategic gains for safeguarding its sea lanes as well as accessing resources from the region.

These initiatives provide China with the future potential to enmesh these countries, though geographically far from China, in its sway thus depriving contenders of the opportunity of influencing. It also fits into the Chinese choke point and sea lane security strategy that has gained critical salience in China's economic growth. These initiatives well as facilitate the building of strategic outposts for safeguarding its sea lanes, mercantile traffic, as well as to spread its influence, a critical requirement of *Shih*. In essence, China has skilfully made several variations to its peaceful rise argument that envelops economic and security cooperation to counter influence exerted by its peer rivals.

MARITIME *MANDALA*

In the 21st century, India's strategic interests have undergone a profound transformation overcoming years of ideological rigidity to an interest-driven autonomy clearly showcasing a systemic transformation. This has been possible partly due to India's choices of globalization resulting in strong economic growth and a desire to restore some of the glorious historical epochs of political, economic and strategic pre-eminence. These strategic choices and the new economic strength have resulted in significant opportunities for increased transactions with the great powers that are fast-evolving into new partnerships, multilateral and bilateral engagements and cooperative initiatives.

The economic and emerging strategic strengths also provide for focused military interactions that offer tactical-operational engagements exemplified by interoperability among the militaries. These are translating into technology transfers for building India's high-technology base. Several of these have spawned defence-technology relations that have accrued immense dividends thus fostering a series of new defence-technological collaborative enterprises. This ensures augmentation of India's existing military industrial infrastructure and adds to India's growing technological strengths. Since the 1990s, India has been nurturing an ascendant strategic profile with maritime engagements with the United States, Russia, France, United Kingdom, Israel, Japan and several countries in the Southeast Asian region. In perspective, India's strategic engagement with several states including the great powers would be an interpretation of the *Mandala* Doctrine. Importantly, the Indo-Pacific Oceans provide the seamless contiguity of strategic space wherein the maritime *Mandala* is enacted by India.

Immediate *Mandala*

The immediate *Mandala* has China and Pakistan, the two contiguous states with whom India has been engaged in wars over boundary disputes that remain unresolved. India has improving relations with China in the political and economic front pivoting on leadership dialogues and expanding trade but there is a strategic disconnect. India's "China threat" and the naming of China as the threat that prompted its 1998 nuclear tests, has been an important factor in Sino-India relations. In March 2000, China's Foreign Minister Tang Jiaxuan grudgingly noted that "generally speaking China and India do not pose a threat to each other ..." and in July 2000, President K.R. Narayanan noted that India and China were "not necessarily rivals".[100] Notwithstanding these statements, both India and China are competitors and engaged in aggressive geostrategic initiatives to counter each other's influence.

Significantly, both China and India are the rising powers in Asia with a potential to shape the security architecture of the region. In that context, China has attempted to balance and box India in the South Asian region with its military-strategic-technical relations with Pakistan, Bangladesh and Myanmar, aimed at strategic encirclement of India. India is concerned about the growing strategic relationship between Beijing and Islamabad premised on nuclear and missile technology transfers to Pakistan. China's relations with the other South Asian countries have been articulated on the basis of a politico-military-economic strategy evident in its strong efforts to contain India, while expanding its own presence in the region through trade, naval access and infrastructure-building projects aiding the smaller states. The ongoing Chinese political, economic, and military initiatives in South Asia and counties in East Africa have led the Indian naval leadership to conclude that the absence of a credible Indian naval capability and sustained naval presence is being exploited by China and it is able to shape the maritime battle space in the Indian Ocean by building strategic relations in "right places".[101]

Pakistan has been India's primary detractor power in the subcontinental context and the two states have engaged in three wars over border and boundary disputes. Pakistan has also engaged in low-intensity conflict, and supported insurgency and separatist movements in India which has generated animosity and mistrust in bilateral relations. Besides, there is very little progress to solve the boundary issues. Further, Pakistan's nuclear and missile capability has resulted in an uneasy deterrence relationship in the region which prompted limited wars as demonstrated by the 2001 Kargil conflict.

Beijing and Islamabad have established bilateral strategic links and their cooperation now covers almost all facets of economy, defence, energy, industry, intelligence-sharing and infrastructure, with military cooperation at its core. The nature and scope of Sino-Pakistan military and nuclear proliferation has been an issue of grave concern for India. Geostrategically, China views Pakistan as an outlet to the Indian Ocean and also as a land corridor to the Gulf and west Asia.[102] Sino-Pakistan naval cooperation has been a major thrust area and a large component of the Pakistan naval hardware is of Chinese origin[103] and naval infrastructure, particularly Gwadar port, has been built with generous Chinese financial and technological assistance. Interestingly, Pakistan had also evinced interest in purchasing nuclear submarines from China.[104] Thus, China is bolstering Pakistan's war-making capability against India and also supporting its nuclear programme as a challenge to Indian dominance in the region.

The conflict-prone nature of India-Pakistan relations and the aggravating Chinese dimension of aiding Pakistan with the deliberate intent to contain India have made it more determined to expand its strategic space. In its quest, India has attempted to hard balance its immediate *Mandala* by engaging several Indian Ocean, Persian Gulf, Southeast Asian and Pacific powers by exploring significant political and economic engagements that have seminal strategic intent and purpose.

Intermediate *Mandala*

In the West, India's intermediate *Mandala* comprises East Africa, the Persian Gulf, and Central Asia. India's engagement with Southwest Asia-Persian Gulf has been quite prominent. Its reliance on its hydrocarbon imports dictates the strong maritime interests in the safety and security of the Straits of Hormuz given the fact that it is India's oil jugular. The presence of Indian diaspora and a substantial remittance economy that it has built over the years reinforces the strong links. India has a pronounced strategy of building close relations with Persian Gulf countries and several Persian Gulf heads of state have been guests of honour in New Delhi including at Indian Republic Day celebrations. Military cooperation with Persian Gulf states is an important aspect of bilateral relations and these interactions have resulted in defence MoUs that envisage military exchanges, training and joint exercises and also provide for military-related hardware.[105]

India's East African engagement came by way of the Indian Navy's deployment for waterfront security and surveillance assistance during the African Union Summit held in Maputo, Mozambique in July 2003.[106] Similarly, the Indian Navy engaged the South African and Brazil navies in trilateral naval exercises under the IBSA (India-Brazil-South Africa) partnership off South Africa.[107] Over all, India has expanded its engagements with the African-Indian Ocean littorals through several maritime initiatives.[108] India-Central Asian Republics' (CAR) engagements pivot on investments in energy. Although the CAR are landlocked, the Indian Navy has contacts with CAR to source ex-Soviet naval hardware and spares. Thus, linkages with CAR are vital for India and figure prominently in the intermediate *Mandala*.

In the East, the intermediate *Mandala* focuses on Southeast Asia. India has enduring economic, trade and diaspora ties with several countries of the region that date back to ancient times. As part of the "Look East" policy, India is engaged in Southeast Asia through political and economic engagements such as the ASEAN Treaty of Amity and Cooperation (TAC) and East Asian Summit (EAS). At another level, India has contributed to several Track II initiatives such as the Council for Security Cooperation in the Asia Pacific (CSCAP), the Bay of Bengal Initiative for Multi-Sectoral Technical and Economic Cooperation (BIMSTEC), Mekong Ganga Cooperation (MGC) Project, and several other bilateral and multilateral initiatives.

Strategic issues too have gained currency in India-ASEAN relations and India's accession to the Southeast Asia Nuclear Weapons Free Zone (SEANWFZ) is a significant example.[109] As part of the ASEAN-India Partnership for Peace, Progress and Shared Prosperity, India is cooperating with several Southeast Asian states in combating international terrorism and transnational crimes and extending its cooperation in capacity-building. At the institutional level, the Indian Navy has developed bilateral maritime relations with all Southeast Asian navies that are premised on ship visits, high-level exchanges, joint exercises and coordinated patrols to maintain order at sea.[110] For instance, the Indian Navy and Singapore Navy have expanded their bilateral cooperation to include issues of interoperability. Similarly, India has bilateral maritime engagements with several Bay of Bengal-ASEAN littorals involving coordinated patrols, ship visits and training arrangements that have gained significant currency in bilateral relations. Similar initiatives have mushroomed with the South China Sea-ASEAN littorals too.

As noted earlier, nearly 55 per cent of India's seaborne trade transits through the Straits of Malacca. India offered assistance to the littoral states of the Straits of Malacca in keeping the Straits safe and secure and has designed and conducted training modules on maritime security with themes of anti-piracy, search-and-rescue, offshore and port security, anti-smuggling and narcotics control, and anti-poaching operations aimed at "capacity-building". ASEAN states also acknowledge India's participation in the Regional Cooperation Agreement on Combating Piracy and Armed Robbery Against Ships in Asia (ReCAAP), the first government-to-government agreement to enhance security of regional waters. It is quite pertinent to note the Indian

Navy humanitarian assistance during the 2004 Indian Ocean Tsunami during which its naval ships, aircraft and helicopters supported rescue and relief operations. This effort was later integrated into the *Operation Unified Assistance* that synergized the maritime forces from the United States, Japan, India and Australia.

Outer *Mandala*

India's strategic engagements with the outer *Mandala*, i.e. Japan, Russia, and the United States have been determined by the norm of synergy of robust relations based on strategic convergence. Strategic dialogues at both political and security level have strengthened ties. Since the mid-1990s, India and Japan have been discussing common security concerns focused on safety and security of sea lanes, combating sea piracy and search and rescue, particularly in the Indian Ocean through which the bulk of Japanese oil transits. With regard to maritime cooperation, the Japanese and Indian maritime forces (navy and coast guard) visit each other's ports and undertake joint exercises.[111]

Significantly, besides the United States and Australia, India is the third country with which Japan has a strategic partnership. India and Japan appear to have taken the strategic initiative to assert greater influence in the Asia-Pacific region. India conducted naval exercises in the South China Sea in 2000, while Japan has stretched its sea-lane defence well beyond the stipulated 1,000 miles towards the Arabian Sea. Because of their geographic locations, the two countries do not appear to compete with each other for influence; instead their strategic geographic areas overlap, covering a large proportion of the Indian Ocean and South China Sea through which their maritime supply chains and energy traffic transit. The recent report that China's new facilities at the Yulin naval base at Sanya on Hainan Island is capable of hosting aircraft carrier groups, several nuclear submarines and amphibious assault ships has added a new dimension to the Asia-Pacific security conundrum. From the Indian and Japanese perspectives, the deployment of the Type 094 Jin class and the Type 093 Shang class attack submarines constitutes a meaningful deterrence and limits Indian and Japanese strategic choices.

As far as Russia is concerned, geostrategic and geopolitical conditions had shaped India's lean towards the former Soviet Union since the 1960s.[112] For New Delhi, an engagement with Moscow helped offset American influence and neutralized that of China. The Soviet Union supported India over Kashmir and acted as a peacemaker between India and Pakistan, brokering the Tashkent agreement. Significantly, Russia dispatched a squadron of nuclear submarines in response to the U.S. decision to dispatch the U.S. Seventh Fleet task force (TF-74) led by nuclear-powered aircraft carrier *USS Enterprise* to move towards the Bay of Bengal to influence events in the 1971 India-Pakistan War.

India's zestful military technical cooperation with Russia with the strong objective of building a robust military platform base has reinforced their bilateral relations. India's defence industrial complex has a large Russian contribution and the Indian Navy has relied on the Soviet Union/Russia for a large number of defence acquisitions. India acquired and continues to acquire a large number of ships, aircraft and submarines from the Soviet Union/Russia. Significant among these acquisitions are the lease of a nuclear submarine (INS Chakra) and the aircraft carrier (INS Vikramaditya). The successful joint production of the Brahmos cruise missile has led India and Russia to work and develop more advanced weapon systems.[113] The India-Russia naval engagements since 2003 code named INDRA have further strengthened cooperation, trust and mutual understanding between the two powers and have reinforced the strategic relationship.[114]

The catalyst to the expanding military cooperation between New Delhi and Washington is substantially driven by the "broad convergence of their security and political interests despite differences over important issues like nuclear non-proliferation".[115] The nuclear tests by India in 1998 led to the temporary suspension of the strategic dialogue that was quickly resumed. The strategic dialogue between the two countries has helped the United States to understand India's nuclear motivations and intentions.[116] India is now negotiating a nuclear deal with the United States for supply of nuclear technology for peaceful purposes under IAEA safeguards.[117]

Common security concerns such as terrorism and piracy at sea and safety of sea lines of communications in the Indian Ocean have provided the required impetus to bring the two navies closer. Indo-U.S. naval relations are witnessing an upswing and this promising relationship has the potential to shape the regional security environment with accents on stability. Since the early 1990s, the U.S. Navy and the Indian Navy have strengthened bilateral naval cooperation through the Malabar series of exercises. The Malabar series has grown in scope and complexity over the years with varying platforms and new missions of interoperability.[118] These exercises are now an annual event for the two navies. In operational terms and common strategic vision, the exercises are symbolic of the enhanced understanding. The bilateral framework has substantially envisaged joint maritime operations such as anti-piracy, safety of sea lanes, anti-drug and gunrunning patrols.

The strategic relations with the United States has enhanced the Indian Navy's prospects to acquire a variety of advanced naval platforms and systems in the ongoing arms procurement package. In strategic terms, the prospect of acquisition of cutting-edge technologies such as submarine rescue facilities, P-3 Orion maritime patrol aircraft, helicopters, laser systems, including training of Indian naval pilots will enhance the Indian Navy's capability. New Delhi and Washington have also signed the General Security on Military Information Agreement (GSOMIA) in January 2002 that facilitates the exchange of defence-related information between the two countries.[119] The India-U.S. relationship also nurtures viable and immensely important relations with Israel that sharpens the leverage of Indian operational naval power. The fact that Israel has emerged as the second largest defence technology and hardware supplier to India is quite crucial for the highly sophisticated platforms and integration technologies to India.[120]

In essence, India's maritime *Mandala* engages potential friends and strategic partners that will be vital to offset the dominant challenge evident in the immediate *Mandala* in the form of China with its growing colossal economic and strategic-military capabilities. However, the interesting debate on India's *Mandala* strategy will be how it can obtain strategic advantage from Russia over China. While Russia continues to be China's important strategic partner, the Russian desire to have India in its trilateral partnership with China to balance the hyper-power of the United States has been limited by India's new strategic links with the United States. Besides, Beijing would be reluctant to accord India an equal partnership in a possible strategic triangle with Moscow. Hence India's quest will be to maximally derive the value additions of the Russian collaboration while balancing its role with operational maritime synergies with the United States and Japan.

The essence of India's maritime *Mandala* thus lies in its robust and dynamic evolution of strategic alliances of the core state with the intermediate and outer powers to determine the *Mandala* balance. The maritime interoperability with the Indo-Pacific region will be India's enduring and viable leverage of power that will add to the competitive gains for India. India is the practitioner par excellence of the *Mandala* in its historical legacy. The maritime *Mandala* that India is now envisioning with the United States, Japan and Russia in Asia Pacific and the countries of Southeast Asia is the evident sign of the evolving power and profile of India's strategic autonomy that comes with its economic and industrial prowess. Its rediscovery comes at a time when its rising power and leverage is quite evident in its maritime engagements with the other maritime powers both in and outside Asia.

SOUTHEAST ASIA

Historical influences, past experiences and the multi-centre polity of ancient Southeast Asia appear to shape the contemporary statecraft in Southeast Asia. Interestingly, the modern-day Southeast Asia represents the "mandalic Southeast Asia" of the traditional Southeast Asian international system in which the states represent the ancient *Mandalas* and each state is an individual entity in its own right that enjoys distinct identity in the region, while the ASEAN represents a modified version of the concept of "chakravartin", i.e. universal monarch, symbolically placing it at the centre. Although ASEAN is not based on the notion of a "Centre" radiating power, it represents the institutional approach linking the others members of the Association. In essence, the member states relate to the ASEAN and are attracted towards it, but conduct their respective independent international relations.

At another level, diplomacy remains fundamental to ASEAN and its members. Interestingly, O.W. Wolters, an eminent historian, observes that "diplomatic flair probably came easily to rulers in multicentered Southeast Asia",[121] a legacy that continues to date. ASEAN diplomacy exhibits an interface of national interest and regionalism with emphasis on consultation and consensus (musyawarah and mufakat), identity-building and collective decision-making, "the ASEAN way".[122] It pivots on mutual respect for national identity, cultural cooperation, economic integration, and security cooperation.[123] The Southeast Asian states have nurtured peaceful, cordial, stable, and enduring relations among themselves that has created a secure environment for the conduct of their bilateral and multilateral international relations. This has been achieved through their adherence to the principles of mutual respect for sovereignty, non-interference in the internal affairs of one another, decision-making by consensus and "prosper thy neighbour" philosophy as enshrined in the Charter of the Association of Southeast Asian Nations.[124]

Regional peace and security is vital for ASEAN member countries both from an individual perspective as well as collectively.[125] ASEAN countries have promoted peace and stability in the broader Asia-Pacific region and supported several initiatives and regional institutions for enhancing regional security. In 1971, the ASEAN states announced the Zone of Peace, Freedom and Neutrality Declaration (ZOPFAN)[126] and identified several regional initiatives for security and to prevent external interferences. These include the Treaty of Amity and Cooperation (TAC) in Southeast Asia, establishing the Southeast Asia Nuclear Weapon-Free Zone (SEANWFZ)[127] in Southeast Asia, and declaring Southeast Asia as a Zone of Peace, Freedom and Neutrality.

ASEAN states, both collectively and individually, have engaged the major powers notwithstanding the competitive nature of their relationships. Instead a sophisticated strategy has been developed that showcases convergence of their interests in which all major powers are considered significant stakeholders, thus preventing any adversarial competition.

ASEAN engagements with China and India, the rising powers in Asia, pivot on several bilateral and multilateral political, diplomatic, economic and security arrangements that have so far produced the desired outcomes leading to regional peace and security that is ever so critical for Southeast Asia. Member states have avoided aligning with the weaker to challenge the dominant power; instead ASEAN has welcomed and supported China and India's participation in regional multilateral institutions such as the ARF, ASEAN Plus Three and East Asia Summit (EAS).[128]

The ASEAN Regional Forum (ARF) has come to serve as a significant security dialogue platform, which includes the five permanent members of the United Nations, five nuclear powers (United States, Russia, China, India, and Pakistan) and European Union. ASEAN has engaged China and India through the ARF that facilitates dialogue and consultations on regional security issues. The "ASEAN Plus Three" serves to tie China, Japan and South Korea with ASEAN, particularly on economic matters. The EAS (ASEAN Plus Three, Australia, India and New Zealand) is a more recent pan-Asian summit meeting first conceptualized in 2005. Interestingly, the ASEAN strategy of engaging and enmeshing China and India has led to the "competitive ascription"[129] demonstrated by the fact that both Asian powers were the first to sign the TAC 2003 and are also signatories to the SEANWFZ.[130]

The 2002 Declaration on the Conduct of Parties in the South China Sea is a multilateral agreement between Brunei, Malaysia, the Philippines, Taiwan, Vietnam and China, based on the convergence of views with the imperative to institutionalize the need to peacefully manage the disputes and prevent tension, suspicion, and misunderstanding that resulted in conflict escalations in the 1970s and the 1980s featuring China and the Philippines and China and Vietnam. As part of their strategy to jointly exploit the resources in the South China Sea, Vietnam, the Philippines and China agreed in 2005 to undertake oil exploration in the disputed areas under a deal known as Joint Marine Seismic Undertaking (JMSU). Under a MoU, the Philippine National Oil Co.-Exploration Corp. (PNOC-EC), China National Offshore Oil Corp. and PetroVietnam entered into a tripartite agreement to undertake data gathering, processing, and interpretation of oil and gas deposits in a part of the South China Sea including the disputed

Spratly Islands. The MoU expired in 2008. For the Philippines, the MoU served the "interest of building and maintaining peace, stability, security and prosperity in the contested areas in the South China Sea".[131]

Most ASEAN countries are reliant on trade for growth and prosperity and wish to harness the benefits of the current trends in globalization that has firm foundations in maritime connectivity. Given the maritime nature of geography and the strategic choke points such as the Straits of Malacca, Sunda and Lombok Straits, a close relationship between sea-based commerce and security is increasingly evident in Southeast Asia. The upward trajectory in regional maritime trade is a welcome sign, but a careful consideration highlights that it is vulnerable to disruption from disorder at sea arising from terrorism, piracy, and other illegal activities such as drug trafficking, gunrunning, human smuggling, maritime theft and fraud, illegal fishing, and pollution. This necessitates order at sea that can be obtained through cooperative engagements with stakeholders.

ASEAN states acknowledge the necessity of multilateral arrangements to enhance the safety and security of maritime traffic in the region. The Regional Cooperation Agreement on Combating Piracy and Armed Robbery Against Ships in Asia (ReCAAP) is the first multilateral government-to-government agreement to enhance security in Asian waters. ASEAN member states and Japan, India, China, South Korea, Sri Lanka and Bangladesh are signatories and the Information Sharing Centre (ISC) is located in Singapore.[132] The Straits of Malacca littorals, i.e. Indonesia, Malaysia, and Singapore, are collectively engaged with China and India for enhancing the safety and security of the Straits. As noted earlier, Beijing has offered financial and technological assistance to improve the safety and security of merchant traffic transiting the Straits of Malacca including technical support for training programmes, capacity-building and hydrographical surveys and to replace navigational aids damaged during the 2004 Indian Ocean Tsunami. India offered to provide security in the Straits of Malacca as well as to design and conduct training modules for "capacity-building" for related aspects of maritime security.

The Shangri-La Dialogue is yet another Track II multilateral initiative that is supported by most Asian security establishments. The forum is unique in that it is "cocooned from the demands of political deliverables"[133] and is highly informal, yet able to deliver consensus. For instance, the Eyes-in-the-Sky initiative involving multilateral coordinated maritime air patrols in the Straits of Malacca emerged as a result of the Shangri-La Dialogue.

At the country level, ASEAN member states are pursuing different engagement strategies that vary from country to country. There are several drivers for such an approach such as the imperatives of strategic autonomy, transforming and diversifying relations, obtaining security assurances, developing strategic partnerships, economic engagements and trade agreements. These engagements are outside the ambit of ASEAN but the members are careful not to develop arrangements that could challenge the sanctity of their relationship with the ASEAN member states as enshrined in the ASEAN Charter.

For instance, Singapore has bilateral security relations with China. In January 2008, the two sides signed the bilateral agreement on defence exchanges and security cooperation that envisages exchanges of personnel, training courses, seminars and port calls.[134] Meanwhile Singapore maintains a neutral position between China and Taiwan and respects the "one China policy", yet it maintains a military contacts with Taiwan for its training requirements. Singapore has a highly developed maritime cooperation agreement with India that includes joint naval exercises, submarine training and bilateral exchanges. India and Singapore have been holding joint exercises for the past fifteen years and these have provided a platform for exchange of information, interoperability and above all contributed to regional stability.

At another level, Vietnam's policy toward India attempts to expand both economic and military ties. In April 2000, Vietnam signed an agreement with India for military hardware and training of the Vietnamese military.[135] Cooperation with Vietnam enables India to position itself astride the sea lanes transiting the South China Sea and in the long run, Vietnamese ports would be critical. Indian naval ships have on a regular basis visited Vietnamese ports on goodwill visits and these visits were useful in showcasing Indian naval shipbuilding capability. In 2000, both Indian and Vietnamese navies carried out joint exercises.[136] The growing relationship between India and Vietnam in part aims to exercise strategic autonomy in Southeast Asia. For Vietnam, Chinese assertiveness and forcible occupation of Vietnam's island territories in the South China Sea are some of the security issues that present challenges to Hanoi and these mutual concerns are potential grounds for greater military cooperation between Vietnam and India.

Myanmar is transforming and diversifying its relations. It has extensive political, economic and military relations with China. The relationship had a significant strategic content pivoting on development of naval facilities, sale of naval hardware to build the Myanmar Navy, signal intelligence networks and other maritime infrastructure with the intent of using these in support of the PLA naval deployments in the Indian Ocean as well as to monitor Indian naval activity. In recent times, Myanmar has begun to court India and what is perhaps more significant is that both Myanmar and India see this as an opportunity to keep issues such as democracy and human rights aside and build good neighbourly relations. The Indian Navy has supplied maritime surveillance aircraft, naval guns and varied surveillance equipment,[137] and the Indian army transferred Howitzers, armoured personnel carriers, artillery guns, mortars and the locally designed advanced light helicopters. Both sides have engaged in coordinated operations against northeastern militant groups along their borders.[138] Significantly, Myanmar had no inhibitions about allowing two Indian naval vessels to carry relief aid to Myanmar in the aftermath of Cyclone Nargis that had battered Myanmar's coastal areas and claimed 140,000 lives.[139] The Myanmar response was significant because it refused similar aid from the United States and France whose ships waited in the Bay of Bengal ready to provide relief but had to abandon the mission.

At another level, Southeast Asian states must contend with Asia's nuclear weapon states. China and India are the nuclear neighbours that possess significant naval and missile capability. The evolving naval order of battle of the PLA Navy and the Indian Navy in the eastern and western flanks of Southeast Asia is potentially unnerving given that the two navies are in the throes of modernization and growing at a rapid pace with assents on power projection platforms such as aircraft carriers, submarines and other surface vessels equipped with advanced weaponry. The nuclear submarines are high on the agenda and the two nuclear powers of Asia are focused on building a credible sea-based deterrent. Meanwhile, the conventional submarines are being fitted out with subsurface missile capability to engage targets at sea and ashore and are increasingly becoming more sophisticated both in terms of stealth and firepower.

The current and the evolving naval nuclear capability of China and India is configured as "second-strike", and is not targeted against any Southeast Asian state. The two nuclear powers have provided the requisite security assurances and commitments that include "no use of nuclear weapons against non-nuclear weapon states". Perhaps what is of concern is that China and India are developing naval nuclear facilities on the peripheries of Southeast Asia, i.e. the Yulin naval base at Sanya on Hainan Island in the South China Sea[140] and Rambilli in the Bay of Bengal.[141] These developments sharpen the Southeast Asian security environment.

The nuclear infrastructure at the Yulin naval base consists of nearly a dozen entrances carved into the rocky hill capable of concealing up to twenty nuclear submarines. Yulin naval base is a fortress at sea astride the shipping sea lanes in the region. The piers around the base can berth aircraft carriers, destroyers, frigates and amphibious assault ships and there are naval-air assets including rapid reaction troops located on the Hainan Island. The depths within a few miles of Hainan Island exceed 5,000 metres and the underwater topography is favourable for nuclear submarines to make a stealthy exit into the open seas. Importantly, the Yulin naval base is a significant staging post that facilitates quick surges by the PLA Navy into the South China Sea and toward the Straits of Malacca in support of its different mission requirements.

The Indian Navy's nuclear infrastructure including nuclear submarine building yard, berthing complex, related maintenance and ancillary facilities are currently located at Vishakhapatnam in the Bay of Bengal. Built with Soviet assistance, the facility served as a staging post for INS Chakra, a Charlie class Soviet submarine acquired on lease in 1988. India is now building a specialist naval base at Rambilli, south of Vishakhapatnam that will be home to both the nuclear and conventional submarines. The Rambilli naval complex is expected to be ready by 2011. The salient features of the Rambilli base is that waters off the base are quite deep and would provide exit-entry stealth to the submarines.

As noted in the earlier chapter, the PLA Navy inventory includes two types of SSBNs; Type 094 Jin class (fitted with twelve JL-2 SLBMs, 8,000-kilometre range) and one Xia class submarine (twelve Julong I SLBM (2,000-kilometre range) with a single 250 KT warhead). The Type 093 Shang class SSN is capable of launching a variety of ordinance including land attack and anti-ship cruise missiles, conventional torpedoes and the super-fast Shkval super-cavitating 200 knots torpedoes. The indigenous Indian naval nuclear submarine designated as ATV is still under development but India has leased an Akula-II class SSBN (12,000 tonnes) currently under construction at the Komsomolsk-on-Amur shipyard in Russia to be commissioned as INS Chakra in 2009.[142]

As early as 2001, the United States had been aware of China's naval nuclear developments at the Yulin base and it engaged in aggressive surveillance and monitoring of construction activity. Apparently, an EP3 surveillance incident in April 2001 was closely related to monitoring developments at Sanya. Acknowledging the existence of the facility and U.S. concerns, Admiral Timothy Keating, Commander U.S. Pacific Command observed that China should not pursue "high-end military options". A U.S. military expert has even called for reinforcing alliances in Asia to counter China's growing military might.[143] The United States' worries also arise from the fact that China would employ anti-access strategies in the South China Sea and this would necessitate access arrangements and enhanced interoperability with Japan, South Korea, Taiwan, the Philippines, and Singapore, including Indonesia and Malaysia.

The nuclear naval developments at Sanya appear to have rattled India too.[144] Indian authorities claimed prior knowledge of the facilities at the Yulin naval base, and the naval leadership commented on the development as a "cause for security concern".[145] It was also observed that, "Though India is not worried about Beijing building a strategic naval base on Hainan Island in the South China Sea, it is concerned about the numbers [submarines]. Nuclear submarines have long legs; it is immaterial where they are based."[146]

China has defended the development at the Yulin nuclear base and the foreign ministry official noted, "We have a vast territorial sea, and it is the sacred duty of the Chinese army to safeguard our security on the sea, the sovereignty of our territorial waters, and maritime rights and interests ... There is no need for the Western countries to be worried, or concerned, or make any irresponsible accusations ... China's national defense and military building will not pose a threat to any country."[147]

The regional naval nuclear developments are bound to impact Southeast Asian countries in several ways. First, the region is known for contested territorial claims between China, Taiwan and some Southeast Asian countries. The possibility of escalation of territorial disputes and the involvement of the militaries could happen if existing conflict management and conflict avoidance measures such as multilateral regional security initiatives and confidence-building measures were to fail. The claimants have so far done well by keeping the military activity low in the South China Sea; however, the possibility of the escalation of the territorial disputes into the military confrontation would be high if sovereignty issues gained currency over regional security arrangements. Further, as energy demands grow, the need for exploration and production of hydrocarbons in the South China Sea will become more intense. The possibility of heightened tensions in the region could arise if claimants conduct exploration activity in disputed areas.

Second, there is increased sensitivity to the issues of safety and security of the sea lanes transiting through the South China Sea-Straits of Malacca, the shortest shipping route connecting Northeast Asia-Southeast Asia-South Asia-Persian Gulf. The issues of safety and security of sea lanes and maritime supply chains through the Southeast Asian strategic choke points is critical for China, Japan, the United States, Korea, and India. China, Japan and Korea are heavily dependent on energy supplies from the Persian Gulf and the energy supply routes transit through the Straits of Malacca, Sunda, Lombok Straits, and the South China Sea. For the United States, its trading routes straddle the South China Sea-Straits of Malacca region resulting in its sensitivities to the sea-lane security. Nearly 50 per cent of Indian trade transits through the Straits of Malacca and any disruption could severely impact its economy. These countries seek greater engagement in the region to safeguard sea lanes that serve as the umbilical cord of their respective economies. Some even seek naval presence including patrolling in the Straits of Malacca and exploring opportunities for access and basing much to the discomfort of the littoral states, i.e. Indonesia, Malaysia and Singapore, who perceive such initiatives as attempts by the extra-regional powers to curtail strategic autonomy.

Third, there is the impact of the military modernization of China and its ripple effects on the arms build-up among Southeast Asian countries. The quest for building national power, deterrence against possible escalation of disputes and competitive process of arms acquisition are some of the drivers for military modernization of Southeast Asian militaries, particularly the navies and air forces. Chinese naval modernization and military developments particularly on the Hainan and Woody Islands has prompted Indonesia, Malaysia, and Vietnam to build substantive military capabilities to thwart any Chinese adventurism. Although Southeast Asian naval and air forces are minuscule both in terms of quality and quantity when compared with China's maritime forces, yet the build-up is seen as a deterrent value against the latter.

Fourth is the issue of the future role and relevance of Southeast Asian regional alliances and bilateral engagements with the United States and the Five Power Defence Arrangements (FPDA). So far, Southeast Asian states have engaged the United States and are quite comfortable with the U.S. presence in Southeast Asia, ostensibly as a balance to the rising profile of China. The Philippines and Thailand enjoy Non-NATO Military Alliance (NNMA) status and Singapore has expanded defence cooperation arrangements with the United States. These states in particular enjoy U.S. support and accrue the relative power that can possibly stand up to China.[148] Notwithstanding that, the United States supports the Southeast Asia-led multilateral institutions such as the ARF to ensure regional peace and strengthen regional security.

The FPDA, established in 1971, is a platform for dialogue and exchange of views on regional security issues between Singapore and Malaysia with Australia, New Zealand and the United Kingdom. It does not include Indonesia. In fact, the genesis of the grouping is traced back to the 1957 Anglo-Malayan Defence Agreement (AMDA) that envisaged a "security umbrella" for independent Malaya and resisted "Indonesia's policy of 'Confrontation' which included military action or terrorist activities in Johor,

Singapore, and Sarawak".[149] In 1994, Singapore's Defence Minister, Lee Boon Yang, observed, "The relevance of the FPDA does not depend on an immediate threat. The FPDA is there to cater to the unforeseen, unanticipated and the most unexpected turn of events."[150] Also, it is important to keep in mind that the FPDA members would be under intense pressure[151] in the event of a conflict in the Spratly Islands involving Malaysian claimed areas.[152]

The Southeast Asian response to Chinese naval nuclear development has been rather muted. For instance, the Philippine Government did not appear to be much concerned about the nuclear facilities at Sanya and noted "all countries in the world are after regional peace and that it's not intended to destabilize peace in the region". Further, "we can be sure a superpower like the US would know about it ... and know how to address it".[153] At the military level, Malaysia plans to base its submarine force at Kota Kinabalu, Sabah in the South China Sea for which a contract has been awarded.[154] Malaysia is acquiring three submarines under a US$972 million deal from the European shipbuilders DCN International and Izar, including an overhauled Agosta 70, an ex-French Navy submarine for initial training.

There are several plausible reasons for the muted response by Southeast Asian countries. First, the Southeast Asian countries have developed significant economic engagements with China and are therefore hesitant to openly express concerns. Second, some of the Southeast Asian militaries have security dialogues, military-technical cooperation and bilateral security arrangements that prevent any articulation by the governments. Third, there is a fear of inviting adverse Chinese reaction and being grouped into the Western camp led by the United States. Fourth, it is ASEAN aspiration to build a security community to serve as a political and diplomatic tool for dispute settlement and expressing concerns would serve no purpose.

The Southeast Asian nations would however be concerned that nuclear submarines have endurance and capability to operate far from home in distant waters and the Chinese and Indian nuclear submarines would naturally be in operation in the South China Sea and the Bay of Bengal. These platforms could in future criss-cross the Southeast Asian sea spaces encompassing the SEANWFZ, particularly the Straits of Malacca and the South China Sea in support of mission requirements. Besides, the Southeast Asian nations also have to factor in the nuclear naval forces of the United States, Russia, United Kingdom, and France who objected to the inclusion of continental shelves and EEZ in the SEANWFZ treaty on the grounds that it imposed significant restrictions on the operational deployment of their navies. These concerns were notable bearing in mind that the sea-based deterrent pivoting on nuclear submarines is the potent segment of the strategic triad.

At the conventional level, there is a keen interest in submarines among Southeast Asian navies. Indonesia has a rich experience in operating submarines and was the first country to acquire submarines in Southeast Asia. In 1965 it decided to dispatch a submarine to Pakistan during the India-Pakistan conflict, but it arrived only after the ceasefire due to the long distance.[155] The current inventory includes two German-built Type 209 vessels. Indonesia is in negotiations with Russia for acquiring the Amur 950 class diesel submarines capable of firing the 290-kilometre range Klub-S cruise missile. Malaysia has contracted from France three Scorpene-class submarines and the first vessel was launched in October 2007 in France. The Singapore Navy operates four Challenger class ex-Swedish Navy submarines and has signed for two Västergötland class diesel submarines from Sweden. Vietnam has two North Korea-built "Yugo" class mini-submarines. Thailand has been debating to develop a subsurface arm for its navy and exploring acquisition from Russia or Israel,[156] or leasing from China.[157]

Southeast Asian navies are fast acquiring submarines clearly highlighting the fact that regional countries must build their respective capabilities in the face of the aggressive submarine developments of the PLA Navy and the Indian Navy whose platforms would criss-cross the Bay of Bengal-Straits of Malacca-South China Sea maritime space. This is sure to result in enhanced subsurface activity in Southeast Asian waters. Adding to these assets will be the U.S. submarine force that transits through these waters which will be quite challenging given that Southeast Asian navies have limited experience in complex submarine operations. Given the density of submarine traffic, it is quite natural that these navies will engage in surveillance and reconnaissance and shadowing and snooping of each other's platforms. These could result in close-quarter situations, which bring the attendant problems of safety of submarines, submarine rescue and the Incidents at Sea Agreement (INCSEA) to prevent escalations including "Hot Lines". Southeast Asian maritime security is further compounded by the ever-increasing shipping traffic through the Straits of Malacca currently pegged at more than 60,000 vessels annually.

A new appreciation of the evolving security environment is critical for Southeast Asian countries bearing in mind the changing strategic vision of China and India.[158] So far China has made significant progress in presenting a benign picture of its peaceful rise and dispelling fears among ASEAN countries about its growing economic and military power and its rising strategic profile. Being a member of the ARF and the EAS, Beijing has argued that it is focused on creating economic linkages and generating interdependence. Similarly, India is also a member of the ARF and EAS but its rise is perceived, in some quarters, as more benign compared to China. For instance, the ASEAN states had expressed grave concern about India's nuclear tests but had also criticized the global powers on their failure to make progress towards nuclear disarmament. Also, India welcomed and signed the SEANWFZ and noted that the treaty was a significant initiative for strengthening security and stability in Southeast Asia as well as a significant effort by the Southeast Asian nations to uphold global efforts at nuclear disarmament. Interesting, it was observed that India's willingness to accede to the SEANWFZ did not arise since it is not a nuclear weapon state, but "the spirit of it will not be lost on the ASEAN countries".[159] It is important to point out that at that time, India did not possess a nuclear submarine and the leased nuclear submarine had been returned to the Soviet Union in 1991.

Unlike India, China supported the SEANWFZ but did not sign on the grounds that the Treaty challenged its sovereignty over the South China Sea. The geographical space envisaged under the SEANWFZ Treaty includes disputed territorial waters, island territories, continental shelf and EEZ in the South China Sea currently claimed and occupied by China but also claimed to various degrees by Brunei, Malaysia, the Philippines, Taiwan, and Vietnam. However, China agreed to support ASEAN's efforts towards realizing the SEANWFZ and announced its readiness to sign various protocols. In essence, Southeast Asian countries seek strict adherence to SEANWFZ by China and India and seek dialogue processes that could include seeking greater transparency on the motivations for naval nuclear developments in their neighbourhood.

This chapter has argued that China, India and Southeast Asia were pre-eminent powers in Asia during ancient times and developed sophisticated political, economic and strategic relations. In the 21st century, the three Asian powers continue to be engaged with each other and are exhibiting a strong continuity from the past.

China is engaged in the region through various political, economic and security initiatives and has attempted to dispel fears among Southeast Asian nations of its rise. It has boundary disputes with several ASEAN countries and has so far endeavoured to resolve these peacefully. Notwithstanding that, the "China Threat" remains among ASEAN states and is a significant driver for the ongoing enhancement of military capabilities in the region.

India has forged close relations with ASEAN countries and this engagement is best reflected through India's "Look East" policy. New Delhi shares ASEAN's vision and its principles of harmonious and good neighbourly relations. Although political and economic linkages are at the forefront of the India-ASEAN relationship, strategic and security issues have gathered momentum and India has consistently supported ASEAN efforts and initiatives at achieving stability and security in the region.

The Southeast Asian nations have so far engaged China and India at equal levels. Although China and India are not rivals and, if current trends are any indicators, are willing to complement each other rather than compete in Southeast Asia, the challenge for Southeast Asia will reach a critical point when the two Asian giants embark on fully utilizing their economic potential and begin to balance each other.

Notes

1. Till the 18th century, Asia had accounted for roughly two-thirds of the world economy. The Industrial Revolution in the early 19th century shifted the weight and the Asian economy declined to less than one-third, reaching its low point by 1950 at only 15 per cent of global income. Lee Kuan Yew, "Asia's Growing Role in Financial Markets", *StraitsTimes*, 3 March 2008.
2. K.K. Beri, *History and Cultures of South-east Asia* (New Delhi: Sterling Publishers Pvt. Ltd., 1994), p. 32.
3. G. Coedes, *The Indianized States of Southeast Asia* (Honolulu: East-West Center Press, 1968), p. 27.
4. O.W. Wolters, *History, Culture, and Region in Southeast Asian Perspectives* (New York: Cornell Southeast Asia Program Publication, 1999), p. 42.
5. For an interesting discussion on the triangulation among China, India and Southeast Asia, see Asad-ul Iqbal Latif, *Between Rising Powers: China, Singapore and India* (Singapore: Institute of Southeast Asian Studies, 2007).
6. John D. Negroponte, "U.S. Policy in Asia: Meeting Opportunities and Challenges", Remarks at the Brookings Institution, Washington, D.C., 28 July 2008.
7. W. Lawrence S. Prabhakar, "The Regional Dimensions of Territorial and Maritime Disputes in Southeast Asia", in *Maritime Security in Southeast Asia*, edited by Kwa Chong Guan and John K. Skogan (New York: Routledge, 2007), pp. 37–40.
8. J.V. Mills, "Arab and Chinese Navigators in Malaysian Waters", in *Southeast Asia-China Interactions* (Kuala Lumpur: MBRAS, 2007), p. 417.
9. Wang Gungwu, "The Nanhai Trade: Chapter I South to Nan-Yueh", in *Southeast Asia-China Interactions*, pp. 69–71.
10. Wang Gungwu, "The Nanhai Trade: Chapter 3 A Mission to Funan", in *Southeast Asia-China Interactions*, p. 80.
11. Ibid., pp. 82–83.
12. Thomas Suarez, *Early Mapping of Southeast Asia* (Singapore: Periplus Editions (HK) Ltd., 1999), p. 48.

13. K. Nilakanta Sastri, *Cola* (Madras: University of Madras, 2000), p. 604; Coedes, *The Indianized States of Southeast Asia*, p. 81.
14. Wang, "The Nanhai Trade", p. 139.
15. For a detailed account of maritime trade developments in China during the Sung period, see Paul Wheatley, "Geographical Notes on Some Commodities Insured in Sung Maritime Trade", in *Southeast Asia-China Interactions* (Kuala Lumpur: MBRAS, 2007), p. 417.
16. Ibid., pp. 183–299.
17. Louise Levathes, *When China Ruled the Seas* (New York: Simon & Schuster, 1994), p. 41.
18. Wheatley, "Geographical Notes on Some Commodities Insured in Sung Maritime Trade", pp. 200–2.
19. Levathes, *When China Ruled the Seas*, p. 43.
20. Ming-Yang Su, *Seven Epic Voyages of Zheng He in Ming China (1405–1433): Facts, Fiction and Fabrication* (Torrence, C.A.: 2005), pp. 133–36.
21. Beri, *History and Cultures of South-east Asia*, pp. 182–224.
22. Tan Ta Sen, "Did Zheng He Set Out to Colonize Southeast Asia", in *Admiral Zheng He and Southeast Asia* (Singapore: Institute of Southeast Asian Studies, 2005), p. 43.
23. Radha Kumud Mookerji, *Indian Shipping: A History of the Sea-borne Trade and Maritime Activity of the Indians from the Earliest Times* (Bombay: Longmans, Green and Co., 1912), pp. 13–22.
24. Ibid., p. 37.
25. Ibid., pp. 72–73.
26. Usha Mehta and Usha Thakkar, *Kautilya and his Arthashastra* (New Delhi: S. Chand & Co., 1980).
27. V.A. Smith, *Early History of India* (Oxford: Oxford University Press, 1924), p. 125, cited in Mookerji, op. cit., p. 79.
28. Several Roman coins were found in South India and these are displayed at the Government Museum, Chennai, India.
29. Suarez, *Early Mapping of Southeast Asia*, p. 61.
30. Mookerji, op. cit., p. 88.
31. Sastri, *Cola*, pp. 207–9.
32. Leong Sau Heng, "Collecting Centres, Feeder Points and Entrepots in the Malaya Peninsula, 1000 B.C.–A.D. 1400", in *The Southeast Asian Port and Polity: Rise and Demise*, edited by J. Kathirithamby-Wells and John Villiers (Singapore: Singapore University Press, 1990), pp. 28–29.
33. B. Arunachalam, *Chola Navigation Package* (Mumbai: Maritime History Society, 2004), p. 22.
34. Ibid., p. 42. George W. Spencer, "Royal Leadership and Imperial Conquest in Medieval South India: The Naval Expedition of Rajendra Chola I, 1025 A.D.", unpublished Ph.D. dissertation, University of California, Berkley, 1967, p. 191. According to Spencer, it is a highly plausible

explanation that Srivijaya kings attempted to strangulate Indian trade with China.
35. B. Arunachalam is of the opinion that these two places may have been in Malaysia keeping in mind the sequence of places attacked.
36. Tansen Sen, "The Yuan Khanate and India: Cross-Cultural Diplomacy in the Thirteenth and Fourteenth Centuries", available at <http://www.ihp.sinica.edu.tw/~asiamajor/pdf/2006ab/13%20AM%20vol19%20Sen.pdf> (accessed 8 January 2008).
37. Coedes, *The Indianized States of Southeast Asia*, p. 28.
38. John F. Cady, *Southeast Asia: Its Historical Development* (New York: McGraw-Hill Book Co., 1964), p. 22, cited in Beri, *History and Cultures of South-east Asia*, p. 37. Coedes, *The Indianized States of Southeast Asia*, p. 27.
39. Beri, *History and Cultures of South-east Asia*, p. 73.
40. Coedes, *The Indianized States of Southeast Asia*, p. 81.
41. D.G.E. Hall, *A History of Southeast Asia*, 4th ed. (London: The Macmillan Press Ltd., 1981), p. 49.
42. Ibid., p. 49.
43. G.K. Rajasuriyar, "Kappal Oddiya Thamilan: The Overseas Exploits of the Thamils & the Tragedy of Sri Lanka", available at <http://www.tamilnation.org/heritage/rajasuriyar.htm> (accessed 30 September 2007).
44. Hall, *A History of Southeast Asia*, p. 23.
45. Jan Wisseman-Christie, "Negara, Mandala and Despotism", in *Southeast Asia in the 9th to 14th Centuries* (Singapore: Institute of Southeast Asian Studies, 1986), pp. 65–93.
46. Roger T. Amis, *Sun-tzu Thw Art of War* (New York: Ballantine Books, 1993), p. 39.
47. Ibid., p. 85.
48. David Lai, "Learning from the Stones: A *GO* Approach to Mastering China's Strategic Concept *Shi*", SSI Monograph PUB 378 (Carlisle, PA: Strategic Studies Institute, U.S. Army War College, 2004), p. 4.
49. Ibid., p. 5. *Bing yi zha li* (war is based on deception), *shang-bing fa-mou* (supreme importance in war is to attack the enemy's strategy), *qi-zheng xiang-sheng* (mutual reproduction of regular and extraordinary forces and tactics), *chu-qi zhi-sheng* (win through unexpected moves), *yin-di zhi-sheng* (gain victory by varying one's strategy and tactics according to the enemy's situation), *yi-rou ke-gang* (use the soft and gentle to overcome the hard and strong), *bishi ji-xu* (stay clear of the enemy's main force and strike at his weak point), *yi-yu wei-zhi* (to make the devious route the most direct), *hou-fa zhi-ren* (fight back and gain the upper hand only after the enemy has initiated fighting), *sheng-dong ji-xi* (make a feint to the east but attack in the west).
50. Roger Boesche, "Kautilya's 'Arthasastra' on War and Diplomacy in Ancient India", *The Journal of Military History* 67, no. 1 (January 2003): 15.

51. A good analysis of the *Mandala* in its historical and regional analysis is done by Rosita Delios, "Mandalas of Security", Humanities and Social Sciences Papers, available at Bond University <http://epublications.bond.edu.au/rosita_dellios/> (accessed 20 January 2008).
52. Wolters, *History, Culture, and Region in Southeast Asian Perspectives*, pp. 48–49.
53. Wisseman-Christie, "Negara, Mandala and Despotism", pp. 65–93.
54. S.J. Tambiah, *World Conqueror and World Renouncer: A Study of Buddhism and Polity in Thailand against a Historical Background* (New York: Cambridge University Press, 1976), cited in Wisseman-Christie, "Negara, Mandala and Despotism", pp. 65–93.
55. Delios, "Mandalas of Security".
56. Narendra Nath Law, *Studies in Indian History and Culture* (Delhi: B.R. Publishing Corporation, 1985), cited in Delios, "Mandalas of Security".
57. Wolters, *History, Culture, and Region in Southeast Asian Perspectives*, pp. 48–49.
58. "A Tribute to Hinduism — War in Ancient India", available at <http://www.hscgmu.org/ebooks/War%20In%20Ancient%20India.pdf> (accessed 9 January 2008).
59. Alastair Iain Johnston, "Is China a Status Quo Power?", *International Security* 27, no. 4 (Spring 2003): 5–56.
60. W. Lawrence S. Prabhakar, "China's Strategic Culture and Current International Dynamics: Perspective from India", paper presented at the international conference on "The Rise of China: Asian and European Perspectives", 23–24 November 2006.
61. Ariel Cohen, "The Russia-China Friendship and Cooperation Treaty: A Strategic Shift in Eurasia?", Asian Studies Center Backgrounder 1459, The Heritage Foundation, 18 July 2001.
62. Alice Lyman Miller, "The Limits of Chinese-Russian Strategic Collaboration", *Strategic Insight*, Center for Contemporary Conflict (CCC), 2 September 2002. Geir Flikke and Julie Wilhelmsen, "Central Asia: A Testing Ground for New Great-Power Relations", Norwegian Institute of International Affairs Report, 2008.
63. Xiang Bin, "Military Exercise in the Pacific Targets China", available at <http://www.china.org.cn/international/opinion/2008-07/01/content_15916848.htm> (accessed 5 July 2008).
64. Cohen, "The Russia-China Friendship and Cooperation Treaty".
65. Yevgeny Bendersky and Erich Marquardt, "The Significance of Sino-Russian Military Exercises", The Power and Interest News Report, 14 September 2005, available at <http://www.pinr.com/report.php?ac=view_report&report_id=366> (accessed 15 December 2007).
66. Vijay Sakhuja, "Peace Mission 2005: Reverberations in India", available at <http://www.ipcs.org/whatsNewArticle11.jsp?action=showView&kValue=1845&status=article&mod=b> (accessed 15 December 2007).

67. Adam Wolfe, "Peace Mission 2007 and the S.C.O. Summit", 10 August 2007, available at <http://www.pinr.com/report.php?ac=view_report&report_id=672&language_id=1> (accessed 15 December 2007).
68. Between 1991 and 1996, Russia sold China weapons worth an estimated US$1 billion per year. Between 1996 and 2001, the rate of sales doubled to US$2 billion per year. Reportedly, the two had signed a military sales package in 1999 that would be worth US$20 billion between 2000 and 2004.
69. Some sub-systems such as Fregat M2EM 3D radar and the MR-90 tracking radar fitted on Project 956E/EM missile destroyer from Russia have been indigenously produced and are fitted on the domestic Type 054A missile frigate (FFG). Similarly, the Chinese versions of the French Sea Tiger ship radar, Crotale air defence system and Tavitac naval command and control systems from France and Italian EW systems are fitted on PLA Navy ships. For more details see, "Russia-China Military Cooperation in Trouble?", 27 August 2007, available at <http://www.domain-.com/industry/defence/20070827_military.htm> (accesed 15 January 2008).
70. Nikita Petrov, "Problems in Russian-Chinese Military-technical Cooperation", *RIA Novosti*, 27 September 2007, available at <http://en.rian.ru/analysis/2007 0925/80780903.html> (accessed 16 December 2007).
71. Michael Pillsbury, *China Debates the Future Security Environment* (Washington, D.C.: National Defense University, 2000), available at <http://www.ndu.edu/inss/books/books%20-%202000/China%20Debates%20Future%20Sec%20Environ%20Jan%202000/pills2.htm> (accessed 10 June 2007).
72. The boundary dispute stretches along the 4,000-kilometre boundary in the north. According to Indian claims, China has occupied 43,180 square kilometres in the Jammu and Kashmir area of which 5,180 square kilometres has been ceded by Pakistan to China under the 1963 China-Pakistan boundary agreement. For its part, China lays claim to some 90,000 square kilometres territory in Arunachal Pradesh. Also see Gurmeet Kanwal, "Scant Progress: India-China Boundary Dispute and Sustained Dialogue", Article no. 1087, 7 May 2008, available at <http://landwarfareindia.org/index.php?action=master&task=87&u_id=7> (accessed 2 July 2008).
73. Discussions with Indian military officers in Delhi, India, March 2008.
74. Yossef Bodansky, "The PRC Surge for the Strait of Malacca and Spratly Confronts India and the US", *Defence and Foreign Affairs Strategic Policy* (30 September 1995): 6–13; Srikanth Kondapalli, "The Chinese Military Eyes South Asia", in *Shaping China's Security Environment: The Role of the People's Liberation Army*, edited by Andrew Scobell and Larry M. Wortzel (Pennsylvania: Strategic Studies Institute, October 2006), pp. 197–282.
75. Japan External Trade Organisation (JETRO), "China Overtakes the US as Japan's Largest Trading Partner", available at <http://www.jetro.go.jp/en/news/releases/20080229066-news> (accessed 24 May 2008).

76. "Chinese Naval Warship Arrives in Tokyo for Visit", available at <http://news.xinhuanet.com/english/2007-11/28/content_7158181.htm> (accessed 10 July 2008).
77. Feng Zhaokui, "Ship Comes Riding High Tide in China-Japan Ties", *China Daily*, available at <http://www.chinadaily.com.cn/opinion/2008-06/23/content_6788831.htm> (accessed 10 July 2008).
78. Katsuro Sakoh, "How Japan Can Do More To Defend Itself", Asian Studies Center Backgrounder 57, The Heritage Foundation, 25 February 1987.
79. Sachie Kanda, "U.S. Navy Chief in Japan Guarded on Role in Iraq Attack", *Japan Today*, 26 September 2002.
80. Vijay Sakhuja, "Japanese Maritime Self Defence Force: Kata and Katana", *Strategic Analysis* XXIV, no. 4 (July 2000).
81. Vijay Sakhuja, "How Far Will the Samurai Swim?", available at <http://www.peaceforum.org.tw/onweb.jsp?pageno=3&webno=3333333711> (accessed 10 July 2008).
82. "Missile Defense System 'Could Harm Stability'", *People's Daily*, 6 June 2007.
83. Gregg A. Rubinstein, "US-Japan Missile Defense Cooperation: Current Status, Future Prospects", available at <http://www.japanconsidered.com/OccasionalPapers/Rubinstein%20USJA%20BMD%20article%20090507.pdf> (accessed 5 July 2008).
84. Charles K. Smith, "Senkaku/Diaoyu Island Dispute Threatens Amiability of Sino-Japanese Relations'", Power and Interest News Report, 3 May 2004.
85. Seongwhun Cheon, "Nuclear-Armed North Korea and South Korea's Strategic Countermeasures", *The Korean Journal of Defense Analysis* 16, no. 2 (Autumn 2004).
86. Michael McDevitt, "Missile Defenses and US Policy Options towards Beijing", Report no. 47, The Henry L. Stimson Center, February 2002.
87. "Statement of the Security Consultative Committee — Alliance Transformation: Advancing United States-Japan Security and Defense Cooperation", available at <http://www.mod.go.jp/e/d_policy/dp16.html> (accessed 10 June 2008).
88. Sudha Ramachandran, "India Promotes 'Goodwill' Naval Exercises", *Asia Times Online*, 14 August 2007, available at <http://www.atimes.com/atimes/South_Asia/IH14Df01.html>. Also see D.S. Rajan, "Is China Wary of India's 'Look-East Policy'?", C3S Paper no. 97, 3 January 2008.
89. "China Sweats Over India Bonding with US, Japan, Aus", *Times of India*, 27 June 2007. Rory Medcalf, "Chinese Ghost Story", *The Diplomat*, February–March 2008, pp. 16–18.
90. Ibid.
91. Ibid.
92. Shirley A. Kan and Larry A. Niksch, "Guam: U.S. Defense Deployments", *CRS Report for Congress*, 16 January 2007.

93. Bernard D. Cole, "Beijing's Strategy of Sea Denial", *China Brief* 6, issue 23 (22 November 2006).
94. Michael Chase and Andrew Erickson, "Information Technology and China's Naval Modernization", *Joint Force Quarterly* 50 (3rd quarter 2008): 24–30.
95. "China's Military Power: An Assessment From Open Sources", Testimony of Richard D. Fisher, Jr., before the Armed Services Committee of the U.S. House of Representatives, 27 July 2005; Victor Corpus, "The Assassin's Mace", *Asia Times Online*, 20 October 2006, available at <http://www.atimes.com/atimes/China/HJ20Ad01.html> (accessed 10 June 2008).
96. Jim Holmes and Toshi Yoshihara, "China's New Undersea Deterrent: Strategy, Doctrine and Capabilities", *Joint Force Quarterly* 50 (3rd quarter 2008): 31–38.
97. Dana R. Dillon and John J. Tkacik, Jr., "China and ASEAN: Endangered American Primacy in Southeast Asia", Asian Studies Center Backgrounder 1886, The Heritage Foundation, 19 October 2005.
98. Mohan J. Malik, "Multilateralism Shanghaied", *IASC Issue*, available at <http://www.strategycenter.net/research/pubID.115/pub_detail.asp> (accessed 24 May 2007).
99. Amis, *Sun-tzu Thw Art of War*, pp. 153–55.
100. Satu P. Limaye, "India-East Asia Relations: India's Latest Asian Incarnation", Occasional Analysis, Pacific Forum, CSIS (3rd quarter 2000). During President K.R. Narayanan's May–June 2000 visit to China to mark the fiftieth anniversary of bilateral relations, Narayanan pressed for speedier progress on resolution of the border dispute. In response, Jiang Zemin, counselled patience, saying that the problem was "left over by history". Narayanan responded that it must not be "left over for history".
101. "China Shaping the Maritime Battlefield: Indian Navy Chief", available at <http://www.zeenews.com/articles.asp?aid=339565&sid=NAT> (accessed 5 January 2008).
102. Sujit Dutta, "China and Pakistan: End of a Special Relationship", *China Report* 30, no. 2 (1994): 127–29.
103. Pakistan Navy Historical Section, *Story of Pakistan Navy, 1947–1972* (Islamabad: Elite Publishers, 1991), p. 79. In September 1970, Vice Admiral Muzaffar Hasan, Commander-in-Chief, Pakistan Navy, led a delegation to China and met Chairman Mao Zedong and Premier Zhou Enlai. Premier Zhou expressed his concern over the situation in East Pakistan and cautioned that the slogan of autonomy could get out of hand and would affect the security interests of both Pakistan and China. The premier advised the Chinese Navy Commander-in-Chief to let Pakistan take whatever could be supplied. He noted, "Helping friends could not be measured in terms of money." However, Premier Zhou Enlai did admit that the Chinese naval hardware was not as sophisticated as those of Western origin. Nevertheless, a large proportion of Pakistan's naval

inventory includes Chinese ships and equipment. The Fuqing class tanker, missile vessels fitted with C801/802 surface-to-surface missiles, the new F22 frigates and development of naval infrastructure are some of the important examples of Sino-Pakistan military cooperation.

104. "Nuclear Deal on Han", *Far Eastern Economic Review*, 6 April 1990, pp. 20–21.
105. Vijay Sakhuja, "Iran Stirs India-US Waters", Article no. 1986, available at <http://www.ipcs.org/US_related_articles2.jsp?action=showView&kValue=1999&military=1016&status=article&mod=b> (accessed 30 March 2008).
106. "Defence Cooperation", Ministry of Defence, available at <http://www.mod.nic.in/ainstitutions/welcome.html> (accessed 30 June 2008).
107. "IBSA Naval Exercise No Precursor To Treaty — Mukherjee", available at <http://www.thaindian.com/newsportal/world-news/ibsa-naval-exercise-no-precursor-to-treaty-mukherjee_10048002.html> (accessed 30 June 2008).
108. "Indian Navy to join War Games with Britain, France", *Saudi Press Agency*, 17 August 2008.
109. Vijay Sakhuja, "India's Growing Profile in Southeast Asia", in *Regional Outlook: Southeast Asia 2008-2009*, edited by Deepak Nair and Lee Poh Onn (Singapore: Institute of Southeast Asia Studies, 2008), pp. 15–18.
110. C. Raja Mohan, "India's Geopolitics and Southeast Asian Security", in *Southeast Asian Affairs*, edited by Daljit Singh and Tin Maung Maung Than (Singapore: Institute of Southeast Asia Studies, 2008), pp. 46–50.
111. Vijay Sakhuja, "Supporting the Malacca Strait Troika: Indo-Japanese Approach to Counter Piracy", *SSPC Brief* 31, 11 April 2005; Nirav Patel, "The Elephant and the Rising Sun: Alliance for the Future", Paper no. 2345, 24 August 2007, available at <http://www.southasiaanalysis.org/%5Cpapers24%5Cpaper2345.html> (accessed 20 January 2008); Lisa Curtis, "India's Expanding Role in Asia: Adapting to Rising Power Status", Asian Studies Center Backgrounder 2008, The Heritage Foundation, 20 February 2007.
112. In the 1960s, Pakistan was an important U.S. ally in Asia and New Delhi was guarded about U.S. relations. Pakistan had allowed the United States to use its northern airfields to operate its U-2 reconnaissance flights over the Soviet Union. India needed strategic depth against China, particularly after the India-China war in 1962. For Moscow, it was also an opportunity to engage New Delhi to offset American influence in Asia as well as neutralize that of China. The Soviet Union supported India over Kashmir and Khrushchev is reported to have stated, "We are so near that if ever you call us from the mountain tops we will appear at your side."
113. Vijay Sakhuja, "Brahmos: Where Will It Hit?", *Asian Defence and Diplomacy* (November 2007).
114. Vijay Sakhuja, "Indra 2005: From Sea to the Desert", Article no. 1854, 5 October 2005, available at <http://www.ipcs.org/whatsNewArticle1_byauthor.

jsp?off=1&keyword=Vijay%20Sakhuja&status=article&mod=b&action=show View> (accessed 24 January 2008).
115. J.N. Dixit, "Indo-US Defence Ties: Convergence of Security and Political Interests", available at <http://news.indiamart.com/news-analysis/indo-us-defence-ties-3981.html> (accessed 18 January 2008).
116. U.S. Deputy Secretary of State Strobe Talbott and India's foreign minister Jaswant Singh conducted the dialogue between India and the United States in the aftermath of India's nuclear tests. This was catalytic in facilitating the new impetus in the bilateral relations and the arrival of strategic consensus in the aftermath of the nuclear tests. It paved the way for President Bill Clinton's much-publicized visit to India and paved the way for the Bush administration to treat India as a strategic partner.
117. "IAEA Safeguards to Cover Civilian Nuclear Facilities", *The Hindu*, 11 July 2008.
118. See the Joint Statement of India-United States with the U.S. Presidential Visit to India, 3 March 2006, available at <http://www.state.gov/p/sca/rls/pr/2006/62418.htm> (accessed 24 May 2007).
119. The United States-India Agreement on Generalized Security of Military Information was signed on January 2002; see "Transforming the US-India Defense and Security Relationship", available at <http://www.state.gov/p/sca/rls/rm/16764.htm> (accessed 24 May 2007).
120. "Israel's Defense Exports Reached $4.4B in 2006", available at <http://www.defenseindustrydaily.com/israels-defense-exports-reached-44b-in-2006-02945/> (accessed 25 May 2007).
121. Walters, *History, Culture, and Region in Southeast Asian Perspectives*, p. 49.
122. Jürgen Haacke, *ASEAN's Diplomatic and Security Culture: A Constructivist Assessment* (London: Routledge Curzon, 2003), pp. 3–4.; Amitav Acharya, *The Quest for Identity: International Relations of Southeast Asia* (Singapore: Oxford University Press, 2000).
123. Lau Teik Soon, "ASEAN Diplomacy: National Interest and Regionalism", *Journal of Asian and African Studies* 25, nos. 1–2 (1990): 114–27.
124. "Charter of the Association of Southeast Asian Nations", available at <http://www.aseansec.org/21069.pdf> (accessed 1 June 2008).
125. Ong Keng Yong, "Achieving Security: The ASEAN Way", *Pointer* 31, no. 1, available at <http://www.mindef.gov.sg/imindef/publications/pointer/journals/2005/v31n1/features/feature1.html> (accessed 24 May 2008).
126. For a discussion on ZOPFAN see Bilveer Singh, *ZOPFAN and the New Security Order in the Asia Pacific Region* (Malaysia: Pelanduk Publications, 1992).
127. Bilveer Singh, "ASEAN, the Southeast Asia Nuclear-Weapon-Free Zone and the Challenge of Denuclearisation in Southeast Asia: Problems and Prospects", Canberra Papers on Strategy and Defence no. 138, Strategic and Defence Studies Centre, Australian National University, Canberra, 2000.

128. Chairman's Statement at the Eleventh ASEAN Summit, "One Vision, One Identity, One Community", Kuala Lumpur, 12 December 2005, available at <http://www.aseansec.org/18040.htm> (accessed 1 June 2008); Sudhir Devare, *India and Southeast Asia: Towards Security Convergence* (Singapore: Institute of Southeast Asian Studies, 2006), p. 155.
129. Evelyn Goh, "Great Powers and Hierarchical Order in Southeast Asia: Analyzing Regional Security Strategies", *International Security* 32, no. 3 (Winter 2007/08): 125.
130. Joint Statement of the Meeting of Heads of State/Government of the Member States of ASEAN and the President of the People's Republic of China, Kuala Lumpur, Malaysia, 16 December 1997, available at <http://www.aseansec.org/2361.htm> (accessed 1 June 2008); see "Instrument of Accession to the Treaty of Amity and Cooperation in Southeast Asia", available at <http://www.aseansec.org/15283.htm> (accessed 1 June 2008). Also see Ong Keng Yong, Secretary-General of Asean, "Advancing the Asean-India Partnership in the New Millennium", India-Asean Eminent Persons Lecture Series, New Delhi, 18 October 2004; S.D. Muni, "China's Strategic Engagement with 'New ASEAN'", IDSS monograph no. 2 (2002): 121.
131. Donnabelle Gatdula, "Joint Exploration Pact Lapses", *Philippine Star*, 12 July 2008.
132. "Factsheet on the Regional Cooperation Agreement on Combating Piracy and Armed Robbery Against Ships in Asia (ReCAAP)", available at <http://app.mot.gov.sg/data/ReCAAP%20factsheet%20_Nov06_%20%5BFINAL%5D as%20of%20281106.pdf> (accessed 1 June 2008). Also see "ReCAAP" at <http://www.recaap.org/index.asp> (accessed 1 June 2008).
133. Teo Chee Hean, "Security Cooperation in Asia: Managing Alliances and Partnerships", *Pointers* 33, no. 2, available at <http://www.mindef.gov.sg/imindef/publications/pointer/journals/2007/v33n2/Security_Cooperation_in_Asia__Managing_Alliances_and_Partnerships.html> (accessed 30 May 2008).
134. "Permanent Secretary (Defence) Signs Agreement on Defence Exchanges and Security Cooperation with China at Inaugural Defence Policy Dialogue", available at <http://www.mindef.gov.sg/imindef/news_and_events/nr/2008/jan/07jan08_nr.html> (accessed 1 June 2008).
135. See "India Aims for Influence in Southeast Asia", at homepage of Stratfor at <http://www.stratfor.com/> (accessed 29 March 2000).
136. Juli A. MacDonald, "South Asia and South East Asia in 2001", *National Strategy Forum Review* (Spring 2001), at website of National Strategy Forum, at <http://www.nationalstrategy.com/nsr/v10n3Spring01/100313.htm>.
137. "Indian Navy to Transfer BN2 Maritime Surveillance Aircraft to Myanmar", available at <http://www.india-defence.com/reports/3179> (accessed 2 June 2008).
138. Vijay Sakhuja, "New Delhi and Myanmar: Nascent Friendship", Article no. 93, 21 November 2006.

139. "Death Toll From Cyclone Nargis is Estimated to be 50,000 or More", <http://www.pdc.org/PDCNewsWebArticles/2008/Nargis/nargis.htm> (accessed 1 July 2008).
140. "Secret Sanya — China's New Nuclear Naval Base Revealed", 21 April 2008, available at <http://www.janes.com/news/security/jir/jir080421_1_n.shtml> (accesed 5 July 2008).
141. Jonathan Manthorpe, "China Builds a Massive Warship Base", *Vancouver Sun*, 2 May 2008.
142. Ilya Kramnik, "Reincarnation of Chakra", available at <http://en.rian.ru/analysis/20080708/113522621.html> (accessed 14 July 2008).
143. "China's New Naval Base Triggers US Concerns", *Agence France-Presse*, 12 May 2008.
144. Rajat Pandit, "India Worried About China's Growing N-Sub Prowess", *Times of India*, 6 May 2008.
145. Jackie Northam, "China's Underground Submarine Base Scrutinized", available at <http://www.npr.org/templates/story/story.php?storyId=90309537> (accessed 6 July 2008).
146. Siddharth Srivastava, "China's Submarine Progress Alarms India", *Asia Times*, available at <http://www.atimes.com/atimes/South_Asia/JE09Df02.html> (accessed 6 July 2008).
147. "China Defends Maritime Rights, But Silent On Nuclear Sub Base Report", *Agence France-Presse*, 6 May 2008.
148. Robert Ross, "China II: Beijing as a Conservative Power", *Foreign Affairs* (March/April 1997).
149. Khoo How San, "The Five Power Defence Arrangements: If It Ain't Broke …", *Pointer* 26, no. 4 (October–December 2000): 2, available at <http://www.mindef.gov.sg/safti/pointer/back/journals/2000/Vol26_4/7.htm> (accessed 16 March 2009).
150. Michael Richardson, "Southeast Asia Maritime Allies Gingerly Keep up Their Guard", *International Herald Tribune*, 23 September 1994.
151. Ian J. Storey, "Malaysia's Hedging Strategy with China", *China Brief* 7, issue 14, available at <http://www.jamestown.org/single/?no_cache=1&tx_ttnews%5Btt_news%5D=4298> (accessed 16 July 2008).
152. Clive Schofield, "An Arms Race in the South China Sea?", *IBRU Boundary and Security Bulletin* (July 1994): 45. Also see Storey, "Malaysia's Hedging Strategy with China".
153. "RP to Sustain Good Relations with China Despite Nuclear Sub Issue", available at <http://www.sunstar.com.ph/breakingnews/2008/05/15/rp-to-sustain-good-relations-with-china-despite-nuclear-sub-issue-11-am/> (accessed 2 July 2008).
154. Roslan Ariffin, "Malaysia's First Scorpene Submarine to be Launched Today", *Bernama*, 23 October 2007.

155. Pakistan Navy Historical Section, *Story of Pakistan Navy, 1947–1972* (Islamabad: Elite Publishers, 1991), pp. 228–29.
156. "LIMA 2007", Event Newsletter vol. 3, December 2006.
157. Wassana Nanuam, "Leasing subs is too expensive", *Bangkok Post*, 6 March 2001. At that time, Thailand's defence minister General Chavalit Yongchaiyudh had suggested that keeping in mind the limited budget, the navy ask China or other European countries for use of their submarines for training.
158. Teo Chee Hean, "Enhancing Security in a Time of Flux", *Pointer* 32, no. 1, available at <http://www.mindef.gov.sg/imindef/publications/pointer/journals/2006/v32n1/features/feature1.html> (accessed 30 June 2008).
159. Satu P. Limaye, "India-East Asia Relations: India's Latest Asian Incarnation", *Policy Forum Online*, 30 November 2000.

8

CONCLUSION

Historically, maritime power has been associated with economic prosperity. During the glorious Greek and Roman eras, the Mediterranean was the centre of maritime power. In the late BC period till the 14th century, Asia emerged as the heart of the commercial world with extensive trade linkages. During the 15th to the 20th centuries, Europe emerged as a major maritime power led by the Portuguese, Dutch, Spaniards, French and English through occupation and subjugation of Asian littorals. With the decline of European colonial domination and the ascent of America, maritime power shifted to the Atlantic. In the 21st century, Asia has emerged as the most dynamic region in economic and strategic terms. There has been a focused attention on economic growth among a number of states in Asia which is reflected in their respective GDP growth rates and booming trade.

In the 21st century, Asia is witnessing a maritime revival led by China and India as they build their maritime power as an important component of their grand strategy to be major strategic players in Asia. These two Asian powers are in fact reliving their ancient maritime pre-eminence pivoting on maritime connectivity, trade, movement of people, culture, religion and ideas. Southeast Asia is significant in the maritime rejuvenation of Asia in the way it was in ancient times that witnessed its importance to China and India and its geographical significance connecting the Indian and the Pacific Oceans, a strategic reality that continues till today.

Maritime developments are integral to the Asian economic and security environment; for many countries in the region, economic vitality depends on safe and secure sea lines of communications that have resulted in greater strategic significance for both merchant and naval shipping. Coastal and offshore resources provide an important means of livelihood for many countries in the region. Thus security is enmeshed in maritime affairs. The regional security concerns are reflected in the arms acquisition programmes that have a strong maritime orientation.

This study has attempted to show that an appreciation of maritime power shapes the power and destiny of a nation. In the past, states have used maritime power to augment their national power and employed it to safeguard national interests. The study has, though very briefly, argued that it is possible to systematically assess the maritime power of countries and through empirical assessments rank the perceived maritime power of states.

Maritime issues are at the forefront of the emerging security environment in Asia. There is a significant change in the strategic thinking of national leaders in China and India that is flavoured with an awareness of the importance of maritime power. Both are committed to building maritime power and believe that, to be credible powers, they must intensify their efforts to build maritime capabilities. A variety of advanced naval platforms and equipment have been added to the naval inventory. The PLA Navy's strategy envisages both offensive and defensive operations and the concepts of limited war under high-tech conditions and the revolution in military affairs are central to Chinese naval thinking. The Indian Navy follows the classical doctrine of *"tous azimuts"* aimed at fighting the battle in the adversary's zone. It has redefined its strategic geography that covers the Indian Ocean and as far as the South China Sea.

There is continuity from the past with regard to the use of navies for political purposes. China has actively supported military exchanges and cooperation with other countries and the PLA Navy has extensive contacts with several countries. As part of naval diplomacy, China has encouraged confidence-building measures with several navies by port calls, joint exercises and naval exchanges. These initiatives have resulted in security dialogues and cooperation with several Asia-Pacific countries. The Indian Navy has been building closer relations with several navies across the globe. Several initiatives are pointers to the fact that the Indian Navy has the capacity and capability to further India's national interests. Power-projection platforms like aircraft carriers, destroyers, submarines and frigates have added to India's prestige and provided the opportunity to showcase India's resolve to safeguard its maritime interests and also to project Indian naval capability. The navy has participated in international fleet reviews, offered humanitarian assistance, carried out disaster relief activities, and conducted anti-piracy patrols and joint exercises aimed at building confidence and trust among regional countries.

Information-based technologies have impacted on the maritime power of China and India. These technologies have also revolutionized the communication process resulting in the growth of complex information networks. The capabilities to use these as a destructive force against enemy computers and networks that support maritime infrastructures is now a reality. It has exposed the vulnerability of navies to information-based warfare, hacker warfare and viruses that have the capability to reduce or even make weapons and sensors defunct. There are several critical deficiencies in the RMA capabilities of India and China and their equipment is at least two generations behind those in the West and systems integration skills are still evolving. However, there is determination and capacity in both China and India to leapfrog some technologies and shape the relative balance of power in their own favour.

While Asian maritime power envisages extensive cooperation to achieve economic dividends and growth, there is also competition that can challenge, or in the worst case, subvert cooperation. In the context of China and India, political disputes remain intractable, but the logic of economic cooperation and the rational choice of a win-win situation leads to increased economic interdependence. The political and diplomatic relations had witnessed incremental progress in confidence-building measures in the 1990s that had come a long way from the acrimony of territorial and boundary disputes. India considers the Indian Ocean as its own sphere of influence and therefore securing control/influence over this area has been one of India's main strategic objectives. This is illustrated by distant naval operations and exercise of influence from the Arabian Sea to the South China Sea. On the other hand, the Chinese have significant economic and strategic stakes in the Indian Ocean and are concerned about the economic lifelines at sea. The strategic priority of planners in Beijing is to consolidate China's influence in the Indian Ocean. In that context, the Indian and Pacific Oceans region emerges as the competitive sea space for China and India.

While the military strategic capabilities of China and India continue to grow and reinforce deterrence against one another, the logic of economic interdependence is a significant driver of the bilateral relations that is premised on the economic agenda. Interestingly, the strategic rivalry of the two rising powers, their increasing focus on naval power and maritime trade with each other and in the region is underlining the expanding scope of Asian maritime power.

There are several implications of the rise of China and India for the Asian littoral, and the Indian and Pacific Oceans. There are crucial strategic implications for the United States, the global super power and for Japan the second largest economic power in the world. The United States and Japan are correlating their economic, strategic and political-diplomatic matrices in response to the rising power of China and India. Although China and India still have a long way to go to build the sinews of comprehensive national power to rival the West and there is a huge multitude of challenges facing them, the potential power that they would possess in terms of domain, range and spheres of national power is substantial. Both aspire to great maritime power status and have embarked on the development of a sophisticated civilian-maritime vision and a strategic-maritime ambition for their respective domains. China and India are investing their resources and capacities in sustained maritime programmes that would be commensurate with their national power quotients.

The intermediate region of Southeast Asia emerges as the crossroads to the core of the rising powers of China and India even as the critical mass of resources, economic-industrial strength and technological excellence migrate to the core. The impact of interactions among China, India and Southeast Asia and the implications of their maritime intersection, carry both benign and negative consequences for the region.

Also in evidence is the civilizational legacy in the operations of the state and statecraft. Significantly, strategic transactions among China, India and Southeast Asia can be better understood through the prisms of ancient schools of thought epitomized in their golden ages. The contemporary political theory is built on the understanding of ancient statecraft professed by Sun-Tzu, Kautilya and the *Mandala* or *Negara* of Hindu-Buddhist construct of religion and polity that was built on the core and periphery construct.

In the 21st century, Southeast Asian states must contend with the rising profile of China (China "threat") and India ("rising" India). So far the Southeast Asian nations have marshalled their diplomatic resources through ASEAN, the ARF, EAS, APEC, and several other bilateral and multilateral economic and security initiatives at both Track I and Track II level. As far as the ARF is concerned, ASEAN occupies the "driver's seat" and is shaping the agenda and providing the direction and this has so far reaped the desired dividends and is also accepted by the participants, but the region has the potential to be the arena of the competitive strategies of China and India. These rising powers will be the major naval powers in Asia and possess significant naval and missile (nuclear and conventional) capabilities. The evolving naval order of battle of China and India on the eastern and western flanks of Southeast Asia, particularly naval nuclear capability, is potentially destabilizing to the Southeast Asian security environment.

These developments have the potential of a ripple effect that could witness an arms build-up in Southeast Asia, which can be the catalyst for Asian insecurity. Also of significance will be how the United States and Japan respond to the evolving strategic profiles of China and India through their respective strategies given that for Southeast Asia, U.S. engagement in Asia remains critical for regional stability.

SELECTED BIBLIOGRAPHY

PRIMARY SOURCES

Defence Agency, Government of Japan. *Defence of Japan 2004, 2005, 2006, 2007.*
Department of Animal Husbandry and Dairying, Ministry of Agriculture, Government of India. "Marine Fishing Policy 2004", 2004.
Department of Planning, Government of the People's Republic of China. "Background Information on China's Recent Military Threats Against Taiwan", March 2007.
Department of Tourism, Ministry of Tourism and Culture, Government of India. "National Tourism Policy 2002".
Directorate of Naval Staff Duties. *BR 1806: Fundamentals of British Maritime Doctrine.* London: HMSO, 1996.
General Political Department, Chinese People's Liberation Army. *China's Army: Ready for Modernization.* Beijing: Beijing Review Editorial Department, 1985.
Government of the People's Republic of China. *China's Shipbuilding Industry in Progress.* Beijing: New Star, 1991.
Indian National Shipowners' Association, Mumbai. *Report on Indian National Shipowners' Association Annual Review: 1998–1999.*
———. *Report on Indian National Shipowners' Association Annual Review: 2005–06.*
Information Office of the State Council, the People's Republic of China. "White Paper on Arms Control and Disarmament", November 1995.
———. "White Paper on Grain Issue in China", October 1996.
———. "White Paper on China's Marine Development Programme", November 1998.
———. *China's National Defense 1998, 2002, 2004, 2006.*
———. "China's Policy on Mineral Resources", December 2003.
———. "China's Space Activities, A White Paper".
Information Warfare Cell, Naval Headquarters, New Delhi. *Indian Naval Doctrine for Information Warfare*, 2001.
Integrated Headquarters, Ministry of Defence (Navy), New Delhi. *Indian Maritime Doctrine (INBR 8)*, 2004.
———. *Freedom to Use the Seas: India's Maritime Military Strategy*, 2007.

Ministry of Defence, Government of India. Annual Report 2004–05, 2005–06, 2006–07, 2007–08.
Ministry of Finance, Government of India. *The Economic Survey 1992–93 to 1998–99.*
———. *Economic Survey 1998–99.*
Ministry of Foreign Affairs, Government of Japan. "Overview of Official Development Assistance (ODA) to China", 2005.
Ministry of Petroleum and Natural Gas, Government of India. Annual Report 2006–07.
Ministry of Shipping, Government of India. Annual Report 2004–05.
———. "National Maritime Development Programme (NMDP)", 2006.
Ministry of Surface Transport, Government of India. *Report on the Working Group for Port Sector for Ninth Five Year Plan (1992–97).*
———. *The Indian Infrastructure Report: Policy Imperatives for Growth and Welfare*, 1996.
———. *Statistics of India's Ship-Building and Ship Repairing Industry: 1998–99.*
Naval Headquarters, New Delhi. *Strategic Defence Review: The Maritime Dimension, A Naval Vision*, 1998.
Pakistan Navy Historical Section. *Story of Pakistan Navy, 1947–1972.* Islamabad: Elite Publishers, 1991.
Planning Commission, Government of India. *The Ninth Five Year Plan (1992–97).*
———. *The Tenth Five Year Plan (1997–2002).*
United Nations. *United Nations Convention on the Law of the Sea.* New York, 1983.

SECONDARY SOURCES

Reports and Papers

Acharya, Amitav and Paul M. Evans. "China's Defence Expenditures: Trends and Implications". Eastern Asia Policy Paper 1. Joint Centre for Asia-Pacific Studies, University of Toronto-York University Ontario, 1994.
Babbage, Ross. "Maritime Security in the Asia Pacific Region: An Australian View". University of Wollengong, New South Wales, Australia, 1995.
Ball, Desmond. "The Post Cold War Maritime Strategic Environment in East Asia". Australian Defence Study Centre, 1994.
Bitzinger, Richard A. and Chongpin, Lin. "The Defence Budget of The People's Republic of China". Staunton Hill Conference Report, 1994.
Bull, Headley. "Sea Power and Political Influence". Adelphi Paper 16, issue 122 (1976): 1–9.
Cheung, Tai Ming. "The Growth of Chinese Naval Power". Pacific Strategic Paper. Singapore: Institute of Southeast Asian Studies, 1990.

Dibb, Paul. "The Emerging Strategic Architecture in the Asia-Pacific Region". Paper prepared for Royal United Services Institute of Australia, February 1996.
Djalal, Hasjim. "The Role of the Users for the Enhancement of the Safety and the Protection of the Strait of Malacca and Singapore in Relation with UNCLOS 1982". Paper presented at the Symposium on the Enhancement of Safety of Navigation and the Environment Protection of the Straits of Malacca and Singapore. Kuala Lumpur, 13–14 March 2007.
Erickson, Andrew S. "China's Military Modernization and its Impact on the United States and the Asia-Pacific". Testimony before the U.S.-China Economic and Security Review Commission, 29 March 2007.
Fisher, Richard D. "Brewing Conflict in the South China Sea". Asian Studies Center Backgrounder 17. The Heritage Foundation, 25 October 1984.
———. "Dangerous Moves: Russia's Sale of Missile Destroyers to China". Asian Studies Center Backgrounder 146. The Heritage Foundation, 20 February 1997.
———. "How America's Friends are Building China's Maritime Power". Asian Studies Center Backgrounder. The Heritage Foundation, 5 November 1997.
Gill, Bates and Lonnie Henley. "China and the Revolution in Military Affairs". Pennsylvania: Strategic Studies Institute, 20 May 1996.
ICC International Maritime Bureau. "Piracy and Armed Robbery Against Ships". Report for the Period 1 January–31 December 1998.
International Labour Organization. "Report on an ILO Investigation into the Living and Working Conditions of Seafarers in the Asia/Pacific Region". Regional Maritime Conference in the Asia/Pacific Region, Singapore, 2002.
Ji, You. "The Evolution of China's Maritime Combat Doctrines and Models: 1949–2001". Working Paper no. 22. Singapore: The Institute of Defence and Strategic Studies, May 2002.
Joshi, Sanjana. "Redefining Japanese Security". Delhi Paper, no. 5. New Delhi: Institute for Defence Studies and Analyses, April 1998.
Jraiw, Kim. "Annex I to the Asian Development Bank and an Integrated Transport System". Infrastructure Division, East and Central Asia Department, Asian Development Bank.
Junnola, Jill R., ed. "Maritime Confidence Building in Regions of Tension". Report no. 2. Washington, D.C.: Henry L. Stimston Centre, May 1992.
Lai, David. "Learning from the Stones: A *GO* Approach to Mastering China's Strategic Concept *Shi*". SSI Monograph PUB 378. Carlisle, PA: Strategic Studies Institute, U.S. Army War College, 2004.
Leva, Charles Di and Sachiko Morita. "Maritime Rights of Coastal States and Climate Change: Should States Adapt to Submerged Boundaries?", Law and Development Working Paper no. 5 (2008).
Meng, Qingxuan and Li Mingzhi. "New Economy and ICT Development in China". Discussion Paper no. 2001/76. World Institute of Development Economics Research, September 2001.

Military Balance 2007–08. London: International Institute for Strategic Studies, 2008.
Morgan, Joseph R. "Porpoises Among the Whales: Small Navies in Asia and the Pacific". Report no. 2. Honolulu: East-West Center, March 1994.
Muni, S.D. "China's Strategic Engagement with 'New ASEAN'". IDSS monograph no. 2, 2002.
Nicholls, R.J., S. Hanson, C. Herweijer, N. Patmore, S. Hallegatte, Jan Corfee-Morlot, Jean Chateau, and R. Muir-Wood. "Ranking of the World's Cities Most Exposed to Coastal Flooding Today and in the Future". OECD Environment Working Paper no. 1 (ENV/WKP(2007)1).
Noer, John H. "Chokepoints: Maritime Economic Concerns in South East Asia". Alexandria, V.A.: Centre for Naval Analyses, March 1996.
Office of Naval Intelligence. *Challenges to Naval Expeditionary Warfare*, 1977.
———. *Worldwide Submarine Challenges*, February 1997.
———. *The Strait of Hormuz: Global Shipping and Trade Implications in the Event of Closure*, 1997.
———. *China's Navy 2007*, 2007.
Office of the Secretary of Defense, U.S. Department of Defense. "Military Power of the People's Republic of China 2006". Annual Report to Congress, 2006.
O'Rourke, Ronald. "China Naval Modernization: Implications for U.S. Navy Capabilities — Background and Issues for Congress". *CRS Report for Congress*, 4 February 2008.
Parris, Edward P. "China's Economy Looks Towards the Year 2000". Chinese Defence Expenditures 1967–1983 in U.S. Congress Joint Economic Committee Report. Washington, D.C., 1986.
Prabhakar, W. Lawrence S. "China's Strategic Culture and Current International Dynamics: Perspective from India". Paper presented at international conference on "The Rise of China: Asian and European Perspectives", 23–24 November 2006.
Roonwal, G.S. "Mineral Resources of the Indian Ocean". Occasional Paper no. 4. New Delhi: Society of Indian Ocean Studies, 2002.
Scobell, Andrew and Larry M. Wortzel, eds. *Shaping China's Security Environment: The Role of the People's Liberation Army*. Pennsylvania: Strategic Studies Institute, October 2006.
Segal, Gerald. "Tying China In (and Down)". IISS/CAFS Conference, 8–10 July 1994.
Sheng, Lijun. "China's Policy Towards the Spratly Islands in the 1990s". Canberra: Strategic and Defence Studies Centre, 1994.
Singh, Bilveer. "ASEAN, the Southeast Asia Nuclear-Weapon-Free Zone and the Challenge of Denuclearisation in Southeast Asia: Problems and Prospects". Canberra Papers on Strategy and Defence no. 138. Canberra: Strategic and Defence Studies Centre, Australian National University, 2000.
Snyder, Scott. "The South China Sea Dispute: Prospects for Preventive Diplomacy". Special Report. United States Institute of Peace, 1996.

Stuart, Douglas T. and William T. Tow. "A US Strategy for the Asia-Pacific". Adelphi Paper 299. London: International Institute of Strategic Studies, 1995.
Sundstorm, Rebecca E. "China's Port Facilities and Maritime Infrastructure: Bo Hai Rim Port Development Strategies for the 21st Century". Nan Huai Chin Scholarship Paper, Spring 1999.
Suri, Vice Admiral R.B. "Shape and Size of the Indian Navy in the Early Twenty First Century". Project Report submitted to the United Services Institution of India, New Delhi, May 1998.
Tkacik, Jr., John J. "China's Quest for a Superpower Military". Asian Studies Centre Backgrounder 2036. The Heritage Foundation, 17 May 2007.
Toth, James E. "Military Strategy and Strategic Geography". Washington: Industrial College of the Armed Forces, 1995.
U.S. Defence Intelligence Agency. "Handbook on Chinese Armed Forces". Washington, D.C., 1976.
Valencia, Mark J. "China and the South China Sea Disputes". Adelphi Paper 298. London: International Institute of Strategic Studies, 1995.
Weeks, Stanley B. "Sea Lines of Communication (SLOC) Security and Access". Working Paper. Institute of Global Conflict and Cooperation, February 1998.
Wilhelm, Jr., Alfred D. "China and Security in the Asia-Pacific Region through 2010". Alexandria, V.A.: Centre for Naval Analyses, March 1996.
World Bank, Washington, D.C. "Global Economic Prospects and the Developing Countries", 1994.
Xu, You and You Ji. "In Search of Blue Water Power: The PLA Navy's Maritime Strategy in the 1990s". *The Pacific Review* 4, issue 2 (1991): 137–49.
Yoshihara, Toshi. "Chinese Information Warfare: A Phantom Menace or Emerging Threat?". Pennsylvania: Strategic Studies Institute, November 2001.
Yung, Christopher D. "People's War at Sea: Chinese Naval Power in the 21st Century". Alexandria, V.A.: Centre for Naval Analyses, March 1996.
Zou, Keyuan. "A Comparative Study of Chinese Basic Maritime Laws: The Mainland and Taiwan". EAI Working Paper no. 17. Singapore: East Asia Institute, December 1998.
———. "Management of Marine Nature Reserves in China: A Legal Perspective". EAI Working Paper no. 86. Singapore: East Asia Institute, January 2002.

Books

Acharya, Amitav. *The Quest for Identity: International Relations of Southeast Asia*. Singapore: Oxford University Press, 2000.
Amis, Roger T. *Sun-tzu Thw Art of War*. New York: Ballantine Books, 1993.
Anand, Commander A. *Information Technology: The Future Warfare Weapon*. New Delhi: Ocean Books, 2000.
Anand, R.P. *Legal Regime of the Seabed and the Developing Countries*. New Delhi: Thomas Press (India) Ltd., 1975.

Arunachalam, B. *Chola Navigation Package*. Mumbai: Maritime History Society, 2004.
Atlas of the World. London: George Phillips Ltd., 1991.
Auer, James E. *The Post War Rearmament of Japanese Maritime Forces, 1945–71*. New York: Praeger Publishers, 1973.
Austin, Greg. *China's Ocean Frontier: International Law, Military Force and National Development*. New South Wales: Allen & Unwin Australia Pte Ltd., 1998.
Bajpai, Kanti and Amitabh Mattoo, eds. *The Peacock and the Dragon: India-China Relations in the 21st Century*. New Delhi: Har-Anand, 2000.
Barkenbus, Jack N. *Deep Seabed Resources: Policies and Technology*. New York: Free Press, 1979.
Bartell, Joyce J. *The Yankee Mariner and Sea Power*. California: University of California Press, 1982.
Basham, A.L. *A Cultural History of India*. Delhi: Oxford University Press, 1975.
Bell, Christopher M. *The Royal Navy, Seapower and Strategy Between the Wars*. London: Macmillan, 2000.
Beri, K.K. *History and Cultures of South-east Asia*. New Delhi: Sterling Publishers Pvt. Ltd., 1994.
Booth, Ken. *Navies and Foreign Policy*. London: Croom Helm, 1977.
Boxer, C.R. *Portuguese Conquest and Commerce in Southern Asia, 1500–1750*. London: Variorum Reprints, 1985.
Brodie, Bernard. *A Guide to Naval Strategy*. New York: Praeger, 1965.
Brown, Lester R. *Who Will Feed China? Wake Up Call for Small Planet*. Washington: Worldwatch Institute, 1996.
Bruce, Robert H., ed. *The Modern Indian Navy and the Indian Ocean*. Perth: Curtin University of Technology, 1989.
Bud, Robert and Philip Gummett, eds. *Cold War, Hot Science: Applied Research in Britain's Defence Laboratories, 1945–1990*. London: NMSI Trading Ltd., 2002.
Buzan, Barry. *Seabed Politics*. New York: Praeger, 1976.
Byce, Vice Admiral Sangram Singh and Rajni Kant Tewari. *Maritime Electronic Warfare: Soft Kill Measures*. New Delhi: Anmaya Publishers, 2007.
Cable, James. *Gunboat Diplomacy 1919–1991*. London: Macmillan, 1994.
Cady, John F. *Southeast Asia: Its Historical Development*. New York: McGraw-Hill Book Co., 1964.
Catley, Bob and Makmur Keliat. *Spratlys: The Dispute in the South China Sea*. Aldershot: Ashgate Publishing Ltd., 1997.
Chatterji, Admiral A.K. *Indian Navy's Submarine Arm*. New Delhi: Birla Institute, 1982.
Cline, Ray S. *World Power Trends and U.S. Foreign Policy for the 1980's*. Colorado: Westview Press, 1980.
Coedes, G. *The Indianized States of Southeast Asia*. Honolulu: East-West Center Press, 1968.

Cole, Bernard D. *The Great Wall at Sea: China's Navy Enters the Twenty-first Century.* Annapolis: Naval Institute Press, 2001.
Collins, Alan. *Security and Southeast Asia: Domestic, Regional, and Global Issues.* Singapore: Institute of Southeast Asian Studies, 2003.
Cottrell, Alvin J. and Associates, eds. *Sea Power and Strategy in the Indian Ocean.* California: Sage Publications Inc., 1981.
Dellios, Rosita. *Modern Chinese Defence Strategy.* New York: St. Martin's Press, 1990.
Deng, Gang. *Maritime Sector, Institutions, and Sea Power of Premodern China.* Westport: Greenwood, 1999.
Deva, Major General Yashwant. *Secure or Perish.* New Delhi: Ocean Books, 2000.
Devare, Sudhir. *India and Southeast Asia: Towards Security Convergence.* Singapore: Institute of Southeast Asian Studies, 2006.
Dismukis, B. and J. McConnell. *Soviet Naval Diplomacy.* New York: Pergamon Press, 1990.
Donaldson, Robert H. and Joseph L. Nogee. *The Foreign Policy of Russia: Changing Systems, Enduring Interests.* Armonk, NY: M.E. Sharpe, 1998.
Dorman, Andrew, Mike Lawrence Smith, and Mathew R.H. Uttley. *The Changing Face of Maritime Power.* New York: St. Martin Press, 1999.
Earney, Filmore C.F. *Marine Mineral Resources.* London: Routledge, 1990.
Eckert, Ross D. *The Enclosure of Ocean Resources.* Stanford: Hoover Institution Press, 1979.
Edgerton, Robert B. *Warriors of the Rising Sun: A History of the Japanese Military.* New York: Norton, 1997.
Elleman, Bruce A. and S.C.M. Paine, eds. *Naval Blockades and Seapower: Strategies and Counter Strategies, 1805–2005.* London: Routledge, 2006.
Erickson, Andrew S., Lyle J. Goldstein, William S. Murray, and Andrew R. Wilson, eds. *China's Future Nuclear Submarine Force.* Annapolis: Naval Institute Press, 2007.
Friedman, Norman. *The Naval Institute Guide to World Naval Weapon Systems.* Annapolis, M.D.: Naval Institute Press, 2006.
Garver, John W. *Protracted Contest: Sino-Indian Rivalry in the Twentieth Century.* Washington: University of Washington Press, 2001.
Ghosh, Sekhar. *Law of the Territorial Sea.* Naya Prakashan: Calcutta Press, 1980.
Godwin, Paul H.B., ed. *The Chinese Defence Establishment: Continuity and Change in the 1980s.* Boulder: Westview Press, 1983.
Gorshkov, S.G. *The Sea Power of the State.* Oxford: Pergamon Press, 1979.
Gray, Colin S. and Roger W. Barnett, eds. *Seapower and Strategy.* Annapolis: Naval Institute Press, 1989.
Greenfield, Jeanette. *China and the Law of the Sea, Air, and Environment.* Germantown Maryland: Sijthoff & Noordhoff, 1979.
———. *China's Practice in the Law of the Sea.* New York: Oxford University Press, 1992.

Griffith, Samuel B. *The Chinese People's Liberation Army*. New York: McGraw Hill, 1968.
Guan, Kwa Chong and John K. Skogan, eds. *Maritime Security in Southeast Asia*. New York: Routledge, 2007.
Gurtov, Mel and Byong-Moo Hwang. *China's Security: The New Roles of the Military*. London: Lynne Rienner Publishers, 1998.
Haacke, Jürgen. *ASEAN's Diplomatic and Security Culture: A Constructivist Assessment*. London: Routledge Curzon, 2003.
Haythornthwaite, Philip J., William Younghusband, and Martin Windrow. *Nelson's Navy*. UK: Osprey Publishing, 1993.
Hill, Admiral J.R. *Maritime Strategy for Medium Powers*. Annapolis: Naval Institute Press, 1986.
Hiranandani, Vice Admiral G.M. *Transition to Triumph: History of the Indian Navy, 1975–1975*. New Delhi: Lancer International, 2000.
Howarth, Peter. *China's Rising Sea Power: The PLA Navy's Submarine Challenge*. New York: Routledge, 2006.
Hyma, Alber. *A History of the Dutch in the Far East*. Ann Arbor: G. Wahr, 1953.
International Petroleum Encyclopedia. Tulsa: Penwell, 1994.
Jackson, Robert. *South Asian Crisis, India-Pakistan-Bangladesh*. London: Chatto & Windus, 1975.
Jeshurun, Chandran, ed. *China, India, Japan and the Security of Southeast Asia*. Singapore: Institute of Southeast Asian Studies, 1993.
Jingzhi, Sun. *The Economic Geography of China*. Hong Kong: Oxford University Press, 1988.
Joffe, Ellis G.H. *The Chinese Army After Mao*. London: Macmillan Press, 1987.
Joshi, Akshay. *Information Age and India*. Delhi: Knowledge World, 2001.
Kane, Thomas M. *Chinese Grand Strategy and Maritime Power*. London: Frank Cass, 2002.
Kathirithamby-Wells, J. and John Villiers. *The Southeast Asian Port and Polity: Rise and Demise*. Singapore: Singapore University Press, 1990.
Kearsley, H.J. *Maritime Power and the Twenty-first Century*. Aldershot: Dartmouth Publishing Company, 1993.
Kenny, Henry J. *An Analyses of Possible Threats to Shipping in Key Southeast Asian Sea Lanes*. Alexandria: Center for Naval Analyses, 1996.
Kim, Dalchoong, Seo-Hang Lee, Jin-Hyun Park, eds. *Maritime Security and Cooperation in Asia Pacific: Towards the 21st Century*. Seoul: Dooilnet, 2000.
Kim, Samuel S., ed. *China and the World: Chinese Foreign Relations in the Post Cold War Era*. Boulder: Westview Press, 1994.
Kohli, S.N. *Sea Power and Indian Ocean: With Special Reference to India*. New Delhi: Tata McGraw-Hill, 1978.
Kondapalli, Srikanth. *China's Naval Power*. New Delhi: Knowledge World, 2001.
Kotkar, Norman. *Horizon History of China*. New York: Heritage, 1969.

Kumar, Anjani, Pradeep K. Katiha, and P.K. Joshi. *A Profile of People, Technologies and Policies in Fisheries Sector in India*. Delhi: Chandu Press, 2004.
Latif, Asad-ul Iqbal. *Between Rising Powers: China, Singapore and India*. Singapore: Institute of Southeast Asian Studies, 2007.
Law, Narendra Nath. *Studies in Indian History and Culture*. Delhi: B.R. Publishing Corporation, 1985.
Levathes, Louise. *When China Ruled the Seas*. New York: Simon & Schuster, 1994.
Lewis, John Wilson and Xue Litai. *China's Strategic Seapower: The Politics of Force Modernization in the Nuclear Age*. Stanford: Stanford University Press, 1994.
Liang, Qiao and Wang Xiangsui. *Unrestricted Warfare*. Beijing: PLA Literature and Arts Publishing House, 1999.
Liang-Yeong, Chiu. *Zheng He: Navigator, Discoverer and Diplomat*. Singapore: Unipress, 2001.
Lindberg, Michael S. *Geographical Impact on Coastal Defence Navies: The Entwining of Force Structure, Technology and Operational Environment*. London: Macmillan Press Ltd., 1998.
Lloyd Richmond M. *Fundamentals of Force Planning*. Vols. 1, 2 and 3. Newport: College Press, 1990.
Lo, Chi-kin. *China's Policy Towards Territorial Disputes: The Case of South China Sea Islands*. London: Routledge, 1989.
Loo, Bernard, ed. *Military Transformation and Strategy: Revolutions in Military Affairs and Small States*. New York: Routledge, 2008.
Luttwak, Edward. *The Political Uses of Seapower*. Baltimore, M.D.: John Hopkins University Press, 1974.
Mack, Andrew. "Key Security Issues in the Asia-Pacific". In *The Post-Cold War Order: Diagnoses and Prognoses*, edited by Richard Leaver and James L. Richardson. Canberra: Allen and Unwin, 1993.
Mahan, Alfred Thayer. *The Influence of Sea Power Upon History 1660–1783*. Boston: Little Brown and Company, 1918.
Malthus, Thomas R. *An Essay on the Principle of Population*. Illinois: Richard D. Irwin Inc., 1963.
Marder, Arthur J. *Old Friends, New Enemies: The Royal Navy and the Imperial Japanese Navy: Strategic Illusions, 1934–1941*. Oxford: Clarendon, 1981.
Marx, Wesley. *The Oceans: Our Last Resort*. San Francisco: Seirra, 1981.
McIntosh, Malcolm. *Japan Re-armed*. London: Frances Pinter, 1986.
Mehta, Usha and Usha Thakkar. *Kautilya and his Arthashastra*. New Delhi: S. Chand & Co., 1980.
Menon, Rear Admiral Raja. *Maritime Strategy and Continental Wars* (London: Frank Cass, 1998.
Moineville, Hubert. *Naval Warfare Today and Tomorrow*. Oxford: Blackwell, 1982.
Montel, Pierre. *Lives of the Pharos*. London: Spring Books, 1974.

Mookerji, Radha Kumud. *Indian Shipping: A History of the Sea-borne Trade and Maritime Activity of the Indians from the Earliest Times*. Bombay: Longmans, Green and Co., 1912.
Muller, Jr., David G. *China as a Maritime Power*. Boulder: Westview Press, 1983.
Mulvenon, James C. and Richard H. Yang, eds. *The People's Liberation Army in the Information Age*. Santa Monica, C.A.: RAND, 1999.
Naidu, G.V.C. *Indian Navy and South East Asia*. Delhi: Knowledge World, 2000.
Naval Aviation: A World History. New Delhi: Birla Institute of Scientific Research, 1985.
Needham, Joseph. *Science and Civilization in China*. Cambridge: University Press, 1954.
Nelson, Harvey W. *The Chinese Military System: An Organizational Study of the People's Liberation Army*. Boulder: Westview Press, 1977.
Niimi, Reiko. *The Problem of Food Security in Japan's Economic Security*. Hampshire: Gower, 1980.
Noer, John H. *Choke Points: Maritime Economic Concerns in South East Asia*. Washington: NDU Press, 1996.
Paleri, Prabhakaran. *Role of the Coast Guard in the Maritime Security of India*. New Delhi: Knowledge World, 2007.
Pannikar, K.M. *Asia and Western Dominance*. London: George Allen and Unwin (India) Private Ltd., 1959.
———. *India and the Indian Ocean*. Bombay: George Allen and Unwin (India) Private Ltd., 1971.
Park, Choon-ho. *East Asia and the Law of the Sea*. Seoul: Seoul National University Press, 1983.
Park, Choon-ho and Jae Kyu Park, eds. *The Law of the Sea: Problems from the East Asian Perspective*. Honolulu: University of Hawaii, 1987.
Pillsbury, Michael, ed. *Chinese Views of Future Warfare*. Washington, D.C.: National Defence University Press, 1997.
———. *China Debates the Future Security Environment*. Washington, D.C.: National Defense University, 2000.
Potter, E.B. *Sea Power: A Naval History*. Annapolis: Naval Institute Press, 1982.
Prabhakar, Lawrence W., Joshua Ho, and Sam Bateman. *The Evolving Maritime Balance of Power in the Asia-Pacific: Maritime Doctrines and Nuclear Weapons at Sea*. Singapore: World Scientific, 2006.
Prakash, Arun. *From the Crow's Nest*. New Delhi: Lancer Publishers, 2007.
Prescott, Victor. *Limits of National Claims in the South China Sea*. London: ASEAN Press, 1999.
Puri, Rama. *India and National Jurisdiction in the Sea*. New Delhi: ABC Publishing House, 1985.
Qasim, S.Z. and G.S. Roonwal, eds. *India's Exclusive Economic Zone: Resources, Exploitation, Management*. New Delhi: Omega Scientific Publishers, 1996.

Qasim, S.Z. and R.R. Nair, eds. *From the First Nodule to the First Mine Site: An Account of the Polymetallic Nodule Project*. New Delhi: Department of Ocean Development, 1988.

Rajavel, N. *Tourism in Andaman and Nicobar Islands*. New Delhi: Manas Publications, 1998.

Ranft, Bryan and Geoffrey Till. *The Sea in Soviet Strategy*. Hong Kong: The Macmillan Press Ltd., 1983.

Ranganathan, C.V. and Vinod C. Khanna. *India and China: The Way Ahead After Mao's India War*. New Delhi: Har-Anand, 2000.

Ray, Animesh. *Maritime India: Ports and Shipping*. Calcutta: Pearl Publishers, 1993.

Reynolds, Clark G. *Command of the Sea: The History and Strategy of Maritime Empires*. New York: William Morrow and Company, 1974.

Roger, N.A.M., ed. *Naval Power in the Twentieth Century*. London: Macmillan, 1996.

Ross, Andrew, ed. *The Military Significance of the Gulf War*. Canberra: Australian Defence Studies Centre, 1991.

Roy-Chaudhary, Rahul. *Sea Power and Indian Security*. London: Brassey's, 1995.

———. *India's Maritime Security*. New Delhi: Knowledge World, 2000.

Sakhuja, Vijay. "India's Growing Profile in Southeast Asia". In *Regional Outlook: Southeast Asia 2008–2009*, edited by Deepak Nair and Lee Poh Onn. Singapore: Institute of Southeast Asian Studies, 2008.

Samuels, Marwyn S. *Contest for the South China Seas*. New York: Methuen, 1983.

Samuels, Richard J. *"Rich Nation, Strong Army": National Security and the Technological Transformation of Japan*. New York: Cornell University Press, 1994.

Sanger, Clyde. *Ordering the Oceans*. London: Macmillan, 1988.

Santhanam, K., ed. *Iraq War 2003: Rise of the New "Unilateralism"*. New Delhi: IDSA and Ane Books, 2003.

Sastri, K. Nilakanta. *Cola*. Madras: University of Madras, 2000.

Schonfield, Hugh J. *The Suez Canal in World Affairs*. London: Constellation Books, 1952.

Seervai, H.M. *Constitutional Law of India*. Bombay: N.M. Tripathi Ltd., 1967.

Segal, Gerald. *Defending China*. New York: Oxford University Press, 1985.

Seiichi, Mariyama and Donna Vandenbrink, eds. *Towards a Knowledge-based Economy: East Asia's Changing Industrial Geography*. Singapore: Institute of Southeast Asian Studies, 2003.

Sharma, R.C. and P.C. Sinha. *India's Ocean Policy*. New Delhi: Khama Publishers, 1994.

Sharpe, Richard, ed. *Jane's Fighting Ships 1995–96, 1996–97, 1997–98, 1998–99, 1999–2000, 2000–01, 2001–02, 2002–03, 2003–04, 2004–05, 2005–06, 2006–07, 2007–08, 2008–09*. Surrey: Jane's Information Group, various years.

———. *Jane's All the World's Aircraft 1996–97*. Surrey: Jane's Information Group, 1996.

———. *Jane's Information Service Sentinel.* Surrey: Jane's Information Group, 1996.

Shultz, Jr., Richard H. and Robert L. Pfaltzgraff, Jr., eds. *The Role of Naval Forces in 21ˢᵗ Century Operations.* Washington: Brassy's, 2000.

Siddiqi, M.A.H. *India in the Indian Ocean: A Geopolitical Study.* Jaipur: Rawat Publications, 1997.

Singh, Bilveer. *ZOPFAN and the New Security Order in the Asia Pacific Region.* Malaysia: Pelanduk Publications, 1992.

Singh, Jasjit, ed. *Kargil 1999: Pakistan's Fourth War for Hashmir.* New Delhi: Knowledge World, 1999.

———. *Oil and Gas in India's Security.* New Delhi: Knowledge World, 2001.

Singh, Jasjit and Swaran Singh. "Trends in Defence Expenditure". *Asian Strategic Review 1996–97.* New Delhi: IDSA, 1997.

Singh, K.R. *Navies of South Asia.* New Delhi: Rupa Co., 2002.

Singh, Pushpinder. *Fly Navy: An Illustrated History of Indian Naval Aviation.* New Delhi: Society of Aerospace Studies, 2006.

Singh, Rear Admiral Satyindra. *Under Two Ensigns.* New Delhi: Lancer International, 1989.

———. *Blueprint to Bluewater: The Indian Navy 1951–65.* New Delhi: Lancer International, 1992.

Smith, George P. *Restricting the Concept of Free Seas.* New York: Kreiger, 1980.

Southeast Asia-China Interactions. Kuala Lumpur: MBRAS, 2007.

Sridharan, Rear Admiral K. *Sea: Our Saviour.* New Delhi: New Age International, 2000.

Su, Ming-Yang. *Seven Epic Voyages of Zheng He in Ming China (1405–1433): Facts, Fiction and Fabrication.* Torrence, C.A.: 2005.

Suarez, Thomas. *Early Mapping of Southeast Asia.* Singapore: Periplus Editions (HK) Ltd., 1999.

Suryadinata, Leo. *Admiral Zheng He and Southeast Asia.* Singapore: Institute of Southeast Asian Studies, 2005.

Swanson, Bruce L. *Eighth Voyage of the Dragon: A History of China's Quest for Seapower.* Annapolis: United States Naval Institute Press, 1982.

Swarztrauber, Sayer A. *The Three Mile Limit of Territorial Sea.* Annapolis: United States Naval Institute Press, 1972.

Tan, Felix B., P. Scott Corbett, and Yuk-Yong Wong, eds. *Information Technology Diffusion in Asia Pacific: Perspectives on Policy, Electronic Commerce and Education.* Hershey: Idea Group Publishing, 1999.

Tan, Tan Chung, ed. *Across the Himalayan Gap: An Indian Quest for Understanding China.* New Delhi: Gyan Publishing House, 1998.

Tanbiah, S.J. *World Conqueror and World Renouncer: A Study of Buddhism and Polity in Thailand against a Historical Background.* New York: Cambridge University Press, 1976.

Tangredi, Sam J., ed. *Globalization and Maritime Power*. Washington: National Defense University Press, 2002.

Till, Geoffrey. *Modern Seapower*. London: Brassey's 1987.

———. *Maritime Strategy and the Nuclear Age*. London: Macmillan, 1994.

———. *Seapower: A Guide for the Twenty-First Century*. London: Frank Cass, 2004.

Toffler, Alvin and Heidi. *War and Antiwar: Survival at the Dawn of the Century*. New York: Warner Books, 1993.

Walbank, F.W. *The Decline of the Roman Empire in the West*. London: Corbett Press, 1946.

Walters, O.W. *History, Culture, and Region in Southeast Asian Perspectives*. New York: Cornell Southeast Asia Program Publication, 1999.

Westcott, Allan. *Mahan on Naval Warfare*. Boston: Prentice Hall, 1991.

Wilson, Carol L. *Coal: Bridge to the Future*. Massachusets: Ballinger, 1975.

Wunderlich, Hans Georg. *The Secret of Crete*. Glasgow: William Collins, Sons and Co., 1976.

Yang, R.H., ed. *China's Military, the PLA in 1992–93*. SCPS PLA Yearbook, 1992. Kaoshiung: National Sun Yat Sen University, 1992.

Yoshihara, Toshi and James R. Holmes, eds. *Asia Looks Seaward: Power and Maritime Strategy*. Westport, Connecticut: Praeger Security International, 2008.

Articles in Journals and Periodicals

Ahrari, M. Ehsan. "Chinese Prove to be Attentive Students of Information Warfare". *Jane's Intelligence Review* (October 1997): 473.

Ai Hongren. "An Inside Look into the Chinese Communist Navy: Advancing towards the 'Blue-Water Challenge'". Hong Kong: Cosmos, 1988. Translated by Joint Publications Research Service of USIS-China (JPRS-CAR-90-052), July 1990.

Arase, David. "A Militarised Japan?". *Journal of Strategic Studies* 18, no. 3 (September 1995): 84–103.

Ball, Desmond. "Introduction". *Journal of Strategic Studies* 18, no. 3 (September 1995): 1–14.

Barnett, Thomas P.M. "India's 12 Steps to a World-Class Navy". *The U.S. Naval Institute Proceedings* (July 2001): 41–45.

Bartlet, Herry C., G. Paul Holman, Jr., and Timothy E. Somes. "The Art of Strategy and Force Planning". *Naval War College Review* 48, no. 2 (Spring 1995): 114–26.

Basistha, Partha Pritam. "Offshore Drilling to provide Shipping with New Dimensions". *Oil Asia Journal* (March–April 2007): 11.

Bateman, Sam. "Maritime Strategy in Asia Pacific". *U.S. Naval Institute Proceedings* (March 1995).

———. "Sea Change in Asia-Pacific". *Jane's Navy International* (October 1996): 26.
Bhardwaj, Atul. "Cruise Missiles and the Changing Naval Strategy". *Journal of Indian Ocean Studies* 9, no. 3 (December 2001).
Bodansky, Yossef. "The PRC Search for the Strait of Malacca and Spratly confronts India and the U.S.". *Defence and Foreign Affairs Strategic Policy* (30 September 1995): 6–13.
Boesche, Roger. "Kautilya's 'Arthasastra' on War and Diplomacy in Ancient India". *The Journal of Military History* 67, no. 1 (January 2003): 15–36.
Boese, Wade. "India Test-Launches Submarine Missile". *Arms Control Today*, 1 April 2008.
Breemer, Jan S. "The End of Naval Strategy: Revolutionary Change and the Future of American Naval Power". *Strategic Review* (Spring 1994).
Britto, Vice Admiral A. "Shipbuilding in India: Yesterday and Today". *Journal of Indian Ocean Studies* (November 1996): 34.
Bussert, James C. "Chinese Naval Sonar Evolves from Foreign Influences". *Signal* (December 2002): 57–60.
Buszynski, Leszek. "ASEAN Security Dilemmas". *Survival* 34, no. 4 (1994).
Buzan, Barry and Gerald Seagal. "Rethinking East Asian Security". *Survival* 36, no. 2 (Summer 1994).
Campbell, David J. "What are the Threats?". *U.S. Naval Institute Proceedings* (March 1996).
Campbell, Kurt and Richard Weitz. "The Limits of U.S.-China Military Cooperation: Lessons from 1995–1999". *The Washington Quarterly* 29, no. 1 (Winter 2005): 169–86.
Chakrabarti, R. "China and Bangladesh". *China Report* 30, no. 2 (1994).
Chand, Naresh. "UAVs for the Indian Navy". *SP's Naval Forces* 3, no. 1: 6–7.
Chand, Prem. "Network-Centric Warfare: Some Fundamentals". *Air Power Journal* 2, no. 1 (Spring 2005).
Chanda, Nayan. "Divide and Rule". *Far Eastern Economic Review*, 11 August 1994.
Chang, Felix K. "Beijing's Reach in the South China Sea". *Orbis* 40, no. 4 (Summer 1996): 353–74.
———. "Conventional War Across the Taiwan Strait". *Orbis* 40, no. 4 (Autumn 1996): 577–607.
Chang, Yihong. "The PLA Strengthens Its Amphibious Capability". *China Brief* 2, issue 9 (25 April 2002).
"Changing Tides in the Indian Ocean". *Jane's Navy International* (November 1997): 39.
Chase, Michael and Andrew Erickson. "Information Technology and China's Naval Modernization". *Joint Force Quarterly* 50 (3rd quarter 2008): 24–30.
Chauhan, Pradeep. "Indian Naval Foreign Cooperation Endeavours". *Journal of Indian Ocean Studies* 15, no. 2 (August 2007): 225–41.

Cheon, Seongwhun. "Nuclear-Armed North Korea and South Korea's Strategic Countermeasures". *The Korean Journal of Defense Analysis* 16, no. 2 (Autumn 2004): 49–78.
Cheung, Tai Ming. "Trends in the Research of Chinese Military Strategy". *Survival* 6, no. 2 (May–June 1987).
"China's Insatiable Energy Needs". *Petroleum Intelligence Weekly*, 3 November 1997.
Chiu, Hungdah. "An Analysis of the Sino-Japanese Dispute over the T'aioyutai Islets". *Occasional Paper/Reprint Series in Contemporary Asian Studies*, no. 1 (1999): 150.
Cloughley, Brian. "Japan Ponders Power Projection". *Jane's International Defense Review* (July 1996).
Cohen, Ariel. "The Russia-China Friendship and Cooperation Treaty: A Strategic Shift in Eurasia?". Asian Studies Center Backgrounder 1459. The Heritage Foundation, 18 July 2001.
Cole, Bernard D. "Beijing's Strategy of Sea Denial". *China Brief* 6, issue 23 (22 November 2006).
Cook, Nick. "All For One: Boeing in India". *Jane's Navy International* (26 March 2008).
Cuomo, Scott A. "US and Indian Navies Close Again". *U.S. Naval Institute Proceedings* (February 2002).
Curtis, Lisa. "India's Expanding Role in Asia: Adapting to Rising Power Status". Asian Studies Center Backgrounder 2008. The Heritage Foundation, 20 February 2007.
Daly, John C.K. "Can the Dragon Swim? The Naval Balance in the Taiwan Strait". *China Brief* 4, issue 2 (January 2004).
Dean, Raleigh. "Japan: The Nature of Sword". *U.S. Naval Institute Proceedings* (November 1998).
Dev, Rear Admiral Krishna. "Indian Shipping in Global Context: A Neglected Industry". *Journal of Indian Ocean Studies* (November 1998).
Dibb, Paul. "The Revolution in Military Affairs and Asian Security". *Survival* 39, no. 4 (Winter 1997–98): 93–116.
Dillon, Dana R. and John J. Tkacik, Jr. "China and ASEAN: Endangered American Primacy in Southeast Asia". Asian Studies Center Backgrounder 1886. The Heritage Foundation, 19 October 2005.
Dimri, Lieutenant Commander B.M. "Naval Diplomacy and UNCLOS III". *Strategic Analysis* (April 1994): 55.
Ding, Arthur S. "China's Defence Finance: Content, Process and Administration". *The China Quarterly* (June 1996).
Djalal, Hasjim, Alexander Yankov, and Anthony Bergin. "Military and Intelligence Gathering Activities in the Exclusive Economic Zone: Consensus and Disagreement II". *Marine Policy* 29, issue 2 (March 2005): 175–83.
Downing, John. "China's Evolving Maritime Strategy". *Jane's Intelligence Review* (2 parts) (March–April 1996).

Dubey, Ajit K. "On the Watch". *Force* (March 2007): 58–60.
Dutta, Sujit. "China and Pakistan: End of a Special Relationship". *China Report* 30, no. 2 (1994): 127–29.
———. "Securing the Sea Frontier: China's Pursuit of Sovereignty Claims in the South China Sea". *Strategic Analysis* 29, no. 2 (April–June 2005): 269–94.
Erickson, Andrew S. and Lyle J. Goldstein. "China's Future Nuclear Submarine Force". *Naval War College Review* 60, no. 1 (Winter 2007): 54–79.
Erickson, Andrew S., Lyle J. Goldstein, and William Murray. "China's Undersea Sentries". *Undersea Warfare* 9, no. 2 (Winter 2007).
Fairclough, Gordon. "Floating Flashpoints". *Far Eastern Economic Review*, 13 March 1997.
Fisher, Jr., Richard D. "China Accelerates Navy Building". *China Brief* 3, issue 15 (13 December 1969).
Flikke, Geir and Julie Wilhelmsen. "Central Asia: A Testing Ground for New Great-Power Relations". Norwegian Institute of International Affairs Report, 2008.
France, Martin E.B. and Richard J. Adams. "The Chinese Threat to US Superiority". *High Frontier Journal* 1, no. 3 (Winter 2005): 1–22.
Garver, John W. "China's Push to the South China Sea: The Interaction of Bureaucratic and National Interests". *The China Quarterly* (December 1992).
Ghosh, Air Commodore C.N. "Revolution in Indian Military Affairs". *Indian Defence Review* (October–December 2001).
Ghosh, P.K. "Revisiting Gunboat Diplomacy: An Instrument of Threat or Use of Limited Naval Force". *Strategic Analysis* 24, issue 11 (February 2001): 2005–17.
Ghosh, S.K. "China's Naval Power". *Strategic Analysis* (July 1971).
Ghoshal, Baladas. "Trends in China-Burma Relations". *China Report* 30, no. 2 (1994).
Gilley, Bruce. "Pacific Outpost: China's Satellite Station in Kiribati has Military Purposes". *Far Eastern Economic Review*, 30 April 1998.
Glover, Peter. "Marine Casualties in the Great Barrier Reef: 'Peacock', 'Bunga Teratai Satu' and 'Doric Chariot'". *MLAANZ Journal* 18 (2004): 55–72.
Godwin, Paul H.B. "From Continent to Periphery: PLA Doctrine, Strategy and Capabilities Towards 2000". *The China Quarterly* 146 (June 1996): 475.
Goh, Evelyn. "Great Powers and Hierarchical Order in Southeast Asia: Analyzing Regional Security Strategies". *International Security* 32, no. 3 (Winter 2007/08): 113–57.
Goldstein, Lyle and William Murray. "International Submarine Rescue: A Constructive Role for China?". *Asia Policy*, no. 5 (January 2008): 167–83.
Grimes, Vincent. "Japanese Maritime Self Defence Force". *Navy International* (April 1991).
Haln, Branley. "Hai Fang" [Maritime Defence]. *U.S. Naval Institute Proceedings* (March 1986): 119.

Harding, Harry. "A Chinese Colossus?". *Journal of Strategic Studies* 18, no. 3 (September 1995): 104–22.

Harris, Stuart. "The Economic Aspects of Security in the Asia/Pacific Region". *Journal of Strategic Studies* 18, no. 3 (September 1995): 32–51.

Hirschfield, Thomas. "The Year of the Rat". *U.S. Naval Institute Proceedings* (May 1996).

Holmes, Jim and Toshi Yoshihara. "China's New Undersea Deterrent: Strategy, Doctrine and Capabilities". *Joint Force Quarterly* 50 (3rd quarter 2008).

Huang, Alexander C. "The Chinese Navy's Offshore Active Defence Strategy, Conceptualization and Implications". *Naval War College Review* 47, no. 3 (Summer 1994): 7–32.

"Indian Navy: Today and Tomorrow". An interview with Chief of Naval Staff Admiral Sureesh Mehta. *Journal of Indian Ocean Studies* 15, no. 1 (April 2007).

Ismail, M. Hanif. "Multi Role Support Vessels: New Key in Small Navy Operations". *Asian Defence Journal* (December 2007): 33.

Jacobs, Gordon. "China's Naval Missiles". *Asian Defence Journal* (October 1990).

Jaitly, P. "Modernising the Indian Navy: Imperatives and Strategy". *SP's Naval Forces* (March 2007): 11–12.

Jiang, Wenran. "China's Growing Energy Relations with the Middle East". *China Brief* 7, issue 14 (11 July 2007).

Johnston, Alastair Iain. "Is China a Status Quo Power?" *International Security* 27, no. 4 (Spring 2003): 5–56.

Jordan, John. "The Japanese Maritime Self-Defence Force". *Jane's Intelligence Review* (1992).

Joshi, Akshay. "A Holistic View of the Revolution in Military Affairs (RMA)". *Strategic Analysis* 22, no. 11 (February 1999): 1743–59.

Kak, Kapil. "Revolution in Military Affairs: An Appraisal". *Strategic Analysis* 24, issue 1 (April 2000): 5–16.

Kalathil, Shanti. "Chinese Media and the Information Revolution". *Harvard Asia Quarterly* (Winter 2002).

Kan, Shirley A. and Larry A. Niksch. "Guam: U.S. Defense Deployments". *CRS Report for Congress*, 16 January 2007.

Kearsley, Harold J. "An Analysis of the Military Threats Across the Taiwan Strait: Fact or Fiction". *Comparative Strategy* 19, no. 2 (April–June 2000): 112.

Keatts, Robert Shawn. "Ancient Mariners". *American Society of Oceanographers Journal* 10, no. 4, available at <www.americanoceanographer.com/PDFs/Archive_K4.pdf>.

Kondapalli, Srikanth. "China's Naval Equipment Acquisition". *Strategic Analysis* 23, issue 9 (December 1999): 1509–30.

———. "Exchanging Concerns". *Sainik Samachar* 52, no. 13 (1–15 July 2005).

Krishnan, S.K.K. "Building Warships is Not Purely a Shipyard Activity Alone". *Force* (December 2007): 30–31.

Liangxiang, Jin. "Energy First: China and the Middle East". *Middle East Quarterly* (Spring 2005).

Lin, Chong Pin. "The Military Balance in the Taiwan Straits". *The China Quarterly* (June 1996): 578.
Lin, Joseph E. "Filling of China's Strategic Oil Reserves Apparently Delayed". *China Brief* 7, issue 14 (12 July 2007).
MacDonald, Juli A. "South Asia and South East Asia in 2001". *National Strategy Forum Review* (Spring 2001).
Mak, J.N. "The Chinese Navy and the South China: A Malaysian Assessment". *Pacific Review* 4, no. 2 (1991).
Mak, J.N. and B.A. Hamzah. "The External Maritime Dimension of ASEAN Security". *Journal of Strategic Studies* 18, no. 3 (September 1995): 123–46.
Martin, Edward L. "Evolving Missions and Forces of the JMSDF". *Naval War College Review* 68 (Spring 1995): 39–67.
McDevitt, Michael. "Missile Defenses and US Policy Options towards Beijing". Report no. 47. The Henry L. Stimson Center, February 2002.
McDougall, Walter A. "Why Geography Matters ... But Is So Little Learned". *Orbis* 47, no. 2 (Spring 2003): 217–33.
Mehta, Sureesh. "The Immediate Need is to Augment and Upgrade Our Capacity for Sustained and Long-Range Airborne Surveillance". *Force* (December 2007): 8–20.
Miller, Alice Lyman. "The Limits of Chinese-Russian Strategic Collaboration". *Strategic Insight*. Center for Contemporary Conflict (CCC), 2 September 2002.
Mitra, N.K. "Advanced Technology and Spirited Workforce led to Successes at Western Offshore". *Oil Asia Journal* (May–June 2007).
Mohan, C. Raja. "India's Geopolitics and Southeast Asian Security". In *Southeast Asian Affairs*, edited by Daljit Singh and Tin Maung Maung Than. Singapore: Institute of Southeast Asian Studies, 2008.
Murugesan, P., T.T. Ajitkumar, and S. Ajmal Khan. "Marine Resources and their Future". *Journal of India Ocean Studies* 13, no. 1 (April 2005): 132–41.
Peele, Reynold B. "The Importance of Maritime Choke Points". *Parameters* (Summer 1997): 61–74.
Porch, Douglas. "The Taiwan Strait Crisis of 1996: Strategic Implications for the United States Navy". *Naval War College Review* 52, no. 3 (Summer 1999): 15–48.
Prakash, Arun. "A Vision of India's Maritime Power in the 21st Century". *Air Power Journal* 3, no. 4 (October–December 2006): 2.
———. "Aware and Secure". *Force* (June 2007): 4.
———. "Time for a Rethink". *Force* (August 2007): 8–9.
———. "The Missing Leg of the Triad". *Force* (September 2007): 28–30.
Pugh, Michael. "Maritime Disputes in the China Seas". *Jane's Intelligence Review Year Book*, 1994–95.
Qasim, S.Z. "History of Ocean Studies in India". *Journal of Indian Ocean Studies* 2, no. 3 (July 1995).

———. "Minerals of the Deep Seabed". *Journal of Indian Ocean Studies* 9, no. 1 (April 2001): 93–99.
Raghuvanshi, Vivek. "India parlays IT expertise into a comprehensive ISR upgrade". *C4ISR Journal* (4 January 2008).
Roonwal, G.S. *Marine Mineral Potential of India and South Africa: A Comparison Journal of Indian Ocean Studies* 2, no. 1 (November 1994).
Rosamond, Jon. "China Completes Joint Exercise with UK Aircraft Carrier". *Jane's Navy International* 112, issue 8 (October 2007): 6.
Roy, Mihir K. "Continental Versus Maritime Strategy: A Requiem". *USI Journal* (1989).
Roy-Chaudhary, Rahul. "The Chinese Navy and Indian Security". *Indian Defence Review* 1 (January 1994): 134.
———. "Ocean/Marine Management in India". *Strategic Analysis* (August 1997): 681.
———. "India's Energy Security and Shipping". *Journal of Indian Ocean Studies* (November 1998).
———. "Huge Demands made on India's Depleted Navy". *Jane's Navy International* (April 1999): 27.
Sakhuja, Vijay. "Maritime Order and Piracy". *Strategic Analysis* 24, issue 5 (August 2000): 923–38.
———. "Dragon's Dragonfly: The Chinese Aircraft Carrier". *Strategic Analysis* 24, no. 7 (October 2000): 1367–86.
———. "Sea Based Deterrence and Indian Security". *Strategic Analysis* 25, issue 1 (April 2001): 21–32.
———. "Naval Diplomacy: Indian Initiatives". *Indian Defence Review* 6, no. 1 (July–August 2003).
———. "Brahmos: Where Will It Hit?" *Asian Defence and Diplomacy* (November 2007).
Sakoh, Katsuro. "How Japan Can Do More To Defend Itself". Asian Studies Center Backgrounder 57. The Heritage Foundation, 25 February 1987.
Sawhney, Pravin and Ghazala Wahab. "Indian Navy Sails in Blue Waters". *Force* (December 2006): 26.
Schofield, Clive. "An Arms Race in the South China Sea?" *IBRU Boundary and Security Bulletin* (July 1994): 45.
———. "Island Disputes in East Asia Escalate". *Jane's Intelligence Review* (November 1996): 517–21.
Scobell, Andrew. "Show of Force: Chinese Soldiers, Statesmen, and the 1995–1996 Taiwan Strait Crisis". *Political Science Quarterly* 115, no. 2 (Summer 2000): 227–46.
Scott, David. "India's Drive for a Blue Water Navy". *Journal of Military and Strategic Studies* 10, issue 2 (Winter 2007–08): 5.
Scott, Richard and Jonathon Weng. "China Launches Type 071 LPD". *Jane's Navy International* 112, issue 2 (March 2007).

Sengupta, Prasun K. "A Builder's Navy Takes Shape". *Asian Defence Journal* (December 1998).
———. "China Commences Building a Helicopter Landing Deck". *Force* (November 2006).
———. "Dual Tasking Ships". *Force* (May 2007): 20–21.
Shambaugh, David. "China's Military in Transition: Politics, Professionalism, Procurement and Power Projection". *The China Quarterly* 146 (June 1996): 291.
Sharma, O.P. "India and the United Nations Convention on the Law of the Sea". *Ocean Development and International Law* 26, issue 4 (1995): 391–412.
Singh, Sanjay J. "India's Maritime Strategy for the 90s". *USI Journal* (July–September 1990): 352–54.
So Kee-Long. "Dissolving Hegemony or Changing Trade Pattern? Images of Srivijaya in the Chinese Sources of the Twelfth and Thirteenth Centuries". *Journal of Southeast Asian Studies* 29 (1998): 300.
Soon, Lau Teik. "ASEAN Diplomacy: National Interest and Regionalism". *Journal of Asian and African Studies* 25, nos. 1–2 (1990): 114–27.
Storey, Ian J. "China's 'Malacca Dilemma'". *China Brief* 6, issue 8 (12 April 2006).
Suryanarayany V. "Sri Lanka's Policy Towards China". *China Report* 30, no. 2 (1994).
Tahiliani, R.H. "Maritime Strategy". *USI Journal* (January–March): 227.
Teo Chee Hean. "Enhancing Security in a Time of Flux". *Pointer* 32, no. 1 (2006).
———. "Security Cooperation in Asia: Managing Alliances and Partnerships". *Pointer* 33, no. 2 (2007).
Thach, Hong Nguyen. "The Spratly Conflict in 1995 Continues Dialogue Amid Tension". *Pacific Research* (November 1995–February 1996).
Thomas, Ticy V. "Ship Recycling Industry in India: Legal Implications". *Maritime Affairs* 2, no. 1 (Summer 2006): 55.
Thomas, Timothy L. "Chinese and American Network Warfare". *Joint Forces Quarterly*, issue 38.
Till, Geoffrey. "Trouble in Paradise: Maritime Links and Threats in the Western Pacific". *Jane's Intelligence Review*. Special Report 7.
Wattanayagorn, Panitan and Desmond Ball. "A Regional Arms Race?" *Journal of Strategic Studies* 18, no. 3 (September 1995): 147–74.
Whiting, Allen S. "The PLA and China's Threat Perceptions". *The China Quarterly* 146 (June 1994): 603.
Woolley, Peter J. and Commander Mark S. Woolley. "The Kata of Japan's Naval Forces". *Naval War College Review* 49, no. 2 (Spring 1996): 59–69.
Xia, Dawai. "Details Emerge of China's Jin SSBN". *Jane's Navy International* 112, issue 9 (November 2007): 4.
Yuan, Jing-Dong. "China's Defence Modernization: Implications for Asia-Pacific Security". *Contemporary Southeast Asia* 17, no. 1 (June 1995): 67–84.

Zalamea, Lieutenant Commander Ulysses O. "Eagles and Dragons at Sea: The Inevitable Strategic Collision Between the United States and China". *Naval War College Review* 41, no. 4 (Autumn 1996): 62–74.

Zhan, Jun. "China Goes to the Blue Waters: The Navy, Seapower Mentality and the South China Sea". *The Journal of Strategic Studies* 17, no. 3 (September 1994): 180–208.

INDEX

A
ABG Shipyard, 148, 149
Academy of Military Sciences (China), 226
Afghanistan, 91
Africa
 in ancient maritime trade, 2, 48, 256
 Chinese naval diplomacy and, 187
 Chinese shipbuilding and, 129, 165n21
 colonial period, 16
 India and, 280
 Indian Ocean and, 56
 source of oil, 130, 203
 source of raw materials, 59, 83, 270
African Union Summit, 280
Akbar the Great, 257
Akiyama Saneyuki, 13
Alang, 160
Alcock & Ashdown Co. Ltd., 147
Aleutian Islands, 72
Alexander the Great, 2, 265
Alexandria, 258
Allahabad, 157
All India Council for Technical Education (AICTE), 239

Andaman Islands
 in Indian geography, 56, 57
 Indian Navy and, 93, 105
 in India-Pakistan war, 66, 202
 MILAN meetings, 198
 offshore oil, 155
 regional shipping, 150
 strategic importance, 107–8, 159
 tourism, 158, 159
 2004 tsunami, 211n84
Andaman Sea, 56, 57
Andhra Pradesh, 153, 155, 160
Anglo-Malayan Defence Agreement (AMDA), 292
Anhui, 137
Annamalai University, 155
Antoninus Pius, Emperor of Rome, 258
Antony, A.K., 99, 203
AP 3000, 8
APEC (Asia Pacific Economic Cooperation), 311
Arabian Sea
 Indian Navy presence in, 97, 196
 India's strategic interests in, 56, 91, 310
 Japanese naval presence in, 272, 282

offshore oil and gas, 107
sea lanes in, 203, 271
Arabs, 2, 255
Arctic Ocean, 36, 37
Argentina, 24–26, 134, 277
Armada Republic Argentina, 25, 26
Arthashastra, 216, 257, 263, 264–66, 267
Art of War, 216, 263, 265
Arunachalam, B., 298n35
Arunachal Pradesh, 109, 300n72
Ascension Island, 25
ASEAN (Association of Southeast Asian Nations), 185, 207n24, 281, 285–88, 294–95, 311
ASEAN Plus Three, 204, 286
ASEAN Regional Forum (ARF), 182, 194, 204, 286, 292, 294, 311
Ashoka the Great, 258, 265
Asian Development Bank, 132
Asia-Pacific region, 58–60, 64n83, 107, 181–83, 253, 282, 284
Associated Chambers of Commerce and Industry of India (ASSOCHAM), 243
Association for Bangladesh-India-Myanmar-Sri Lanka-Thailand Economic Cooperation (BIMST-EC), 194
Association for Relations Across the Taiwan Straits (ARATS), 184, 185
Atlantic Ocean, 16, 57, 142, 232, 277, 308
Augustus, Emperor of Rome, 258
Aurangzeb, 257
Australia
in Asia-Pacific region, 58, 59
in East Asia Summit, 286

Five Power Defence Arrangements, 292
Great Barrier Reef, 42
joint naval exercises, 274
maritime power, 22
relations with China, 78, 131
relations with India, 198
relations with Southeast Asia, 254
relations with the United States, 274
2004 tsunami, 193, 197, 282
Aviation Week, 226
Azhical, 160

B

Baghdad, 245n8
Bagramayan, Hovhannes, Marshal, 11
Bahamas, 134, 277
Balboa, 277
Baltic and International Maritime Council (BIMCO), 192
Baltic Sea, 10, 11
Bangaram Island, 159
Bangladesh
anti-piracy agreement, 287
fishing industry, 152
in India-Pakistan conflicts, 98
in India's maritime geography, 56
relations with China, 187, 271, 279
relations with India, 44, 157, 197
ship recycling industry, 160
Baotou, 137
Barak River, 157
Barbers, 162
Barus, 258
Basham, A.L., 265

Batang Hari River, 261
Bateman, S.W., 32n68
Bay of Bandon, 260
Bay of Bengal
   in ancient maritime trade, 259, 260
   China's strategic interests in, 271
   Indian Navy presence, 97, 98, 196, 198, 236, 271, 289–90
   in India's maritime geography, 56
   nuclear submarines in, 293
   offshore oil and gas, 107
   Tamil Tigers and, 213n104
   tourism development, 158
   U.S. Navy and, 202, 236
Bay of Bengal Initiative for Multi-Sectoral Technical and Economic Cooperation (BIMSTEC), 281
Baypore, 160
Beidou satellites, 231
Belarus, 100
Bengal, 254
Bhagirathi River, 157
Bharat Electronics Limited (BEL), 101, 241
Bharti Shipyard, 148, 149
Bihar, 157
Bindusara, 265
Black Sea, 2, 11
Boeing, 104, 243
Bohai Bay, 142
Bohai Rim, 134
Bolgatty Island, 159
Bombay. *See* Mumbai
Bombay Steam Navigation Company, 161

Bonin Islands, 72
Book of Lord Shang, 263
Booth, Ken, 195
Border Peace and Tranquillity Agreement (BPTA), 270
Borneo, 56
Bosnia, 216
Brahmaputra River, 157, 158
Brazil, 22, 131, 134, 198, 200, 280
Britain. *See also* British Royal Navy; Falklands War (1982)
   Chinese computer hackers and, 227
   colonial possessions, 16, 39, 65, 111n2
   Five Power Defence Arrangements, 292
   history of maritime thought, 7–8
   Indian Ocean and, 3
   Japan and, 12, 13–14
   maritime power, 4, 7, 9–10, 22–23, 308
   nuclear capabilities, 67, 96, 293
   relations with India, 98, 100, 198, 199, 278
   trade with Mogul empire, 257
   UNCLOS III and, 43
British Army, 8
British Military Doctrine, 8
British Royal Navy
   in British maritime power, 7–8
   in development of Indian Navy, 16, 90
   in Falklands War, 25–26
   joint exercises, 186, 200, 236, 254
   technological advancement, 238
Brown, Lester R., 134

Brunei, 51, 52, 183, 286, 295
Buddhism, 260, 261, 266
Buenaventura, 134
Buenos Aires Container Terminal, 134
Burma, 16, 258. *See also* Myanmar
Bush, George W., 304n116

C

Cable, James, 177
Cady, John F., 260
Calcutta, 147, 151, 162
Callao, 134
Cambodia, 39, 207n17, 258, 259
Canada, 22, 101
Canada-United Kingdom-United States (CANUKUS) Naval Data Transmission Working Group, 219
Cape of Good Hope, 57, 91, 93
Caranzalem, 160
Caribbean Sea, 10
Central Asia, 280, 281
Centre for Development of Telematics (India), 241
Chaiya, 259
Chalukya kingdom, 15, 257
Cham kingdom, 267
Chandragupta Maurya, Emperor, 257, 263, 265
Chengdu, 226
Chengzu, Emperor, 256
Chennai, 151, 162, 297n28
Chen Shui-bian, 185
Chera kingdom, 15, 258
Chiang Kai-Shek, 71, 112n20
Chi Haotian, General, 189, 209n52
Chile, 134, 152, 187
China. *See also* China-India relations; China-Japan relations; China-Pakistan relations; China-Russia relations; China-Taiwan relations; China-United States relations; PLA (People's Liberation Army); PLA Navy
  ancient maritime power, 3, 14, 47–48, 70, 175–76, 251–56, 262
  anti-piracy agreement, 287
  coastal regions, 86–87, 126, 127
  computer hacking incidents, 226–27
  determinants of maritime power, 22, 60
  energy supply, 83–84, 107, 130, 185
  environmental protection, 139
  European dominance over, 14, 65, 111n1
  fishing industry, 134–35, 152, 163
  information technology in, 223–24
  inland waterways, 135–37
  international maritime agreements and, 48–51
  marine tourism, 137–40
  maritime economic policies, 126–45
  maritime geography, 55–56, 59
  military spending, 89–90, 109, 183
  nuclear capabilities, 86, 113n32, 286, 293
  peacekeeping operations, 182, 207n17
  port infrastructure, 131–34

relations with Southeast Asia, 253–54, 285–96
seafaring workforce, 142–45
shipbuilding industry, 75, 78, 127–29, 163, 165 (nn13, 21)
shipping industry, 129–31, 163
space programme, 230–33
Special Economic Zones, 86, 125
territorial claims, 42, 48–49, 51–53, 286
theories of statecraft, 263–64
tsunami relief, 193, 211n73, 287
2008 Beijing Olympics, 139, 140, 227
China-ASEAN dialogue, 183, 207n24
China Association of the National Shipbuilding Industry (CANSI), 128, 129
China Coordination Council for Overseas Seamen Employment (COSE), 144
China-India relations
  Indian exports, 131, 153
  naval diplomacy, 181
  rivalry and strategies, 182, 270–74
  Tamil merchant guilds, 258
  war and border disputes, 109, 122n197, 191, 233, 303n112
China Information Technology Report, 224
China International Contractors' Association (CHINCA), 144
China-Japan relations
  historical factors, 12, 13, 111n1
  military diplomacy, 181
  PLA Navy and, 176, 185, 191, 270
  rivalry and strategies, 182, 191, 268, 272–74
  role of the United States in, 87
China Maritime Surveillance (CMS), 80
China National Computer Network Emergency Response Technical Team (CNCERT), 227
China National Electronic Import and Export Corporation, 230
China National Offshore Oil Corporation (CNOOC), 142, 286
China National Research Centre for Intelligence Computing Systems, 226
China National Tourism Administration (CNTA), 138
China Ocean Mineral Resources R&D Association (COMRA), 141
China-Pakistan relations
  boundary agreement, 300n72
  Gwadar port project, 84, 277, 280
  India and, 279–80
  Karakoram Highway, 271
  military assistance, 302n103
  naval diplomacy, 187
  nuclear cooperation, 109, 273, 280
  signal monitoring facilities, 231
China Precision Machinery Import and Export Corporation, 230

China-Russia relations
  military and technical
    cooperation, 15, 75,
    80, 181, 192, 269–70,
    300nn68–69
  naval diplomacy, 187
  rapprochement, 72
China Shipbuilding Industry
  Corporation (CSIC), 129
China Shipping Group (CSG),
  143
China's National Defense, 181,
  183
China State Shipbuilding
  Corporation (CSSC), 129
China-Taiwan relations
  international maritime
    agreements, 50–51
  Russia and, 192
  threats of invasion, 80–81,
    84–86, 176, 182, 184–85,
    207n26, 270
  United States and, 48, 66, 184,
    188–89, 274–75
China Tourism Association, 138
China Tourism Management
  Institute, 138
China Tourism News, 138
China Travel and Tourism Press,
  138
China-United States relations
  Hurricane Katrina, 193
  naval encounters, 176, 188–91
  rivalry and strategy, 182, 187,
    268, 274–76, 290–91
  Taiwan issue, 48, 66, 78, 83,
    85, 184, 274–75
China Wide Web, 223
Chinese Academy of Fishery
  Science (CAFS), 135

Chinese Academy of Social
  Sciences (CASS), 273
Chinese Maritime Authority, 142
Chirac, Jacques, 161
Chittagong, 187
Chola empire, 3, 15, 257, 258–59,
  262
Cholas, 175
Chongqing, 137
Chulamani Varmadeva Vihara,
  261
Chungshan Institute of Science
  and Technology, 85
Chunxiao gas field, 185
climate change, 43–44
Cline, Ray S., 21
Clinton, Bill, 304n116
CNTA Information Center, 138
CNTA Logistics Center, 138
coastal populations, 37, 60n2
Coates, Nigel, Rear Admiral, 201
Cochin, 147, 151, 158, 159, 160
Cochin Shipyard Limited (CSL),
  99, 147, 148
Cohen, William, 189, 209n52
Cold War, 11, 67, 188, 201
Colombia, 134
Colombo, 187, 212n84
Commission of Science,
  Technology and Industry
  for National Defense
  (COSTIND), 128, 129,
  226
Committee on Maritime
  Education and Training
  (CMET) (India), 162
Compass Navigation Satellite
  System, 231
Confederation of Indian Industry
  (CII), 242

Conference on Interaction and Confidence-Building Measures in Asia (CICA), 182
Congo, 207n19
Container Security Initiative (CSI), 204
Coordinating Body on the Seas of East Asia (COBSEA), 139
Coordination Council for Overseas Seamen Employment of China (CCOSEC), 143
Corbett, Sir Julian, 7–8
Cornell University, 184
Coromandel coast, 258
COSCO (China Ocean Shipping Company), 129, 143
COSCOMAN (COSCO Manning Cooperation Inc.), 143
COSTIND University of Electronic Science and Technology, 226
Council on Security Cooperation in Asia and Pacific Region (CSCAP), 182, 194, 281
Crestone Company, 185
Crete, 2, 29n2
Cristobal, 277
Crowder, William, Vice Admiral, 200
Cultural Revolution, 49, 72, 89
Cyclone Nargis, 197, 289
Cyclone Sidr, 197

D
Dai Qingmin, General, 222
Da Lac Reef, 185
Dalai Lama, 190
Dalian Maritime University, 144
Dalian Port, 133
Daoism, 263
Davis Engineering, 101
Dayawan, 84, 87
DCN International, 98, 293
Deccan plateau, 156
Defence Electronics Research Laboratory (DLRL), 241
Defence Imagery Processing and Analysis Centre (DIPAC), 239
Defence Research and Development Organization (DRDO), 96, 149, 240, 241
Dellios, Rosita, 267
Democratic Party of Japan, 274
Democratic Progress Party (DPP), 185
Deng Xiaoping, 15, 70, 72, 138
Deng Xiaoping on Tourism, 138
Denmark, 100
Department of Electronics (DoE) (India), 234
Department of Ocean Development (DOD) (India), 154
Department of Space (DoS) (India), 234
Dhubri, 157
Diaoyutai Islands, 52–53, 55, 81, 142, 185, 272
Diego Garcia, 27
Directorate General for Information Warfare (India), 234
Directorate General of Shipping (India), 161, 162
Directorate of Foreign Cooperation (DFC) (India), 199
Directorate of Information Technology (DIT) (India), 241

Directorate of Naval Design
   (DND), 105
Djibouti, 198
Dongshan Island, 184
Drake, Sir Francis, 7

E
East Asia Summit (EAS), 194,
   274, 281, 286, 294, 311
East China Sea, 51, 55, 142, 185,
   192
East India Company, 111n2
Ecuador, 134
EEZs (Exclusive Economic Zones)
   in sea power, 16, 21, 22, 44–47,
      178, 179
   UNCLOS III and, 29, 38,
      42–43
Egypt, 1, 2, 198, 257, 258
Electronics Corporation of India
   Limited (ECIL), 233
English Channel, 7, 10
English language, 144, 161
Ensenada International Terminal,
   134
environmental issues, 43–44, 139,
   160–61, 171n130
Eritrea, 198
Erlangga, 267
Essar Shipping, 151
Ethiopia, 2
Europe, 182, 187, 227, 252, 277,
   308
European Union, 232, 286

F
Fa Hsien, 255
Falklands War (1982), 24–26, 82
Fernandes, George, 91
Fiji, 22

Fisher, Admiral Jackie, 8
fishing
   in China, 134–35
   EEZs and, 45–46
   in India, 152–54, 164, 171n130
   Law of the Sea and, 41
   sea power and, 11, 19
Five Power Defence Arrangements
   (FPDA), 292
Fleet Ship Management, 162
food security, 125, 134–35
FOSMA (Foreign Owners Ship
   Managers Association), 162
France
   colonial possessions, 51, 52, 65,
      111n2
   defence contracts, 294
   humanitarian missions, 289
   maritime power, 4, 10, 22,
      308
   military literature, 226
   navy, 9, 186, 200, 236, 238
   nuclear capabilities, 67, 96,
      293
   relations with India, 102, 160,
      198, 199, 278
   tourism industry, 138
   trade in Indian Ocean, 3
Fujian Militia, 80
Fujian province, 134
Funan, 254–55, 260
*Fundamentals of British Maritime
   Doctrine, BR 1806*, 8

G
Galileo global positioning system,
   232
Galle, 212n84
Ganges River, 157, 158
Gao Zong, Emperor, 255

Garden Reach Shipbuilders and
    Engineers (GRSE), 106, 147,
    148–49
Gates, Robert, 64n83, 99
General Security on Military
    Information Agreement
    (GSOMIA), 284
Germany
  Chinese computer hackers and,
    227
  Indian Navy and, 100, 102, 198
  maritime power, 4
  military literature, 226
  naval engagements, 11
  World War II, 14
Gia Long, Emperor, 51
globalization, 4, 5–6, 18, 66,
    124–26, 142
Glonass system, 231
Goa
  fishing industry, 153
  inland waterways, 157
  marine tourism, 158, 159, 160
  oceanography institute, 154
  port and shipyards, 147, 151
Goa Shipyard Limited (GSL), 106,
    147, 148
Godavari River, 157
Gorshkov, Admiral Sergei, 11–12
GPS (global positioning system),
    231, 232
Grain Issue in China, 135
Grand Canal, 137
Great Barrier Reef, 42
Great Eastern Shipping Company,
    151
Greater Sunda Islands, 72
Great Wall of China, 137
Greece, 1, 2, 144, 175, 257, 308
Greenpeace, 161

Grove, Eric, 195
Guam, 27, 72, 274–75
Guangdong, 137
Guangdong province, 84
Guangxi, 137
Guangzhou, 138, 259
Guangzhou Naval Academy, 77
Guayaquil, 134
Guizhou, 137
Gujarat, 147, 151, 153, 155, 160
Gulf of Mannar, 54
Gulf of Oman, 84
Gulf of Siam, 260
Gulf War, First (1990–91)
  conduct of, 26–27
  effects on China and India,
    216–17, 225, 227–28, 244
  as showcase of technological
    warfare, 23, 220
  U.S. defence spending and, 28
Gulf War, Second (2003-), 27–28,
    216, 245n8
Gupta empire, 257
Gwadar Deep Sea Project (GDSP),
    84, 277, 280

H
Hague Peace Conferences, 48
Hainan Island
  nuclear naval base, 282, 289–91,
    292
  piracy, 192
  PLANAF deployments, 77, 83
  signals intelligence stations, 233
  tourism, 139
  U.S. Navy incident, 189
Haiti, 207n19
Haldia, 157
Hall, Kenneth, 261, 262
Han dynasty, 254

Hangzhou, 255
Han Xu, 49
Haribhanga River, 44
Hasan, Muzaffar, Vice Admiral, 302n103
Hawaii, 187
HDW (Howaldstwerke-Deutsche Werke), 102
Heilongjiang, 136
Hideyoshi, Toyotomi, 267
Himalayas, 156, 191, 270
Hindustan Aeronautics Limited (HAL), 99, 102, 104, 106
Hindustan Copper Limited, 155
Hindustan Shipyard Limited (HSL), 147, 148
Hindustan Zinc Limited, 155
Hippalus, 258
Honduras, 22
Hong Kong
  British naval presence, 39
  in China-United States relations, 190
  Chinese shipping industry and, 144
  marine tourism, 139–40
  piracy, 192
  port, 134, 137
  Tiananmen Square rally, 224
Hooghly Dock & Port Engineers Limited, 147
Hooghly River, 157
Hormuz, 3
How Far is War from Us?, 229
Huaihe, 136
Huangdao, 84
Huanghua Port Construction Project, 133
Huangpu, 136
Hubei, 137

Hu Jintao, 70, 84
Hunan, 137
Hurricane Katrina, 193
Hussein, Saddam, 27

I
IAEA (International Atomic Energy Agency), 283
IBSAMAR (IBSA Maritime), 200
Imperial Japanese Navy, 13
Incidents at Sea Agreement (INCSEA), 294
India. *See also* China-India relations; Indian Navy; India-Pakistan relations; India-Russia relations; India-United States relations
  ancient maritime power, 1, 15, 175–76, 251–54, 256–59
  anti-piracy agreement, 287
  colonial history, 16, 65
  determinants of maritime power, 22, 60
  economic rise, 92
  energy supply routes, 280
  fishing industry, 152–54, 164, 171n130
  information technology industry, 233–34
  inland waterways, 156–58
  international maritime agreements and, 53–54, 204–5
  marine tourism, 158–60
  maritime economic policy, 145–63
  maritime geography, 56–57, 59
  military spending, 108–9
  nuclear capabilities, 95–97, 279, 283, 285, 293, 304n116

offshore oil and gas, 107, 155–56
peacekeeping operations, 176, 195
port infrastructure, 146, 151–52, 164
relations with Japan, 12, 198, 199, 200, 278, 282, 284
relations with Southeast Asia, 253, 281–82, 286, 295–96
seafaring workforce, 161–63
shipbuilding industry, 146–49, 163–64, 256–57
shipping industry, 149–51, 164
ship recycling industry, 160–61
space programme, 239–42
Special Economic Zones, 125
strategic interests, 40, 90–93
territorial disputes, 44
2004 tsunami, 193, 197
Zheng He's voyages, 256
India, Brazil and South Africa (IBSA), 200, 280
India Hydrocarbon Vision-2025, 156
Indian Air Force, 201, 243
Indian Coast Guard, 148
Indian Institute of Maritime Studies (IIMS), 162, 163
Indian Institutes of Technology (IITs), 155, 242
Indian Maritime Doctrine (IMD), 68, 105, 195
Indian Maritime University, 162
Indian National Database of Seafarers (INDoS), 161
Indian Naval Academy, 239
Indian Naval Doctrine for Information Warfare (INDIW), 221, 235

Indian Navy
aircraft carriers, 97–99
aviation arm, 82, 102–4
development of, 16, 32 (nn65, 69), 65–68, 90
diplomacy, 194–205, 309–10
force structure and inventory, 94–97, 98–104, 294, 295
International Fleet Review, 191, 194
intrusions into Chinese waters, 49, 191
joint exercises, 186, 199–200, 280, 281, 288
MILAN, 194, 198
military engagements, 98, 104
Myanmar and, 288–89
role of merchant fleet, 105
roles and missions, 106–8, 118n129, 176–77
size, 68, 94–95
strategic thinking, 93–94, 110, 309
technological warfare capabilities, 234–39, 310
2004 tsunami, 282
Indian Ocean
China's strategic interests in, 84, 270–71, 288
geography, 56–57, 261
Indian naval deployments, 98, 310
India's strategic interests in, 40, 90, 93–94, 203, 278
monsoon winds, 258
oceanographic exploration, 142, 154–55
Portuguese and, 3
satellite communications, 231, 232

source of raw materials, 83
Soviet presence in, 36
trade and, 3, 16–17, 37
2004 tsunami, 44, 79, 92, 193, 197, 211n73, 287
during World War II, 14
Indian Ocean Naval Symposia (IONS), 194, 198–99
Indian Ocean Rim-Association for Regional Cooperation (IOR-ARC), 194
Indian Rare Earths Ltd., 155
Indian Space Research Organisation (ISRO), 234, 239, 240, 249n93
India-Pakistan relations
 air force encounters, 201–2
 growth of Indian military and, 233
 Kargil conflict, 203, 279
 1965 war, 66
 1971 conflict, 66, 98, 104
 other countries and, 66, 278–80, 282–83
 transfer of Karachi, 151
 2001 conflict, 240
India-Russia relations
 defence contracts, 100, 103, 105, 106
 energy cooperation, 156, 203
 joint naval exercises, 198, 199, 278
 nuclear naval cooperation, 96, 290
 Pakistan and, 282–83, 303n112
India-United States relations
 China and Japan and, 273
 conflicts with Pakistan and, 202, 303n112
 defence contracts, 98, 99

 imports of Indian fish, 153
 India's nuclear programme and, 283, 304n116
 Israel and, 274, 284
 joint naval exercises, 199, 200–1, 204–5, 236, 283
 multilateral maritime initiatives, 204
 post-September 11, 203
 tsunami relief efforts, 282
Indonesia
 in ancient times, 258, 266
 in Asia-Pacific region, 58
 Confrontation, 292–93
 fishing industry, 152
 Malacca Strait patrols, 39, 292
 maritime geography, 22, 41, 56, 57
 naval engagements, 66, 202, 294
 navy, 215, 294
 relations with China, 187
 relations with India, 198, 200
 relations with Russia, 294
 relations with the United States, 291
 2004 tsunami, 197
Industrial Revolution, 252, 296n1
Indus Valley civilization, 256
Influence of Sea Power Upon History, 1660–1783, 8, 13
Information Warfare, 225
Information Warfare (IW) (India), 241
Inland Waterways Authority of India (IWAI), 156–57
Inland Waterway Transport (IWT) (India), 146
Institute of Asia Pacific Studies, 273

Integrated Network-Electronic
  Warfare (INEW), 222
Intergovernmental Panel on
  Climate Change (IPCC), 43
International Law of the Sea, 48
International Maritime Bureau
  (IMB), 192
International Maritime Defence
  Exhibitions (IMDEX), 194
International Maritime
  Organization, 162
International Seabed Authority,
  141
International Seapower
  Symposium, 194
International Ship and Port
  Security Code (ISPS), 204,
  205
Internet, 223–24
Iquique, 134
Iran, 39, 188, 273
Iraq, 26–27, 27–28, 216, 220–21,
  225
iron ore, 131, 137
Irrawaddy River, 271
Ishiba, Shigeru, 191
I'sing, 255, 260
ISMERLO (International
  Submarine Escape and Rescue
  Liaison Office), 192
Israel
  defence industry, 101, 106, 216,
    242, 294
  Law of the Sea Convention and,
    41
  relations with India, 199, 274,
    278, 284
Italy, 4, 14
Izar, 293
Izvestia, 11

J

Jambi, 261
Jammu, 300n72
Jamshedpur, 155
Janatha Vimukti Perumuna (JVP),
  201
Jane's Defence Weekly, 226
Japan. *See also* China-Japan
    relations; Japanese Maritime
    Self Defence Force (JMSDF)
  anti-piracy agreement, 287
  in Asia-Pacific region, 58
  attempted Mongol invasions,
    256
  dependence on maritime trade,
    37
  dietary habits in, 45
  fishing industry, 135, 152
  maritime power, 10–11, 12–14,
    193, 253
  naval engagements, 10–11
  relations with India, 153, 198,
    199, 200, 278, 282, 284
  relations with Southeast Asia,
    254, 267, 286
  relations with the United States,
    188, 272–73, 274
  sea lanes important to, 56, 107
  shipbuilding industry, 12,
    13–14, 127, 128, 148,
    163, 165n13
  shipping industry, 144
  strategic interests, 40
  territorial claims, 42, 52–53
  tsunami relief, 211n73, 282
  in World War II, 52
Japanese Maritime Self Defence
    Force (JMSDF)
  Indian Navy and, 200, 201,
    236, 238

PLA Navy and, 77, 272
size and technological
    superiority, 68, 71, 95, 215
tsunami relief efforts, 193
United States and, 274, 275
Japanese Overseas Corporation
    Fund, 132
Jaswant Singh, 304n116
Java, 258, 266
Java Sea, 260
Jawaharlal Nehru Port, 151
Jawaharlal Nehru University
    (JNU), 239
Jharkhand, 157
Jiangsu province, 129, 137
Jiangxi, 137
Jiang Zemin, 70, 302n100
Jinan, 137
Jinmen, 48, 66, 184, 207n25
Johor, 292–93
Joint Marine Seismic Undertaking
    (JMSU), 286
Jones Act, 28

K
Kalimantan, 56
Kambujadesa, 259
Kandla, 151
Kanpur, 242
Kanyakumari, 155
Karachi, 151, 187, 192, 202
Karakoram Highway, 271
Karnataka, 153, 158, 160
Kashmir, 109, 282, 300n72,
    303n112
Kautilya, 180, 216, 263, 265–66,
    311
Kearsley, H.J., 33n83
Keating, Timothy, Admiral, 191,
    290

Kedah, 259, 261
Kenya, 197, 198
Kerala, 153, 157, 158, 159, 160
Kerala State Minerals Corporation,
    155
Kerala Tourism Development
    Corporation (KTDC), 159
Khaireddin Pasha, 18
Khetri, 155
Khruschev, Nikita Sergeevich,
    303n112
Kickleighter, Claude, 212n93
Kiribati, 231
Kismayu, 197
Kochi, 147, 151, 158, 159, 160
Koda, Yoji, Vice Admiral, 201
Kohli, S.N., Admiral, 33n73
Kolkata, 147, 151, 162
Kollam, 155, 157
Konkan, 159
Korea, 12, 111, 267. *See also*
    North Korea; South Korea
Korean War, 49, 89, 190
Kosovo, 207n19, 216
Kota Kinabalu, 293
Kottapuram, 157
Krishna River, 157
Kuala Lumpur, 203
Kublai Khan, 12, 256
Kunming, 271
Kurile Islands, 72
Kuwait, 26, 198
Kyushu, 188

L
Lakshadweep Islands, 56, 57, 93,
    105, 107, 150, 159
Lal Bahadur Shastri College of
    Advanced Maritime Studies
    and Research, 161

Langkawi, 159
Langkawi International Maritime and Aerospace Exhibition (LIMA), 194
Lanzhou, 137
Latin America, 83, 130, 133, 134, 187
Law of the Sea Convention, 18, 40–43, 49, 53, 54, 141
Lebanon, 207n19
Lee Boon Yang, 293
Lee Teng-Hui, 184
Liberation Army Daily, 225
Liberia, 207n19
Libicki, Martin, 229
Libya, 22
Ligor, 259
Lirquen, 134
Liu Huaqing, 15, 72, 77
Liu Kui-li, 83
Lockheed Martin, 243
Lombok Strait, 55, 56, 57, 59, 287, 291
London Naval treaties, 13
Lothal, 256
L&T Pipavav Shipyard, 148, 149
LTTE (Tamil Tigers), 201, 213n104
Luanshan, 84, 87
Luttwak, Edward, 177
Luzon, 192

M
Macao, 3
Mackinder, Sir Halford John, 37
Madagascar, 198
Madhvendra Singh, Admiral, 119n137
Madras, 151
Mahan, Alfred Thayer, 8–10, 13, 16, 28–29, 33n73, 37
Maharashtra, 153
Maipe, 160
Makassar Strait, 55, 56, 57
Malabar Coast, 159, 258
Malabar naval exercises, 199, 200–1, 204–5, 236, 283
Malacca, 3, 267
Malacca Straits. *See* Straits of Malacca
Malay Peninsula, 259, 260, 261
Malaysia
  in Asia-Pacific region, 58
  Five Power Defence Arrangements, 292–93
  Malacca Strait patrols, 39, 292
  maritime geography, 56
  navy, 215, 293, 294
  relations with China, 187, 276
  relations with India, 198
  relations with the United States, 291
  Tamil merchants in, 258
  territorial claims, 51, 52, 82, 183, 286, 295
  tourism, 159
  2004 tsunami, 197
Maldives, 43, 197, 198, 201, 211n84
Malta, 41
Malthus, Thomas Robert, 45
Manama, 39
mandala, 263, 264–67, 278–84, 311
Manila, 273
Manila Declaration on the South China Sea, 185–86
Manmohan Singh, 91, 108, 122n197

Manzanillo, 134
Mao Zedong, 70, 71, 72, 73, 112nn18–19, 302n103
Maputo, 280
Mariana Islands, 72
marine exploration, 42–43, 46, 141, 142, 154–55
marine resources
 in Chinese economic policy, 140–42
 economic role, 125
 EEZs and, 44–47
 in Indian economic policy, 154–56
marine tourism, 137–40, 158–60
Maritime Engineering and Research Institutes, 162
maritime power
 calculations of, 19–20, 20–23
 concepts, 4–17, 27
 economic dimension, 124–26
 foreign policy and, 175–80
 role of geography in, 35–37
 role of technology, 23, 124–25, 215–44
Maritime Safety Agency (MSA), 80, 144
Maritime Security Program, 28
Marmugao Port, 151
MASES (China Marine & Seamen Service Corp.), 143–44
MASSA (Maritime Association of Shipowners Shipmanagers and Agents), 162
Master Hsun, 263
Master Huai Nan, 263
Master Kuan, 263
Master Mo, 263
Mataram, 261
Matsu, 48, 184, 207n25

Mauritius, 198
Mauryan empire, 15, 257, 258
Mazagon Dockyard Limited (MDL), 100, 101, 102, 147, 148
Mediterranean, 1–2, 15–16, 91, 251, 252, 277, 308
Megasthenes, 257
Mehta, Sureesh, Admiral, 243
Meiji Restoration, 12
Mekong Ganga Cooperation (MGC), 281
Melaka, 3, 267
merchant shipping
 role in China's economy, 129–31
 role in India's economy, 149–51, 164
 role of geography, 37, 38
 seafaring labour, 144, 161, 162
 threat of piracy, 37, 40
Mexico, 134, 187, 277
Middle East, 83, 129, 153, 160, 255, 270
Military Maritime Consultative Agreement (MMCA), 189, 190, 209n52
Military Sealift Command (MSC), 28
Ming Dynasty
 influence on present, 268
 Japanese attempt to conquer, 111n1
 maritime power, 14, 70, 262
 trade policies, 256
 Zheng He's voyages, 176, 270
Minicoy Islands, 57
Ministry of Communication (China), 143
Ministry of Defence (DoD) (India), 147, 200

Ministry of External Affairs (India), 199, 227
Ministry of Foreign Trade and Economic Cooperation (MOFTEC) (China), 144
Ministry of Railways (India), 146
Ministry of Shipping (India), 145, 162
Ministry of Surface Transport (MoST) (India), 147
Ministry of Tourism (India), 160
Minjiang, 136
Minoan civilization, 2
Mischief Reef, 183, 233
Mogadishu, 197
Mogul empire, 257
Moluccas, 260
Money Island, 51
Mongolia, 12
monsoons, 258, 260
Morsky Sbornik, 11
Mountbatten, Louis (1st Earl Mountbatten of Burma), 90
Mozambique, 198, 280
Mukherjee, Pranab, 91, 122n197, 204, 205
Mullen, Mike, Admiral, 204
Mumbai
  Chinese naval visit, 191
  Indian Navy fleet, 202
  inland waterways, 157
  maritime training institutes, 161, 162, 239
  port and shipyards, 147, 151
Musharraf, Pervez, 84
Musi River, 260
MV Alondra Rainbow, 203
MV Limburg, 254
Myanmar
  Cyclone Nargis, 197, 289

Indian Navy and, 198, 289
maritime geography, 56, 57
navy, 288
relations with China, 109, 231, 271, 277, 279

N
Nakhon Si Thammarat, 258
Nalanda, 260
Nandas, 265
Napoleon I, Emperor of the French, 35
Napoleonic wars, 3–4
Narayanan, K.R., 279, 302n100
Naresvara, 267
National Democratic Alliance (NDA), 91
National High Technology Research and Development Programme (China), 230
National Highway Authority of India (NHAI), 146
National Inland Navigation Institute (NINI) (India), 157
National Institute of Oceanography (NIO) (India), 154, 155
National Institute of Port Management (NIPM) (India), 162
National Institute of Water Sports (NIWS) (India), 160
National Maritime Development Programme (NMDP) (India), 145, 150–51
National Maritime Policy (NMP) (India), 145, 150
National Metallurgical Laboratory (India), 155

National Security Council (India), 227
National Ship Design Research Centre (NSDRC) (India), 147
NATO (North Atlantic Treaty Organization), 26, 200, 248n72, 277
Natuna Islands, 55
Natwar Singh, 204
Naval Institute of Computer Applications (NICA), 239
Naval Physical Oceanographic Laboratory (NPOL), 101
naval power
  air forces and, 25, 26–27, 28, 82
  force structuring, 68–70
  foreign policy dimensions, 177–81, 195
  humanitarian role, 44, 181
  land warfare and, 1, 7–8
  maritime community and, 25
  and maritime power, 4, 19, 20, 22–23, 23–24, 27
  new security environment and, 18, 59
  nuclear capabilities, 24
  piracy and, 1
  role of geography in, 36, 38
  sea-space-shore (S3) continuum, 66, 67
  security of trade routes and, 66
  technological innovation and, 5, 18
  theories of, 7–17
Navy Enterprise Wide Network (NEWN), 238
Nearchos, Admiral, 2
Needham, Joseph, 48

negara, 266–67, 311
Nehru, Jawaharlal, 17, 90
Netherlands, 3, 12, 111n2, 257, 308
Network Centric Operations (NCO), 236
network-centric warfare (NCW), 221, 225, 234, 235–36
New Delhi, 198, 212n93, 238, 280
New Mangalore, 151
New Mumbai, 161
New Zealand, 286, 292
NIC (National Infomatics Centre) (India), 227
Nicobar Islands
  ancient name, 259
  in Indian geography, 56, 57, 204
  Indian Navy and, 93, 105
  in India-Pakistan war, 66, 202
  MILAN meetings, 198
  offshore oil, 155
  regional shipping, 150
  strategic importance, 107–8, 159
  tourism, 158, 159
  2004 tsunami, 211n84
Ningbo Port, 133
Northeast Asia Cooperation Dialogue (NEACD), 182
Northern Wars, 10
North Korea, 187, 273, 275
Norway, 144
nuclear weapons
  Britain and France, 67, 96, 293
  China, 15, 73–74, 86, 96
  as deterrent, 24, 66, 67
  development, 219
  possessed by India, 95–97

Index

Russia, 286, 293
United States, 96, 286, 293

O

Ocean Agenda 21 (China), 126
Oc Eo, 260
Oil and Natural Gas Corporation (ONGC), 122n193, 148, 149, 155, 156
Oil India, 155
Okinawa islands, 55, 185
Okinawa Treaty, 53
Okinotorishima, 42
Oman, 39, 198, 200
Ombai Wetter Strait, 55
ONGC Videsh Limited (OVL), 156
Operation Cactus, 201
Operation Desert Shield/Desert Storm, 26–27, 28, 220, 225
Operation Enduring Freedom (OEF), 220, 225, 274
Operation Iraqi Freedom (OIF), 27–28, 220, 225
Operation Pawan, 201
Operation Restore Hope, 197
Operation Sagittarius, 203
Operation Unified Assistance, 282
Opium Wars, 14, 110n1
Orissa, 153, 155
Oshima, 148
Owens, William, 229

P

Pacific Ocean
  Chinese presence, 277
  Indian navy and, 16
  links to Atlantic and Indian oceans, 57
  mineral resources, 46
  satellite communications, 231, 232, 233
  seabed and other exploration, 141, 142
  strategic importance, 39, 93, 203, 278
  territorial disputes in, 42
  U.S. territories, 276
  during World War II, 14
Pakistan. *See also* China-Pakistan relations; India-Pakistan relations
  maritime geography, 56
  navy, 165n21
  nuclear capabilities, 279, 286
  relations with China, 193
  relations with the United States, 303n112
  ship recycling industry, 160
  territorial claims, 54
Pakistan Navy, 90
Palau Islands, 72
Palawan Islands, 55
Palembang, 255, 260
Palk Bay, 54, 213n104
Palk Strait, 54
Panama, 22
Panama Canal, 10, 277
Panama Ports Company, 134
Panikkar, K.M., 7, 18
Panjim, 160
Paracel Islands
  Chinese military installations, 52, 77, 82, 233
  disputes over, 51, 183–84, 276
  location, 55, 57
Paradeep, 151
Parameters, 226
Pardo, Arvid, 41

Partnerships in Environmental Management for the Seas of East Asia (PEMSEA), 139
Patani, 260
Patna, 157
Pattle Island, 51
Pearl Harbor, 14
Pearl River, 136, 137
Pearl River Delta, 134, 137
Pentagon, 245n8
People's Armed Police (PAP), 80
Perry, Matthew C., Commodore, 12
Persia, 2, 15, 251, 252, 255, 257, 259
Persian Gulf. *See also* Gulf War, First (1990–91); Gulf War, Second (2003-)
   ancient links with China, 255, 256
   China's energy supplies, 84, 130, 270
   Indian naval deployments in, 98
   India's strategic interests in, 91, 194, 280
   Japanese presence, 272
   as part of Indian Ocean, 56
   Royal Indian Marine and, 16
   source of oil, 57, 59, 83, 203, 291
   U.S. military presence, 39, 40
   wars, 26–27
   Yinhe incident, 188
Peru, 134, 187
Peter the Great, 10
PetroVietnam, 286
Philippine National Oil Co.-Exploration Corp. (PNOC-EC), 286

Philippines
   fishing industry, 152
   maritime geography, 22, 41, 72
   military inventory, 83
   relations with China, 81, 183, 187, 233, 276, 293
   relations with the United States, 274, 291, 292
   seafaring workforce, 142
   sea lanes to, 56
   territorial claims, 51, 52, 81, 82, 183, 286, 295
Phoenicians, 2, 257
Phuket, 159
Pierce, Franklin, 12
piracy
   Chinese efforts against, 192–93
   in historical times, 258
   incidents, 203
   international agreement to fight, 194, 277, 281, 287
   interstate tensions and, 178, 254
   naval buildups to fight, 1, 3, 92
   threat to merchant shipping, 37, 40
Piracy Reporting Centre, 203
PLA (People's Liberation Army)
   in China's rise, 268
   computer hacking activities, 226–27
   diplomatic role, 181
   India and, 109, 122n197, 271
   posture towards Taiwan, 207n26
   Russian military hardware and, 192
PLA Academy of Electronic Technology, 226
PLA Air Force, 208n26
PLA Naval Air Force (PLANAF), 77

PLA Navy
  China's space programme and, 232
  deficiencies, 77–78, 87–88, 193, 275
  development, 65–68, 70–73, 110
  diplomacy, 181–94, 272, 309
  force structure and inventory, 72–81, 294, 300n69
  joint exercises, 269
  leadership, 15, 112n19
  nuclear submarines, 15, 73–74, 276
  Pakistan and Myanmar and, 271, 277, 288
  role and mission, 81–87, 184–85, 208n26
  size, 68
  technological warfare capabilities, 86, 222, 225–30, 310
PLOTE (People's Liberation Organization of Tamil Eelam), 201
Poland, 105
Pondicherry, 111n2, 153
Port Blair, 198
ports
  in China, 131–34
  climate change and, 43
  in India, 146, 151–52, 164
  in Pakistan and Myanmar, 84, 271, 277, 280
  role in globalization, 5
  role in maritime power, 10, 124
  technology and, 5–6
  warm water, 10, 36
Port Said, 277

Portugal, 3, 12, 65, 111n2, 151, 257, 308
Powell, Colin, 204
Proliferation Security Initiative (PSI), 204
Prueher, Joseph, Admiral, 189
Ptolemy, 258
Punic Wars, 2
Punjab, 265

Q
Qatar, 198
Qiantang, 136
Qin Gang, 273
Qingdao, 84, 139
Qingdao Port, 133
Qing Dynasty, 111n1
Qinhuangdao Port, 133
Quanzhou, 259
Quemoy, 48, 66, 184, 207n25
Quilon, 155, 157

R
Rafael Advanced Defence Systems Limited, 242
Rajabagan Dockyard Central Inland Water Transport Corporation, 147
Rajaraja I, 258
Rajasthan, 155
Rajendra Choladeva I, 175, 252, 259
Rambilli, 289, 290
Ramta, 106
Rann of Kutch, 156
Red Sea, 56, 93, 277
Regional Cooperation Agreement on Combating Piracy and Armed Robbery Against Ships in Asia (ReCAAP), 194, 277, 281, 287

Ren-Song, Emperor, 14
Republic of Singapore Navy, 200, 215, 238, 274, 281, 288, 294
Rig-veda, 257
RIMPAC (Rim of the Pacific) exercises, 269
Robert Island, 51
Rocky Island, 233
Rojdestvensky, Zinovy, Admiral, 11
Roman empire, 2–3, 175, 257, 258, 297n28, 308
Rotterdam, 133
Rowen, Henry, 212n93
Royal Air Force, 8, 25
Royal Indian Marine (RIM), 16
Royal Indian Navy, 90
Royal Malaysian Air Force, 82
Russia. *See also* China-Russia relations; India-Russia relations
  in Asia-Pacific region, 58
  defence industry, 216, 231, 294
  fishing industry, 135
  geographical constraints, 36
  history of maritime thought, 10–12
  international maritime agreements and, 49
  military literature, 226
  naval power, 10–11, 22–23, 67, 75, 96
  navy, 186, 269
  nuclear power, 286, 293
  relations with Japan, 10–11, 13
Russian Navy, 79, 200
Russo-Japanese war, 13
Ryukyu Islands, 52, 53, 72

S
Sabah, 56, 293
Sachana, 160
Sacotra, 3
Sadiya, 157
Safety of Life at Sea (SOLAS), 205
San Diego, 187
San Francisco Treaty, 52
Sanya, 139, 282, 289, 291, 293
Sarawak, 293
Satavahnas, 15
Sato Tetsutaro, 13
Satyam Technologies, 242
Saudi Arabia, 26
Scarborough Shoal, 183
Science of Military Strategy, 226
seafaring labour, 124, 142–45, 161, 162
sea power, 4, 8–10, 16–17, 19–20
Sea Power of the State, 11
Seleucus, 265
Senkaku Islands, 52–53, 55, 81, 142, 185, 191, 272
Seychelles, 198
Shalimar Works Ltd., 147
Shandong Peninsula, 49, 269
Shandong province, 84, 129
Shanghai, 79, 133, 137, 138, 140, 191, 233
Shanghai Cooperation Organization (SCO), 182, 192, 269, 274
Shanghai Maritime University, 144
Shangri-La Dialogue, 194, 287
Shen Weiguang, 225
Shenzhen, 139
Shenzhen Dapeng Bay Yantian Port, 133
shih, 263, 267–68, 277–78
Shi Lang, Admiral, 78
Shimoneasky Treaty, 53

shipbuilding
  in China, 75, 78, 127–29
  historical developments in, 219
  in India, 146–49
  in Japan, 12, 13–14
  role in sea power, 12, 19
Shipping Corporation of India, 145, 151, 162
Shirakaba gas field, 185
Shi Yunsheng, Admiral, 77
Sichuan, 137, 232
Sikkim, 271
Silk Route, 252
Sindh, 265
Singapore. *See also* Republic of Singapore Navy
  anti-piracy body, 287
  Five Power Defence Arrangements, 292–93
  geographical and geopolitical location, 56, 58
  Malacca Strait patrols, 39, 292
  port, 133
  relations with China, 288
  relations with India, 194, 198, 200
  relations with the United States, 274, 291, 292
  shipping industry, 144
Sino-Japanese war, 13, 53
Smith, Vincent, 258
Society for International Information Technologies, 226
Soekarno, 202
Somalia, 37, 197
Song Dynasty, 14, 70, 255
South Africa, 187, 198, 200, 280
South Asia Association for Regional Cooperation (SAARC), 194, 201

South China Sea
  in Chinese geography, 55
  Chinese military installations, 52, 77, 82, 186, 231, 233, 290
  Chinese strategic interests in, 50, 142, 176, 191, 233, 276
  Declaration on the Conduct of Parties, 184, 286
  hydrocarbon reserves, 142, 291
  India and, 57, 91, 93, 203, 282, 310
  nuclear submarines in, 293
  piracy in, 192
  territorial disputes in, 51–53, 81–82, 182, 291, 295
Southeast Asia
  ancient links with China, 253, 254–56, 262
  ancient maritime powers, 1, 15, 48, 175–76, 251–54, 259–62
  arms race, 292
  China-India relations and, 285–96
  colonial period, 16
  imports of Indian fish, 153
  military cooperation within, 181
  relations with India, 253, 281, 284
  sea lanes in, 37, 59, 107
  source of oil, 130
  source of raw materials, 83, 270
  strategic importance, 39, 91
  theories of statecraft, 263, 266–67
  tourism, 160
  Zheng He's voyages, 256
Southeast Asia Nuclear Weapons Free Zone (SEANWFZ), 281, 285, 286, 293, 295

South Georgia, 24
South Korea
  anti-piracy agreement, 287
  in ASEAN Plus Three, 286
  in Asia-Pacific region, 58
  fishing industry, 152
  naval power, 71, 77, 215
  relations with the United States, 40, 274, 291
  shipbuilding industry, 127, 128, 163
  shipping industry, 144
Southwest Asia, 16
Soviet Navy, 11, 75
Soviet Union. *See also* Russia
  Cold War strategies, 67, 188, 201
  India and, 96, 103, 105, 295, 303n112
  military hardware, 216, 225
  role in China's nuclear programme, 73
Space Tracking and Control Station, 231
Spain, 186, 257, 308
Spanish Armada, 7
Spratly Islands
  bases of claims, 52
  China and, 81, 83, 183–84, 185, 233, 276, 286–87
  claimant countries, 51
  Five Power Defence Agreement and, 293
  location, 55, 56, 57
  military installations on, 82, 233
Spring and Autumn of Master Lu, 263
Sriharikota, 239
Sri Lanka
  anti-piracy agreement, 287
  historical links, 258, 261
  maritime jurisdiction, 39, 54, 56
  relations with China, 187
  relations with India, 198, 200, 201
  2004 tsunami, 197, 211n84
Sri Lankan Navy, 106
Srivijaya, 3, 47, 175–76, 255, 256, 258–62, 267
State Oceanic Administration (SOA), 127
St. Helena, 25
Straits Exchange Foundation (SEF), 184, 185
Straits of Bab-al-Mandeb, 84, 93
Straits of Hormuz
  China's energy supplies and, 84, 277
  critical importance, 39, 57, 59, 107
  India's strategic interest in, 93, 280
Straits of Malacca
  in ancient times, 252, 255, 260
  ASEAN states and, 287
  geography, 55, 261
  Japanese presence, 272
  joint patrols and exercises, 39, 176, 281, 292
  level of traffic, 294
  nuclear submarines and, 293
  piracy, 193, 203
  strategic importance to China, 59, 83–84, 271, 276–77, 290, 291
  strategic importance to India, 57, 91, 93, 107, 203–4
Strategic Defence Review (SDR), 195
Strategy Research Centre, 226

Index

Sudan, 2, 198, 207n19
Suez Canal, 3, 57, 277
Sulawesi, 56
Sumatra, 57, 204, 255, 258, 259, 260, 261
Sundarbans, 157
Sunda Strait, 55–56, 57, 59, 260, 287, 291
Sung Dynasty, 255, 256, 259, 270, 297n15
Sun Shihai, 273
Sun Tzu, 180, 216, 226, 263, 265, 277, 311
Sun Yat-sen, 14, 48
Supreme Court of India, 153, 161
Su Zhiqian, Rear Admiral, 186
Sweden, 294
Syria, 273

T
Tadri, 160
Taipei, 207n26
Taiwan. *See also* China-Taiwan relations
 air and naval power, 71, 83, 85, 112n20, 190, 291
 in Asia-Pacific region, 58
 computer hacking incidents, 226
 fishing industry, 135
 geographical location, 55, 72
 the Internet and, 224
 Japan and, 272
 law on maritime rights and jurisdiction, 50
 Manchu conquest, 78
 military spending, 87, 190
 shipping industry, 144
 Singapore and, 288
 territorial claims, 51, 52, 53, 183, 286, 295
 tsunami relief, 211n73
 U.S. support for, 48, 66, 188–89, 274–75
Taiwan Strait crises, 66, 85, 184–85, 189
Taiwan Straits, 55, 84–85, 184, 185, 275
Takuapa, 259
Talbott, Strobe, 304n116
Talpatti Island, 44
Tamil merchants, 258
Tamil Nadu, 153, 155, 160, 162, 211n84
Tang Dynasty, 255
Tang Jiaxuan, 279
Tanjavur, 259
Tanzania, 187, 197, 198
Tarawa, 231
Tata Consultancy Services, 242
Taylor, James F., Admiral, 27
Ten Degree Channel, 57
terrorism, 37, 40, 92, 178, 254
Thailand
 in Asia-Pacific region, 58
 fishing industry, 152
 maritime geography, 56, 57
 navy, 215, 294
 relations with China, 165n21, 187
 relations with India, 198, 200
 relations with the United States, 274, 292
 Tamil merchants in, 258
 tourism, 159
 2004 tsunami, 197
Theatre Missile Defence (TMD), 272
1000 Ship Navy (TSN), 204
Three Gorges Dam, 137
Tiananmen Square incident, 224

Tibet, 271
Toffler, Alvin, 229
Tokugawa Shogunate, 12–13
Tolani, 162
Torres Strait, 55
Trafalgar, Battle of, 3
Training Ship Chanakya, 161
Trang, 259
Treaty for Good Neighbourliness, Friendship and Cooperation, 269
Treaty of Amity and Commerce (TAC), 12, 281, 285, 286
Trincomalee, 212n84
Tristan da Cunha, 25
Tsushima, Battle of, 11, 13
Turkey, 41
Tuticorin, 151, 160

U

Udaipur, 155
Ukraine, 100
UNCLOS (UN Convention on the Law of the Sea) III
  China and, 49, 50
  effect on interstate relations, 58, 177–78
  effect on naval diplomacy, 196–97
  Exclusive Economic Zones, 5, 29, 47, 52, 196–97
  framework, 40–43
  India and, 54, 194
UN Department of Peacekeeping Operations, 182
UNEP (United Nations Environment Programme), 139
United Arab Emirates, 198
United Kingdom. *See* Britain

United Nations (UN)
  ASEAN Regional Forum and, 286
  China and, 49
  humanitarian operations in Somalia, 197
  peacekeeping operations, 176, 182, 195, 207n17
  sanctions against Iraq, 26
  seabed exploitation regime, 49, 141
  U.S.-led war on terror and, 274
United Nations Food and Agriculture Organization (FAO), 45
United States. *See also* China-United States relations; Gulf War, First (1990–91); Gulf War, Second (2003-); India-United States relations
  in Asia-Pacific region, 58, 64n83
  Chinese computer hackers and, 226
  Cold War strategies, 67, 188, 201, 303n112
  defence industry, 216
  energy supply routes, 277
  history of maritime thought, 8–10
  humanitarian missions, 197, 282, 289
  information technology in, 224
  international agreements and, 41, 49
  Japan and, 12, 13–14
  maritime power, 4, 22, 188, 253
  maritime strategy, 178–79
  military engagements, 26–28
  military exchanges, 181, 198, 199, 200–1

nuclear capabilities, 96, 286, 293
port infrastructure, 133
post-Cold War hegemony, 269, 274
relations with Japan, 188, 272–73, 274
South China Sea disputes and, 51
space programme, 232
strategic interests, 39, 40
UNCLOS III and, 43
War on Terror, 216, 272
Univan, 162
Unrestricted Warfare, 226
UN Seabed Committee, 49
UPA (United Progressive Alliance), 91
Uruguay Navy, 25
U.S. Air Force, 26
U.S. Marine Corps, 26
U.S. Naval Institute Proceedings, 226
U.S. Navy
  aircraft under development, 243
  in China-Taiwan relations, 48
  in Gulf wars, 28
  Indian Navy and, 199, 204–5, 236, 238
  joint exercises, 199, 200–1, 204–5, 236, 274, 275
  PLA Navy and, 75, 176, 188
  technological warfare and, 71, 221, 233
U.S. Ready Reserve Force (RRF), 28
USS Cole, 254
USS Kitty Hawk, 188, 189–90, 275
USS Reuben James, 190

Uttar Pradesh, 157

V
Vajpayee, Atal Bihari, 91
Valinokan, 160
Valparaiso, 134
Varun Shipping, 151
Venezuela, 41, 134
Veracruz, 134
Very Large Crude Carriers (VLCCs), 56, 78, 160, 165n13
Vietnam
  in Asia-Pacific region, 58
  fishing industry, 152
  military inventory, 82–83, 294
  relations with China, 182, 276
  relations with India, 288
  sea lanes, 56
  territorial claims, 51, 52, 81, 183, 286, 295
Vietnam People's Air Force, 82–83
Vietnam War, 27
Vishakhapatnam, 147, 160, 162, 202, 290
Voluntary Intermodal Sealift Arrangments (VISA), 28
Voroshilov Naval Institute, 15
Vriksha-Ayurveda, 257
V Ships, 162

W
Wallem, 162
Wang Lingyun, 224
Wang Zhiyuan, Lieutenant General, 78
Weapons and Electronic System Engineering Establishment (WESEE), 242
Wen Jiabao, 90

West Asia Maritime, 151
West Bengal, 147, 153, 157
Western Pacific Naval Symposium (WPNS), 194
West River, 137
Who is the Next Target?, 229
Who Will Feed China: A Wake Up Call for a Small Planet, 134
Who Will Win the Next War?, 229
Wolters, O.W., 267, 285
Woody Island, 52, 83, 233, 292
World Bank, 132, 136
World Expo 2010, 140
World Tourism Organization, 138
World War I, 4, 11
World War II, 4, 11, 14, 25, 52, 97
World Watch Institute, 134
Worli, 161
Wu Bangguo, 84

X
Xiamen, 134, 139
Xian, 138
Xichang Launch Facility, 232
Xijiang, 137
Xinjiang, 271
Xu Qi, Captain, 206n6

Y
Yalong Bay, 139
Yalu River, 49, 111n1
Yangshan Port, 133
Yangtze River, 136, 137
Yangtze River Delta, 134

Yao Zhilou, Rear Admiral, 77
Yasukuni Shrine, 272
Yellow River, 137
Yellow Sea, 51, 55, 111n1, 137, 139, 188
Yinhe, 188
Yokosuka naval base, 188
Yongle Emperor, 256
Yuan Dynasty, 259
Yu Guoquan, 228
Yuktikalpataru, 257
Yulin naval base, 282, 289–91, 293
Yunnan, 137, 271
Yusuf, Ismail, 161

Z
Zhang Lianzhong, Admiral, 74
Zhang Xiangmu, 128
Zhang Yan, Rear Admiral, 192
Zhang Zhao Zhong, 229–30
Zhanjiang Port, 133
Zhao Nanqi, General, 271
Zhejiang province, 84, 129
Zheng He, 3, 51, 252, 256, 268, 270
Zhengzhou, 137
Zhenhai, 84, 87
Zhou Enlai, 232, 302n103
Zhoushan Island, 84
Zhoushan Port, 133
Zhu Yuanzang, 256
Zimmer, Heinrich, 265
Zone of Peace, Freedom and Neutrality (ZOPFAN), 285

ABOUT THE AUTHOR

Vijay Sakhuja is Visiting Senior Research Fellow at the Institute of Southeast Asian Studies (ISEAS), Singapore. Currently he is Director (Research), Indian Council of World Affairs, a leading think-tank in New Delhi. A former Indian Navy officer, Vijay Sakhuja received his Doctorate from the Jawaharlal Nehru University, New Delhi. He has been on the research faculty of the Centre for Air Power Studies, Observer Research Foundation, and Research Fellow at the Institute for Defence Studies and Analyses, and United Service Institution of India, all in New Delhi. Vijay Sakhuja has published books, monographs, and policy briefs on issues of geopolitics, maritime security, politics of the Arctic, climate change and diplomacy. His research areas include Asia-Pacific security, maritime and naval developments, politics of the High North, climate change debate, and marine risk analyses. He is the author of *Confidence Building from the Sea: An Indian Initiative* and co-editor of *Nagapattinam to Suvarnadwipa: Reflections on the Chola Naval Expeditions to Southeast Asia* and *Fisheries Exploitation in the Indian Ocean: Threats and Opportunities*, both published in 2009.